D1028918

Transportation:
The Domestic System

ROBERT C. LIEB
Northeastern University

Reston Publishing Co., Inc.
A Prentice-Hall Company
Reston, Virginia

Library of Congress Cataloging in Publication Data

Lieb, Robert C.
    Transportation: the domestic system.

    Includes bibliographies and index.
    1. Transportation—United States.   2. Transportation
and state—United States.   I. Title.
HE203.L48   380.5'0973   77-5432
ISBN 0-87909-843-0

© 1978 by
Reston Publishing Co., Inc.
A Prentice-Hall Company
Reston, Virginia 22090

10   9   8   7   6   5   4   3   2

Printed in the United States of America

To Lorraine, Kristin, and Smokey

Contents

Contents

Contents

Preface

Our national transportation system is quite dynamic. In recent years numerous institutional and technological changes have occurred, and many problems have surfaced which have demanded the attention of both the public and private sectors. This book has been written to assist students and practitioners in comprehending the complexity of the domestic transportation system.

The book doesn't attempt to provide final answers to all of the diverse transportation problems of contemporary life. Rather, it seeks to identify those problems while providing background information to assist the reader in analyzing the issues and alternatives involved. Hopefully, the book will provide sufficient stimulus to the reader to promote further study of the field. Such continued study is essential to those who have career goals in transportation because they will find that there are no simple solutions to our transportation problems.

I have attempted to offer a readable and comprehensive treatment of domestic transportation which might be useful to people with a variety of backgrounds including business, economics, and government. While the primary focus of the book is intercity transportation, attention is also devoted to the transportation systems of our metropolitan areas. The book takes a balanced approach to transportation by considering not only the views of carrier management, but also those of public officials and consumers of transportation services. The study of transportation should be as exciting and dynamic as the field itself. I have attempted to convey this feeling in the book.

Preface

To facilitate the development and flow of material, the book is organized into six parts. Part One identifies the significance and role of transportation in our society, and also defines the perspective of the shipping public as it views transportation alternatives. Part Two concentrates on the development, structure, and cost and service characteristics of the several modes of intercity carriage. These chapters serve as the foundation for the public policy and management-oriented problem discussions of subsequent chapters. Part Three focuses on the interaction of cost and demand considerations in the transportation pricing process. It also gives attention to the rate-making procedures employed by intercity carriers. Part Four examines the role of various government units in the regulation and promotion of intercity carriage. The development of the extensive government involvement in transportation is traced, and the difficulties inherent in such a complex private-public interrelationship are discussed. Part Five provides an in-depth review of a number of management problems and public policy issues. The book concludes with Part Six which devotes attention to transportation within our metropolitan areas. The institutions, problems, and government policies which relate to metropolitan transportation are examined, as is the interface which exists between the intercity and metropolitan transportation systems.

The contributions of many people have been most valuable in the development of this book. Among the foremost contributors to this effort have been my past and present students at Northeastern University. Their enthusiasm for transportation has made our interaction most enjoyable, and it has proven quite inspirational. Similarly, my contacts with representatives of carriers, shippers, industrial associations, and government agencies have proven invaluable.

I also greatly appreciate the contributions of many of my colleagues to this project. I'm especially indebted to my fellow faculty members at Northeastern, Frederick J. Stephenson and James F. Molloy, for their reviews and encouragement. Other valuable reviews were provided by: Steven D. Grossman, Texas A & M University; Grant M. Davis, University of Arkansas; John C. Spychalski, Pennsylvania State University; and Jay A. Smith, University of North Florida.

I'd also like to express my thanks to A. Stuart Horton of Reston Publishing Company for his assistance in both the development of the manuscript and coordination of review efforts.

The most important contributions, however, were made by my wife, Lorraine, and our daughter, Kristin. Lorraine edited and proofread the manuscript, and both she and Kristin were most understanding concerning the time I devoted to the book. Consequently, it was truly a family project.

Robert C. Lieb
Northeastern University

PART
1

Transportation:
Its Scope and Function

CHAPTER
1

Transportation and Its Role in Society

Our nation's transportation system has a pervasive impact on each of us. It not only influences our personal mobility and the prices that we pay for goods and services, but is also a major determinant of where we choose to live and work. At the same time, individuals affect the transportation system through such actions as their purchase of transportation services and their ever-increasing commitment to the automobile. In turn, automobile use has significant implications with respect to contemporary concerns involving pollution, congestion, and energy conservation.

Although this two-directional pattern of influence is quite meaningful in terms of the realization of both personal and national goals, the transportation system and its operations are little understood by the general public. Historically, the public has tended to take the existence of transportation services for granted, and public interest has only been stimulated by such incidents as carrier bankrupties, strikes, or accidents. However, in recent years public awareness of transportation issues seems to have increased as our national transportation problems have been more widely publicized. One often hears such questions as: If a railroad declares bankruptcy, why doesn't the federal government allow it to be liquidated, rather than waste taxpayers' money keeping it alive? Or, transit service in this town is terrible. Why doesn't the company buy some new equipment, increase service, and lower fares to attract additional passengers?

Superficially there is great appeal in such suggestions. However, because of the complexity of our nation's transportation system, and due to public dependence upon it, there are no simple solutions to these problems. The basic purpose of this book is to illustrate this complexity and to provide sufficient background to allow the reader to become conversant with the issues involved.

ECONOMIC SIGNIFICANCE OF TRANSPORTATION

Development of an adequate transportation system is essential to a nation's economic progress. As an integral part of national production and distribution systems, an adequate transportation network is necessary to provide a means of servicing domestic and international markets. This is of primary importance in the early stages of economic development because it promotes an accumulation of capital, which allows the economy to progress from the subsistence level at which most production is consumed locally. Transportation and other government programs, such as education and health care, necessarily compete for public expenditures, particularly in underdeveloped countries. There are indications, however, that a balanced approach to expenditures in these areas, rather than a disproportionate concentration of government outlays in one area, leads to a more desirable growth pattern.[1]

Naturally, as an economy expands, its demand for transportation facilities and services increases. This typically leads to an increasing flow of capital from both the public and private sectors into transportation.

Federal, state, and local government transportation expenditures have grown steadily in the United States, and have played a major role in fostering the development of the country's extensive transportation system. One source has estimated that throughout the years aggregate government expenditures for our domestic transportation system have exceeded $486.7 billion. In 1975 alone, such outlays exceeded $32.6 billion (see Table 1–1).

The extent of private sector participation in financing transportation development varies from country to country. In the United States such private investment exceeds $200 billion.

The combination of public and private transportation expenditures helps promote regional specialization and division of labor, which in turn fosters large-scale production. These factors combine to lower raw material and finished goods prices in the economy and to increase the availability of goods throughout the nation. National commodity flows necessitate the emergence of large-scale distribution patterns, with market areas for specific commodities being at least partially determined by transportation

Table 1–1

Summary of 1975 Government Spending for Intercity Transport Systems and Facilities[a] **(in millions)**

	Federal	State and Local	Total
Airways	$1,759	—	$ 1,759
Airports	316	$ 1,450	1,766
Airline Subsidy	60	—	60
Highways	5,276	21,384	26,660
Waterways	512	625	1,137
Railroads[b]	660	655	1,315
Total	$8,583	$24,114	$32,697

[a] The 1975 figures are for the fiscal year in some cases and for the calendar year in others.
[b] Preliminary estimates of the Association of American Railroads.

SOURCE: Association of American Railroads, Economics and Finance Department, *Government Expenditures for Highway, Waterway, and Air Facilities and Private Expenditures for Railroad Facilities* (Washington, D.C.: the Association, 1976), p. 2; also, additional data supplied by the Association.

prices. In underdeveloped countries the emergence of national trade patterns is critical in triggering the movement from regional self-sufficiency to a national economy.

The availability and prices of transportation services in an economy has a decided impact on overall price levels, because transportation costs comprise part of the total market price of any item. This cost component reflects both the movement of raw materials to a point of production and the flow of finished products to consumers. On the average, 20 cents of every consumer dollar is absorbed by transportation costs.[2] However, the significance of transportation costs, as related to the wholesale prices of products, varies considerably among commodities. For some bulk commodities, such as sand and gravel, transportation outlays comprise more than half the wholesale price; on other items, such as business machines, the ratio is less than 1 percent.[3] As discussed in later chapters, the price (rate) charged for moving a particular commodity from origin to destination is a function of several factors, including the value of the commodity, its handling characteristics, the distance of the shipment, and the quantity of the commodity to be moved.

While transportation influences the overall price level as an input in practically every economic activity, it also has a positive effect on prices due to the regional specialization and division of labor that it fosters. These factors tend to lower the prices of goods in the economy, as does

5

the fact that a well-developed transportation system opens distant markets for producers, thereby promoting greater competition and broader consumer choice.

Additionally, the improved access and greater alternative use that result from expansion of the transportation network can have a positive effect on land values. For example, this is often observed in the suburbs of metropolitan areas following expansion of a freeway or transit system that provides improved access to the core city. Conversely, transportation can have a negative impact on property values. The environmental degradation which affects properties that abut freeways and airports and the adverse effects of automobile congestion and emissions on the quality of urban life are contemporary illustrations of such problems.

SOCIAL AND POLITICAL SIGNIFICANCE OF TRANSPORTATION

A nation's transportation system is not only shaped by economic considerations but by social and political factors as well. Thus, transportation policy cannot be formulated or critiqued in a purely economic context. A variety of social and political considerations is examined in the following discussion.

Social Significance

A viable transportation network contributes to improved living standards through promotion of regional specialization, and tends to broaden the perspectives of the nations and individuals involved. This cultural diffusion, fostered at the national or international level, is desirable, because it works toward the promotion of mutual understanding.

At the local level, the social impact of transportation is more obvious. For example, freeway systems and mass transit have permitted many people to enjoy suburban living while still having access to the educational, cultural, and social attractions of the core city. Similarly, many of these people are employed in the city, yet reside in the suburbs. However, the separation of home and work locations is a mixed blessing. In most cities this necessitates massive commutation, which intensifies the pollution and congestion problems of the core area. Extensive highway building programs in urban areas have also led to neighborhood disruption and the dislocation of many businesses and families.

As implied in the preceding discussion, the existence of transportation facilities plays a major role in the determination of industrial and residential location patterns. Consequently, considerable attention is being devoted by all levels of government to the patterns of development that result from government expenditures for particular forms of transportation facilities. The intention of such analysis is to integrate transportation programs into broader plans for community and regional development so that development can be managed in an orderly fashion.[4]

Several aspects of transportation's negative impact on society have already been discussed. Two additional negative factors deserve mention. Transportation accounts for approximately one-half of the volume of petroleum products consumed in the United States.[5] This issue may be expected to attract growing attention as concern with energy conservation escalates. Also, accidents in the various forms of transportation annually generate an awesome toll in property damage, injuries, and death. The greatest offender, the automobile, was responsible for more than 45,000 deaths per year during the 1970–1975 period.[6] In response to these problems, growing national attention has been focused on the promotion of transportation safety. The scope of governmental involvement in safety and environmental issues is discussed in Chapter 17.

Political Significance

Because of the importance of transportation in the realization of governmental goals, it has always attracted considerable political attention. The significance accorded transportation at the national level was illustrated by the establishment of the cabinet-level Department of Transportation (DOT) in 1967. Similarly, nearly one third of the states have organized departments of transportation.[7]

Government involvement has often been precipitated by the inability of the private sector to finance an adequate rate of transportation system growth. Additionally, government powers must frequently be exercised to secure feasible routes or to provide facilities, such as waterways, that would not generate sufficient rates of return to attract private capital.

Government outlays for transportation facilities have often been used to promote national unity. In the United States during the 1860s, the financial assistance and land grants provided by various governmental units facilitated the construction of a transcontinental railroad system, which was specifically aimed at promotion of closer ties between the western area of this country and the rest of the union. The Canadian national government was similarly motivated in building railroad facilities into its western provinces.

Another major reason for governmental involvement in transportation is its military significance. Centuries ago, military considerations played a major role in the development of the highway system of ancient Europe. More recently, the construction of the Interstate Highway System was partially motivated by a congressional desire to improve our national defense capabilities. Similarly, much of the federal expenditure for waterway development has been related to defense concerns. In fact, the Statement of National Transportation Policy, which is discussed in Chapter 12, clearly specifies the importance to be given to national defense considerations in formulating transportation policy.

The overall significance of transportation to the realization of economic, social, and political goals has led to the emergence of a pattern of extensive government promotion and regulation of transportation at the federal, state, and local levels. The promotional aspects, at least in financial terms, have already been discussed. The regulatory aspects of government involvement will be examined following a brief look at the nature of the domestic transportation industries.

DOMESTIC TRANSPORTATION SYSTEM

The United States benefits from the existence of a highly developed and extensive transportation network. In most instances we have a choice of several different modes (or forms) of transportation to service our needs. The businessman contemplating a trip from New York to Boston may choose between airline, railroad, bus, or private automobile as a means of intercity travel. Each mode has distinctive cost and service characteristics; for example, air travel is typically faster than bus or rail passenger service, but it also tends to be more expensive. Consequently, the traveler is faced with a series of *tradeoffs*. He must decide the relative importance of such factors as speed, convenience, and cost in making his modal selection. His choice will be influenced by such factors as the value he places on his time and the size of his expense account.

Similarly, those wishing to ship freight, whether industrial or governmental shippers or individuals concerned with moving their personal belongings to a new home, are generally faced with several different modal alternatives. Additionally, in both freight and passenger movements the individual may also typically choose among several companies in a given mode of carriage. Or the shipper may decide to provide the service himself by, for example, leasing or purchasing a truck rather than using a *for-hire carrier* (one which is in the business of selling transportation services in the marketplace). The individual who chooses to provide the service himself is said to be engaged in *private carriage*. That is, his primary business is not selling transportation service. Rather, the shipper has decided, after making the kinds of tradeoffs discussed above, that he can better meet his transportation needs by providing the service for himself.

8

The farmer moving his produce to the market in his own truck and the local department store making deliveries in its own vehicles provide illustrations of private carriage. In a noncommercial context, each of us engages in private carriage when we choose to drive to work or to the shopping center rather than take a bus.

Market Share of Intercity Carriers

The several basic modes of carriage that play prominent roles in the intercity movement of passengers and freight are highway carriage (buses, trucks, and automobiles on public highways), railroads, airlines, water carriers, oil pipelines, and freight forwarders. Forwarders function in a middleman capacity, linking shippers and companies that provide for-hire services in the other modes.

The market shares of both freight and passenger traffic controlled by the several modes of intercity carriage have shifted dramatically throughout the years as a result of a number of factors, including technological changes, regulation, and government financing of expansion of our national transportation system. The causes and effects of these shifts are discussed in detail in Chapters 3 through 7.

In the freight sector (see Table 1–2), the railroad industry's market share declined from 61.3 percent of intercity ton mileage (1 ton mile is 1 ton of freight moved 1 mile) in 1940 to 36.8 percent in 1975. During the same period, the market share controlled by the oil pipeline industry more than doubled; it now ranks second among the modes in terms of

Table 1–2

Intercity Freight Market Share by Mode (percent of freight ton miles)[a]

	1940	1950	1960	1970	1975[c]
Railroads	61.3	56.2	44.1	39.7	36.8
Oil Pipelines	9.5	12.1	17.4	22.3	24.2
Motor Carriage	10.0	16.3	21.8	21.3	21.3
Water[b]	19.1	15.4	16.7	16.6	17.1
Air		0.03	0.07	0.18	0.19

[a] Includes mail and express.
[b] Includes inland and Great Lakes traffic.
[c] Percentages do not total 100 percent due to rounding.

SOURCE: Transportation Association of America, *Transportation Facts and Trends* (Washington, D.C.: the Association, 1976), p. 8.

percentage of intercity ton mileage carried. This fact surprises many people, due to the limited range of commodities that are suited to pipeline movement. However, the volume of traffic handled by oil pipelines is merely reflective of the tremendous utilization rate of petroleum products in the United States. The speed and flexibility of the trucking industry have contributed to the expansion of its share of the intercity freight market from 10.0 percent in 1940 to 21.3 percent in 1975. The market share of domestic water carriage, which is primarily composed of bulk and liquid commodity movements, has stayed relatively constant since 1940. At the same time, air freight has expanded greatly in terms of absolute ton mileage, but still comprises less than 1 percent of intercity ton mileage.

Significant modal shifts have also occurred in intercity passenger travel. The automobile has emerged as the dominant mode of intercity passenger carriage; in recent years it has annually accounted for approximately 86 percent of intercity passenger mileage. The balance of intercity passenger movements are handled by the commercial airlines, railroads, bus companies, and water carriers. Table 1–3 traces the market-share changes

Table 1–3

Intercity Commercial Passenger Market Share by Mode (percent of passenger miles)

	1940	1950	1960	1970	1975
Air	3.2	14.1	42.1	73.0	77.5
Bus	27.2	34.6	25.6	16.9	14.5
Rail	66.2	49.5	28.7	7.8	5.7
Water	3.4	1.8	3.6	3.3	2.3

SOURCE: Transportation Association of America, *Transportation Facts and Trends* (Washington, D.C.: the Association, 1976), p. 18.

experienced by intercity commercial passenger carriers between 1940 and 1975. The dominance of air passenger carriage in this field is obvious, as is the precipitous decline of rail passenger traffic, and the more limited decline of the bus industry.

Scope of the System

One measure of the scope of the domestic transportation system is the intercity route mileage of the various modes (see Table 1–4). The causes of the expansion or contraction of the intercity route mileage of the individual modes are examined in Chapters 3 through 6.

10

Table 1–4

Intercity Route Mileage Within the Continental United States, 1960 and 1974 (statute mileage)

	1960	1974
Highways[a]	557,729	681,646
Airways	293,003	307,783
Railroads	217,552	200,916
Oil Pipeline	190,944	223,583
Inland Waterways[b]	25,253	25,543

[a] Does not include more than 2 million miles of rural roads.
[b] Excludes the Great Lakes.

SOURCE: Transportation Association of America, *Transportation Facts and Trends* (Washington, D.C.: the Association, 1976), p. 31.

Our nation also possesses an extensive urban transportation network. In addition to the route mileage specified in Table 1–4, approximately 115,000 route miles of transit operations exist in urban areas.[8] This includes bus, trolley, commuter rail, and subway operations. The urban transportation system also includes approximately 600,000 miles of urban streets that serve the transportation needs of metropolitan residents.[9]

Another measure of the scope of the domestic transportation system is the vehicle stock of the various modes. The highway system of the United States is traveled by approximately 104.8 million automobiles, 24.6 million trucks, 356,800 school and noncommercial buses, and 90,100 commercial buses. The railroad system has an equipment stock of approximately 1.7 million freight cars, 7,100 passenger cars, and 30,200 locomotives. There are roughly 153,300 aircraft in this country. Finally, nearly 25,500 barges and towboats travel our waterway system and nearly 600 ships ply deepwater routes.[10]

In utilizing this extensive transportation system, Americans paid more than $139 billion for freight transportation services and nearly $163 billion for passenger travel in 1974.[11] Each year such transportation outlays are approximately one-fifth of our Gross National Product.[12]

GOVERNMENT PROMOTION AND REGULATION

The economic, social, and political significance of transportation has prompted considerable government involvement in both promoting the development of transportation and its regulation. Each of these governmental roles is examined briefly in the following discussion.

11

Promotion

As noted earlier in this chapter, various governmental units have become extensively involved in funding the development of our national transportation system. These promotional outlays have not only involved construction of facilities such as highways, airports, and waterways, but have also influenced the pace of technological development in the various modes. The federal Department of Transportation plays the central role in government financing of technological development in transportation. Since its creation in 1967, the department has financed a wide variety of research and development efforts, ranging from adaptation of aircraft technology to railroad locomotives to the initial development of a supersonic passenger transport (SST). The importance of governmental expenditures in fostering such technological development cannot be overstated, because it can be quite significant in determining the relative roles to be played by the various modes of carriage in the future.

Regulation

The involvement of government in U.S. transportation also includes a rather extensive pattern of safety and economic regulation. These regulations have evolved over a period of years at both the federal and state level and have been primarily justified on the basis of protection of the public interest. An illustration of the scope of these regulations is provided by the fact that, in the economic sphere, the regulation of interstate carriers generally encompasses such factors as determination of the markets they serve, their ability to introduce new services, the prices they charge, carrier mergers, and the issue of securities. Similarly, in the area of safety such factors as vehicle weights, operating speeds, operator qualifications, and the number of consecutive hours operators are permitted to work are controlled. The development of these regulations and their specific nature are discussed in subsequent chapters. However, it is important that the reader understand as early as possible that the extent of economic and safety regulation plays a major role in determining the structure and performance of the domestic transportation network. This is particularly important if the reader wishes to analyze current issues as he progresses through this book. In fact, the most controversial area of domestic transportation policy in recent years has involved the question of whether such extensive regulations actually protect the public interest or harm it. This issue is addressed again following those chapters that specify the nature of present regulation.

Transportation Policy Development

At this point, attention should also be given to the process by which national transportation policy is formulated. Figure 1–1 illustrates this process with respect to regulatory policies. In enacting the laws that serve as the foundation for economic and safety regulation of transportation, Congress acts as the basic formulator of national transportation policy. Inputs to this law-making process are provided by any number of parties, including the DOT, the president, and various lobby groups representing

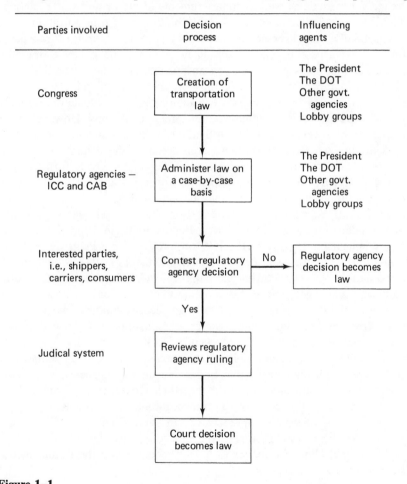

Figure 1–1

The Process of Formulating and Implementing Regulatory Policies in Transportation

such interests as shippers, carriers, environmentalists, and consumers. The final output of this interaction may be the passage of a statute that in some way influences our national transportation system. If the law pertains to an aspect of economic regulation, it is likely that it will require administration by a federal regulatory agency, such as the Interstate Commerce Commission (ICC) or the Civil Aeronautics Board (CAB). These agencies were created by Congress to function in this administrative and regulatory capacity. The ICC has jurisdiction over the economic aspects of several modes of interstate carriage, including railroads, oil pipelines, and surface freight forwarders, as well as some segments of motor and water carriage. The CAB has similar regulatory responsibilities in air transportation.

Essentially, these agencies administer the economic aspects of transportation law on a case by case basis. They influence the policy formulation process in that many provisions of transportation law have been drafted by Congress in rather vague terms, thus providing considerable latitude for regulatory agency interpretation. For many years the regulatory agencies played a parallel role in administering safety regulations. However, these responsibilities were transferred to the DOT following its creation in 1967.

When individual cases are being considered by the regulatory agencies, shippers, carriers, and other interested parties may provide formal inputs to the agency by filing position papers or appearing at hearings. In certain instances the agency's decisions may be appealed on legal grounds in the court system. Some cases pertaining to transportation matters are ultimately heard by the Supreme Court. For example, in 1966 the Supreme Court upheld the legality of the ICC's approval of the Penn Central consolidation.[13] The Regional Rail Reorganization Act of 1973, which created a mechanism for restructuring the bankrupt railroad system of the Northeast, was challenged before the Supreme Court as being unconstitutional. However, the Court ruled against railroad security holders who had instituted the suit and found the congressional action to be constitutional, thereby paving the way for the reorganization.[14]

A parallel transportation policy development process also occurs at the state level, with state legislative bodies, regulatory agencies, and courts interacting in a pattern similar to that of their federal counterparts.

The preceding discussion of the transportation policy formulation process was by no means comprehensive. In fact, Chapter 11 is devoted entirely to this matter. However, the preceding brief introduction to this matter should allow the reader to quickly comprehend the significance of such daily news releases as

The Boston & Maine Railroad today petitioned the ICC to allow it to abandon 200 miles of track in northern New England.

or,

Today the Department of Transportation recommended to the Civil Aeronautics Board that it reduce domestic air fares by 10 percent.

SUMMARY

The transportation system of the United States is an important component of the nation's economic, social, and political structure, and thus influences many aspects of our daily lives. Conversely, individual decisions concerning such matters as the purchase of transportation services from for-hire carriers and the use of private automobiles affect the development of the transportation system.

The United States has an extensive transportation network that has evolved through a joint system of public and private expenditures. Due to transportation's importance in the realization of personal and governmental goals, extensive governmental involvement has emerged in both the promotion and regulation of transportation. The promotional expenditures of various governmental units play a major role in financing the growth and maintenance of the national transportation network. Furthermore, the economic and safety regulations that have been applied to transportation have had a pervasive impact on the structure and performance of the transportation industry.

NOTES

1. Wilfred Owen, *Strategy for Mobility* (Washington, D.C.: Brookings Institution, 1964), pp. 191–94.
2. Roy J. Sampson and Martin T. Farris, *Domestic Transportation: Practice, Theory, and Policy,* 3rd ed. (Boston: Houghton Mifflin Company, 1975), p. 8.
3. Ibid.
4. For an interesting discussion of this matter, see Wilfred Owen, *The Accessible City* (Washington, D.C.: Brookings Institution, 1972), pp. 114–35.
5. U.S. Department of Transportation, Office of the Secretary, *Energy Statistics: A Supplement to the Summary of National Transportation Statistics* (Springfield, Va.: National Technical Information Service, 1973), p. 67.
6. U.S. Department of Transportation, Office of the Secretary, *A Statement*

of National Transportation Policy (Washington, D.C.: Government Printing Office, 1975), p. 35.

7. James W. Bennett and William J. Dewitt, "The Development of State Departments of Transportation—A Recent Organizational Phenomena," *Transportation Journal,* XII, No. 1 (Fall, 1972), p. 12.

8. American Transit Association, *'70–'71 Transit Fact Book* (Washington, D.C.: the Association, 1971), p. 12.

9. U.S. Department of Transportation, Office of the Secretary, *A Summary of National Transportation Statistics* (Springfield, Va.: National Technical Information Service, 1973), p. 21.

10. Transportation Association of America, *Transportation Facts and Trends* (Washington, D.C.: the Association, 1976), p. 30.

11. Ibid., pp. 4–5.

12. Ibid.

13. Pennsylvania Railroad Company–Merger–New York Central Railroad Company, 327 ICC 475 (1966).

14. United States Railway Association, *Preliminary System Plan* (Washington, D.C.: U.S. Railway Association, 1975), I, p. iv.

SELECTED REFERENCES

Bigham, Truman C., and Merrill V. Roberts. *Transportation Principles and Problems,* 2nd ed. New York: McGraw-Hill Book Company, 1952.
Chapter 1. "General Significance of Transportation," pp. 1–13.
Chapter 2. "Transportation and Production," pp. 17–28.
Chapter 3. "Transportation and Exchange," pp. 29–48.

Daggett, Stuart. *Principles of Inland Transportation,* 4th ed. New York: Harper & Row, Inc., 1955.
Chapter 2. "The Effects of Improved Transportation on Industrial Society," pp. 12–27.

Fair, Marvin L., and Ernest W. Williams. *Economics of Transportation and Logistics.* Dallas, Tex.: Business Publications, Inc., 1975.
Chapter 1. "The Transportation System of the United States," pp. 1–18.
Chapter 2. "Transport and Economic Development," pp. 19–32.
Chapter 3. "Transport and Sociopolitical Development," pp. 33–47.

Kneafsey, James T. *The Economics of the Transportation Firm: Market Structure and Industrial Performance.* Lexington, Mass.: D.C. Heath & Company, 1974.
Chapter 1. "Introduction: The Domestic Transportation Industries," pp. 1–14.

Lansing, John B. *Transportation and Economic Policy.* New York: Free Press, 1966.
Chapter 1. "The Objectives of Policy," pp. 3–11.
Chapter 2. "The Economic Functions of Transportation," pp. 12–26.

Locklin, D. Philip. *Economics of Transportation,* 7th ed. Homewood, Ill.: Richard D. Irwin, Inc., 1972.
Chapter 1. "Economic Significance of Improved Transportation," pp. 1–18.
Chapter 2. "The Transportation System of the United States," pp. 19–48.

Norton, Hugh S. *Modern Transportation Economics,* 2nd ed. Columbus, Ohio: Charles E. Merrill Publishing Company, 1963.
Chapter 1. "Transportation: An Economic, Social and Political Function," pp. 3–18.

Owen, Wilfred. *The Accessible City.* Washington D.C.: Brookings Institution, 1972.
Chapter 5. "Combining Transportation and Community Development," pp. 114–35.

Owen, Wilfred. *Strategy for Mobility.* Washington, D.C.: Brookings Institution, 1964.
Chapter 3. "Transportation Requirements for Development," pp. 44–85.

Pegrum, Dudley F. *Transportation: Economics and Public Policy,* rev. ed. Homewood, Ill.: Richard D. Irwin, Inc., 1968.
Chapter 1. "Transportation and the Economy," pp. 3–23.

Sampson, Roy J., and Martin T. Farris. *Domestic Transportation: Practice, Theory, and Policy,* 3rd ed. Boston: Houghton Mifflin Company, 1975.
Chapter 1. "The Role of Domestic Transportation," pp. 1–16.

U.S. Department of Transportation, Office of the Secretary. *Energy Statistics: A Supplement to the Summary of National Transportation Statistics.* Springfield, Va.: National Technical Information Service, 1973.

U.S. Department of Transportation, Office of the Secretary. *Summary of National Transportation Statistics.* Springfield, Va.: National Technical Information Service, 1973.

DISCUSSION QUESTIONS

1. Why have federal, state, and local government units played such an active funding role in transportation development?
2. Discuss briefly the relative roles played by Congress, the Department of Transportation, and the regulatory agencies in formulating and administering national transportation policy.
3. Distinguish between the promotional and regulatory roles that the federal government plays in transportation.

CHAPTER

2

Transportation: The Shipper's Perspective

Although this book focuses primarily on the structure, regulation, and performance of the domestic transportation industries, it is important that the perspective of the shipping public be included. Each of us, at various times, acts as a shipper. We may contact a household goods carrier to move our belongings to a new home or send a trunk full of books and clothes to a family member who is away at school. However, the scope of our individual transactions is greatly overshadowed by the shipping activities of large corporations. For example, it has been estimated that on any given day Ford Motor Company has approximately 50,000 finished vehicles in transit and almost 1 billion finished parts bound for assembly plants and parts depots. Additionally, the company ships over 14 million tons of raw materials and semifinished parts each year.[1] It is important that the significance of transportation to shippers, both large and small, be understood not only in dollar terms but also as a means of realizing company objectives. Achievement of this understanding will make later chapters concerning carrier and governmental actions more meaningful. Consequently, this chapter concentrates on the industrial shipper.

In the typical manufacturing firm, transportation expenses rank third in dollar outlays, behind direct materials and direct labor.[2] Due to the scope of their business, many companies have substantial transportation budgets. For example, Eastman Kodak Company's transportation budget annually exceeds $75 million.[3] Naturally, when such sums of money are involved, understanding transportation options available to the firm and integrating transportation planning with other company activities is of the utmost importance. These matters are explored in this chapter.

PHYSICAL DISTRIBUTION MANAGEMENT

The emergence of national and international markets for many products, particularly in the post-1960 period, has necessitated the development of complex distribution patterns. Indicative of the scope of the distribution networks of many large companies is the Hershey Foods Company, which serves customers at more than 65,000 locations.[4] Product lines have increased in scope, and multiple manufacturing and distribution locations have become commonplace in U.S. industry. At the same time, the application of the total systems concept to the business enterprise has resulted from recognition of the fact that a company's success is quite dependent upon the smooth interaction of numerous organizational components, such as transportation, marketing, and production. It has become obvious that these functions, as well as many others, must not be approached in isolation, but rather must be managed in a systematic fashion so as to realize the goals of the total organization.

In a transportation context this has led to the emergence of the concept of *physical distribution* or *logistics management*. Definitions of this concept abound. However, the one accepted in this book is that

> Physical distribution is the management of movement, inventory control, protection, and storage of raw materials and processed or finished goods to and from the production line.[5]

This necessarily includes transportation, materials handling, industrial packaging, warehousing, inventory control, and location analysis. It has been estimated that expenditures for such activities generally range between 20 and 50 percent of sales for most firms.[6]

Physical Distribution Activities

Adoption of the physical distribution management approach necessitates a major shift in organizational thinking because, historically, control over this range of activities has been quite dispersed. For example, it was not uncommon for a company's production department to be responsible for inventory control, while the traffic department managed transportation activities, and industrial engineering controlled packaging and material-handling techniques. This fragmentation of authority often led to organizational conflicts and suboptimal performance. A desire to integrate these activities has led many companies to appoint a director or vice-president of physical distribution. This individual is responsible for coordinating and controlling physical distribution activities, and in most instances the department heads who previously controlled these functions report to the director. Due to the importance of this position, considerable attention must be devoted to staffing it. The individual selected should be well versed not only in distribution activities but also in many other phases of his company's operations.

There are considerable differences in the range of responsibilities assigned to physical distribution executives in various companies. These differences may be well justified. In fact, there is no generally accepted pattern for physical distribution organization. In addressing this organizational issue the individual company must necessarily consider the needs created by such factors as its market structures, product lines, locational patterns, cost characteristics, and competitive situation. A thorough assessment of these considerations improves the likelihood of the emergence of a pattern of physical distribution controls that are well suited to the company's needs.

The interrelationship of physical distribution activities creates a situation in which a company is faced with a series of *tradeoff* possibilities. For example, often a choice must be made between the use of two different modes of for-hire carriage. Typically, air freight rates would be higher than those charged by motor carriers; if transportation cost minimization was the basic concern, motor carriage would be selected. However, the higher freight rates of air carriage might be *traded off* against the fact that air service is generally faster and its packaging requirements are often less stringent. Additionally, the use of air freight might improve customer service levels while reducing inventory requirements (due to shorter delivery cycles) at various distribution points. In this instance the total cost of air freight distribution might actually be lower than the total cost of distribution by motor carriage.

In physical distribution such choices are numerous, and decisions are necessarily influenced by a variety of factors, including the company's customer service standards and production schedules.

The following discussion further examines the transportation or traffic component of physical distribution management, and illustrates its interaction with other corporate activities. Systematic management of these interactions, regardless of the organizational structure adopted by a company, can lead to significant improvements in both cost control and customer service levels. The coverage given these topics is by no means exhaustive, but rather serves to clarify the role of transportation in the corporate setting.

Traffic

Transportation is usually the most costly component of physical distribution management.[7] In attempting to control transportation outlays, those involved in the industrial traffic or transportation function have a broad range of responsibilities. The most obvious of these is arranging for transportation of materials to processing or manufacturing facilities and of finished products to the next link in the distribution channel. Finished goods movements may involve several basic distribution patterns. The finished product may be shipped directly to the ultimate consumer or to a warehouse for storage; in other cases it might be shipped to distributors. Generally, fulfillment of these varied transportation needs necessitates reliance upon for-hire carriers to at least a limited degree. Consequently, those in traffic departments often arrange for the purchase of transportation services, which is not the simple task that many people assume it to be. Selections must be made not only among modes, but also among carriers within a mode. The ultimate carrier selection, however, should be approached on a multidimensional basis. Besides rate differences, the traffic department must also be concerned with differences in service offerings, routings, speed, reliability, packaging requirements, and the likelihood of loss and damage. Each factor has direct implications with respect to both cost and customer service. In such instances it is also the responsibility of the department to inform those in other functional areas of the *trade-off* possibilities and the cost of certain policy alternatives. This might involve such issues as the cost of shifting from a three- to two-day customer delivery pattern, or the amount of money that could be saved through consolidation of shipments (as discussed later, as the weight of a shipment increases, transportation charges tend to decline on a per unit of weight basis).

In companies that have adopted the physical distribution management concept, the director or vice-president of physical distribution often interacts with such parties as the director of marketing in assessing the merits of these matters.

Traffic responsibilities related to a shipment do not cease once the carrier has been contacted. Shipping documentation must be prepared, such as the bill of lading. This serves as the basic contract between carrier and shipper, and specifies such factors as the names of the parties involved, commodities and quantities shipped, routing, rates, and carrier liabilities. At some later date, the department may also be involved in such activities as tracing the shipment, processing loss and damage claims, and auditing carrier freight bills for accuracy. Auditing may either be conducted internally or by companies that specialize in this function. The benefits of freight bill auditing are often substantial. For example, Scovill Manufacturing Company estimates that it recovers between $130,000 and $140,000 in transportation charges each year as the result of its audit.[8]

The traffic department can also play an active role in promoting changes in carrier rates and service. By negotiating with carriers and making presentations before carrier rate bureaus and regulatory agencies, those involved in traffic may influence the level of transportation costs incurred by the company. This is one area in which the purchasing power of large shippers can effectively be used to their advantage. This matter is discussed in detail in Chapter 9.

Often the traffic department is responsible for arranging the movement of personal belongings of transferred employees to new locations and for making travel arrangements for employees traveling on company business. The department may also be involved in the operations of a private transportation fleet possessed by the company, and it often becomes involved in company location decisions. These last two matters are discussed later in this chapter.

Traffic's Interaction with Other Activities

The interaction of traffic with other company activities is quite varied. A sampling of these relationships is provided in the following discussion.

Close interaction between traffic and marketing personnel is essential. It is the responsibility of the traffic department to inform marketing personnel of such information as the cost of altering established customer service standards. For example, shifting from a three- to two-day delivery standard may attract additional customers, but the increase in transportation costs that it necessitates may outweigh the additional revenues that it generates.

Traffic can also be of assistance in the delineation of company markets. In some instances, the transportation cost burden of serving distant markets may well preclude the possibility of serving such markets profitably. The characteristics of carriers serving markets must also be conveyed to marketing personnel so they can quote realistic delivery dates. At the same time, marketing must convey information to traffic personnel concerning such matters as future volume projections, new markets to be served, and specific promotional programs that would create any *irregular* demands on the traffic department. A two-way communications flow of this nature between traffic and marketing is essential not only in planning and controlling transportation activities, but also in realizing marketing objectives.

Traffic can also assist in the reduction of inventory costs. The dollar cost associated with carrying inventory includes not only the cost of capital committed to inventory, but also the costs associated with storage,

22

handling, obsolescence, taxes, and insurance. These costs naturally vary from company to company; one source has estimated that they may total 25 percent of average inventory value.[9] One means of reducing inventory costs involves the use of either faster modes of carriage or express service. As indicated earlier, this will increase transportation costs, but inventory costs will tend to fall because inventory in transit will be reduced. Additionally, inventory requirements at various distribution points may be lowered by development of a faster delivery cycle. Analysis of the total cost of such actions is necessary before a decision can be properly made.

Traffic can also play a role in the development of packaging standards for a company. Insight into the handling characteristics of the various modes is quite useful in the design of protective packaging specifications. Traffic should also furnish advice concerning the form in which products should be shipped (e.g., should assembled products or components be shipped?). In many instances there are substantial differences in the freight rates which apply to these items, and it may be beneficial to the company to establish assembly operations near major markets to take advantage of the transportation cost differential.

The design of a company's material-handling system must necessarily influence and be influenced by shipping considerations. Attention must be given to such factors as whether the company plans to use pallets or containers in its shipping. These factors influence the types of equipment, such as conveyors and forklifts, selected for movement within company-operated facilities, and play a role in the design of the physical layout of facilities.

Any number of additional illustrations of traffic's interaction with other company activities, such as production scheduling and finance, could be provided, but these interactions are quite similar to the *trade-off* situations already discussed.

PRIVATE CARRIAGE

A growing number of shippers have instituted private carriage operations. Many of these operations are of limited scope, such as delivery operations for local dairies and department stores, but some are both multimodal and interstate in scope. An indication of the scale of some private operations was provided by a 1967 national survey of companies engaged in private carriage. Approximately two-thirds of the 1,800 responding companies reported that they moved at least half their company's freight by private carriage.[10] Seventy percent of these companies operated their fleets on an interstate basis, and 20 percent had runs of over 1,000 miles.[11] One example of an extensive company commitment to private carriage is

Phillips Petroleum Company, which maintains 4,900 rail cars, 3,000 trucks, and 2,000 automobiles.[12] Similarly, other companies have established private barge, pipeline, railroad, and aircraft operations.

Private carriage frequently offers potential savings in transportation costs. One Boston-based paper company was able to reduce transportation outlays by 45 percent by using leased trucks.[13] Similarly, Scoville Corporation reported savings of $285,000 per year following its switch to private carriage.[14] Although many other examples of transportation cost savings generated in this manner might be cited, the conversion to private carriage is often precipitated by service considerations. Potentially, private carriage offers better service because of flexibility of routes and schedules, greater speed, and reduction of loss and damage. It also provides the company with access to transportation equipment when it needs it. This access is not automatic when dealing with for-hire carriers, particularly if the shipper needs specialized equipment such as tank trucks or refrigerated rail cars.

The most frequently used form of private carriage is trucking. Studies have indicated that the use of private truck operations tends to increase with the size of the firm up to very large companies, which typically rely less heavily on private carriage. Indications are that medium-sized shippers, those which generate 4,000 to 20,000 tons per year, rely most heavily upon company-owned trucking.[15] Shippers that generate smaller volumes are unable to utilize privately owned vehicles intensely enough to justify the equipment investment. Larger shippers, due to their buying power, often are able to use this leverage with carriers to obtain the rates and services that they desire. In many instances, firms that have moved into private carriage still use common carriage, particularly for meeting peak volume requirements.

Traffic's Involvement

The personnel of a company's traffic department typically become involved in private carriage at two levels. The first of these is at the decision-making level in determining whether the establishment of company-owned transportation capabilities is justified. Second, if a decision is made to move into private carriage, the traffic department may become involved in the operation of the private fleet.

The traffic department should play a major role in the analysis of the feasibility of private carriage. Studies of carrier cost structures and rate patterns, and analysis of service offerings and market coverage should be undertaken. Also, the total cost of both purchasing and operating private carriage must be projected. This involves consideration of capital outlays related to equipment acquisition and maintenance facilities, and operating

24

cost elements such as fuel, operator compensation, supervision, maintenance, and licensing. Similarly, the comparative costs of equipment purchase versus leasing should be explored. As previously noted, however, service considerations may outweigh cost factors. Consequently, historical data concerning such matters as carrier delivery patterns and loss and damage claims should be developed, and these should be compared with projections related to company-owned operations. Compilation of this information improves the likelihood of the traffic department being able to effectively interact with other functional areas, including marketing and finance, in addressing this important issue.

In those companies in which private carriage has become a reality, the traffic department generally supervises the operation of the private fleet. Supervision may entail numerous activities, such as scheduling of equipment utilization and operating personnel, development of routes to be used, formulation of shipment consolidation plans, and arrangement of interplant and warehouse transfers. The last matter is important, because one major problem area related to the use of private carriage is the sparsity of two-directional moves. Thus many companies employing private fleets incur a considerable volume of empty mileage. One study of this issue indicated that nearly 57 percent of private trucking movements had empty backhauls.[16] However, careful analysis and planning of all company movements, both intracompany and to customers, can improve equipment utilization. Additionally, many companies engaged in private truck and barge operations solicit exempt commodities (commodities that are not subject to the economic jurisdiction of regulatory agencies) as backhauls. The specific nature of these exemptions is examined in Chapters 4 and 5. Solicitation of this traffic allows private carriage not only to serve in a cost reduction or service improvement capacity, but also enables it to function as a revenue generator.

INDUSTRIAL LOCATION

Company decisions concerning the location of facilities, whether manufacturing plants, warehouses, or distribution points, play an important role in determining both a company's cost structure and its ability to serve customers. Inappropriate location decisions are costly to reverse, particularly if a company has chosen to build rather than lease facilities. Additional costs are generated by such matters as labor turnover, hiring and training of new personnel at a different location, and moving expenses. Consequently, location decisions cannot be treated casually.

Analysis of company location decisions should be a continuing process due to the dynamic nature of the markets served by many companies. A number of companies have created standing committees composed of representatives of various functional areas to periodically review these matters. Outside assistance may also be obtained, in many cases at no cost, through chambers of commerce, utility companies, and carriers.

Location Variables

Location decisions are typically approached at two levels: (1) the selection of a general geographic area, and (2) the choice of a site within a given community. Proceeding on this basis, the decision makers must consider a variety of factors, which often vary by location. Among these are the comparative cost and availability of labor, energy, raw materials, capital, property, and transportation. Additional attention must be given to such matters as access to markets, living conditions, tax rates, and community services offered in various locations. Naturally, the personal preferences of the decision makers also play important roles in this process.

The relative significance of the various decision-making variables differs across industries. Throughout the years considerable study has been made of the influence of various factors on industrial location. Manufacturing locations of some industries, such as the steel and paper, tend to be drawn toward the source of raw materials, which lose a considerable portion of their weight in the manufacturing process.[17] In contrast, the dominant location variable that operates in the apparel industry appears to be market access, while climate has played the major role in selection of locations for flight testing in the aerospace industry.[18]

Only by considering the broad range of location variables in a comprehensive manner can a company hope to optimize its location decisions. In the academic setting, increasing attention has been devoted to this topic, as well as to the role that government can play in influencing both location and growth patterns. A number of universities have established programs in regional sciences to focus on this matter.

Traffic's Influence on Location

A company's traffic or transportation staff often plays an active role in the location decision-making process. Documentation of raw material and finished product flows to and from existing facilities and projections of shifts necessitated by modifying location patterns are of the utmost importance. Similarly, comparative studies of both service availability and carrier rates in various prospective locations should be undertaken. Carrier schedules, equipment availability, and likely delivery times to various customer and company locations must also be examined. Overall impact on the company's transportation budget must be projected. Of course, this must be weighed against changes in other nontransportation cost categories.

A number of quantitative techniques, such as simulation, can facilitate this analysis. A discussion of the nature and capabilities of the various mathematical formulations is clearly beyond the scope of this book, but it should be noted that many firms, including the H. J. Heinz Company, Whirlpool Corporation, and Miles Laboratories, have effectively used quantitative methods to improve their physical distribution efforts.[19]

SUMMARY

This chapter has focused on the perspective of the industrial shipper. It should now be clear that the management of a shipper's transportation function is often a quite complex task involving a variety of responsibilities. Among these are carrier selection, shipment consolidation, routing, and rate negotiations. In many companies it also includes management of the firm's private carriage operations and participation in industrial location decisions. The transportation outlays of many companies are substantial, and knowledge of available options can have considerable dollar and service significance.

The complexity of emerging distribution patterns and pressures to control costs while meeting customer service standards have led many companies to adopt the concept of physical distribution management. Acceptance of this concept leads to the integration of transportation, materials handling, industrial packaging, warehousing, and inventory control. It should be remembered, however, that there is no generally accepted pattern of physical distribution organization. A thorough assessment of such matters as market structures, product lines, cost characteristics, and the competitive environment improves the likelihood of the creation of a system of physical distribution controls that is well suited to company needs.

NOTES

1. Charles A. Taff, *Management of Physical Distribution and Transportation,* 5th ed. (Homewood, Ill.: Richard D. Irwin, Inc., 1972), p. 15.

2. Roy J. Sampson and Martin T. Farris, *Domestic Transportation: Practice, Theory, and Policy,* 3rd ed. (Boston: Houghton Mifflin Company, 1975), p. 4.

3. Jack W. Farrell, "Distribution Dynamics at Work: Eastman Kodak Company," *Traffic Management,* X, No. 11 (November, 1971), p. 41.

4. Jack W. Farrell, *Physical Distribution Case Studies* (Boston: Cahners Publishing Company, 1973), p. 273.

5. Taff, op. cit., p. 8.

6. Donald J. Bowersox, Edward W. Smykay, and Bernard J. Lalonde, *Physical Distribution Management,* rev. ed. (New York: Macmillan Publishing Co., Inc., 1968), p. 13.

7. Sampson and Farris, op. cit., p. 245.

8. Jack W. Farrell, "Distribution Dynamics at Work: Scovill Manufacturing Company," *Traffic Management,* IX, No. 1 (January, 1970), p. 48.

9. James L. Heskett, Nicholas A. Glaskowsky, Jr., and Robert M. Ivie, *Business Logistics: Physical Distribution and Materials Management,* 2nd ed. (New York: Ronald Press Company, 1973), p. 20.

10. Robert M. Butler, "Preliminary Data on Private Trucking Show 77% Don't Haul Exempt Commodities," *Traffic World,* CXXX, No. 12 (June 17, 1967), p. 50.

11. Ibid.

12. Jack W. Farrell, "Distribution Dynamics at Work: Phillips Petroleum Company," *Traffic Management,* VIII, No. 1 (January, 1969), p. 63.

13. Kenneth Flood, "Decision Making in Private Carriage," in *Private and Unregulated Carriage* (Evanston, Ill.: Northwestern University, Transportation Center, 1963), p. 63.

14. Farrell, "Distribution Dynamics at Work: Scovill Manufacturing Company," p. 47.

15. Walter Y. Oi and Arthur P. Hurter, Jr., *Economics of Private Truck Transportation* (Dubuque, Iowa: William C. Brown Company, 1965), pp. 182–84.

16. Highway Research Board, "Line Haul Trucking Costs in Relation to Vehicle Gross Weights," Bulletin 301 (1961), p. 83.

17. For an extensive discussion of location theory, see Walter Isard, *Location and Space-Economy* (Cambridge, Mass.: The MIT Press, 1956), especially pp. 24–54.

18. Gunnar Alexandersson, *Geography of Manufacturing,* Foundations of Economic Geography Series (Englewood Cliffs, N.J.: Prentice-Hall, Inc., 1967), pp. 73, 99.

19. Harvey N. Shycon and Richard B. Maffei, "Simulation—Tool for Better Distribution," *Harvard Business Review,* XXXVII, No. 6 (November–December, 1960), pp. 65–75; also, James F. Piechosowski, "Miles . . . What If . . . ?" *Distribution Worldwide,* LXXV, No. 5 (May, 1976), pp. 24–27, and Joy V. Sterling, "Whirlpool . . . What If . . . ?" *Distribution Worldwide,* LXXV, No. 5 (May, 1976), pp. 32–35.

SELECTED REFERENCES

American Electric Power Service Corporation. *How to Find a Plant Site Without Losing Your Mind.* New York: the Corporation, 1969.

Arizzi, Vincent V. "The Role of the Corporate Staff Transportation Group in Medium and Large Diversified Manufacturing Organizations," *Transportation Journal,* XIV, No. 2 (Winter, 1974), pp. 41–52.

Ballou, Ronald H. *Business Logistics Management.* Englewood Cliffs, N.J.: Prentice-Hall, Inc., 1973.
Chapter 1. "An Overview of Business Logistics," pp. 4–29.

Bartlett, Hale C. *Readings in Physical Distribution,* 3rd ed. Danville, Ill.: Interstate Printers and Publishers, 1972.
Part I. "Nature of Physical Distribution Management," pp. 5–40.
Part II. "Organizing for Physical Distribution," pp. 43–60.

Bowersox, Daniel J., Edward W. Smykay, and Bernard J. Lalonde. *Physical Distribution Management,* rev. ed. New York: Macmillan Publishing Co., Inc., 1968.
Chapter 1. "Physical Distribution Management," pp. 1–19.
Chapter 2. "Marketing and Physical Distribution Interaction," pp. 20–31.

Davis, Grant M., and Joseph Rosenberg. "Physical Distribution Management —A Collage of 1973 Observations," *Transportation Journal,* XIII, No. 4 (Summer, 1974), pp. 50–56.

DeHayes, Daniel, Jr., and Robert L. Taylor. "Moving Beyond Physical Distribution Organization." *Transportation Journal,* XIII, No. 3 (Spring, 1974), pp. 30–41.

Farrell, Jack W. *Physical Distribution Case Studies.* Boston: Cahners Publishing Company, 1973.
Chapter 1. "Gearing the Organization for Physical Distribution," pp. 1–44.
Chapter 2. "Logisitcs in the Giant Companies," pp. 45–147.

Flood, Kenneth. *Traffic Management,* 2nd ed. Dubuque, Iowa: William C. Brown Company, 1963.
Chapter 1. "The Buying and Selling of Transportation Service," pp. 1–23.
Chapter 2. "Company Operated Transport," pp. 24–51.

Greenhut, Melvin L. *Plant Location in Theory and Practice.* Chapel Hill, N.C.: University of North Carolina Press, 1956.
Part I. "Review of Location Theory," pp. 3–100.
Part II. "A General Theory of Plant Location," pp. 251–91.

Heskett, James L., Nicholas A. Glaskowsky, Jr., and Robert M. Ivie. *Business Logistics: Physical Distribution and Materials Management,* 2nd ed. New York: Ronald Press Company, 1973.
Chapter 1. "Logistics in the Economy," pp. 5–24.
Chapter 2. "Logistics in the Enterprise," pp. 25–56.

Isard, Walter. *Location and Space-Economy.* Cambridge, Mass.: The MIT Press, 1956.
Chapter 2. "Some General Theories of Location and Space Economy," pp. 24–54.

Johnson, James C. *Readings in Contemporary Physical Distribution.* Tulsa, Okla.: Commerce Press, 1974.
Part I. "Physical Distribution Overview," pp. 1–53.
Part III. "The Transportation Elements of Physical Distribution," pp. 109–211.

Oi, Walter Y., and Arthur P. Hurter, Jr. *Economics of Private Truck Transportation.* Dubuque, Iowa: William C. Brown Company, 1965.

Sampson, Roy J., and Martin T. Farris. *Domestic Transportation: Practice, Theory, and Policy,* 3rd ed. Boston: Houghton Mifflin Company, 1975.
Chapter 16. "Traffic Management's Role in the Decision-Making Mechanism," pp. 255–71.
Chapter 17. "Traffic Control Decisions and Activities," pp. 273–88.
Chapter 18. "Traffic Management's Relationship to Other Operating Decisions," pp. 289–99.

Smykay, Edward W. *Physical Distribution Management,* 3rd ed. New York: Macmillan Publishing Co., Inc., 1973.
Chapter 1. "Physical Distribution Management," pp. 1–21.
Chapter 2. "Marketing and Physical Distribution Interaction," pp. 22–45.

Taff, Charles A. *Management of Physical Distribution and Transportation,* 5th ed. Homewood, Ill.: Richard D. Irwin, Inc., 1972.
Chapter 1. "Conceptual Framework," pp. 3–19.
Chapter 2. "Organizing for Physical Distribution," pp. 20–36.
Chapter 8. "Make or Buy Decisions," pp. 166–95.

DISCUSSION QUESTIONS

1. To what extent can shippers (consumers of transportation services) influence the characteristics of the for-hire transportation marketplace? Be specific and give illustrations where applicable.

2. Explain the concept of physical distribution management, and discuss its importance to the typical large manufacturing firm.

3. Develop a checklist of the factors that should be considered by a company in selecting a location for a new production facility.

4. Assume that you are the director of physical distribution for a manufacturing firm. The finance committee of your company is considering the possibility of financing a private truck fleet to handle the company's transportation needs. You have been asked to make a presentation to the committee that examines both the potential benefits and problems that might be encountered in operating such a private fleet. What would you tell them?

PART 2

Modes of Intercity Carriage

CHAPTER
3

The Railroad Industry

In recent years, the problems of the railroad industry have been widely publicized. Many people were stunned by the 1970 bankruptcy of the largest U.S. railroad, the Penn Central. Before that turmoil had quieted, Congress found it necessary to create a quasi-public corporation, Amtrak, to assume the financial burden of continued intercity rail passenger service. More recently, Congress enacted the Regional Rail Reorganization Act of 1973 to facilitate a financial restructuring of seven bankrupt railroads in the Northeast, including the Penn Central.

Based on this chain of events, one might conclude that the railroad industry is no longer a significant component of the national transportation system, but is merely a financial drain on taxpayers. However, as noted in Chapter 1, the railroads still generate more intercity freight ton mileage than any other mode. Also, it should not be assumed that the financial condition of the railroads of the Northeast is indicative of the status of the aggregate industry. For many years there have been significant regional differences in railroad profitability because of variances in regional economic growth rates, commodity flows, length of hauls, and competitive intensity. At the same time, rail technology's inherent capabilities in moving large-volume bulk loads, coupled with its comparative energy efficiency, indicate that the railroads will continue to be a major component of our national transportation system for many years to come.

The Railroad Industry

This chapter examines the development and structure of the railroad industry, and highlights its strengths and problems. Many of these problems are examined in greater detail in later chapters.

DEVELOPMENT OF THE SYSTEM

Throughout the years, technological developments have led to major shifts in the market positions of the various forms of carriage. Typically, the newer technologies have offered speed, flexibility, and cost advantages over earlier modes; consequently, some traffic has been diverted to the newer modes. In most cases this has led to long-term adjustments in market shares as competitive reactions have surfaced in the marketplace. However, in some instances the technological change has been so great that it has overwhelmed existing competitors. This was the case during the last half of the nineteenth century following the emergence of rail technology.

Early Railroad Competition

Prior to the introduction of railroad services, economic development had been closely tied to available waterways. A variety of vessel types, including flatboats, barges, and steamboats, used the waterway system. Service was slow and expensive.[1] The canal-building era, which commenced in the 1820s, attempted to inject an element of flexibility into the waterway network to promote more widespread economic growth. The success of some early canal projects, such as the Erie Canal, which linked the Hudson River and the Great Lakes, in stimulating economic development led to heavy state government spending for canal construction. However, overbuilding occurred, and many of the canals built during the period were financial disasters.

Highway travel at that time was quite restricted due to limited federal and state expenditures for highway development; the private sector was unable to generate adequate funds for significant highway expansion. The shortcomings of early road-building techniques and the vulnerability of many roads to adverse weather conditions also hindered travel.

The application of the steam engine to locomotives during the 1830s ushered in what was to be an extremely competitive period in transportation. Most early rail lines were local, and often initially served in a feeder capacity to water and highway carriage. However, it soon became apparent that this new technology, with its speed and flexibility advantages, offered potential competition to the highway and waterway modes. As rail operations expanded, intermodal competition increased in intensity.

Table 3–1

Railroad Mileage Operated in the United States

Year	Mileage
1830	23
1840	2,818
1850	9,021
1860	30,626
1870	52,922
1880	93,262
1890	166,703
1900	192,556
1910	240,831
1920	259,941
1930	260,440
1940	233,670
1950	223,779
1960	217,552
1970	206,265
1974	200,916
1975	200,000

SOURCE: Data supplied by the Department of Commerce and the Association of American Railroads.

Railroad mileage expanded rapidly in the post-1830 period (see Table 3–1), and numerous end-to-end consolidations led to the emergence of the first railroad systems.[2]

Throughout that expansionary period the bulk of the capital that financed railroad development came from the private sector. However, as the strengths of rail service became apparent, state and local governments used tax concessions, loans, security guarantees, and land grants as enticements to railroads to lay new track. Railroads also began to attract attention at the national level. In fact, during the Civil War, railroads were used as a means of securing the West to the Union. Federal assistance in the form of massive land grants was extended to a number of railroads to facilitate the building of a transcontinental linkage, which was completed in 1869. Thus a precedent was set that involved the use of railroads as an instrument of public policy.

The financial inducements led not only to tremendous expansion of the railroad network, but also provided an opportunity for financial mismanagement. A number of early railroad promoters amassed sizable fortunes by swindling railroad investors.[3] Such actions and growing concern for protection of the public interest against discrimination and other monopoly-related abuses ultimately led to federal regulation of the industry. With the passage of the Act to Regulate Commerce in 1887, the Interstate Commerce Commission was created to regulate interstate rail carriage, and the pattern of extensive federal regulation of transportation was initiated.

Resurgence of Intermodal Competition

By 1900, rail carriage was the dominant mode of both intercity freight and passenger movements. There is considerable debate as to whether the diversion of traffic from water and highway carriage to the railroads was caused by the superior characteristics of rail technology or by predatory behavior in the marketplace. In any event, rail service became dominant, and from 1900 to 1920 the transportation competition that did exist was primarily intramodal in nature. At that time, federal regulation of railroads was strongly oriented toward promotion of competition among rail carriers.

The competitive position of the railroad industry has changed drastically since then. Government expenditure programs that have financed highway, waterway, and airport–airway expansion and the emergence of the newer forms of technology have led to significant competitive inroads. Trucks, barges, pipelines, airplanes, buses, and private automobiles now compete for traffic that was once tightly controlled by the railroads. The market share of intercity ton mileage handled by the railroads has been halved, and rail passenger service has declined to minimal significance. The industry has responded to these developments with technological changes, service innovations, service cutbacks, and mergers, but its financial condition in the post-World War II period has at best been marginal. This has prompted many questions concerning the future role of railroads in the national transportation system. Specific policy issues that will influence this role are addressed in subsequent chapters.

INDUSTRIAL AND FINANCIAL STRUCTURE

Our nation's railroads provide service over an extensive physical network that includes approximately 200,000 miles of rail lines and 325,000 miles of track. Figure 3–1 provides a map of the contemporary railroad system. In conducting their operations the railroads utilize more than 30,000 locomotives, approximately 1.7 million freight cars, and nearly 7,100 passenger cars.[4]

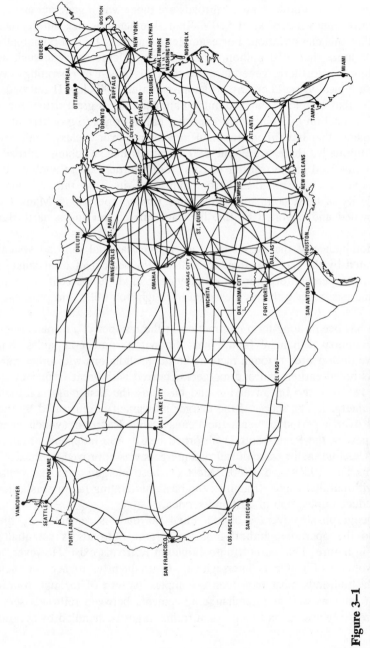

Figure 3–1

U.S. Railroad Mainlines—Routes Between Principal Cities

SOURCE: U.S. Department of Transportation.

The Railroad Industry

Although the railroad industry might appear to be a grouping of homogeneous companies, in reality it consists of several quite different components. Predominant among these are the 52 class I railroads. According to ICC standards, class I railroads are those which generate annual operating revenues in excess of $10 million. Tremendous size differentials exist within this classification. For example, some class I carriers annually earn little more than $10 million, whereas several large carriers, such as the Burlington Northern, generate more than $1 billion in operating revenues in a typical year. There are also approximately 300 class II railroads, companies that earn less than $10 million annually. To a great extent these companies function in an auxiliary capacity, either originating or terminating shipments that have their line haul movements over a class I railroad line. Additionally, there are about 200 terminal and switching railroads primarily involved in the transfer of cars from one railroad to another, or in the movement of cars to and from industrial sites and railroad lines. The majority of these companies have quite limited operations. Many are jointly owned and operated by the line haul carriers serving a particular area.

The dominance of the class I railroads in our national railroad system is illustrated by the fact that they account for 96 percent of total mileage operated, 94 percent of railroad employment, and 99 percent of both freight and passenger traffic as measured in freight ton miles and passenger miles.[5]

There has been a long-term contraction in the number of railroads serving this country. Financial failure has eliminated some companies, but most have disappeared through mergers and consolidations with other railroads. As noted earlier, railroad mergers occurred with great frequency in the late 1880s, often on an end-to-end basis, as the first major railroad systems emerged. The scope of the merger movement is illustrated by the fact that over a period of years the Pennsylvania Railroad (which later became part of the Penn Central) absorbed nearly 600 independent companies. A second major wave of railroad mergers was approved by the ICC during the late 1950s and 1960s. Most of these mergers involved companies with parallel route structures; the basic motivating factor was a desire to reduce duplication of cost and service.

The geographical coverage of individual railroads is regulated by the ICC, and the operating authority of the largest railroads is essentially regional in nature. That is, no transcontinental railroads exist. However, a sizable volume of traffic is interregional. Consequently, to service such traffic, the railroads must rely upon a complex pattern of through routes and joint rates as well as interchange agreements between railroads serving different regions. Even though such traffic might be handled by several railroads en route from origin to destination, the shipper need only contact the originating carrier. Although the existence of these intercarrier agreements facilitates the movement of interregional traffic, these movements do cause problems for the industry. The interchange process itself is time consuming and tends to slow service. Also, in most instances it is not economically feasible to unload a railroad car and reload the shipment into the car of a connecting railroad. Instead, loaded cars are interchanged. That is why we see so many different company names on cars in a single train as we sit impatiently at railroad crossings. These cars must ultimately be returned to the company that owns them, and this tends to promote empty mileage and poor equipment utilization.

The railroad industry has taken several collective steps to improve this situation. The most significant action was the establishment of Railbox in 1974. Railbox is an industry-sponsored company that operates a free-floating boxcar fleet financed on the basis of individual railroad guarantees. Railbox cars, which numbered more than 7,300 in 1976, flow freely over the lines of participating railroads and do not have to be expedited back to a particular home base. This reduces the cross-hauling of empty cars and promotes better equipment utilization.

Congress has also periodically addressed the railroad equipment shortage issue, and there have been several congressional proposals to create a government-owned national freight car fleet that would be leased to rail carriers. As in the Railbox system, these cars would float throughout the railroad network. These proposals, however, have not yet managed to attract sufficient legislative support.

Capital Needs

The railroad industry's net investment in plant and equipment is approximately $29.5 billion.[6] Participation in the industry on a large scale necessitates heavy fixed investment in such areas as rolling stock, terminal facilities, and the right-of-way. Only the railroads and oil pipelines own and maintain their rights-of-way. In all other forms of carriage at least part of the right-of-way expense is borne by some governmental unit. Railroads also pay substantial property taxes on their rights-of-way. Competitive forms of carriage are not similarly burdened because of public ownership of the infrastructures that they use.

In such an industry a company's ability to remain competitive through modernization and expansion is greatly dependent upon its ability to sell securities and borrow funds in the capital markets. However, a company or an industry's access to the capital markets is dependent upon its financial performance. This has been a constant problem of the railroad industry in the post-World War II period. Contrary to widely held beliefs, the railroad industry in the aggregate is profitable. However, when the level of railroad profitability is related to the industry's investment base, it yields a rather anemic rate of return on investment (see Table 3–2). Not once since 1944 has the aggregate rate of return for the railroad industry reached 5 percent. The average rate of return on investment for American industry in general during the same period ranged from 9 to 12 percent.[7]

Table 3–2

Rate of Return on Investment, Class I Railroads, 1944–1975 (%)

	United States	Eastern District	Southern District	Western District
1944	4.70	4.37	5.45	4.82
1951	3.76	3.47	4.74	3.76
1955	4.22	4.19	5.45	3.86
1960	2.13	1.55	2.97	2.40
1965	3.69	3.32	4.16	3.87
1970	1.73	Deficit	4.50	3.02
1971	2.12	Deficit	4.36	3.51
1972	2.34	0.11	4.61	3.34
1973	2.33	0.07	4.61	3.30
1974	2.70	0.46	4.73	3.66
1975	1.20	Deficit	3.98	2.66

SOURCE: Association of American Railroads, *Yearbook of Railroad Facts* (Washington, D.C.: the Association, 1976), p. 20.

Consequently, railroads have experienced difficulty in *competing* in the capital markets. As also shown in Table 3–2, railroad profitability has varied widely in different regions of the country, with the eastern district registering the most dismal record.

A prolonged lack of capital infusion leads to a deterioration of plant and equipment and a resultant decline in traffic. In recognition of this capital-access problem, on several occasions the federal government has established short-term loan guarantee programs to assist railroads in securing funds. These programs met with mixed response in the industry; in retrospect they appear only to have postponed eventual financial crisis. For example, all the major recipients of loan guarantees granted under the provisions of the Transportation Act of 1958 subsequently declared bankruptcy.[8] Similar efforts, which give little or no attention to the problems that have limited the carriers' ability to refinance, seem doomed to failure. This issue is discussed further in Chapter 13.

Regulation

The railroads are regulated as common carriers, and their interstate operations are subject to regulation by the ICC (economic matters) and the Department of Transportation (safety). Similar controls of intrastate operations exist at the state level.

Regulatory coverage of the railroad industry is extensive. Although the railroads are not restricted as to the commodities that they might carry, the following economic aspects of the industry are regulated by the ICC: entry into markets, abandonment of service, initiation of new service offerings, pricing, issue of securities, and carrier mergers.

The recent financial deterioration of many railroads has led to considerable debate concerning the desirability of such extensive regulation. Critics have contended that overregulation is the most serious problem faced by the industry. Among those calling for a substantial reduction in regulation have been the Department of Transportation and the Council of Economic Advisors.[9]

For many years the most frequently criticized aspects of railroad regulation have been ICC controls over abandonment of service and carrier pricing. One basic problem faced by the industry has been its inability to expeditiously abandon noncompensatory freight services, particularly branch lines. Although the ICC has permitted abandonment of some rail lines, it has historically been reluctant to permit complete curtailment of rail services into many areas. This has been particularly true in areas that generate bulk traffic, such as sand, gravel, and coal, which in many cases is not subject to extensive intermodal competition. Such forced continuance of noncompensatory services was cited by many sources as a major cause of the financial collapse of the railroad system of the Northeast. As discussed later in this chapter, the government reorganization of the financially troubled carriers substantially reduced that burden.

Railroad rate making is also subject to ICC controls, and the commission has often been criticized as being unresponsive to competitive dynamics.[10] The railroads long advocated more liberal ICC pricing controls. In the aftermath of the Northeast railroad crisis, Congress addressed the pricing issue in the Railroad Revitalization and Regulatory Reform Act of 1976. Among other things, the statute gave the railroads considerably greater pricing flexibility. The nature of these changes and their significance to the industry are examined in Chapter 13.

41

COST AND SERVICE CHARACTERISTICS

The following discussion examines both the cost and service characteristics of the railroad industry. Particular attention is devoted to the competitive significance of these factors.

Railroad Costs

The total cost structure of the railroad industry is characterized by a very large fixed-cost component. It has been estimated that nearly two thirds of the industry's costs are unrelated to volume.[11] This fixed-cost component is comprised of heavy expenditures for long-lived assets such as rolling stock, terminal facilities, right-of-way, and yearly related outlays in interest, depreciation, and property taxes. Additionally, the industry has a large overhead burden in nonoperating salaries that is unrelated to volume.

Such an industry is often referred to as a declining-cost industry because, as output increases over some broad range, average unit costs tend to decline as fixed costs are allocated over an increasing number of units. Public utilities tend to have similar cost structures. In these industries, it is in the best interest of suppliers to attract additional volume, which results in lower average costs. These cost savings may ultimately be shared with consumers in the form of lower prices.

In contrast to the railroad industry, all other modes of intercity carriage, except oil pipelines, have total cost structures that are much less heavily weighted with fixed costs.[12] That is, total cost is much more responsive to the volume of traffic handled. One basic reason for this structural cost difference is that in the other modes the major system cost element, the right-of-way, is not directly borne by the carriers. In some instances, user charges, including tolls and gasoline taxes, have been imposed by various governmental units. However, the aggregate amount of these charges is generally closely related to business volume. One example is provided by the trucking industry in which gasoline taxes are levied on a per gallon consumed basis. As a trucker's traffic volume increases, it is likely that his mileage and gasoline tax payments will increase, and hence the direct relationship between volume and cost.

Because of these differences in modal cost structures, the railroad industry possesses a theoretical pricing advantage over competitive modes. Naturally, in the long run, all costs must be covered and a reasonable rate of return on investment must be earned. However, in the short run, as long as the revenues generated by traffic cover the variable cost of providing the service and make some contribution to fixed cost, it makes sense for the railroad to solicit the traffic. Other forms of carriage with higher variable costs per output unit theoretically may be placed at a pricing disadvantage under these circumstances. However, except in exempt carriage, prices are regulated in transportation, and for many years the ICC was reluctant to allow such *variable cost* pricing by the railroads due to its possible negative impact on competitive forms of carriage. The enactment of the Railroad Revitalization and Regulatory Reform Act of 1976 marked a significant movement toward greater carrier pricing freedom.

In comparing rates, shippers would find that rail rates tend to be higher than those of both water carriers and oil pipelines where competition exists among these modes (see Table 3–3). Rail rates also tend to be higher than

Table 3–3

Average Revenues per Ton Mile, Intercity Modes, 1960–1974 (cents)

Year	Rail[a]	Motor[b]	Water[c]	Oil Pipeline	Air[d]
1960	1.40	6.31	—	0.315	22.80
1965	1.27	6.46	0.346	0.279	20.46
1970	1.43	7.46	0.303	0.271	21.91
1971	1.59	7.85	0.339	0.285	22.58
1972	1.62	8.00	0.328	0.285	22.75
1973	1.62	8.24	0.378	0.290	23.31
1974	1.85	9.00	—	0.321	25.92

[a] Includes Amtrak and Auto-Train.
[b] Class I motor carriers.
[c] Barge lines operating on the Mississippi River and its tributaries.
[d] Domestic scheduled airlines.

SOURCE: Transportation Association of America, *Transportation Facts and Trends* (Washington, D.C.: the Association, 1976), p. 7; also, p. A-6 of the 1974 edition of *Transportation Facts and Trends*.

the rates of motor carriers in short-haul markets, but often are lower than motor carrier rates for large shipments moving long distances. Due to significant speed and price differences, minimal freight competition exists between rail and air carriers. It must be remembered, however, that these are generalizations, and the relative prices of the modes will vary depending on the commodities to be shipped, the markets to be served, and the distances to be traveled. The role of the regulatory agencies in controlling the extent of price competition among the modes in a given market should also be remembered.

The Railroad Industry

Railroad Service

In assessing the merits of competitive forms of freight carriage, shippers are naturally concerned with service as well as price differentials. In this regard, service is multidimensional, consisting of such factors as speed, reliability, and equipment availability.

In freight movements (passenger carriage and Amtrak are discussed separately), railroads offer both carload and less-than-carload (LCL) services. Historically, LCL service has tended to be rather slow compared to less-than-truckload (LTL) services offered by motor carriers. Consequently, there has been a long-term shift in such traffic to motor carriage, and small shipments have declined in importance to the railroads. The railroads also tend to suffer a speed disadvantage to motor carriage in carload service in short-haul markets. However, rail service is faster than water carriage in most cases, and over long distances certain rail services, such as through container trains, can be speed competitive with motor carriage.

Another factor which is important to the shipper is the incidence of loss and damage in the various modes of carriage. In that regard the railroads have experienced increasing difficulty in recent years. In fact, between 1960 and 1973 railroad freight claims nearly doubled.[13] At least part of the increase was caused by the industry's deferral of maintenance expenditures due to depressed earnings.

As discussed earlier in this chapter, the industry has also been troubled by equipment shortages, which have further eroded shipper confidence.

Due to a combination of competitive pressures and its own inherent capabilities, rail carriage has primarily become involved in long-distance, large-volume movements of low-valued, high-density commodities. Products of forests, mines, and agriculture, all exhibiting the low-value, high-density characteristics, are the major products transported by the railroads. The long-distance nature of railroad freight service is illustrated by the fact that the average length of railroad hauls in 1974 was 533 miles compared to 280 miles in trucking.[14] Reflecting the large-shipment concentration of railroad traffic, the average load moved by the railroads in 1975 exceeded 61 tons.[15]

To offset some of the service and price disadvantages encountered in the marketplace, the railroads have developed a number of service innovations in recent years. Foremost among these have been the expansion of the piggybacking and unit train services. Piggybacking (TOFC for trailer on flatcar, COFC for container on flatcar) involves the line-haul movement of loaded highway trailers or containers on flatcars, with local pickup and delivery performed by truck. This service combines the best characteristics of both modes, the line-haul efficiencies of rail carriage with the pickup and delivery speed and flexibility of motor carriage. The unit train is essentially a rent-a-train concept. An entire train of specialized equipment (often shipper-owned cars) is rented to a single shipper for a specified time period. Rates are quoted on the entire train movement, and services are typically conducted between a raw material source and a processing point. In most instances, no attempt is made to solicit a back-haul movement. Several such unit train agreements exist in the utilities industry involving the movement of coal from mines to electric power generating stations.

AMTRAK

As government spending programs have promoted the expansion of our highway and airway systems, intercity rail passenger service has diminished in importance. The railroads carried 77 percent of all for-hire intercity passengers in the United States in 1929, but their share of this traffic declined to 7.2 percent by 1970.[16] If this passenger volume is expressed as a percentage of all intercity travel, including automobile trips which dominate such movements, railroads account for less than 1 percent of passenger volume.[17]

The reasons for the precipitous decline in rail passenger service are numerous. They include the expansion of the other modes of intercity carriage, our growing national affluence, and our society's ever-increasing commitment to the automobile. As the shift in passenger preference accelerated following World War II, many railroads incurred sizable deficits in passenger operations. At the same time, railroad management was reluctant to commit scarce capital to declining passenger operations, and consequently service deteriorated. The ICC responded to these developments by permitting the railroads to discontinue nearly one third of intercity passenger trains between 1958 and 1970. Although these actions partially alleviated the problem, they did not prevent deficits. In fact, between 1963 and 1970 the aggregate passenger service deficit of the railroads exceeded $400 million annually.[18]

In response to this problem, and undoubtedly prompted by the June 1970 bankruptcy of the Penn Central, which had annually incurred approximately one third of the annual passenger loss, Congress enacted the Rail Passenger Service Act in October 1970.[19] This legislation created a quasi-public company, the National Railroad Passenger Corporation (Amtrak), to manage the national intercity rail passenger service network. Amtrak was charged with the development of a modern and efficient pas-

45

senger network that would ultimately operate on a profitable basis.

Amtrak initiated service in May 1971 over a reduced passenger network, which had been jointly determined by the Department of Transportation, Congress, and Amtrak's board of incorporators. Figure 3–2 illustrates the scope of the Amtrak network. Carriers that had previously served the routes included in the initial Amtrak network were given the option of becoming affiliated with Amtrak or continuing the services independently. If the carriers chose not to become a party to the Amtrak agreement, they were not to be permitted to drop any of those services for a period of at least five years. Three railroads, the Denver & Rio Grande Western, the Rock Island, and the Southern Railway chose not to become affiliated with Amtrak, and continued to operate passenger service independently.

The carriers that opted to become affiliated with Amtrak were assessed entry fees based on their prior passenger service losses. Such payments totaled $197 million; these funds, coupled with congressional appropriations, provided the initial funding of the new passenger system. Under the Amtrak agreement, individual railroads actually provide the service on a contractual basis with Amtrak.

In the years following its incorporation Amtrak has succeeded in reversing the long-term decline of intercity rail passenger service ridership. The equipment fleet has been upgraded, primarily through congressional grants and loan guarantees, and service has improved according to such standards as on-time arrivals. The relationship between Amtrak and the contracting railroads has also improved after some early disputes concerning such matters as the scheduling of passenger and freight trains. However, one continuing controversy has involved the level of compensation to be given the railroads for provision of passenger service.[20] Existing contracts call for cost reimbursement, but do not include a rate of return on investment. The railroads have called for such an increment in future contracts, but Congress and Amtrak have not agreed to that stipulation.

Although ridership figures and service levels have improved, Amtrak has shown little promise of becoming a profitable venture. Its losses have grown steadily, and in 1975 they exceeded $300 million.[21] These deficits have led to continued Amtrak dependence upon congressional operating subsidies. In turn, Amtrak's dependence on Congress is partially responsible for the mounting deficits. Although by law Amtrak is permitted to discontinue any services at its own discretion, in recent years Congress has made continued Amtrak funding dependent upon Amtrak's commitment to continue all existing runs. Additionally, Congress has required Amtrak to add at least one experimental run per year. A continuation of such congressional actions will only serve to perpetuate overextension of Amtrak's resources, while frustrating its ability to achieve long-term self-sufficiency.

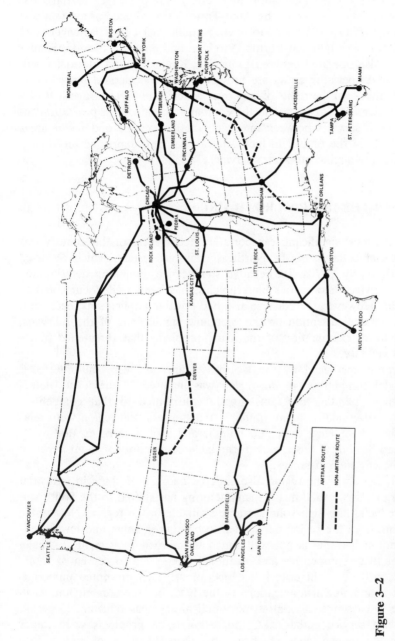

Figure 3–2

Intercity Rail Passenger Routes—Amtrak and Others

SOURCE: U.S. Department of Transportation.

47

Auto-Train

One major service innovation in intercity rail passenger carriage has been the initiation of service by Auto-Train. This private corporation was granted authority by the ICC to operate trains that carry passengers and their automobiles between Lorton, Virginia, and Sanford, Florida. Similar service is also operated between Louisville, Kentucky, and Florida. Locomotives and operating crews are provided on a contractural basis by the railroads that own the rights-of-way over which Auto-Train travels. Ridership has increased steadily, and the company operates at a profit. Expansion of such services between major population centers and resort areas seems likely in the future. In fact, Amtrak has also expressed an interest in initiation of similar auto-ferry service.

THE NORTHEAST RAILROAD CRISIS

One of the most significant transportation occurrences of this century was the financial collapse of the Northeast railroad system, which occurred during the early 1970s. Its negative significance, including deteriorating railroad services and carrier bankruptcies, has been well documented in the media. However, the collapse also had positive implications, because it focused national attention on the economic significance of the railroads, and led to an examination of the many problems that threatened future railroad viability.

The problems faced by the Northeast railroads were multifaceted.[22] Intermodal competition in the region was intense. As previously noted, government spending programs greatly contributed to that competitive intensity. Additionally, many traffic flow patterns in the region were relatively short haul (less than 300 miles), and motor carriage, due to its speed and flexibility, was a quite formidable competitor for many types of traffic moving such distances.

The railroads of the region also suffered because of shifts in industrial location patterns. Much heavy manufacturing has shifted to the South and West, reducing the high-volume traffic available in the region. New traffic emanating from the region has tended to be high in value and low in volume, and such traffic is not well suited to railroad movement. In many instances these competitive and locational factors led to decreased traffic density, particularly in branch-line operations. This prompted numerous railroad abandonment applications to the ICC; but the commission, as in the case in passenger discontinuance applications, was reluctant to permit broad-scale service cutbacks. Complicating these problems were rather questionable management practices, including diversion of capital into nonrailroading ventures, and low labor productivity among the region's railroads compared to class I railroads in general.[23] Finally, the burden of passenger service losses in the pre-Amtrak period also drained much needed capital from the Northeast railroads.

Bankruptcies

This combination of problems led to continued cash flow and refinancing difficulties for the railroads of the region, and ultimately resulted in the bankruptcy of seven major carriers by 1973. Those railroads declaring bankruptcy were the Ann Arbor, the Boston and Maine, the Central of New Jersey, the Erie Lackawanna, the Lehigh Valley, the Penn Central, and the Reading. Collectively, these carriers served 19 states and the District of Columbia, while earning nearly 18 percent of the industry's revenues and employing nearly 20 percent of the industry's workforce.[24] Because of public dependence upon continued rail services in the region, these lines were not liquidated; rather, each entered court-supervised reorganization proceedings in hopes of becoming a viable railroad.

However, by early 1973 it was apparent that the individual reorganizations were not working. Services continued to deteriorate, cash flow and deferred maintenance problems persisted, and deficits grew. As a result, Congress considered a number of courses of action, including nationalization, that might be used to rehabilitate rail services in the Northeast.

Regional Rail Reorganization Act

After considering a variety of restructuring plans, which had been suggested by such parties as the Department of Transportation, the ICC, several congressmen, and a number of railroad executives, Congress in late 1973 enacted the Regional Rail Reorganization Act.[25] The bill was signed into law by President Ford in January 1974.

The legislation created two new organizations that were to bring about an unprecedented collective reorganization of the region's bankrupt railroads. One was a government agency, the United States Railway Association (USRA), which functioned as the planning and financing agency in bringing about the restructuring. The second organization was the Consolidated Rail Corporation (Conrail), which was to operate the restructured system as a private, for-profit organization.

To facilitate the reorganization, Congress provided nearly $3 billion in federally guaranteed loans, direct loans, and direct grants. Included in this total was $180 million to subsidize nonprofitable lines that might otherwise be abandoned. Also included was $250 million in job protection funds for workers who would be displaced.

The Railroad Industry

Working in conjunction with the Rail Services Planning Office of the ICC and the Department of Transportation, the USRA was charged with development of a final system plan, which would be subject to congressional approval. The task faced by USRA was monumental. There was no precedent for a reorganization of this scale. The number of lines and facilities to be evaluated in the development of the final system plan, which was to preserve essential rail services while equitably reimbursing previous security holders, was mind-boggling. At the same time, political pressures were immense, particularly from elected officials whose districts were faced with a decrease or loss of rail services.

Essentially, the planning process was a classic confrontation between public and private interest. For years the railroads of the Northeast, and many other regulated carriers, have been used as instruments of public policy. Governmental desire to promote competition and service continuity has often led to carriers being forced to continue noncompensatory services. In the long run, such action may run counter to the public interest by draining essential capital from private companies. Although resolution of this conflict is difficult and multidimensional, it is also essential.

After nearly two and a half years of planning, Conrail initiated operations on April 1, 1976. Conrail officials estimated that the company, whose operations encompassed 17,000 miles of track, would be profitable by 1980. It is too early to evaluate the likelihood of that contention. However, the significance of that matter should not be underestimated. It may well determine whether or not railroad nationalization will become inevitable in the Northeast. On the national level, related governmental actions may have a similar effect.

SUMMARY

The railroads of the United States have been troubled by many problems in recent years. A combination of competitive factors and government spending programs has led to a significant reduction in the industry's share of intercity freight movements. Intercity rail passenger service has been assumed by Amtrak, a quasi-public corporation, and the long-term downward ridership trend has been reversed; but deficits persist.

Nevertheless, rail carriage is still the dominant form of intercity freight movements as measured in terms of intercity ton mileage. As such, it remains a very important component of our national transportation system.

Due to financial problems the railroad system of the Northeast has undergone an unprecedented collective structural and financial reorganization. The degree of success of the reorganization program will determine if the rail system of that region will remain in the private sector. The reorganization has also served to increase public awareness of the economic importance and problems of the railroad industry. In the long run this may well have a positive impact on the industry because of the re-examination of government policies toward the railroads which this has prompted.

NOTES

1. D. Philip Locklin, *Economics of Transportation,* 7th ed. (Homewood, Ill.: Richard D. Irwin, Inc., 1972), p. 95.

2. U.S. Congress, Senate, Committee on Interstate and Foreign Commerce, Special Study Group on Transportation Policies in the United States, *National Transportation Policy* (Doyle Report), 87th Cong., 1st Sess., 1960 (Washington, D.C.: U.S. Government Printing Office, 1961), p. 232.

3. Dudley F. Pegrum, *Transportation: Economics and Public Policy,* 3rd ed. (Homewood, Ill.: Richard D. Irwin, Inc., 1973), pp. 55–56.

4. Transportation Association of America, *Transportation Facts and Trends* (Washington, D.C.: the Association, 1976), p. 30.

5. Association of American Railroads, *Yearbook of Railroad Facts* (Washington, D.C.: the Association, 1976), p. 2.

6. Ibid., p. 56.

7. Jerome B. Cohen and Sidney M. Robbins, *Financial Manager* (New York: Harper & Row, Inc., 1966), p. 230.

8. George W. Hilton, *The Transportation Act of 1958* (Bloomington, Ind.: Indiana University Press, 1969), pp. 87–90.

9. "Program to Pare Regulatory Powers Nearing Completion by Nixon Task Force," *Wall Street Journal,* New York, May 26, 1971, p. 3; also, U.S. Department of Transportation, Office of the Secretary, *Executive Briefing: Transportation Regulatory Modernization and Assistance Legislation* (Washington, D.C.: the Department, 1972), pp. 1–4.

10. U.S. Department of Transportation, Office of the Secretary, *Rail Service in the Midwest and Northeast Region* (Washington, D.C.: U.S. Government Printing Office, 1974), p. 10.

11. Roy J. Sampson and Martin T. Farris, *Domestic Transportation: Practice, Theory, and Policy,* 3rd ed. (Boston: Houghton Mifflin Company, 1975), p. 57.

12. Ibid.

13. Data supplied by the Freight Claims Division of the Association of American Railroads.

14. Transportation Association of America, op. cit., p. 14.

15. Association of American Railroads, op. cit., p. 42.

16. National Railroad Passenger Corporation, "Amtrak News," Washington, D.C., 1972, p. 1.

17. Transportation Association of America, op. cit., p. 18.

18. Association of American Railroads, op. cit., p. 21.

19. Rail Passenger Service Act of 1970, Public Law 91–518 (1970).

20. "Penn Central Presses Amtrak for Higher Fees," *Wall Street Journal,* New York, May 21, 1973, p. 2.

21. Association of American Railroads, op. cit., p. 62.

22. U.S. Railway Association, *Preliminary System Plan* (Washington, D.C.: the Association, 1975), I, p. 3.

23. Railroad labor relations have been quite controversial throughout the years, and labor agreements have a decided impact on worker productivity and carrier costs. These issues are discussed in depth in Chapter 15.

24. U.S. Railway Association, op. cit., I, p. i.

25. Regional Rail Reorganization Act of 1973, Public Law 93–236 (1973).

SELECTED REFERENCES

Baumol, William J. "Payment by Performance in Rail Passenger Transportation: An Innovation in Amtrak's Operations," *Bell Journal of Economics,* VI, No. 1 (Spring 1975), pp. 281–98.

Conant, Michael. "Structural Reorganization of the Northeast Railroads," *ICC Practitioners' Journal,* XLIII, No. 2 (January–February 1976), pp. 207–23.

Fogel, Robert W. *Railroads and American Economic Growth.* Baltimore, Md.: Johns Hopkins Press, 1964.

Harbeson, Robert W. "Some Policy Implications of the Northeastern Railroad Problems," *Transportation Journal,* XIV, No. 1 (Fall 1974), pp. 5–12.

Hilton, George W. *The Transportation Act of 1958.* Bloomington, Ind.: Indiana University Press, 1969.

Hilton, George W. *The Northeast Railroad Problem.* Washington, D.C.: American Enterprise Institute for Public Policy Research, 1975.

Locklin, D. Philip. *Economics of Transportation,* 7th ed. Homewood, Ill.: Richard D. Irwin, Inc., 1972.
Chapter 6. "The Era of Railroad Building," pp. 109–41.

Nelson, James C. *Railroad Transportation and Public Policy.* Washington, D.C.: Brookings Institution, 1959.

Norton, Hugh S. *Modern Transportation Economics,* 2nd ed. Columbus, Ohio: Charles E. Merrill Publishing Company, 1971.
Chapter 2. "Railroads, Motor Carriers, and Air Carriers," pp. 18–30.

Pegrum, Dudley F. *Transportation: Economics and Public Policy,* 3rd ed. Homewood, Ill.: Richard D. Irwin, Inc., 1973.
Chapter 2. "Elements of a Modern Transportation System," pp. 22–45.
Chapter 3. "Development of Transportation in the United States," pp. 46–70.

The Penn Central and Other Railroads. A report to the Senate Committee on Commerce, 92nd Cong., 2nd Sess., 1972. Washington, D.C.: U.S. Government Printing Office, 1972.

Sampson, Roy J., and Martin T. Farris. *Domestic Transportation: Practice, Theory, and Policy,* 3rd ed. Boston: Houghton Mifflin Company, 1975.
Chapter 2. "The Development of Transportation," pp. 17–39.
Chapter 4. "Land Carriers," pp. 53–61.

Task Force on Railroad Productivity. *Improving Railroad Productivity.* A report to the National Commission on Productivity and the Council of Economic Advisers. Washington, D.C.: Task Force on Railroad Productivity, 1973.

U.S. Railway Association. *Final System Plan,* 2 vols. Washington, D.C.: U.S. Government Printing Office, 1975.

DISCUSSION QUESTIONS

1. Discuss briefly the cost structure of the railroad industry.
2. Explain the reasons for the necessity of traffic interchange in the railroad industry, and outline the problems that such interchange causes.
3. What were the pressures that led to the creation of Amtrak; in your opinion, what role should the company play in the future intercity transportation network?
4. What factors led to the Northeast railroad reorganization? What were the functions of the U.S. Railway Association and Conrail in the reorganization?

CHAPTER

4

The Highway System

Another major component of the national transportation network, highway carriage, is the subject of this chapter. Primary attention is devoted to for-hire freight movement by truck, but attention is also given to passenger carriage by bus and automobile.

Motor carriage has shared transportation's rapidly expanding public profile. National attention was attracted by the 1974 strike of independent drivers in the trucking industry, which was caused by the limited availability and rising prices of diesel fuel during the Arab oil embargo. We have also witnessed extensive media coverage of consumer group and Department of Transportation (DOT) criticisms of Interstate Commerce Commission (ICC) policies in regulating the trucking industry. Similarly, while we as consumers have faced steadily rising gasoline prices and have begun to consider alternative means of travel, federal and state agencies have devoted increasing attention to analyzing the propriety of existing highway funding programs. Government pressures have also been directed at Detroit to produce more energy efficient automobiles.

It is the purpose of this chapter to explore the industry structure of intercity highway carriage, and to focus attention on the contemporary strengths and problems of this system. Local or urban highway transportation is examined in depth in Chapters 19 and 20.

DEVELOPMENT OF THE SYSTEM

Little highway development occurred in this country prior to 1800. Most that did take place was in the form of turnpike or toll roads financed by private capital. Many toll roads were financial successes, but it was apparent that private capital was inadequate to meet the highway needs of the country's expanding economy.

Initial Government Funding

Responding to this need, Congress in 1797 authorized the construction of a National Pike to connect major population centers. Yearly federal highway appropriations followed this action, and the highway system expanded to approximately 27,000 miles by 1830.[1] However, during the 1830s, a dispute over states' rights and the desirability of federal involvement in the internal affairs of the states led to a curtailment of federal highway spending. Further development of the highway system was viewed as a state function, but most states lacked the financial capability of promoting such development. Consequently, highway expansion decelerated and received relatively little attention until the latter part of the century.

The lobbying efforts of farmers, railroads, and bicyclists led several states to create highway departments and to increase state funding of highway programs in the 1890s, but the real impetus for renewed highway expansion was the invention of the internal combustion gasoline engine. As automobile ownership increased during the early 1900s, growing attention was devoted to highway expansion. Rekindled state interest in highway programs was illustrated by the creation of state highway aid laws in 45 states by 1915.[2] However, state funding of highway projects was still rather limited.

Expansion of Federal Funding

Federal involvement in highway construction was renewed in the Federal-Aid Road Act of 1916, which established a program of federal–state cooperation in highway construction that continues to the present. The statute established a program of formula grants under which states were allocated federal highway funds on the basis of several variables, including state population and area. To qualify for these grants, the states were required to establish state highway departments to cooperate with the federal government.[3]

The Highway System

Highway expansion continued following World War I. The growth was financed by a combination of federal, state, and local government outlays. Gasoline taxes were levied in many states and soon became a major source of state highway funds. Underlying these levies was a basic philosophy that relies upon users to pay for publicly provided facilities. Such user charges still generate much of federal and state funding for highway programs.

As the highway system both expanded and improved in quality, the number of people attracted to for-hire trucking and bus operations steadily increased. Intermodal competition grew in intensity during the 1920s, and the competitive impact of the highway modes began to be felt by the railroads. The ICC, concerned not only with the diversion of traffic from the railroads but also with questionable competitive practices in trucking, called for federal regulation of trucking as early as 1925.[4] By that time, a number of states had already enacted regulations governing intrastate motor carriage.

Competitive conditions between truckers and railroads intensified even further with the onset of the Depression. Highway building programs were expanded to stimulate the economy, and the number of people engaged in for-hire highway carriage increased dramatically. Ultimately, these conditions led to the passage of the Motor Carrier Act of 1935, which established ICC control over many aspects of interstate highway carriage. The scope and coverage of these regulatory controls are discussed later in this chapter.

National priorities dictated suspension of federal aid highway projects during World War II. As a result, highway expansion slowed considerably during the conflict. Even in the years immediately following the war, material and personnel shortages continued to severely restrict highway programs. It was not until the early 1950s that the pace of highway development accelerated appreciably.

Post–World War II Highway Expansion

The most significant highway development since World War II has been the building of the Interstate Highway System, which is illustrated in Figure 4–1. This high-speed, limited-access highway network, which was designed to link most major cities and state capitals, was originally approved by Congress in 1944, but financing was not finalized until 1956. The Interstate will ultimately extend 42,500 miles. Ninety percent of the cost of constructing the Interstate has been financed by the federal government. The federal share has been funded through the Highway Trust Fund, which was created for that purpose in 1956. The fund accumulates revenues from a federal gasoline tax and other federal highway excise taxes. The system was originally scheduled for completion by 1969, but a series of delays extended the completion date to 1990. Expenditures for the Interstate have exceeded $56 billion, making it the largest peace-time public works program in our country's history. The high-quality roads of the Interstate have not only reduced highway travel times, but have also lowered vehicle operating costs.

The federal role in highway expansion has not been limited to the Interstate Highway System. It also includes the ABC Program, which covers primary and secondary (farm to market) highways and the extension of primary routes into urban areas. The federal share of highway construction costs under this program is 70 percent (up from 50 percent prior to 1974). In total, the federally aided highway system covers about 20 percent of our nation's aggregate street, road, and highway mileage of 3,684,000 miles.[5]

The role of state and local government in financing highway expansion and improvement should not be underestimated. In fact, such outlays far outweigh federal highway expenditures. The relative highway funding role of these governmental units is illustrated by the fact that, of the $26.7 billion spent for highways in 1975, $21.4 billion was appropriated by state and local government; the federal share was $5.3 billion.[6]

Trucks now move approximately 21 percent of intercity freight ton mileage, while intercity buses carry more passengers than any other mode of for-hire carriage (airlines register more passenger miles due to the long-haul nature of many of their passenger trips). The speed and convenience of the automobile have led to its emergence as the dominant form of inter-city passenger carriage, accounting for nearly 87 percent of intercity passenger mileage.[7]

Development of the contemporary highway network has yielded enor-mous benefits to our nation. Because of the transportation cost savings that the network has generated, it has tended to lower the prices of many goods while increasing their availability. It has also given our population unparalleled mobility. However, the highway system has also had tremen-dous costs. From a purely economic standpoint, more than $375 billion was spent for highway purposes by governmental units between World War II and the end of 1975.[8] Social costs have also been substantial. Air pollution has become a national concern, and more than 40,000 people lose their lives on our highways each year, while millions are injured. Our great reliance upon highway modes, particularly the automobile, has ac-celerated the depletion of precious energy resources. Consequently, a major challenge in the years to come will be a reassessment of national transportation priorities and a determination of appropriate highway spend-ing levels, given society's other goals.

57

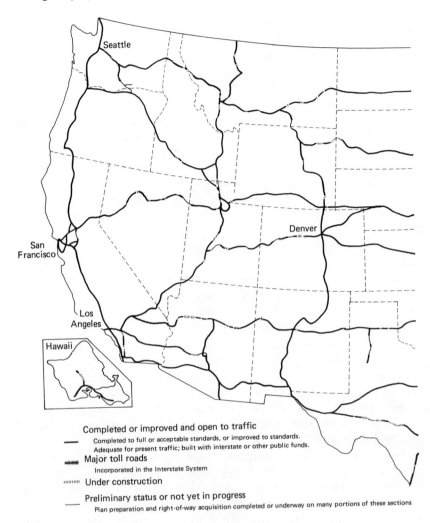

Figure 4–1

The Interstate Highway System

SOURCE: U.S. Department of Transportation, Federal Highway Administration.

INDUSTRIAL AND FINANCIAL STRUCTURE

Intercity movement of freight by truck, which accounted for approximately 21 percent of intercity freight ton mileage in 1974, involves both for-hire and private carriage. Included in for-hire carriage are both regulated motor

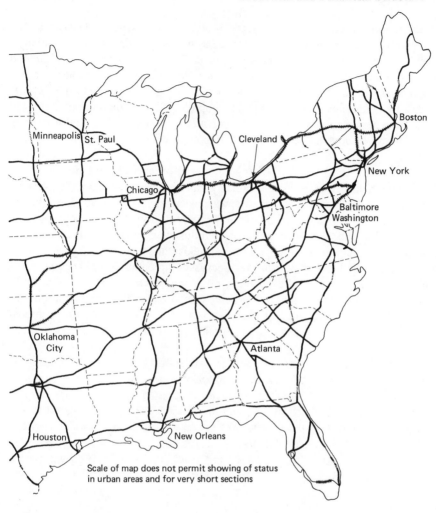

Scale of map does not permit showing of status
in urban areas and for very short sections

carriers and carriers that are exempt from the economic controls of regulatory agencies. The nature and significance of these exemptions are discussed later in this chapter. It has been estimated that nearly two thirds of intercity truck ton mileage is carried by private and exempt carriers, with the balance being moved by regulated carriers.[9]

The number of interstate motor carriers subject to ICC regulation decreased steadily from 20,872 in 1945 to approximately 14,500 in 1975.[10] Mergers are the major reason for the long-term contraction in the number of regulated motor carriers. Because of the geographical and commodity restrictions faced by ICC-regulated motor carriers (discussed later in the chapter), mergers have often provided a means of broadening a company's market and commodity authority. The ICC controls mergers of regulated carriers and has approved hundreds in recent years. End-to-end mergers, which have tacked together the individual geographical operating authorities of companies, have been quite popular; such combinations have led to the emergence of several motor carriers with transcontinental operating authority. In contrast, as noted in Chapter 3, no railroad has such authority.

While the total number of regulated motor carriers has declined, the number of larger firms in the industry has increased substantially. Among those concerned with this trend toward growing concentration in the industry has been the Department of Transportation. The agency has contended that the cost structure of the industry is such that economies of scale (see Chapter 8) appear to be nonexistent in the industry, and without such cost benefits substantial decreases in competition are not justified.[11] Proponents of the merger movement have countered the DOT arguments with claims that competitive conditions, both intramodal and intermodal, have made mergers necessary, and that mergers have promoted service economies. Federal merger policies and their impact are discussed in Chapter 16.

The ICC classifies regulated motor carriers on the basis of annual gross operating revenues. In 1974, the number of class I carriers (those annually earning more than $3 million) was 830; class II carriers (those earning between $500,000 and $3 million) numbered 2,588.[12] Regulated motor carriers earning less than $500,000 are categorized as class III carriers. As is the case in the classification of railroads according to revenues, there are substantial size differentials in the trucking industry. The emergence of large-scale trucking companies is illustrated by the fact that 368 regulated motor carriers earned gross revenues in excess of $10 million in 1974.[13]

Additionally, the ICC categorizes motor carriers according to the types of commodities that they are permitted to carry. In total, the ICC maintains 17 different commodity classifications for truckers.[14] The largest carrier grouping consists of general freight carriers who are permitted to haul a wide variety of packaged goods that are referred to as general commodities. However, the operating rights of these carriers typically exclude certain freight, such as heavy machinery, household goods, heavy or dangerous materials, or other freight requiring special handling or special equipment. These commodities are usually handled by specialized carriers.

Besides the regulated and private carriage components of the intercity motor carrier industry, there is another group of truckers, which is often referred to as the owner–operators. These truckers are primarily engaged in the for-hire movement of exempt agricultural products. Additionally, some owner–operators are involved in the truckload movement of regulated commodities under subcontract with regulated carriers. In operating on a subcontract basis, the owner–operator receives a percentage of the total revenues paid to the regulated carrier (under whose operating authority the owner–operator is working) by the shipper. It has been estimated that there are approximately 100,000 owner–operators, most of whom operate one truck.[15] However, although the scale of the individual operation is relatively small, it is believed that owner–operators collectively carry between 25 and 40 percent of intercity trucking tonnage.[16]

Regulation

The Motor Carrier Act of 1935 established ICC control over a variety of the economic and safety aspects of interstate motor carriage. Control over economic aspects still rests with the ICC, but control over safety matters has since been transferred to the DOT.

Under the provisions of the act, all motor carriers serving interstate routes on a for-hire basis are classified as common, contract, or exempt carriers. *Common carriers* hold themselves out to the general public, which they have authority to serve. Their operating rights may be for regular route service (over designated highways on a regular basis) or irregular route service between designated points or areas on a nonscheduled basis. *Contract carriers* operate under continuing contracts with one or more shippers. *Exempt carriers* are those engaged in certain commodity movements or types of operation that are considered to be outside the economic jurisdiction of the ICC. Included are trucks used exclusively for transportation of unmanufactured agricultural commodities or newspapers, and vehicles used incidental to air carriage.

Scope of ICC Regulation

Among those aspects of regulated motor carrier operations controlled by the ICC are entry into common and contract carriage, prescription of commodities to be carried, specification of routes to be traveled and points to be served, pricing, mergers, and the issue of securities. The development of these regulatory controls is discussed in Chapter 12.

Recent years have witnessed controversy concerning ICC regulation of trucking. In particular, the commodity restrictions imposed by the ICC have been challenged as promoting low capacity utilization and excessive costs. Similarly, routing limitations have been attacked as not only generating excessive costs and time delays, but also as causing unnecessary fuel consumption. ICC policies on pricing have also been questioned by the DOT, which has sought both more liberal entry policies for the industry and a greater degree of price competition. These issues are discussed further in Chapter 13.

State Regulation

Regulation of intrastate motor carriage rests with state authorities. Although there are considerable differences in the economic regulation of motor carriage on a state-by-state basis, state controls are often quite similar to the pattern of controls that exists at the federal level. In the area of motor carrier safety, state governments regulate such matters as licensing, speed, and vehicle weights and lengths.

Capital Needs

The average net investment per firm of class I intercity motor carriers was slightly more than $2.2 million in 1973.[17] In contrast, that same year the average net investment of class I railroads (those generating annual operating revenues in excess of $5 million) exceeded $400 million.[18] Reflection on these figures indicates that there are considerable scale differences between the two modes; consequently, motor carriers tend to have rather different capital requirements than those of railroads, as discussed in Chapter 3.

The most important factor that leads to these differences in average investment is the fact that highways, the major cost element of the total motor carrier system, are financed by various government units, whereas railroads own and maintain their own rights-of-way. Motor carriers contribute to the financing of highways through a variety of user payments, but they are not individually burdened with investment in highway facilities.

Because there are many comparatively small companies and because their related capital requirements are limited, much trucking industry financing is accomplished without reliance on capital markets. Capital for smaller companies is frequently provided by a few individuals, and in many instances a large part of the capital invested represents reinvested earnings of the business. However, as noted earlier, concentration is increasing in the industry, and the emergence of large companies, such as Associated Transport, Consolidated Freightways, and Yellow Freight, will lead to a growing industry participation in capital markets through the issue of securities.

Although regulated intercity motor carriers transport less than one half the volume of traffic carried by the railroads, the aggregate operating revenues of the motor carriers exceed those of rail carriers. In 1975 regulated motor carriers generated $21.4 billion in operating revenues, compared to $15.4 billion for the railroads.[19] To a great degree, this reflects a difference in the composition of the traffic carried by the two modes. The majority of the traffic moved by the railroads consists of heavy bulk commodities that move at low rates, whereas the truckers dominate the carriage of manufactured goods that have higher absolute rates.

As discussed in Chapter 3, a major factor in a company's or industry's ability to obtain financing in the capital markets is its rate of return on investment. Table 4–1 contains a summary of return on investment data

Table 4–1

Rate of Return on Net Investment, Class I Intercity Motor Carriers of Property, 1960–1974

Year	Rate of Return (%)
1960	11.53
1961	17.83
1962	19.22
1963	18.53
1964	20.22
1965	22.56
1966	20.90
1967	15.07
1968	21.18
1969	17.44
1970	13.90
1971	17.17
1972	16.28
1973	15.14
1974	11.16

SOURCE: U.S. Interstate Commerce Commission, *89th Annual Report to Congress* (Washington, D.C.: U.S. Government Printing Office, 1975), p. 126, and additional information supplied by the commission.

generated by class I intercity motor carriers in recent years. In contrast, the aggregate rate of return on investment for U.S. industry has ranged between 9 and 12 percent during the same period.[20] This fact, coupled with the long-term growth of industry traffic and profitability, has tended to provide the industry with needed capital access. It must be remembered, however, that it is difficult to generalize about the financial condition of several thousand motor carriers. Naturally, differences in earnings, volume, and growth prospects of individual companies can lead to major differences in ease of capital access.

COST AND SERVICE CHARACTERISTICS

The cost and service characteristics of the motor carrier industry are examined in the following discussion. Particular attention is devoted to the competitive significance of these factors.

Motor Carrier Costs

As discussed in Chapter 3, the cost structure of the motor carrier industry is substantially different than that of rail carriage in that it is much more heavily weighted with variable costs. Therefore, the total cost structure of the industry is quite responsive to the volume of traffic handled. Because of the *current* nature of the majority of motor carrier costs, these carriers are rather restricted in terms of the limits within which they can reduce rates below fully allocated costs to meet competition. This explains the long-standing opposition of the industry to efforts to promote variable-cost pricing in cases of competition between motor and rail carriers. Further attention is devoted to this matter in Chapter 8.

Major Cost Elements

Several of the major cost elements of the industry deserve mention. Approximately 60 cents of each revenue dollar earned by common and contract carriers is absorbed by wages and fringe benefits.[21] Employee compensation has increased dramatically in recent years, largely through the bargaining efforts of the Teamsters. Consequently, motor carrier management has devoted considerable attention to improving worker productivity, which has tended to lag behind that of employees in the other modes of carriage. Labor productivity in the various modes of intercity carriage is discussed in depth in Chapter 15.

Another major element of cost in the industry is highway user payments. For their use of the nation's highway system in 1973, truck owners (private and for hire) paid more than $7.1 billion in federal and state highway use taxes.[22] Approximately $4.5 billion of this total was paid to state governments. There are several different forms of highway use tax. At the state level, the major highway user charges consist of motor fuel taxes and truck and trailer registration fees. The major categories of federal highway use payments are motor fuel taxes and excise taxes on new trucks, trailers, tires, and tubes. For a given vehicle class, user fees vary substantially from state to state. Sizable variations also exist in the user charges levied on various vehicle classes. The American Trucking Association estimated that the annual state and federal highway tax paid by trucks in 1973 varied from an average of $124 for a gasoline-powered pickup truck (5,000 pounds) to an average of $3,941 for a diesel-powered five-axle combination truck (72,000 pounds).[23]

There has been a long-standing controversy concerning the adequacy of the highway use payments made by for-hire motor carriers. The carriers contend that they are assessed a disproportionate share of highway cost responsibility; critics suggest that they underpay. Numerous cost allocation methods might be used in judging the cost responsibilities of various vehicle classes so as to establish equitable user charges. Each method is quite complex, and the basic assumptions concerning the costs and benefits realized by users and nonusers are debatable. A comparison of these techniques and the results that they generate would be interesting, but such a task is obviously beyond the scope of this book. However, the last major highway cost allocation study conducted by the Department of Transportation contended that the users of automobiles and light trucks tended to be overcharged in user payments, while those owning buses operating in intercity service and owners of diesel-powered combination trucks tended to be undercharged.[24] These conclusions have been challenged by the American Trucking Association, and the controversy has not yet been resolved.

One additional cost element of significance in motor carriage is the expenditure for fuel. Major increases in fuel costs precipitated by energy shortages have necessitated several freight rate increases in motor carriage in recent years. These fuel cost increases are passed along to shippers through rate increases, but if continued they threaten to impair the competitive position of motor carriage, which has a proportionately higher fuel consumption rate than rail carriage.

Operating Ratio

One measure of the revenue needs and financial condition of a motor carrier is its operating ratio. This ratio expresses a percentage relationship between the operating expenses and operating revenues of the company. The greater the spread between operating expenses and revenues, the larger the amount of residual revenue that is available to cover nonoperating expenses such as interest payments and income taxes. Any remaining revenues are profits.

Much attention is devoted to prevailing operating ratios in the trucking industry; these figures are often used as a criterion for proving the need for rate increases before the ICC. As discussed earlier in this chapter, the percentage of nonoperating expenses to total expenses is quite low in motor carriage compared with the magnitude of nonoperating expenses incurred by railroads. As a result, it is possible for a motor carrier to operate profitably with an operating ratio in the low nineties. There is general agreement among motor carriers that a company's stability and service are impaired when its operating ratio rises above 95 percent. Between 1950 and 1974, the annual operating ratios of classes I and II intercity motor carriers of general freight varied between 93 and 98 percent.[25] In contrast, for railroads, with a much greater percentage of nonoperating expenses, the ratio approaches the mid-seventies.

Although the operating ratio provides some indication of the operating condition of a company, it must be remembered that it does not consider how efficiently resources are being used. Nor does it differentiate between the carrier whose costs are high due to inefficiency and one whose operating ratio is high because of circumstances beyond its control, despite the carrier's efficient use of resources.[26]

Motor Carrier Rates and Price Competition

The average revenue per intercity ton mile realized by class I intercity motor carriers was 8.3 cents in 1973.[27] This was approximately five times the average revenue per ton mile earned by railroads that same year. At first glance, it would appear that there is little price competition between these two modes. However, such average figures reveal little about the actual degree of competition in a given market situation. Generalizations can be drawn about the relative rates of regulated motor carriers and railroads in several different settings. As a result of differences in both terminal and line-haul expense characteristics, truck rates are generally lower than rail rates on small shipments and on short hauls. However, in intermediate- to long-distance moves of high-valued commodities there tends to be considerable parity in the rates of railroads and regulated motor carriers. In contrast, in long-haul volume movements of bulk commodities, motor carriers are typically unable to quote rail-competitive rates. Nevertheless, it must be remembered that rate differences are only one decision variable considered by shippers in making modal selections.

Regardless of rate differences, several recent studies have indicated that regulated motor carriers of general commodities do not appear to be particularly competitive with railroads due to the markets in which the motor carriers specialize. This contention appears to be partially substantiated by the fact that much of the traffic handled by these carriers consists of small shipments, with the average weight per shipment handled being 1,600 pounds.[28] Due to their generally slower service, the railroads have ceased to be a competitive factor in the movement of such small shipments. As a result, it appears that the most intense competition experienced by regulated motor carriers exists in the form of private carriage, which tends to compete for the most attractive (high-rated) LTL traffic. In a given market, additional competition is also encountered from other regulated motor carriers, including contract carriers. To a lesser extent, there is also competition between regulated motor carriers operating over long distances and air freight movements. Although the average revenue per ton mile of airlines is now more than double that of motor carriage, some air carriers have expressed growing interest in air cargo and have initiated experimental fare reductions. In response to the long-term challenge of air cargo, a number of motor carriers, including Consolidated Freightways and Navajo Freight Lines, have established air freight forwarding subsidiaries to share in the possible growth of such service.

There appears to be strong competition between owner–operators engaged in exempt commodity movements and railroads. It has been estimated that owner–operators might annually divert between 80 and 120 billion ton miles of traffic from the railroads.[29] These truckers tend to compete more on a price basis with the railroads, while their regulated counterparts tend to place more emphasis on service competition. In exempt commodity movements by truck, prices fluctuate substantially over time, and the pricing decisions of owner–operators have often been attacked as being irrational. Some credibility was given to this charge by a national survey of owner–operators in which nearly 30 percent of the respondents admitted that they did not know their operating cost per mile.[30] Regardless of this fact, owner–operators remain a major competitive force in the industry, and shippers appear to be generally satisfied with their prices and service.

Motor Carrier Service

As discussed earlier, regulated motor carriers of general commodities are heavily engaged in the less-than-truckload (LTL) shipment business. The ICC has estimated that these carriers transport four times the small shipment tonnage and generate twice the intercity small shipment revenues of all other regulated carriers combined. Domination of this segment of intercity freight movements poses some problems for motor carriers. Handling costs on small shipments are quite high. Typically, a motor carrier will provide pickup service on small shipments in the originating city. The shipment then moves through one or more consolidation and/or break bulk terminals en route to its final destination. Delivery service is also generally provided at the destination city. Due to the flow pattern of these shipments, handling of each shipment occurs several times, and labor costs are quite high as is the susceptibility of the shipment to loss and damage. It has been estimated that nearly 20 percent of the operating revenues of general commodity carriers is absorbed by the costs of terminal (sorting) operations.[31] Because of these factors, the rates on small shipments have risen dramatically in recent years, and carriers contend that the rate structure is still depressed.

For statistical purposes, the ICC defines truckloads (TL) as shipments weighing over 10,000 pounds. It is in the movement of such shipments over intermediate and long distances that competition between motor carriers and railroads increases. In truckload movements, the shipment generally travels directly from shipper to consignee with no terminal handling or consolidation activity. This naturally leads to a comparative speed advantage of TL versus LTL movements.

Length of Haul and Load Factor

The average load of class I intercity motor carriers was 12.8 tons in 1973, up from 8.4 tons in 1945.[32] At the same time, there were considerable differences in the load patterns experienced by motor carriers in various regions of the country. During 1973, the average load of these carriers ranged from 9.4 tons in New England to 15.6 tons in the Rocky Mountain Region.[33] These regional variances reflect any number of factors, including the regional commodity mix and competitive conditions prevailing in each region.

The average length of haul of class I intercity motor carriers also varies substantially by region, with New England registering 157 miles and the Rocky Mountain Region averaging 395 miles.[34] The national average for the year was 276 miles, up from 177 in 1945, reflecting not only the growth of national markets but also expansion of carrier operating authorities.[35]

Commodities Carried

The composition of truck traffic is quite different from that carried by the railroads. As discussed in Chapter 3, the majority of rail tonnage consists of products of mines, forests, and agriculture. Less than one third of rail traffic is comprised of manufactured products. In contrast, in excess of 85 percent of the truckload tonnage originated by class I motor carriers consists of manufactured products.[36] The degree of motor carrier control over high-valued commodity movements is illustrated by the fact that during 1974 truckers delivered 73.2 percent of all radios, televisions, and phonograph records, 82.3 percent of all clothing, and 84.0 percent of all office and accounting machines.[37] Additionally, truckers now deliver the largest percentage of such mineral products as sand, gravel, and crushed stone. Truckers (primarily exempt operators) also now deliver the majority of livestock and fresh fruit and vegetables to major markets.

Other Service Characteristics

Due to the nature of their operations and the extensive coverage of the national highway system, motor carriers tend to have a decided speed advantage over other forms of intercity carriage, excluding air freight. This is particularly true in short-distance markets, but the development of the Interstate System has also enabled truckers to become speed competitive with railroads in many long-haul markets. Speed of service is a major variable to be considered by shippers of high-valued goods, which lead to very high inventory carrying costs. The sooner such goods are delivered, the sooner the customer payment cycle is likely to begin.

Another important aspect of motor carrier service to be considered by shippers is the packaging requirements for shipments. Generally, these are less stringent in motor carriage than they are in rail service. Improvements in truck tires and suspension systems have led to quite smooth riding characteristics. These factors have contributed to a long-term decline in motor carrier loss and damage claims expressed as a percentage of revenues. For class I intercity common carriers of general freight, claims were reduced from 2.46 percent in 1945 to 1.27 percent in 1973.[38] Naturally, this is important to shippers in meeting customer service standards. The reduction of the claim rate as a percentage of motor carrier revenue should not mislead one to believe that loss and damage claims are of little importance in trucking. In fact, in a typical year aggregate claims paid by intercity motor carriers exceed $200 million.[39] Consequently, a high-priority item in the industry is continued improvement of cargo security systems.

A major strength of the motor carrier industry is the extensive coverage of the highway network. Because of this, the great majority of industrial shippers have door-to-door trucking services available to them. In contrast, many industrial sites are off-line from rail facilities. Additionally, shippers often find a greater number of motor carriers than rail carriers in a given market, resulting in a greater choice of carriers in trucking than in rail carriage.

Although motor carriers do have advantages over rail service in both flexibility and accessibility, they are at a distinct capacity disadvantage to railroads. Given existing regulation of truck weights and the nature of contemporary truck design, motor carriers can seldom carry more than 30,000- to 50,000-pound payloads. In contrast, the carrying capacity of modern railroad freight cars often exceeds 150,000 pounds.

The trucking industry has attempted to strengthen its competitive position through a variety of innovations. Of major importance has been the development of twin trailers, which are pulled by a single power unit. These operations provide up to one third greater productivity per vehicle combination. Such operations are now permitted in 35 states. This development, coupled with the use of lighter and stronger materials in vehicle construction, has led to an increase of more than 120 percent in ton miles carried per power unit in intercity service over the past 25 years.[40] These factors have tended to offset some of the capacity disadvantage suffered by truckers in competing with railroads. One further service development in the industry has been the growing investment in specialized equipment, such as bulk and liquid commodity carrying units, which are aimed at the specific needs of certain shipping groups.

PASSENGER CARRIAGE

Passenger travel on the national highway system occurs in both private automobiles and buses. As noted earlier, automobiles dominate intercity passenger travel, accounting for more than 87 percent of intercity passenger mileage. The relative roles of these two forms of passenger carriage are examined in the following discussion.

Intercity Bus Operations

Most of the companies presently engaged in intercity bus operations began in short-route automobile passenger service. Others began as a form of substituted service for expensive railroad passenger operations in low-density areas. The extent of railroad involvement in early bus operations is illustrated by the fact that, during the early 1930s, railroads had a financial interest in companies operating 50 percent of Greyhound's route mileage.[41]

The intercity bus industry's growth has paralleled that of the national highway system, and buses account for approximately 14.5 percent of commercial intercity passenger mileage. Buses carry more passengers than either rail or air service, but they register fewer passenger miles than air carriers due to the substantial difference in the average passenger trip length between the two modes (120 miles for bus passengers, 684 for airline passengers).[42]

Although the industry's structure has been affected by the numerous mergers that have occurred throughout the years, there are still more than 1,000 bus companies operating on an interstate basis and subject to the economic regulation of the ICC. These companies provide intercity service to more than 40,000 communities, many of which are not served by either rail or air carriers.

Two dominant bus systems have emerged in intercity service. These are the Greyhound and Transcontinental Bus systems (Continental Trailways). Greyhound is the largest intercity bus operator in the country, with more than 5,000 buses serving a 100,000 route mile system. Transcontinental accounts for more than one fourth of all intercity bus mileage through the operations of more than 40 affiliated companies. Both of these carriers provide transcontinental service and offer connections with many smaller companies. Extensive interline arrangements exist in the industry, making it possible for passengers to purchase through tickets to most destinations.

Regulation

Bus operators engaged in intercity service are subject to economic regulation by the ICC and safety regulation by the DOT, as well as state regulation of intrastate operations. Among those aspects of industry operations regulated by the ICC are entry, rates, and mergers. Carriers are also classified by the commission according to revenues; in 1974 there were 84 class I intercity motor carriers of passengers (at least $1 million in average annual gross operating revenues). In aggregate, these carriers earned $909 million in 1974.[43] The bulk of this total was generated by intercity passenger fares in regular route service, 14 percent was provided by package express service, and an additional 13 percent represented charter revenues.[44] The rate of return on net investment for this group of carriers has ranged between 11 and 15 percent in recent years.[45]

Cost and Service Characteristics

Because most of the highway system's cost structure is financed by the governmental units that provide the highways, the majority of bus costs are variable in nature, with more than 50 percent of operating expenses being comprised of labor costs.[46] User taxes paid by class I carriers to federal, state, and local governments have annually exceeded $100 million in recent years.[47]

The ICC gives considerable attention to the operating ratios of regulated bus companies. It has been suggested by the ICC that an operating ratio of 85 percent or less before income taxes would be appropriate for the industry. The industry operating ratio was considerably above this in 1974, reaching 93 percent.[48]

In short-distance markets, buses are generally speed competitive with other modes of intercity passenger carriage. In longer-haul markets, buses tend to register slower speeds than both rail and air service. However, recent highway improvements have reduced the magnitude of this disadvantage. Intercity bus operations are quite competitive with other for-hire modes on a price basis. In 1974, the average revenue per revenue passenger mile of the bus industry was 4.41 cents, compared to 7.52 cents for airlines and 5.85 cents for Amtrak.[49] Additionally, intercity bus operations appear to be an efficient user of petroleum products relative to the other modes of passenger carriage. A 1973 National Science Foundation study said that buses generate about 85 intercity passenger miles per gallon of fuel, compared to 48, 40, and 16 passenger miles for rail, automobile, and airlines, respectively.[50] However, regardless of energy considerations, the real competitor of the bus industry is the private automobile, which continues to attract an increasing share of intercity passenger traffic. Representatives of the bus industry are also concerned with the long-run threat posed by the heavily subsidized operations of Amtrak.

Private Automobiles

The American love affair with the automobile is a well-documented phenomenon. Automobile registrations exceeded 106 million in 1975, up from 33 million in 1940, and the percentage of our aggregate personal consumption expenditures spent on automobiles has increased steadily. Two- or three-automobile families are no longer rarities. Access to the private automobile provides a degree of convenience and flexibility that cannot be matched by the modes of for-hire passenger carriage.

Although we generally think of the automobile in terms of local movements within a given metropolitan area, as discussed in Chapter 3, it has become the dominant mode of intercity passenger carriage. The tremendous expansion and upgrading of intercity highway facilities following World War II, coupled with design improvements in the automobile, have strengthened the role of the automobile by making long-distance driving safer, faster, and less tiring.

As the prices of new automobiles and gasoline have increased, the cost of owning and operating automobiles has naturally risen. DOT recently estimated that the cost of owning and operating a standard-sized automobile is approximately 18 cents per passenger mile, assuming slightly more than one passenger per trip.[51] In contrast, as noted earlier in this chapter, the average fare per passenger mile charged by for-hire carriers ranges between 4 and 8 cents. Based on these figures, the automobile would appear to be a rather high cost mode of intercity passenger carriage. However, it should be realized that the addition of a second, third, or fourth passenger to the automobile for the trip reduces the per passenger mile cost dramatically. Consequently, for many intercity family trips, the automobile is quite price competitive with for-hire carriage. Its speed, flexibility, and convenience also offer value to the traveler.

Critics have often argued that individuals irrationally select the automobile for such trips because they are not aware of the total capital and operating costs on a per mile basis. Although it may be true that the individual is not aware of all costs, it is questionable whether or not total costs are relevant to such modal selection decisions. A more relevant consideration is the marginal cost of operation, because the individual has already committed himself to the ownership of the vehicle for multiple trip purposes (e.g., to drive to work or to the shopping center). If the individual were to compare the marginal cost of intercity trips by automobile with the tickets of for-hire carriers, the automobile would often represent a quite rational choice.

The role of the automobile as a form of intercity passenger carriage may well change over time due to rising gasoline costs and energy shortages. However, even during the 1973–1974 energy crisis, more intercity passenger miles were registered in automobiles than had been driven during the previous year. Rising gasoline prices are naturally a deterrent to automobile usage, but it does not appear that the increases have been of a sufficient magnitude to significantly alter travel patterns. Intensification of our national energy problems and restriction such as gasoline rationing would necessitate some modal switching behavior, but a major shift in travel patterns would cause severe capacity problems in the other modes of intercity carriage. Therefore, any national attempt to deemphasize the automobile as a form of intercity passenger carriage will have to be coupled with related adjustment of the passenger-carrying capabilities of the for-hire modes.

SUMMARY

Our nation's highway system has played a steadily increasing role in meeting our national transportation needs. As government highway spending programs have accelerated, the highway network has both expanded and improved in quality. For-hire trucking has attracted a steadily increasing movement of high-value freight.

In intercity passenger carriage, the automobile has become the dominant form of transportation. Automobiles annually account for approximately

87 percent of intercity passenger mileage. At the same time, intercity bus operations have surpassed the railroads in terms of passenger volume handled.

There is no question that the highway modes will continue to play major roles in our national transportation system. However, several factors, including environmental concerns and an increasing sentiment to decelerate highway building programs, may combine to limit their future growth. Government policy decisions concerning each of these matters will have a decided impact on the relative roles to be played in the future by the highway modes.

NOTES

1. Charles A. Taff, *Commercial Motor Transportation,* 4th ed. (Homewood, Ill.: Richard D. Irwin, Inc., 1969), p. 12.

2. Roy J. Sampson and Martin T. Farris, *Domestic Transportation: Practice, Theory, and Policy*, 3rd ed. (Boston: Houghton Mifflin Company, 1975), p. 30.

3. Taff, op. cit., p. 16.

4. Motor Bus and Truck Operations, 140 ICC 685 (1928); also, Coordination of Motor Transportation, 182 ICC 263 (1932).

5. U.S. Department of Transportation, Office of the Secretary, *A Statement of National Transportation Policy* (Washington, D.C.: U.S. Government Printing Office, 1975), p. 6.

6. Association of American Railroads, *Government Expenditures for Highway, Waterway, and Air Facilities and Private Expenditures for Railroad Facilities* (Washington, D.C.: the Association, 1975), p. 8.

7. Transportation Association of America, *Transportation Facts and Trends* (Washington, D.C.: the Association, 1976), p. 18.

8. Association of American Railroads, op. cit., p. 8.

9. D. Daryl Wyckoff and David H. Maister, *The Owner–Operator: Independent Trucker* (Lexington, Mass.: D.C. Heath & Company, 1975), p. 2.

10. American Trucking Associations, *American Trucking Trends, 1975* (Washington, D.C.: the Associations, 1975), pp. 1 and 9.

11. U.S. Department of Transportation, Office of the Secretary, *Executive Briefing: Transportation Regulatory Modernization and Assistance Legislation* (Washington, D.C.: the Department, 1972), pp. 45–50.

12. American Trucking Associations, op. cit., p. 9.

13. Ibid.

14. Grant M. Davis, Martin T. Farris, and Jack J. Holder, Jr., *Management of Transportation Carriers* (New York: Praeger Publishers, Inc., 1975), p. 69.

15. Wyckoff and Maister, op. cit., p. 1.

16. Ibid.

17. American Trucking Associations, op. cit., p. 18.

18. Association of American Railroads, *Yearbook of Railroad Facts* (Washington, D.C.: the Association, 1976), p. 56.

19. American Trucking Associations, op. cit., p. i; also, Association of American Railroads, op. cit., p. 13.

20. Jerome B. Cohen and Sidney M. Robbins, *Financial Manager* (New York: Harper & Row, Inc., 1966), p. 230.

21. American Trucking Associations, op. cit., p. 28.

22. Ibid., p. 1.

23. Ibid., p. 23.

24. U.S. Department of Transportation, Federal Highway Administration, Bureau of Public Roads, *Allocation of Highway Cost Responsibility and Tax Payments, 1969* (Washington, D.C.: the Department, 1970), pp. 1–3.

25. American Trucking Associations, op. cit., p. 19.

26. Taff, op. cit., p. 177.

27. American Trucking Associations, op. cit., p. 23.

28. D. Daryl Wyckoff, "Which Truckers Compete with Us?" *Modern Railroads*, XXIX, No. 11 (November 1974), p. 65.

29. Ibid., p. 66.

30. Ibid.

31. Ibid., p. 65.

32. American Trucking Associations, op. cit., p. 32.

33. Ibid.

34. Ibid.

35. Ibid.

36. D. Philip Locklin, *Economics of Transportation*, 7th ed. (Homewood, Ill.: Richard D. Irwin, Inc., 1972), p. 644.

37. American Trucking Associations, op. cit., p. 14.

38. Ibid., p. 26.

39. "A New Note in the Freight Claims Dirge," *Traffic World*, CXLII, No. 13 (March 28, 1970), p. 7.

40. American Trucking Associations, op. cit., p. 30.

41. Taff, op. cit., p. 429.

42. Transportation Association of America, op. cit., p. 15.

43. U.S. Interstate Commerce Commission, *89th Annual Report to Congress* (Washington, D.C.: U.S. Government Printing Office, 1975), p. 126.

44. Ibid.

45. Ibid.

46. National Association of Motor Bus Operators, *The Intercity and Suburban Bus Industry, 1973–1974* (Washington, D.C.: the Association, 1974), p. 20.

47. Ibid., p. 18.

48. Interstate Commerce Commission, op. cit., p. 126.

49. Transportation Association of America, op. cit., p. 7.

50. National Science Foundation, *Energy Intensiveness of Passenger and Freight Transport Modes, 1950–1970,* as cited by the National Association of Motor Bus Operators, op. cit., p. 4.

51. U.S. Department of Transportation, Federal Highway Administration, Office of Highway Planning, Highway Statistics Division, "Cost of Owning and Operating an Automobile, 1976" (Washington, D.C.: the Department, 1976), p. 2.

SELECTED REFERENCES

Alderson, V. Ray. "Adaption of the Motor Carrier Industry to Present and Prospective Supplies of Fuels." *Transportation Journal,* XIII, No. 3 (Spring 1974), pp. 20–23.

American Trucking Associations. *1975 Financial Analysis of the Motor Carrier Industry.* Washington, D.C.: the Associations, 1975.

Fair, Marvin L., and Ernest W. Williams. *Economics of Transportation and Logistics.* Dallas, Tex.: Business Publications, Inc., 1975.
Chapter 7. "Intercity Passenger Logistics," pp. 103–22.

Felrice, Barry. U.S. Department of Transportation, Federal Highway Administration. *Financing Federal-Aid Highways Revisited.* Washington, D.C.: the Department, 1976.

Hudson, William J., and James A. Constantin. *Motor Transportation: Principles and Practices.* New York: Ronald Press Company, 1958.

Lamkin, Jack. "Organization and Competition in Transportation: The Agricultural Exempt Sector." *Transportation Journal,* XIII, No. 1 (Fall 1973), pp. 30–37.

Locklin, D. Philip. *Economics of Transportation,* 7th ed. Homewood, Ill.: Richard D. Irwin, Inc., 1972.
Chapter 28. "Highway Transportation," pp. 642–65.

Nelson, James R. "Motor Carrier Regulation and the Financing of the Industry." *ICC Practitioners' Journal*, XLI, No. 4 (May–June 1974), pp. 436–57.

Sampson, Roy J., and Martin T. Farris. *Domestic Transportation: Practice, Theory, and Policy*, 3rd ed. Boston: Houghton Mifflin Company, 1975. Chapter 4. "Land Carriers," pp. 53–70.

Smith, Jay A. "Concentration in the Common and Contract Motor Carrier Industry—A Regulatory Dilemma." *Transportation Journal*, XII, No. 4 (Summer 1973), pp. 30–48.

Taff, Charles A. *Commercial Motor Transportation*, 4th ed. Homewood, Ill.: Richard D. Irwin, Inc., 1969.
Chapter 2. "Highways," pp. 12–51.
Chapter 5. "Types of Operations," pp. 109–32.
Chapter 18. "Commission Policy—Operating Authority and Mergers," pp. 402–28.
Chapter 19. "Intercity Passenger Operations," pp. 429–55.

U.S. Department of Transportation, Federal Highway Administration, Office of Highway Planning, Highway Statistics Division. "Cost of Owning and Operating an Automobile, 1976." Washington, D.C.: the Department, 1976.

Wyckoff, D. Daryl, and David H. Maister. *The Owner–Operator: Independent Trucker*. Lexington, Mass.: D.C. Heath & Company, 1975.

DISCUSSION QUESTIONS

1. What are user charges? How are they applied in motor carriage, and what is the function of such charges?
2. Distinguish between common, contract, and exempt motor carriage; explain the significance of each in the transportation marketplace.
3. Discuss the importance of owner–operators in intercity trucking operations.
4. Compare the cost structure of the motor carrier industry with that of the railroad industry.

The Oil Pipeline and
Water Carriage Industries

Attention now shifts to two major modes of intercity freight transportation, oil pipelines and water carriage, which are little understood by the general public. The recent financial problems of the railroad and airline industries and the energy implications of motor carriage have given these modes high public profiles, but the oil pipeline network and water carriage continue to function in relative obscurity.

It may well be surprising to the reader to learn that the oil pipeline network of the United States extends more than 220,000 miles and that it carries approximately one quarter of intercity freight ton mileage on an annual basis. It is also likely that the reader is unaware that the U.S. waterway system is the most extensive in the world. It consists of nearly 24,000 miles of navigable waterways, and commodity movements over the system account for approximately 16 percent of annual intercity ton mileage.

This chapter focuses on the nature of these two industries, and examines their relative roles in our national transportation system.

OIL PIPELINE INDUSTRY

In the following pages, the development, industrial and financial structure, and cost and service characteristics of the oil pipeline system are examined.

The discussion is limited to companies primarily involved in the for-hire pipeline movement of petroleum products.

Development of the System

The oil pipeline industry began in 1865 in the oil fields of western Pennsylvania. A number of entrepreneurs financed short 2-inch diameter pipelines to feed oil to barge and rail facilities located several miles away. The pipelines offered lower rates than horse-drawn wagons, and soon attracted a substantial share of short-haul crude oil traffic. As had been the case in the early years of railroading, the profitability of the first pipeline companies attracted many new entrants into the business, and cutthroat competition and bankruptcies became commonplace.[1]

The high risk associated with investment in pipeline facilities and the threat of bankruptcy led to a growing reluctance on the behalf of many financiers to invest in pipeline operations. As a result, the industry came to be dominated by the oil companies and their subsidiaries, which needed uninterrupted transportation service. Many smaller independent companies were later consolidated into such organizations as the National Transit Pipeline Company, which was controlled by Standard Oil.

Emergence of Trunk Lines

Until the late 1870s the oil pipelines were primarily limited to short-haul gathering activities that connected with other modes for line-haul carriage. However, as pipeline technology progressed, it became possible to move crude oil over longer distances by pipeline. This led to the construction of several 6-inch diameter trunk lines, which carried crude oil more than 100 miles.[2] When these ventures proved successful, the major oil companies took the next logical step and connected their large refineries directly to the oil fields by pipeline. Consequently, much of the longer-haul crude oil traffic was diverted from rail and barge movements. Thus the pipelines emerged as a viable competitor for this traffic in intercity markets.

The growth of the oil pipeline network continued to parallel that of the oil industry, and the system expanded steadily into the twentieth century. Throughout that period of growth, pressures increased to make interstate oil pipelines common carriers. Supporters of that proposal believed that such action would provide small independent oil producers and refiners with nondiscriminatory access to this mode. Congressional acceptance of the concept was signified by the passage of the Hepburn Act of 1906, which gave the Interstate Commerce Commission (ICC) economic jurisdiction over for-hire interstate oil pipeline carriage. The scope of ICC regulation of oil pipelines is discussed later in this chapter; the pressures that led to this regulation are examined in detail in Chapter 12.

Emergence of Products Lines

Prior to 1930, pipeline carriage of oil had been limited to the movement of crude oil because of pipeline leakage problems, which made the movement of refined products such as gasoline impractical.[3] However, welding techniques improved, and product lines became a reality. Because of that development, oil pipelines began attracting an increasing percentage of such product movements from other modes.

Federally Funded Oil Pipelines

During World War II, two major oil pipeline projects were financed and operated by the federal government. These pipelines were built to provide the capacity to handle overland oil movements from Texas to the Northeast. Prior to the war, much of the traffic moved in coastwise tankers, but the activity of enemy submarines off our coasts made the continuance of this practice unfeasible. One federally funded pipeline project, the Big Inch, carried crude oil from Longview, Texas, to the New York–Philadelphia refining area. The system, which extended 1,340 miles and cost $78 million, operated from 1943–1945. The other project, the Little Inch, extended 1,475 miles and cost $67.3 million.[4] This line basically ran parallel to the Big Inch and moved *products* from the Texas Gulf Coast refineries to the New York area during 1944 and 1945. The Little Inch was somewhat revolutionary in that its 20-inch diameter made it the first large-diameter products line; it provided an impetus toward larger-diameter pipelines following the war. Both federally financed pipeline projects were sold to private interests following the war and were later converted to natural gas lines.[5]

Growth of Large-Diameter Pipelines

Before World War II, the majority of oil pipelines had diameters of less than 10 inches. However, as pipeline technology progressed, the desirability of larger-diameter pipelines became apparent. Because of the technical characteristics of pipelining, the larger the diameter of the pipe, the lower the per unit cost of transportation, assuming good utilization. In recent years there has been a decided trend toward the use of large-diameter pipe. By 1968 there were nearly 20,000 miles of oil pipeline that exceeded 12 inches in diameter, and 42-inch pipelines had appeared.[6]

As the volume of oil consumption has risen in this country, making large-diameter pipelines feasible, oil companies have often jointly financed pipeline projects over common routes. Such joint financing under *undivided interest* agreements has lowered financing costs by reducing duplicate investment, and has promoted cost efficiencies due to better pipeline utilization. Under joint financing agreements, pipeline capacity and profits are typically prorated on the basis of each participating company's investment in the project.

Alaskan Pipeline

Probably the most significant development in the oil pipeline industry in the post-World War II period has been the construction of the Alaskan Pipeline. In 1968 one of the richest oil and gas areas in the world was discovered on the North Slope of Alaska. To bring this oil to the lower 48 states, a consortium of seven oil producers and pipeline companies formed the Alyeska Pipeline Service Company to design, construct, and maintain the pipeline. After successfully defending the pipeline project in a series of court challenges related to environmental concerns and the property rights of native Alaskans, Alyeska spent more than three years building the pipeline system. The completed system stretches nearly 800 miles from Prudhoe Bay on the Arctic Ocean to Valdez on Alaska's southern coast. At Valdez the oil is loaded aboard tankers for shipment to West Coast refineries.

The Alyeska system, which utilizes 48-inch pipe, cost more than $6.4 billion and was the largest construction project ever undertaken by private industry.[7] When operating at capacity, the system will transport approximately 2 million barrels per day, or roughly 15 percent of daily domestic demands.[8]

Contemporary Pipeline System

The expansion of the domestic oil pipeline system has continued to parallel the growth of the oil industry. By 1975 oil pipeline mileage exceeded 220,000 miles, with nearly one half of this mileage consisting of products pipelines for the movement of various refined products. During that year oil pipelines accounted for 24.6 percent of intercity freight ton mileage. Of the intercity modes, only the railroads generated more ton mileage. The relative volume handled by pipelines might seem somewhat surprising, but it reflects the tremendous consumption rate of petroleum products in this country for both consumer and industrial purposes.

Pipelines now account for approximately 45 percent of all oil traffic, with railroads carrying about 3 percent and the balance split almost equally between water and motor carriage.[9] The efficiencies of pipeline movements have led to consideration of the movement of other commodities through pipelines. In fact, by 1970 there were more than 100 slurry pipelines in the United States, which used water as a propellant to move coal, gilsonite, limestone, sulfur, and metal concentrates.[10] However, most of these lines are relatively short and quite limited in their application. Some attention has also been devoted to the future potential of pipelines as movers of hollow capsules filled with such commodities as wheat and chemicals. However, given the present capital requirements of the industry, and innovations in other modes of carriage such as unit trains offering attractive volume rates, it does not appear likely that such pipeline services will be commercially feasible in the foreseeable future.

Industrial and Financial Structure

By 1974 there were 101 oil pipeline companies that were regulated as common carriers by the Interstate Commerce Commission. The industry is still dominated by the major oil producers and their subsidiaries. This dominance is illustrated by the fact that more than two thirds of the crude oil pipeline mileage in the U.S. is owned or controlled by 20 major integrated oil companies.[11] However, there are a limited number of independents in the industry; they are primarily involved in the movement of refined products. One interesting development in this area has been the establishment of pipeline subsidiaries by several railroads, including the Southern Pacific, the Sante Fe, and the Burlington Northern. These railroad-controlled pipelines have not only provided the railroads with a means of recapturing some traffic that had been lost to the pipelines, but have also diverted some oil traffic that previously moved in the company's less efficient tank cars.[12]

Regulation

Federal regulation of interstate oil pipeline operations was established by the Hepburn Act of 1906, which created a pattern of regulation quite similar to that which had been earlier applied to the railroads.[13] The ICC is vested with control over oil pipeline rates of common carriers and personal discrimination is forbidden. Reporting requirements have also been established. However, entry into the industry is not controlled by the ICC, nor are line extensions. Theoretically, this provides free entry into the industry. Realistically, the substantial capital costs and the difficulties inherent in acquiring the necessary rights-of-way constitute quite formidable nonregulatory entry barriers. Other areas in which the regulation of oil pipelines is not as extensive as it is for railroads include the following: (1) there is no control over pipeline abandonment, (2) there is no control over the security issues of pipeline companies, and (3) there is no regulation of consolidations and acquisitions of control, but pipelines are subject to the antipooling provisions of the Interstate Commerce Act. The safety aspects of interstate oil pipeline operations are administered by the Department of Transportation, and the industry has an admirable safety record.

More than half the states have adopted some form of regulation pertaining to oil pipelines. Generally, these states require common carrier status of companies operating on an intrastate basis. Some states impose common carrier status as a prerequisite to exercise the right of eminent domain to acquire property for pipeline rights-of-way.[14]

Capital Needs

The net investment in the oil pipeline industry exceeds $10 billion. It has been estimated that between 80 and 90 percent of the total investment in the industry consists of pipelines and rights-of-way.[15] Earnings of the industry have been quite stable, averaging 7 to 8 percent on net investment on an annual basis. In pipeline rate cases the ICC has tended to allow an 8 percent rate of return for crude oil lines and a 10 percent return for product line operations.[16] One reason for different treatment of crude and product lines is the higher risk associated with handling the more valuable refined products. The maximum earnings of shipper–owners (parent oil companies that ship by the pipeline) were limited to 7 percent by the ICC and a Justice Department consent decree signed by a number of pipeline companies in 1940.[17] The consent decree was accepted by the companies following a Justice Department investigation of alleged rebating practices involving the major oil producers.

The consistent earnings of oil pipelines and their affiliation with the major oil producers have provided these companies with a steady flow of investment capital, and pipeline securities tend to be highly regarded in the investment community. Consequently, the industry has not been troubled by the cyclical capital shortages that have plagued carriers in other modes in recent years. The historical financial strength of the oil pipeline industry has enabled it to remain the only mode of carriage in this country that has never received any form of government subsidization.

Cost and Service Characteristics

The cost and service characteristics of the oil pipeline industry are examined in the following discussion. Particular attention is devoted to the competitive implications of these factors.

The Oil Pipeline and Water Carriage Industries

Oil Pipeline Costs

The aggregate cost structure of the oil pipeline industry is characterized by a large fixed-cost component. Because of the substantial fixed investment in pipeline and right-of-way, the industry resembles the railroad industry in that, as volume increases, average costs per unit of output tend to decline steadily over a broad range of output. Also, as noted earlier, as the diameter of a pipeline increases, given steady high-volume utilization, costs per unit of output tend to decline. Because of these two factors, there is a strong incentive for the industry to use large-diameter pipelines when possible and to attempt to operate at high levels of traffic volume.

The industry is highly automated, having fewer than 15,000 employees. The use of more efficient pumping equipment and large-diameter pipe, increases in long-haul movements, and improvements in detecting pipeline failure have all contributed to major increases in industry productivity. Similarly, the development of more durable pipe that is highly resistant to corrosion has substantially reduced industry maintenance costs. As a result of these various factors, average rates of the pipeline industry have remained almost constant since 1945.[18]

The cost structure of the industry is such that it gives oil pipelines a substantial cost advantage over competing modes (except water carriage) on large-volume movements of petroleum products. Reflecting their lower costs, pipelines tend to have lower rates on high-volume petroleum shipments than either rail or motor carriage. For example, the typical long-haul pipeline rate is 10 to 20 percent of railroad rates for similar movements.[19] The rates of water carriers tend to be lower than those of pipelines. However, larger-diameter pipelines (in excess of 30 inches) appear to be cost competitive with water carriage.[20] Nevertheless, pipelines are often used in a feeder capacity in connection with water carrier operations.

Oil Pipeline Service

To the shipper of either crude or refined petroleum, the pipeline system offers a continuous, uninterrupted mode of carriage that is unaffected by weather conditions. Excluding movement over gathering lines, the average length of crude oil movement by pipeline is 302 miles; the average length of product movement is 345 miles.[21] Many movements requested by petroleum shippers involve origins and destinations on the lines of different pipeline companies. In some cases the movement from the producing field to the refinery involves the lines of five or six different companies. To facilitate these movements, pipeline companies have established a complex system of through tariff rates. Because of the existence of interline agreements, the refiner or purchaser of petroleum has a broad choice of suppliers; conversely, the owners of crude oil or refined products are given a wider market for their products.

Pipeline companies specify a minimum tender size (the minimum quantity of petroleum acceptable for shipment); this typically ranges between 10,000 and 100,000 barrels. These tender-size guidelines are subject to review by the ICC, which has in the past scaled these requirements down so as to prevent discrimination against smaller shippers.

DOMESTIC WATER CARRIAGE

There are several distinct forms of domestic water carriage: (1) movements over the inland waterways, which consist of the river and canal system of the country; (2) movements on the Great Lakes; and (3) domestic deep-sea transportation, which includes coastal shipping between ports of the Pacific coast and between ports on the coastline of the Gulf of Mexico and the Atlantic seaboard, and intercoastal shipping between ports on the Pacific coast and the ports of the Gulf of Mexico and the Atlantic coast.[22] The following discussion examines the significance of domestic water carriage and explores the nature of the industry. Because this book is primarily concerned with domestic transportation, limited attention is devoted to international shipping by water carriage.

Development of the System

The waterway system has played an important role in the development of the United States. This was particularly true in the prerailroad period. Overland travel was generally slow and expensive and often dangerous. Initially, coastal water carriage by ship served as the major link between the colonies, which were clustered along the coastline.

As settlement proceeded inland, natural lakes and rivers provided access to new lands. In subsequent years the waterways served as channels of commerce for various forms of rafts and boats, which moved excess farm production to colonial markets.

Although the natural waterway system was extensive, geographical and navigational limitations led to public efforts to improve and expand the system. The rivers of the United States have historically been owned and controlled by the federal government in the name of the people, and federal funding has promoted the bulk of waterway development. As early as 1789, federal monies were appropriated for harbor improvements; in the years that followed, numerous federal river and harbor projects were initiated.[23]

Canals

State participation in the promotion of waterway development during the formative years of our nation primarily involved canal building. The era of canal building, which witnessed the construction of more than 4,400 miles of artificial waterways linking various bodies of water, really began with the completion of the Erie Canal in 1825. The canal, which was built by the state of New York at a cost of nearly $7 million, stretched 364 miles and linked Buffalo on Lake Erie with Albany on the Hudson River.[24] It provided low cost transportation between the East and the West. Consequently, it diverted much of the traffic eastward that had previously moved from the West down the Mississippi River to New Orleans. The canal was a great success, and not only was an important factor in promoting development of the West, but also led to the emergence of New York City as an important commercial center on the Atlantic coast.

The financial success of the Erie Canal and the widespread desire for low-cost transportation led to construction of canals in many other states. Some of those projects were financially viable, but many were economic failures that placed heavy financial burdens on the sponsoring states. By 1880 the superiority of rail carriage and the inability of most canal projects to generate adequate toll revenues had led to the abandonment of more than half of all canal mileage.[25] The present domestic waterway system contains fewer than 700 miles of canals.

Steam Technology

While canal building was increasing the scope and coverage of the waterway system, the introduction of steam technology to water transportation was revolutionizing the mode of carriage. The relative increase in speed introduced by the steamboat and its ability to undertake upstream journeys led it to a position of transportation dominance prior to the Civil War. Steamboat traffic, particularly on the Mississippi and Ohio rivers, grew steadily into the 1850s, when the competition of railroads began to have an impact. Railroads had outgrown their role as feeders to water facilities, and were now actively competitive with water operations over longer routes. Within a decade following the Civil War, steamboats had practically disappeared, and railroads had clearly emerged as the leading mode of both passenger and freight movement.

Resurgence of Water Carriage

The near-monopoly power of the railroads in many markets at the turn of the century was a matter of considerable public concern. In response to this situation, the federal government took both regulatory and financial action. From 1900 to 1920, Congress substantially tightened railroad regulations (as discussed in Chapter 12), thereby strengthening the relative competitive position of water carriers. At the same time, federal outlays for waterway development, which were made yearly following the Civil War, increased substantially. Although many of these outlays were considered primarily as conservation measures, their secondary effect was the improvement of the waterways for commercial purposes. One measure of the extent of federal commitment to waterway development is the fact that more than $213 million was appropriated for such projects between 1900 and 1940.[26]

The resurgence of water carriage was slow but steady, and by the 1930s approximately 15 percent of intercity freight was moving over the U.S. waterway system.[27] Barge operations had made sizable inroads on bulk and liquid commodity movements that had previously been carried by rail, and the railroads advocated federal regulation of water carriage to ease the competitive intensity. Congress responded to these conditions with the passage of the Transportation Act of 1940, which, among other things, established ICC control over certain aspects of domestic water carriage. These regulatory controls are discussed later in this chapter.

Public financing of waterway development and improvement has continued (see Table 5–1). It should be noted that expenditures for multiple-purpose waterway projects are not included in the table. Most new construction is carried out by the Army Corps of Engineers with congressional funding from general tax revenues. This contrasts sharply with federal funding of highway and airport–airways programs, which are primarily financed through user-charge programs and administered by DOT.

Several major waterway projects have been completed during the past two decades. Foremost among these have been the St. Lawrence Seaway and the Arkansas–Verdigris River project. The seaway, which was completed in 1959, stretches 160 miles from Lake Ontario to Montreal, providing deep-sea access to traffic from lake ports. It is capable of servicing both deep-water ocean vessels and shallow-draft vessels. The project was jointly financed by the United States ($131 million) and Canada ($340 million); it is the only waterway in the country to experiment with the user-charge concept, which has often been proposed for other domestic waterways. Tolls levied on users of the seaway were to be used to retire

Table 5-1

Public Expenditures for Waterway Development (in millions)

	Federal[a]	State and Local[b]	Total
Prior to 1955	$3,914.4	$1,195.0	$5,109.4
1955	110.1	154.0	264.1
1960	293.5	237.0	530.5
1965	399.5	276.0	675.5
1970	360.7	444.0	804.8
1971	407.5	504.0	911.5
1972	436.1	527.0	963.1
1973	482.3	601.0	1,083.3
1974	516.5	625.0	1,141.5
1975	512.5	625.0	1,137.5

[a] Includes inland waterways, intracoastal waterways, Great Lakes and coastal harbors —obligations for construction, operation and maintenance of channels and harbors, locks and dams, alteration of bridges over navigable rivers, advanced engineering and design, and other minor costs related to navigation. The table does not include construction and operating expenditures for navigation on the Tennessee River as reported by the Tennessee Valley Authority ($363 million through fiscal 1974) and the U.S. portion of construction costs for the St. Lawrence Seaway ($134 million through fiscal 1975).
[b] State and local expenditures for years 1955–1973 are for water transport and terminal facilities. Expenditure figures are not available prior to 1955 and since 1973, so the figures presented in the table for those years are estimates.

SOURCE: Association of American Railroads, *Government Expenditures for Highway, Waterway, and Air Facilities and Private Expenditures for Railroad Facilities for Railroad Facilities* (Washington, D.C.: the Association, 1975), p. 10.

the bonds that were issued to finance the project, but to date revenues and traffic volume have not met expectations.[28]

The Arkansas–Verdigris River project was built by the Corps of Engineers over a period of 12 years at a cost of $1.2 billion. It consists of a 440-mile channel that extends from the Mississippi River across Arkansas to the outskirts of Tulsa, Oklahoma. Even though the channel cannot service deep-water vessels, it does provide access to ocean-bound traffic through New Orleans. Completion of the project has stimulated considerable industrial growth along its route, and it has been estimated that it will ultimately save shippers approximately $40 million per year.[29]

The propriety of such waterway projects has been a source of controversy in recent years. As federal outlays have come under closer scrutiny and as the relative roles of the various modes have received more attention, DOT has expressed the opinion that most, if not all, the economically justified opportunities for significant waterway extensions have been exploited.[30] However, as noted by DOT, there is no shortage of proposed waterway projects, reflecting their desirability to both the sponsoring politicians and their respective constituents.

Contemporary Waterways Network

The combination of a vast natural waterways system and sizable public outlays has yielded a domestic waterway network that is the most extensive in the world. Excluding seacoasts and Great Lakes routes, by 1975 the network consisted of 24,000 miles of navigable waterways, of which nearly 20,000 miles are in commercial use. In 1975, this system moved 17.1 percent of intercity ton mileage.[31] The nature of carriers operating over this system and their cost and service characteristics are discussed in the following sections.

Industrial Structure

Domestic water transportation consists of several major industrial components: companies conducting barge services on the river and canal portion of the inland waterway system, companies conducting steamship and ferry operations on the Great Lakes, and companies providing ocean-going vessel services in coastal and intercoastal transportation.

Inland Waterway Operations

Barge operations, which consist primarily of multiple-barge *tows* pushed by a power unit, comprise the most significant segment of domestic water carriage; they account for approximately 11 percent of intercity freight ton mileage.[32] More than 1,250 companies provide services on a for-hire basis. Of these, approximately 70 regular route common carriers and fewer than 50 contract carriers are regulated by the ICC. The remaining 1,100 companies operate as exempt carriers, and engage in the unregulated movement of bulk and liquid commodities. The origin and exact nature of these exemptions are discussed later in this chapter. Additionally, more than 400 companies, such as public utilities, oil companies, and food processors, conduct private barge operations. It should be noted that the Interstate Commerce Act permits both private and regulated water carriers to act as exempt carriers on back-haul movements.

In total, about 4,100 towboats or tugs and more than 25,000 barges are involved in operations over the river and canal network.[33] There are several large companies engaged in for-hire barge operations, but the typical operator is a relatively small businessman in transportation terms. Because of the scale of the typical barge operation and the limited regulatory entry controls in this form of carriage, it is often assumed that entry into such operations is relatively easy. However, the cost of a modern towboat is several million dollars, so capital entry barriers are rather significant.[34]

Great Lakes and Deep-Sea Operations

The second major component of domestic water carriage operations consists of movements on the Great Lakes. An additional 5 percent of intercity freight ton mileage moves on the Great Lakes by freighter or ferry services. About 70 commercial harbors exist on the lakes, and the traffic flow consists primarily of ore and grain movements. Opening of the St. Lawrence Seaway has provided lake ports with access to service by all but the largest ocean-going vessels, and has stimulated the growth of import–export traffic.

The third component of the domestic water system is coastal (along either the Pacific coast or the Atlantic coast, or between Atlantic and Gulf Coast ports), and intercoastal (connecting East and West coast ports through the Panama Canal or around South America). Historically, the federal government has restricted such services to vessels that are built, owned, and operated by U.S. citizens. Such stipulations, both here and abroad, are generally referred to as *cabotage* laws. The related guidelines that cover the U.S. situation are contained in the Jones Act (also known as the Merchant Marine Act), which was passed in 1920.

A considerable volume of coastal traffic moves by barge, with the remainder moving by regular cargo ship. Prior to World War II, 19 companies offered package and volume service on intercoastal movements.[35] These services were interrupted by the war, and the business never really recovered. Contributing to its decline was increasing rate and service competition from railroads, oil pipelines, and motor carriers. Traffic volume moving over the intercoastal routes has dwindled, and the number of companies serving the routes has similarly contracted. According to the ICC, this is the only segment of regulated domestic water carriage that has experienced major financial difficulties in recent years.[36]

Commission Classification of Carriers

In regulating domestic water carriage, the ICC classifies carriers into three groups based on annual gross operating revenues. Class A carriers are those with annual operating revenues in excess of $500,000; class B carriers generate operating revenues between $100,000 and $500,000; class C carriers generate annual operating revenues of less than $100,000. Commission reports indicate that in recent years the number of class A and B carriers has declined slightly and that the aggregate freight revenues of these two classes of carriers have averaged $450 million.[37]

Regulation

Responsibility for the economic regulation of domestic water carriage was given to the ICC by the Transportation Act of 1940. A regulatory pattern was adopted which was quite similar to that which had been applied to the railroads. Major provisions of the act stipulate regulation of the following aspects of the industry: entry into common and contract carriage, common carrier rate making (contract carriers must publish minimum rates only), and carrier mergers.

However, a significant difference exists between the regulation of railroads and water carriage in that all water carriers of bulk commodities are exempt from regulation provided that not more than three commodities are carried in the same vessel or tow. Liquid cargo movements are similarly exempt from regulation. The combined effect of these exemptions and the existence of private carriage is that only 10 percent of domestic water carriage traffic is subject to ICC regulation.[38]

The U.S. Coast Guard, now a component of the federal Department of Transportation, enforces federal maritime safety regulations and is charged with provision of navigational aids. It is also responsible for enforcing the antipollution laws that apply to the waterway system.

Capital Needs

The major cost element of the domestic water carriage industry—the right-of-way—is provided, maintained, and operated primarily at public expense. Government spending for these purposes has averaged slightly more than $1 billion annually in recent years. Unquestionably, these outlays strengthen the competitive position of water carriers by opening new markets and reducing operating costs. As discussed earlier in the chapter, the only instance in which waterway user charges are levied in domestic water carriage is on movements through the St. Lawrence Seaway.[39]

Competitive modes have long contended that these public outlays, if not recovered through user charges, give water carriage an artificial price advantage in intermodal competition. Water carriers have countered by claiming that waterway expenditures generally have multiple purposes, such as promotion of national defense, flood control, or improved irrigation, and that commercial water carriage is an indirect beneficiary. In any event, several legislative proposals to create a broad waterways user-charge program have failed, and creation of such a program seems unlikely in the near term.[40]

It has been estimated that the total private sector net investment in domestic water carriage (private plus for-hire) is slightly more than $2 billion.[41] Of this, approximately $456 million represents the net investment of the class A and B inland and coastal waterways carriers subject to the ICC.

According to the ICC, the financial condition of regulated water carriers appears to be generally sound. The aggregate rate of return on net investment of all class A and B water carriers operating on the inland and coastal waterways has ranged between 6 and 10 percent in recent years.[42]

Conglomerate Involvement

One factor that has contributed to this financial strength is the recent inflow of capital to the industry from nontransportation companies. Some of the largest barge operations have been acquired by conglomerate (multiindustry) companies, and the capital backing of the conglomerates has led to equipment modernization and related operating cost reductions.[43] This movement of conglomerate companies into for-hire transportation is the subject of considerable controversy; it is discussed at length in Chapter 16.

Barge Mixing Rule

Another factor that increased the financial stability of regulated water carriage was the suspension of the *barge mixing rule*. Under the provision of the Transportation Act of 1940, if a barge operator mixed exempt and regulated commodities in the same tow of barges, the exempt commodities would be brought under the published regulated rate structures of the ICC. Additionally, the law stipulated that no more than three exempt commodities could be carried in a single tow.

As more powerful towboats were developed, which made tows of 40 or more barges possible, it became prohibitively expensive for barge operators to keep towboats and crews waiting while they accumulated enough barges with regulated or exempt cargoes to make up a tow. Because of this, beginning in 1959, industry representatives filed several petitions with the ICC to suspend the mixing rule. Each petition was rejected, but finally in 1967 Congress granted a waiver of the mixing rule pending investigation. The mixing rule was abolished in 1973; this has contributed to reduced capital needs, improved barge service, and lower operating costs within the industry.[44]

Cost and Service Characteristics

The following discussion examines the cost and service characteristics of domestic water carriage. Particular attention is devoted to the competitive significance of these factors.

Water Carrier Costs

Extensive governmental participation in the construction, operation, and maintenance of domestic waterways significantly lowers the cost structure of firms that perform water transport services. Because the right-of-way is provided at minimal carrier expense, the major capital outlays of carriers are related to vessel ownership and terminal facilities.

The cost structure of inland and coastal water carriers is lightly weighted with fixed costs, the majority of costs being variable in nature. In that respect, their cost structure resembles that of trucking rather than that of railroads or oil pipelines. The unit costs of water carriers in moving freight tend to be considerably lower than those of competitive modes (with the possible exception of pipelines in certain instances). Several factors combine to make water carriage such a low-cost mode: the public provision of the right-of-way, extremely low operating costs, and the favorable impact on unit costs of handling large-volume shipments, which further reduces the already low overhead expenses per unit.

In contrast, the capital investment of water carriers involved in Great Lakes and intercoastal shipping tends to be much larger than that of the typical barge operator because of the relative costs of the vessels employed —freighters and tankers versus barges. This sector of the industry consequently has a cost structure that exhibits, as do the cost structures of the railroad and pipeline industries, a significant difference between fully distributed and variable costs.[45]

Major Cost Elements. Line-haul costs in inland and coastal water carriage tend to be quite low not only because the industry is very energy efficient, but also because of the introduction of more powerful towboats (some up to 9,000 horsepower versus 700 horsepower in the 1930s) has increased possible tow lengths and reduced labor requirements. Terminal costs and the costs of loading and unloading tend to be proportionately higher.

A lack of information concerning exempt and private water carriage makes it impossible to comment on their operating ratios. However, the ICC reports that class A and B carriers operating on the inland and coastal waterways, taken collectively, had average operating ratios between 85 and 90 for the years 1969–1974.[46] The fact that these carriers could report high operating ratios and yet register average rates of return on net investment between 6 and 10 percent during the same period attests to the low nonoperating cost structure of this sector of the industry. During the same period, regulated coastal and intercoastal carriers reported average operating ratios between 89 and 100 percent. As noted earlier, on the average, these carriers earned 4 to 8 percent, reflecting, among other things, higher capital costs.[47]

Water Carrier Rates and Competitive Pricing. It is difficult to generalize about the rate structure of the domestic water carrier industry because of the diversity of water carrier services and the existence of major exemptions. However, each year the ICC calculates an average revenue per ton mile figure for regulated class A and B barge operators on the Mississippi River system. This figure was 0.378 cents in 1973.[48] This is approximately one fourth the average revenue per ton mile earned by railroads during that same year; but comparison of these figures is of limited value, because it fails to reflect the impact of rail–water competition over a given route. Where such competition has existed between regulated carriers, water carriers have traditionally attempted to establish prices that were about 20 percent below rail rates.[49] The ICC has tended to allow this differential. Under these circumstances, shippers must weigh this price difference against several other factors, including the relative speeds and route distances of the two modes. Where competition exists between exempt water carriers and railroads, the ICC has tended to allow the railroads to meet the prices of the exempt carriers.[50]

In some markets, competition has also developed between water carriage and oil pipelines on petroleum traffic. Improvements in the pumping technology and the use of wide-diameter pipe have allowed the pipelines to quote rates that are quite competitive with water carriage over long-distance movements.

There is also a certain degree of competition between water carriers engaged in common and contract carriage. Where such competition exists, the rates of common carriers tend to be higher than the rates of contract carriage.

Some joint rail–water rate making also exists. Such agreements, which effectively extend the markets that might be served by individual carriers, are subject to ICC approval.

Water Carrier Service

Domestic water carriage primarily serves industries that generate, process, or consume bulk-loading commodities. These commodities do not tend to be time sensitive, and their shippers trade off the relative slowness of water carriage for its low price. A limited number of commodity categories account for the majority of water traffic. It has been estimated that 80 percent of water carriage ton mileage is generated by four commodity categories: (1) petroleum and petroleum products, (2) coal and coke, (3) sand and gravel, and (4) iron ore and steel.[51] As indicated by the average length-of-haul figures registered by water carriers operating over the various segments of the U.S. waterway system, water carriers are generally engaged in long-distance movements. During 1974 these figures were river and canal movements, 359 miles; Great Lakes operations, 540 miles; and domestic deep-sea traffic, 1,383 miles.[52]

Typically, water traffic moves in large quantities, taking advantage of a major strength of the mode—its ability to handle large-volume shipments. In barge operations, waterway improvements and introduction of towboats with up to 9,000 horsepower have combined to yield astounding capacity. Dry-cargo barges have capacities ranging from 800 to 3,000 tons; tank barges have capacities ranging from 1,000 to 3,800 tons. Given these barge capacities and towboat capabilities, tow loads of 30,000 to 50,000 tons are not uncommon.[53] In contrast, 20 years ago a tow of 10,000 tons was considered huge. These capacity figures are more meaningful when it is realized that some barges are capable of carrying as much bulk traffic as 40 railroad cars, and that tows consisting of 40 to 50 barges are possible.

In coastal and intercoastal service there have been several recent changes in service offerings. Much of this traffic now moves in unitized loads relying upon loaded container or trailer movements on containerships. This has not only reduced loading and unloading times, but has also lowered longshoring costs and reduced loss and damage. Probably the most dramatic innovation in water carriage in recent years is the development of barge-carrying, ocean-going ships. This system, LASH (lighter aboard ship), has provided shippers located on practically any segment of the inland waterway system with access to seaports and inland water destinations throughout the world. Barges having capacities ranging from 250 to 750 tons are moved along the inland waterways to a deep-water port.[54] There they are loaded upon ocean-going vessels for ocean movement. Upon arrival at the destination port, the barges are unloaded from the mother ship and moved by towboat to their final destination. This service was introduced on a limited basis in 1969. Although the concept has some application in domestic movements, its primary purpose will be to serve international markets.

Shipper Assessment of Water Carriage. In considering the possible use of water carriage, the shipper is confronted by the fact that the capacity strength and low rate structure of the mode are offset to varying degrees by certain disadvantages inherent in the mode. For example, even under ideal conditions water operations generally operate between 8 and 15 miles per hour.[55] Contributing to this relative slowness is waterway congestion at some key locks during certain seasonal peaks. Also, some segments of the waterway system are impassable during winter months. Additionally, many water routes are quite circuitous, which effectively increases origin–destination times.

Because of the geographical limitations of the waterway system, services are not readily available at all locations, and the cost and time involved in the transfer from rail or truck to water carrier are often prohibitive. However, frequent shippers and receivers of bulk-loading commodities often locate facilities on waterways to assure access to water service. Finally, in employing the services of water carriers, shippers will find that the carrier's liability is more limited than that of carriers of other modes; the shipper must often take a marine insurance policy to assure total coverage.

Despite these disadvantages, domestic water carriage has maintained a relatively stable share of intercity freight ton mileage in recent years, and it continues to serve as a major component of our national transportation network.

International Shipping

This book is primarily concerned with domestic transportation. However, a steadily growing number of U.S. companies have entered international markets; consequently, some mention of international ocean shipping is justified.

In planning international ocean movements the shipper is confronted with massive documentation problems, limited carrier liability (necessitating additional marine insurance coverage), and a variety of carrier services. The shipper of dry cargo will generally deal with companies engaged in *liner* services—regularly scheduled, common-carrier-type voyages between regular ports of call. These companies operate vessels that usually have cargo-carrying capacities of 10,000 tons or more. Rates for such services are determined by carrier conferences subject to approval by the Federal Maritime Commission. Typically, a dual rate system is used whereby shippers who agree to ship by conference lines exclusively are given lower rates than other shippers. One major development in liner services in recent years has been the emergence of containerships, which handle unitized loads. These ships have not only reduced loading and unloading time, but also have cut labor expense and cargo loss and damage.

If the shipper must move shipload lots of bulk commodities, he will likely consider the use of a tramp steamer. These vessels operate as contract carriers on a charter basis. The charters are of varying durations, and the tramp operator tends to follow the flow of commerce rather than conduct regularly scheduled, regular-route services. Also, the rates of tramp operators tend to fluctuate dramatically due to changing demand and supply conditions.

Tanker services are also offered on a charter basis, but many such vessels are owned by the petroleum companies. The emergence of supertankers that provide carrying capacity of up to 250,000 deadweight tons has led to a series of questions concerning both their economic and environmental impact. The Deep Water Port Act of 1974 directed the Department of Transportation to determine the requirements for constructing facilities capable of handling supertankers in U.S. waters.

The United States Merchant Marine

Throughout the years, a major objective of the federal government in addressing international shipping has been the maintenance of a strong merchant marine fleet not only to serve an economic role, but also to provide support in times of national emergency. Only ships built in the United States and owned and staffed by U.S. citizens can be registered as U.S. vessels. This registration is significant because only registered U.S. vessels are eligible for federal subsidies, which are administered by the Federal Maritime Administration. These subsidies, which averaged $500 million per year between 1973 and 1975, take two forms:[56] (1) construction differential subsidies to make the purchase of U.S.-built vessels more attractive, and (2) operating differential subsidies primarily to offset the lower crew costs of foreign vessels.

Even with these subsidy programs, the U.S. merchant marine has declined significantly in terms of both fleet size and cargo volume handled. Between 1950 and 1975 the U.S. fleet declined from 1,145 to 660 vessels of over 1,000 gross tons in size.[57] Approximately 400 of these are dry-cargo vessels, and more than 200 are tankers (the tankers are primarily engaged in domestic service).[58] Additionally, the federal government owns approximately 600 vessels that are kept in an inactive reserve fleet. As the fleet size has contracted, the volume of our country's international commerce handled by U.S. ships has also declined from 42 percent in 1950 to roughly 6 percent in 1975.[59]

In an attempt to revitalize our merchant marine fleet, Congress passed the Merchant Marine Act of 1970, which was to add 300 ships to the private fleet by 1980 through more liberal subsidy payment, tax incentives, and government loan guarantees.[60]

SUMMARY

Oil pipelines play a dominant role in domestic petroleum movements. The steady earnings of the industry and its affiliation with the major oil companies have allowed the industry to continuously modernize and automate, thereby keeping costs relatively low. In the long run, the industrial base may well expand into movements of other commodities on a broad scale. At the present, however, such movements are generally of an experimental nature. Therefore, the industry's main contribution to the economy in the immediate future will likely be the provision of continuous, low-cost petroleum carriage. The industry's participation in the joint financing of the Alaskan pipeline project will at least temporarily alleviate some of the energy problems faced by our nation.

Domestic water carriage has benefited from recent regulatory changes and a capital infusion from conglomerate companies. The industry's cost structure, which benefits from major public spending for waterways, is generally lower than that of competitive modes. Although the mode suffers some competitive disadvantage due to such factors as the limitations of the waterway network, climatic conditions, and relative slowness, technological improvements and federal construction projects have combined to alleviate some of these problems. Consequently, both the regulated and exempt sectors of the industry will continue to play a major role in the intercity movement of bulk and liquid commodities.

NOTES

1. J. L. Burke, "Oil Pipelines' Place in the Transportation Industry," *ICC Practitioners' Journal*, XXXI, No. 7 (April 1964), p. 782.

2. Ibid., p. 783.

3. Fred S. Steingraber, "Pipeline Transportation of Petroleum and Its Products," in *Transportation: Principles and Perspectives* by Stanley J. Hille and Richard F. Poist (Danville, Ill.: Interstate Printers and Publishers, 1974), p. 147.

4. D. Philip Locklin, *Economics of Transportation*, 7th ed. (Homewood, Ill.: Richard D. Irwin, Inc., 1972), p. 608.

5. Ibid.

6. Ibid., p. 609.

7. Richard D. James, "Alaska Pipeline's Estimated Cost Is Boosted Again," *Wall Street Journal*, New York, June 23, 1975, p. 4.

8. Alyeska Pipeline Service Company, "Oil from the Arctic," Cleveland, Ohio, 1973. (Brochure)

9. Roy J. Sampson and Martin T. Farris, *Domestic Transportation: Practice, Theory, and Policy*, 3rd ed. (Boston: Houghton Mifflin Company, 1975), p. 68.

10. "Pipeline Transportation Technology," *Handling and Shipping*, X, No. 1 (January, 1969), p. 66.

11. Locklin, op. cit., pp. 607–608.

12. Robert C. Lieb, "Intermodal Ownership: Experience and Evaluation," *ICC Practitioners' Journal*, XXXVIII, No. 5 (July–August, 1971), p. 752.

13. Companies engaged in the movement of natural gas by pipeline are regulated by the Federal Power Commission.

14. Burke, op. cit., p. 787.

15. Ibid., p. 801.

16. Charles F. Phillips, *The Economics of Regulation*, rev. ed. (Homewood, Ill.: Richard D. Irwin, Inc., 1969), p. 276.

17. John Guandola, *Transportation Law* (Dubuque, Iowa: William C. Brown Company, 1965), p. 215.

18. Burke, op. cit., p. 785.

19. Ibid., p. 782.

20. Sampson and Farris, op. cit., p. 69.

21. Transportation Association of America, *Transportation Facts and Trends* (Washington, D.C.: the Association, 1976), p. 14.

22. Additionally, there are noncontiguous services between the mainland of the United States and offshore parts of the country, including Alaska, Hawaii, Puerto Rico, Guam, American Samoa, and the U.S. Virgin Islands. However, these services are regulated by the Federal Maritime Commission and are treated more in the manner of international rather than domestic services.

23. Sampson and Farris, op. cit., p. 35.

24. Locklin, op. cit., p. 97.

25. Ibid., p. 102.

26. Charles W. Howe, *Inland Waterway Transportation: Studies in Private and Public Management and Investment Decisions* (Baltimore, Md.: Johns Hopkins Press, 1969), p. 9.

27. Dudley F. Pegrum, *Transportation: Economics and Public Policy*, rev. ed. (Homewood, Ill.: Richard D. Irwin, Inc., 1968), p. 67.

28. Association of American Railroads, *Government Expenditures for Highway, Waterway, and Air Facilities and Private Expenditures for Railroad Facilities* (Washington, D.C.: the Association, 1975), p. 9.

29. "What? Oklahoma a 'Coastal' State?" *U.S. News and World Report*, LXX, No. 8 (February 22, 1971), p. 60.

30. U.S. Department of Transportation, Office of the Secretary, *A Statement of National Transportation Policy* (Washington, D.C.: the Department, 1971), p. 7.

31. Transportation Association of America, op. cit., p. 8.

32. Sampson and Farris, op. cit., p. 72.

33. Transportation Association of America, op. cit., p. 30

34. Sampson and Farris, op. cit., p. 72.

35. Paul T. McElhiney, *Transportation for Marketing and Business Students* (Totowa, N.J.: Littlefield, Adams & Company, 1975), p. 105.

36. U.S. Interstate Commerce Commission, *86th Annual Report to Congress* (Washington, D.C.: U.S. Government Printing Office, 1972), p. 49.

37. U.S. Interstate Commerce Commission, *89th Annual Report to Congress* (Washington, D.C.: U.S. Government Printing Office, 1975), p. 27.

38. Thomas Gale Moore, *Freight Transportation Regulation* (Washington, D.C.: American Enterprise Institute for Public Policy Research, 1974), p. 32.

39. User fees are also charged for movements through the Panama Canal, which is administered by the U.S. government.

40. Carlo J. Salzano, "Nation's Barge, Towing Industry Girds for New Fight Against User Charges," *Traffic World*, CLXIV, No. 1 (October 6, 1975), p. 18.

41. Sampson and Farris, op. cit.. p. 72.

42. U.S. Interstate Commerce Commission, op. cit., p. 127.

43. "Teacher's Pet," *Forbes*, CVII, No. 5 (March 1, 1971), pp. 50–1.

44. For a discussion of this issue, see U.S. Department of Transportation, *Implementing Transportation Policy* (Washington, D.C.: the Department, 1973), pp. 8–9.

45. Phillips, op. cit., pp. 325–26.

46. U.S. Interstate Commerce Commission, *86th and 89th Annual Reports*, pp. 139 and 127, respectively.

47. U.S. Interstate Commerce Commission, *86th and 89th Annual Reports*, pp. 140 and 127, respectively.

48. U.S. Interstate Commerce Commission, *Transport Economics*, I, No. 3 (1974), p. 15.

49. Phillips, op. cit., p. 328.

50. George W. Hilton, *The Transportation Act of 1958: A Decade of Experience* (Bloomington, Ind.: Indiana University Press, 1969), p. 76.

51. "New: Traffic Jams on U.S. Rivers," *U.S. News and World Report*, LXXI, No. 2 (September 20, 1971), p. 68.

52. Transportation Association of America, op. cit., p. 14.

53. "Bulk Transportation: A Barge Tow Hauling 50,000 Tons of Grain," *Handling and Shipping*, X, No. 6 (June 1969), p. 101.

54. "A State-of-the-Arts Report on Technology in Water Transportation," *Handling and Shipping*, XIII, No. 1 (January 1972), p. 75.

55. U.S. Department of Transportation, Office of the Secretary, *Summary of*

National Transportation Statistics (Springfield, Va.: National Technical Information Service, 1973), p. 47.

56. Association of American Railroads, op. cit., p. 11.

57. McElhiney, op. cit., p. 99.

58. Ibid.

59. Sampson and Farris, op. cit., p. 371.

60. Ibid.

SELECTED REFERENCES

American Waterway Operators, Inc. *Big Load Afloat*. Washington, D.C.: American Waterway Operators, Inc., 1965.

Burke, J. L. "Oil Pipelines' Place in the Transportation Industry." *ICC Practitioners' Journal*, XXXI, No. 7 (April 1964), pp. 780–802.

Howe, Charles W. *Inland Waterway Transportation: Studies in Private and Public Management and Investment Decisions*. Baltimore, Md.: Johns Hopkins Press, 1969.

Jantscher, Gerald R. *Bread upon the Waters: Federal Aids to the Maritime Industries*. Washington, D.C.: Brookings Institution, 1974.

Johnson, A. M. *Petroleum Pipelines and Public Policy, 1906–1959*. Cambridge, Mass.: Harvard University Press, 1967.

Labor–Management Maritime Committee. *The U.S. Merchant Marine Today: Sunrise or Sunset?* Washington, D.C.: the Committee, 1970.

Lawrence, Samuel A. *United States Merchant Shipping Policies and Politics*. Washington, D.C.: Brookings Institution, 1966.

Locklin, D. Philip. *Economics of Transportation*, 7th ed. Homewood, Ill.: Richard D. Irwin, Inc., 1972.
Chapter 26. "Pipelines," pp. 607–621.
Chapter 31. "Water Transportation," pp. 722–744.

McDowell, Carl E., and Helen M. Gibbs. *Ocean Transportation*. New York: McGraw-Hill Book Company, 1954.

Meyer, R. Charles, and Harold Handerson. "A Critique of the Rationales for Present U.S. Maritime Programs." *Transportation Journal*, XIV, No. 2 (Winter 1974), pp. 5–16.

"Pipeline Transportation Technology." *Handling and Shipping*, X, No. 1 (January 1969), pp. 64–66.

Sampson, Roy J., and Martin T. Farris. *Domestic Transportation: Practice, Theory and Policy*, 3rd ed. Boston: Houghton Mifflin Company, 1975.
Chapter 4. "Land Carriers," pp. 53–70.
Chapter 5. "Water, Air, and Other Forms of Carriage," pp. 71–87.

"A State-of-the-Arts Report on Technology in Water Transportation." *Handling and Shipping*, XIII, No. 1 (January 1972), pp. 74–76.

Steingraber, Fred S. "Pipeline Transportation of Petroleum and Its Products," in *Transportation: Principles and Perspectives* by Stanley J. Hille and Richard F. Poist (Danville, Ill.: Interstate Printers and Publishers, 1974), pp. 143–67.

DISCUSSION QUESTIONS

1. Explain the concept of undivided interest as it applies to the oil pipeline industry.
2. In several transportation regulatory statutes, Congress has granted certain exemptions from regulation. What are these exemptions, and what is their significance in the transportation marketplace?
3. Discuss the barge *mixing rule* and outline its importance to domestic water carriers.
4. Discuss the ability of barge operators to be competitive with other modes of freight movement on the basis of both price and service characteristics.

CHAPTER

6

The Airline Industry

Throughout the years, the airline industry has attracted considerable public attention. The speed and globe-shrinking characteristics of this mode are fascinating, and the extensive promotional efforts of the airlines would not allow us to forget this mode if we wanted to.

Speed and glamour aside, however, the public profile of the airline industry has been dominated by negative factors in recent years. Among the problems that have troubled the industry have been the steadily escalating costs of jet fuel and the industry's related cost spiral. These and other difficulties have combined to cause severe financial problems for a number of major airlines. While this has occurred, the pricing and entry control policies of the Civil Aeronautics Board (CAB) have been widely criticized as running counter to consumer interests. Considerable public attention has also been drawn to the airline industry's division of judgment about the wisdom of using reduced-fare plans to stimulate traffic.

While enduring such problems and criticisms, the airline industry has emerged as the dominant form of for-hire intercity passenger movement in the United States, nearly doubling the passenger mileage registered by intercity buses. Air cargo movements have also increased steadily in both volume and significance to the shipping public.

This chapter explores the industry structure of air carriage, and devotes attention to the contemporary strengths and problems of the mode.

103

DEVELOPMENT OF THE SYSTEM

Since the inception of manned aircraft flight in this country in 1903, the development of commercial aviation has had a strong connection with government and military endeavors. Although experimentation continued following the successful efforts of the Wright brothers, it took World War I to trigger large-scale development and production of aircraft. During the war years, much of the productive capacity of the automobile industry was redirected into production of more than 17,000 aircraft under federal contracts. The number of pilots trained by the military during this period exceeded 10,000.[1]

United States involvement in the war clearly demonstrated the future military significance of aircraft, and thereby established a pattern of joint military–industry development efforts that continues to the present.

Following the war, surplus planes were sold to private parties (including many ex-military pilots), and small-scale commercial operations surfaced. In 1918 the federal government initiated experimentation with airmail service. By 1924 the government provided continuous day and night transcontinental airmail service.[2] The feasibility of such service having been demonstrated, the Kelly Act of 1925 permitted the Post Office Department to award airmail contracts to private companies. The significance of this legislation in promoting the growth of commercial aviation cannot be overstated. By the mid-1930s, airmail contracts (which included a major subsidy element) comprised the bulk of the aviation industry's operating revenues.[3] Furthermore, the Kelly Act and several later statutes also stimulated expansion of passenger services by requiring companies that were awarded airmail contracts to provide passenger facilities as well.

Throughout this early period in aviation history, the federal government assumed responsibility for developing and operating the national airway system. This responsibility continues to the present time, whereas the bulk of the responsibility for the construction and operation of airport facilities rests with municipalities and public authorities.

Commercial aviation continued to expand during the 1930s, but at a slow pace. Passenger carriage was still in its infancy, and aircraft development efforts were limited. During this period many carriers experienced financial difficulties and air safety deteriorated. These factors contributed to passage of the Civil Aeronautics Act of 1938, which created the Civil Aeronautics Board (CAB) and established an extensive pattern of federal regulation of commercial air carriage to be administered by the board.

With the onset of World War II, increased government spending led to accelerated efforts in aircraft design and rapid expansion of the national aircraft fleet. During the conflict the number of people exposed to air travel grew dramatically, setting the stage for expansion of commercial airline capacity and demand in the post-World War II period.

The years immediately following the war witnessed rapid expansion of route mileage by the trunk lines and establishment of extensive cargo operations by these carriers. The trunk lines also introduced coach service during that period, which provided still another stimulus to passenger growth. The base of the industry also broadened with the establishment of a group of local service lines to provide links between smaller communities and major cities, and with the initiation of service by a number of all-cargo airlines.

In the years that have followed, the technology of the industry has changed dramatically with the advent of faster and more efficient jet aircraft and the introduction of jumbo passenger planes, such as the Boeing 747 and the Douglas DC-10. Internationally, supersonic flight has become a reality.

The U.S. airport–airway system has expanded tremendously, and the airway system now extends more than 300,000 statute miles.[4] The extensive coverage of the major airline routes in the continental United States is illustrated in Figure 6–1. There are more than 12,700 landing areas in the United States, including 1,280 heliports and 459 seaplane bases. Of the landing areas, 8,164 are privately owned and operated and 4,536 are publicly owned.[5] Scheduled and nonscheduled carriers provide passenger and cargo service to 722 certified airports.[6] The remaining landing areas are commonly used only by general aviation.

A significant portion of the recent expansion of the airport–airways system has been financed by user charges created by the Airport–Airway Development Act of 1970. Prior to that time, user payments were relatively limited in domestic aviation.

Air carriage of passengers and cargo has expanded steadily (see Table 6–1). Airlines now account for more than 75 percent of for-hire intercity passenger mileage in the United States, and handle nearly 80 percent of all first class intercity mail.[7] Additionally, air carriers have attracted a steadily increasing volume of high-value cargo.

INDUSTRIAL AND FINANCIAL STRUCTURE

The net investment in airlines engaged in scheduled operations in the United States exceeds $13 billion. These firms employ more than 290,000 workers and utilize more than 2,200 jet and piston-driven aircraft in providing passenger and freight services. Approximately 80 percent of the industry's operating revenues, which exceeded $15.2 billion in 1975, are

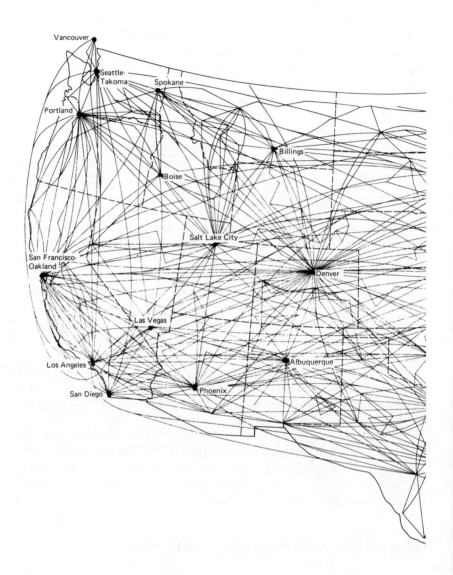

Figure 6–1

Major Airline Routes in the Continental United States

SOURCE: U.S. Civil Aeronautics Board.

Table 6–1

Passenger and Cargo Statistics, U.S. Scheduled Airlines, 1961–1975

Year	Revenue Passengers Enplaned (000)	Revenue Passengers Miles (000,000)	Cargo Ton Miles (000)
1961	63,012	39,831	1,093,343
1962	67,817	43,760	1,308,023
1963	77,403	50,362	1,453,967
1964	88,520	58,494	1,751,106
1965	102,920	68,677	2,303,131
1966	118,061	79,889	2,900,941
1967	142,499	98,747	3,426,117
1968	162,181	113,958	4,167,064
1969	171,898	125,420	4,690,355
1970	169,922	131,710	4,984,197
1971	173,677	135,652	5,108,616
1972	191,349	152,406	5,495,072
1973	202,208	161,957	6,035,200
1974	207,458	162,919	6,121,751
1975	205,062	162,810	5,892,605

SOURCE: Air Transport Association, *Air Transport, 1976* (Washington, D.C.: the Association, 1976), p. 12; also, p. 26 of the 1972 edition.

generated by passenger services.[8] An additional 5 to 6 percent of operating revenues originate in freight and express services, with the balance representing such revenue sources as airmail contracts and government subsidies.[9]

Carrier Classifications

Commercial aviation is in reality a hybrid, being composed of a variety of carrier types and operations. The Civil Aeronautics Board, the federal agency that regulates the economic aspects of the industry, classifies airlines into nine different groups. Some carriers are double counted due to the diverse nature of their operations. The major carrier groupings are domestic trunk lines, international and overseas lines, local service lines, all-cargo lines, supplemental air carriers, air taxi operators, and air freight forwarders.[10]

Domestic Trunk Lines

Foremost among these groups is the domestic trunk line category, which consists of carriers that have permanent operating rights between major population centers within the United States. There are 11 of these carriers, including such familiar names as Eastern Air Lines, United Airlines, and American Airlines. This group might be considered to be the backbone of the commercial aviation industry because of its major role in linking high-density cities. Operating in this capacity, the trunk lines generate nearly 80 percent of the industry's revenue passenger mileage. Although 19 trunk lines were originally certified by CAB in 1938, the number has declined to 11, primarily as a result of carrier mergers. Normally, in high-density passenger markets several trunk lines operate in direct competition. The extent of this competitive atmosphere is illustrated by the fact that all but 11 of the 100 largest domestic city-pairs are served by two or more trunk lines.[11] In addition to their domestic operations, eight trunk lines also provide service between the United States and foreign countries, excluding Canada.

Local Service Lines

Local service lines were created in the mid-1940s when CAB certified 23 carriers to provide air services in and between areas of lesser traffic density. They were also to provide connections between smaller population centers and major airports. In performing this latter service, the local carriers function in a *feeder* role relative to the domestic trunk lines. The number of local service lines has been reduced to nine through carrier failures and mergers. Included among the local service lines are such companies as Allegheny Airlines, Ozark Airlines, and Piedmont Airlines. Often, local service lines are awarded sole operating rights over a particular route because the CAB believes that potential passenger volume in such markets is not sufficient to support competitive service. Because of the light-density markets served by the local service lines, and the resulting low load factor realized in many of their operations, the financial viability of the majority of local service carriers continues to be dependent upon annual subsidies awarded by the CAB.

All-Cargo Lines

Three all-cargo lines, Airlift International, Flying Tiger, and Seaboard World Airlines, provide freight services, under limited certificates, between specified areas in the United States or between the United States and desig-nated foreign countries. The all-cargo lines provide no passenger service, and in many markets are in direct competition with the freight services offered by passenger airlines. Bankruptcies have reduced the number of all-cargo lines since their inception in the 1940s, but the remaining carriers have benefited from the strong growth rate of air cargo volume in recent years.

Supplemental Air Lines

Soon after the passage of the Civil Aeronautics Act of 1938, a group of nonscheduled carriers was granted an exemption from the economic regulation of the act by the CAB. This group of carriers has evolved into 13 supplemental airlines, which are presently authorized by the CAB to conduct unlimited charter operations involving both passengers and freight. In providing passenger services these carriers are permitted to charter aircraft to tour operators, who in turn sell package tours to individual members of the general public. CAB regulations generally prohibit the supplemental carriers from selling tickets to individuals. However, in recent years the CAB has been under considerable pressure from Congress and consumer groups to permit the supplementals more flexibility in this regard.

By far the most significant activity of supplemental operators is passenger charters in international service. Supplementals have attracted more than 25 percent of passenger traffic in the North Atlantic markets; this has led the regularly scheduled commercial airlines to call for more stringent regulation of charter operations by the CAB.[12] This matter is discussed further later in this chapter.

Air Taxis

There are more than 2,600 air taxi operators which utilize light planes that are restricted to flights involving less than 30 passengers or a 7,500-pound payload.[13] These carriers have been granted a CAB exemption and are not therefore subject to general economic regulation by the board. However, they are required to register with the CAB and must maintain a required level of liability insurance. Air taxis normally serve low-density traffic points that do not have sufficient population to support a local service line. About 80 percent of the passengers carried by these lines are connecting with major airlines.[14]

In 1966, the CAB modified its route policies and allowed some local service lines to compete directly with trunk lines. As the local service lines sought to shift their schedules into higher-density routes, the CAB permitted air taxis to replace them in many low-density, short-haul markets. Air taxis have established service to more than 60 of these points, and they generally provide more frequent service and better schedules than the local service lines that they replaced.[15] Carriers providing these services are part of a special group within the air taxi class that is known as *commuter air carriers.* Unlike other air taxi operators, they maintain published schedules and provide at least five round trips per week between two or more points, or carry mail. There were slightly more than 200 commuter airlines in operation in 1973.[16]

Although air taxi operators are generally thought of as passenger carriers, many of these companies conduct freight services. One such company, Federal Express, which entered the industry in 1972, has established national operations handling primarily packages that weigh less than 50 pounds. The company offers a variety of services, including next-day delivery, and has attracted a sizable volume of traffic that previously was handled by the regularly scheduled carriers.

Air Freight Forwarding

The final industry grouping consists of indirect air carriers or air freight forwarders. More than 300 air freight forwarders are certified by the CAB.[17] These companies are engaged in local pickup, consolidation, and delivery of air cargo. The certificates of some air freight forwarders are limited to either domestic or international operations, but more than half of them hold both forms of authority. A complete discussion of air freight forwarder operations and regulations is contained in Chapter 7.

Regulation and Promotion

The Civil Aeronautics Act of 1938 established the present regulatory structure of air transportation. The statute sought to stabilize conditions in the still-infant industry. During the period immediately preceding the passage of the act, the industry was in a rather chaotic state. Operating problems were widespread, accidents were increasing at an alarming rate, and several major carriers were faced with the prospect of bankruptcy.

The act created the CAB to act in both a regulatory and promotional capacity with respect to commercial air carriage. The board was given independent status and was required to report to Congress, as was the Interstate Commerce Commission. It was granted authority over such matters as fares and rates, routes served, operating rights, mergers, and subsidy payments. It was also charged with promoting development of international air transportation. In that capacity, the CAB, subject to presidential approval, grants foreign operating certificates to U.S. carriers and U.S. operating permits to foreign carriers.

In recent years, the CAB has been subject to growing criticism concerning its economic regulation of air carriage. It has been charged that the CAB has discouraged price competition between carriers, thereby fostering expensive service competition, which increases consumer costs. Other critics have contended that the CAB has been overly concerned with protection of the regulated carriers and has given inadequate attention to consumer interests. Convinced that these charges were accurate, the federal Department of Transportation submitted a broad aviation deregulation bill to Congress in 1975.[18] The specific nature of the DOT proposals is discussed in Chapter 13.

The Federal Aviation Administration (FAA), which is a component of the Department of Transportation, is charged with development and enforcement of safety regulations in air transportation. It also develops and operates the airways and administers the federal airport program. On an annual basis the FAA handles more than 20 million planes throughout the airway system.[19] Another federal agency, the independent National Transportation Safety Board, is responsible for investigation of fatal airline crashes. The board plays a similar role with respect to the other modes of transportation.

State Regulation

The federal government, through the FAA, has the power to regulate all interstate or intrastate flying to the extent that it may be necessary to protect interstate, overseas, or foreign air commerce. This greatly limits the authority of the states in the field of air safety.

However, with respect to economic regulation, the powers of CAB are limited to jurisdiction over interstate, overseas, and foreign commerce as well as the carriage of mail. This leaves the field of intrastate commerce by air to the jurisdiction of the states. Consequently, individual states can certify carriers for intrastate air service, and can similarly regulate the fares charged in these operations. Given this ability, 28 states have chosen to regulate at least some economic aspects of intrastate air carriage.[20]

Capital Needs

Various governmental units have played major roles in financing the growth and development of the U.S. airport–airways system. The federal government has played the predominant role in this regard. Until 1970, when the Airport–Airways Development Act was passed by Congress, the national airways system was maintained by the federal government at minimal costs to the users of the system. However, the 1970 act created a system of user charges that have been levied on airline passengers, shippers, general aviation, and the airlines so that the airways might be self-supporting. The act also provided for continued federal funding of both airway operation and airport development. Illustrating the magnitude of the federal commitment in this area is the fact that the federal budget for fiscal 1975 included $1.7 billion for Federal Aviation Administration operation of the airways system.[21] Public authorities and local governments generally own and operate the airports. In many instances the fees charged for landing aircraft, office and operational space, and maintenance and administrative quarters do not repay the operating costs of the airport.

Even when the fees repay operating costs, they commonly do not cover capital costs.[22] Consequently, the airline industry has historically benefited from the financing of the major cost element of the industry—the airport–airways system—by various governmental units, which until recently levied quite limited charges on system users.

Airline Capital Requirements

Prior to World War II, the capital requirements of most commercial airlines were modest, and many airlines were closely controlled by individuals or small groups that had little dependence on outside sources of capital.[23] However, as the scale of the industry increased, and jets and wide-bodied aircraft were introduced, capital requirements increased tremendously. As a result, it has been necessary for many carriers to rely quite heavily upon the financial markets for capital. This has required the major airlines to sell securities (primarily bonds) to attract capital in the investment community. An indication of both the trend in the method of financing and the aggregate capital needs of the scheduled airlines is provided by the fact that the long-term debt of the industry increased by nearly 250 percent between 1960 and 1975, reaching $5.53 billion in 1975.[24]

Reliance upon external sources of financing focuses the attention of the investment community on the performance and potential of those companies seeking financing. One indication of the financial strength of a company is its rate of return on investment. In 1961, the CAB set 10.5 percent as a *fair and equitable* target annual rate of return on investment for the scheduled airline industry. This standard was increased to 12 percent in 1970.[25] However, troubled by overcapacity, steadily rising costs, pressures to purchase the newest generation of equipment, and a softening of demand in the early 1970s, the airlines only achieved the CAB's target rate of return once between 1960 and 1976. Table 6–2 illustrates airline earnings between 1950 and 1975.

Airline Subsidies. The federal government has played a major role in promoting the development of commercial aviation in the United States. One significant component of this government role has consisted of airmail payments, which have historically included a sizable subsidy element. In the years prior to the passage of the Civil Aeronautics Act of 1938, to a great extent the Post Office Department based its airmail contract awards on carrier needs rather than the real value of the services performed. Later this practice was incorporated into the 1938 act.[26]

In 1951, Congress stipulated that future airmail payments were to be disaggregated into *service mail pay,* which represents fair payment for services rendered, and susbidy.[27] Two years later, the CAB was given

Table 6–2

Rate of Return on Investment, U.S. Scheduled Airlines, 1950–1975

Year	Rate of Return (%)
1950	11.2
1955	11.8
1960	2.8
1965	11.2
1970	1.5
1971	3.5
1972	4.9
1973	5.1
1974	6.4
1975	2.5

SOURCE: Charles F. Phillips, *Economics of Regulation,* rev. ed. (Homewood, Ill.: Richard D. Irwin, Inc., 1969), p. 505; also Air Transport Association, *Air Transport, 1976* (Washington, D.C.: the Association, 1976), p. 22.

administrative responsibility for the subsidy element of airmail payments; it has carried out this responsibility since that time.[28] Table 6–3 traces these payments, by carrier classification, between 1954 and 1975.

As the figures indicate, the CAB has moved toward elimination of carrier subsidy whenever possible. It should be noted that, with the exception of subsidies to Northeast Airlines for services provided to New England between 1964 and 1968, trunk lines have not been subsidized since 1959. The bulk of recent subsidy payments has been directed to the local service lines to help them achieve reasonable profitability while serving routes that are not directly compensatory.

COST AND SERVICE CHARACTERISTICS

Although modern jet aircraft represent multimillion dollar investments, such fixed costs as interest, depreciation, and amortization comprise a relatively small percentage of the industry's cost structure. It has been estimated that nearly 80 percent of the industry's cost structure is variable in nature.[29] Contributing to this situation is the provision of airways and airports by various governmental units. While charges are levied on the users of these system elements, these payments, such as landing fees, are variable with operations.

Table 6-3

Estimated Subsidy Payments, by Carrier Groups, All Certified Carriers, Fiscal Years 1955–1975 (in thousands)

Fiscal Year	Alaskan	Hawaiian	Helicopter	International	Local Service	Trunkline[a]	Grand Total
1955	$7,902	$ 293	$2,656	$3,757	$22,358	$2,773	$39,739
1960	8,670	330	4,930	—	51,498	—	65,428
1965	8,162	995	3,358	—	61,273	3,475	77,263
1966	6,508	1,124	1,170	—	58,148	3,089	70,039
1967	5,938	567	—	—	54,189	2,477	63,171
1968	5,895	—	—	—	47,982	1,343	55,220
1969	5,420	1,022	—	—	40,513	—	46,955
1970	4,917	—	—	—	34,262	—	39,179
1971	4,631	—	—	—	58,615	—	63,246
1972	2,242	—	—	—	64,484	—	66,726
1973	4,374	—	—	—	64,555	—	68,929
1974	4,345	—	—	—	68,508	—	72,853
1975	4,294	—	—	—	59,790	—	64,084

[a] Trunkline accruals for 1964–1968 reflect local service operations in New England area.

SOURCE: U.S. Civil Aeronautics Board, *Subsidy for United States Certified Air Carriers* (Washington, D.C.: the Board, 1971), p. 11, and data supplied by the Civil Aeronautics Board.

The Airline Industry

Major Cost Elements

The cost of labor is the most significant cost element of the domestic airline industry, accounting for nearly 40 percent of total airline operating costs. In recent years airline employee compensation has grown at an annual rate exceeding 10 percent, which far surpasses the rate of compensation growth of employees in most other industries. Airline employees have the highest annual level of compensation in the transportation industries, reaching more than $17,000 in 1975.[30] These compensation increases have led to sharp increases in unit labor costs within the industry. Another airline employee cost that is not reflected in compensation figures is the cost of lost business related to strikes. The industry has experienced numerous strikes in recent years. These work stoppages are typically conducted on a single carrier basis and can have a quite debilitating impact on a given carrier. This issue is discussed in detail in Chapter 15.

Fuel Costs

A major problem faced by the nation's airlines has been the rapidly rising cost of fuel. This problem was accentuated by the price increases that resulted from the Arab oil boycott of 1973. Evidence of the severity of the problem is provided by the average price per gallon of jet fuel, which increased from 12 to 32 cents between 1973 and 1975.[31] As a result, even though U.S. carriers used less jet fuel in 1975 than they had in 1973, the fuel bill was $1.6 billion higher in 1975.[32] During the 1973–1974 energy crisis, the magnitude of fuel price increases and fuel shortages led airlines to ground some aircraft and cut back flights to achieve higher load factors on continued flights. Future escalation of fuel costs may lead to pressures to make such cutbacks permanent.

User Payments and Airport Fees

As discussed earlier in this chapter, user charges in the aviation industry increased significantly in 1970 with enactment of the Airport–Airways Development Act. The bulk of user fees collected under this statute are borne directly by the traveling public in the form of excise taxes on passenger tickets and freight waybills. Although the airlines do not directly bear these costs, the taxes increase airline ticket prices and cargo rates. In recent years the development trust fund has generated a surplus, and the airlines have called for a reduction in fees, which might lead to lower airline prices.[33]

Airports also levy fees on airlines to support runways, taxiways, apron areas, terminal buildings, parking facilities, and airport access roads. These fees have increased more than 300 percent over the past decade; landing fees have also grown significantly.[34]

Equipment Costs

As discussed earlier in this chapter, equipment costs in the airline industry comprise a relatively low percentage of the industry's cost structure, but they are by no means trivial. Between 1960 and 1970 jet aircraft ranged in price between $5 and $7 million, not including the investment in parts, equipment, and crew training and orientation.[35] The newer wide-bodied jets are considerably more expensive; Boeing's 747 sells for more than $20 million.

Another element of equipment cost for domestic airlines is in the market pressure to buy the latest planes available. Service competition within the industry has led to considerable emphasis on new equipment. This has necessitated frequent refinancing of major capital outlays and selling off of equipment far before its useful life is realized. Many of these planes historically were sold to local service lines or supplemental carriers.[36] However, as the newer, larger planes are replaced, they are generally sold to foreign operators.

Fares and Price Competition

Collective pricing behavior plays a far more limited role in domestic air carriage than it does in surface transportation. In fact, air carriers must receive CAB permission before they can engage in collective discussions on such matters as fares. While the CAB has traditionally relied upon the initiative of individual carriers in the establishment of fares (subject to board approval), it has not fostered extensive price competition within the industry. Trunk line competition therefore has tended to have a service orientation, with emphasis being placed on frequency of service, equipment flown, and a variety of accessorial services.

Scheduled air fares have climbed steadily over the last decade, but they have risen considerably slower than the Consumer Price Index. Average revenue per revenue passenger mile is significantly higher in domestic airline operations than it is in intercity rail or bus operations (see Table 6–4). But, over the past decade, rail and bus fares have increased at a more rapid pace than air fares. However, once again caution must be used in comparing these figures because of their lack of market specificity. In fact,

Table 6–4

Average Revenue per Revenue Passenger Mile, Intercity Common Carriers (in cents per mile)

Year	U.S. Scheduled Airlines[a]	Class I Railroads[b]	Class I Buses
1965	6.06	3.18	2.88
1966	5.83	3.18	2.89
1967	5.64	3.19	2.98
1968	5.61	3.39	3.18
1969	5.79	3.61	3.39
1970	6.00	3.91	3.60
1971	6.32	4.26[c]	3.83
1972	6.40	4.75	3.98
1973	6.63	4.75	4.05
1974	7.52	5.22	4.41
1975	7.68	5.61	4.79

[a] Includes first class and coach. For 1974 the average revenue per revenue passenger mile in first-class service was 10.56 cents and 7.05 cents in coach.
[b] Includes both first-class and coach service.
[c] Beginning in 1971, railroad figures include Amtrak and independent railroad operations.

SOURCE: Air Transport Association, *Air Transport 1976* (Washington, D.C.: the Association, 1976), p. 27; Association of American Railroads, *Yearbook of Railroad Facts,* (Washington, D.C.: the Association, 1976), p. 34.

some promotional programs of domestic air carriers have established air fares that are quite competitive with bus and rail fares in high-density passenger markets. The fare structure of international air transportation is discussed later in this chapter.

Although the domestic airlines have traditionally maintained a two-class system of fares, first class and coach, they have periodically engaged in special promotional programs. These programs have been primarily directed at the nonbusiness traveler, and have sought to increase revenues by inducing additional travel. Some promotions, such as night-coach flights and special rates for weekend and other off-peak travel, have been highly attractive to the public and successful for the airlines. However, others, less well designed, have diluted total industry revenues.[37]

Because of Department of Transportation challenges pertaining to the potential discrimination inherent in such programs as family plans and youth fares, the airlines phased out many of these programs in the early 1970s. However, the excess capacity generated by the recessionary pressures of the early 1970s and the simultaneous delivery of wide-body air-craft led to a new generation of similar promotional fare programs.[38]

Airline Service

The basic differentiating factor of air transportation is its speed. Air-craft speeds far surpass those of competitive modes of surface carriage, and tend to give air carriage a decided advantage, particularly in long-distance markets.

However, several factors tend to offset some of the line-haul speed advantage of air carriage. One factor is the airport access–egress problem. The traveler must get to and from the airport. Air transportation ex-periences peaking of demand that coincides roughly with the peaking of travel in urban transportation during the morning and evening rush hours. If the airport is located near center city, it leads to a mix of urban and air travelers at peak hours. Consequently, this adds considerable time to air travel on a door-to-door basis. The individual making the line-haul journey by automobile does not have to contend with this problem. Nor do rail and bus travelers who board at suburban terminals. Conversely, some airports, such as those in Houston and New Orleans, are located considerable dis-tances from center city. As planes have become larger and more space has been needed to accommodate the aircraft, the trend toward outlying air-ports has accelerated. Suburbanization had already consumed large masses of property; conseqeuntly, some new air facilities have had to locate 20 to 25 miles from the center city. Once again, many travelers find that this adds considerable time to their total trip.

Another factor that offsets some of the line-haul speed advantage of air travel is airport congestion. Many domestic airports are operating at flight levels that approach their maximum capacity. Community resistance and environmental concerns have made it increasingly difficult to expand air-port capacity. As a result, congestion has become a fact of life at many major commercial air facilities. This also tends to be a problem during adverse weather conditions. Frequent air travelers have usually experienced *stacking* over some airport caused either by traffic peaks or poor visibility. In all fairness, it should be noted that even though air carriage is some-what more vulnerable to weather conditions than are competitive modes, it has compiled an excellent reliability record. In one recent year only 2.7 percent of scheduled airline mileage was canceled.[39]

Because of the combination of factors that offset some of the line-haul speed advantage of air carriage, airlines are more susceptible to competition from auto, bus, and rail operations in short-distance markets than they are in long-distance operations. The airline speed differential is so great in serving long-distance markets that it easily offsets the cumulative effects of the previously mentioned factors, even when stop-offs at intermediate cities are included. The extent of airline participation in long-distance travel markets is indicated by the average length of passenger haul for the scheduled airlines, which has increased steadily from 667 miles in 1965 to 810 in 1975.[40]

Customer Options

Several factors, including duplicate CAB route awards, competitive pressures to increase service frequency, and airline use of promotional fares, have combined to give the air traveler numerous options. Generally, the traveler has a choice of carriers over a particular route. Of the 400 largest domestic city-pairs served by commercial aviation, 365 are served by at least two carriers.[41] In most markets the traveler also has a choice of numerous flights throughout the day. Promotional fare programs have also had an impact on consumer choice. For example, in one recent year a family of four flying between New York and Puerto Rico had a choice of more than 40 possible fare combinations.[42] In attempting to differentiate their service offerings from those of competitive carriers, airlines spend proportionately more on advertising and public relations than competitive modes.[43]

Load Factors and Capacity Limitation

Given the multimillion dollar investment represented by the modern jet liner, airlines are naturally concerned with equipment utilization. One measure of utilization is the revenue passenger load factor. This figure expresses the relationship between available seat miles and revenue passenger miles realized. Table 6–5 contains the load factor figures for U.S. scheduled airlines between 1965 and 1975. Load factors fluctuated between 48.5 and 58.0 percent during that period. The relatively low load factors of 1970–1971 reflect the recession and the simultaneous delivery of larger-capacity equipment. The higher load factor figures of more recent years have been influenced by traffic growth and capacity limitation agreements, which the CAB permitted in some long-distance markets that were served by several carriers. These capacity reductions, and those triggered by the energy crisis, led to significant increases in carrier load factors in those markets. The board, at least temporarily, considered such agreements to be a useful regulatory tool.[44] However, the Justice Department and other critics have charged that such agreements have a negative competitive impact. These charges, coupled with pressures for more liberalized entry into domestic air markets, reduce the likelihood of

Table 6–5

Revenue Passenger Load Factor, U.S. Scheduled Airlines, 1965–1975[a]

Year	Load Factor (%)
1965	55.2
1966	58.0
1967	56.5
1968	52.6
1969	50.0
1970	49.7
1971	48.5
1972	53.0
1973	52.1
1974	54.9
1975	53.7

[a] These figures are aggregate, including trunk line and local service carriers. For the same period, trunk line load factors ranged from 48.3 to 58.5 percent. As might be expected, local service lines registered somewhat lower load factors, ranging from 42.9 to 52.7 percent over the same time span.

SOURCE: Air Transport Association, *Air Transport, 1976* (Washington, D.C.: the Association, 1976), pp. 12–13.

capacity limitation agreements being used on a broad scale in the near future.

Airline Safety

As indicated in Table 6–6, there was considerable hazard involved in the early years of commercial aviation. During those years, the passenger fatality rate experienced in air carriage exceeded that of other modes of intercity for-hire carriage. However, improvements in both aircraft technology and the air traffic control system have led to a situation in which the airline safety record compares favorably with that of bus and rail systems. The absolute number of fatal accidents is now relatively low in commercial aviation, averaging 5.4 annually over the past decade.[45]

As discussed earlier in this chapter, the Federal Aviation Administration maintains broad responsibilities in promoting air safety. Included are certification of aircraft, airmen, and airports. The FAA has been subject to some criticism in recent years related to fatal crashes involving equip-

The Airline Industry

Table 6-6

Passenger Fatalities in Intercity Transportation, Rate per 100 Million Passenger Miles, 1940-1975

Year	Domestic Scheduled Air Carriers[a]	Rail	Bus	Auto
1940	30.00	3.40	n/a	n/a
1945	22.00	1.60	n/a	n/a
1950	1.14	0.58	0.18	2.9
1955	0.75	0.07	0.18	2.7
1960	0.93	0.16	0.13	2.2
1965	0.38	0.07	0.16	2.4
1970	0.00	0.09	0.19	2.1
1971	0.16	0.53	0.19	2.1
1972	0.13	0.56	0.17	1.9
1973	0.10	0.07	0.17	1.7
1974	0.13	0.08	0.06	1.3
1975	0.09	0.08	0.02	1.2

n/a = not available.
[a] The fatality rate of general aviation is quite high, reaching 42.06 per 100 million plane miles in 1974.

SOURCE: Air Transport Association, *Air Transport, 1976* (Washington, D.C.: the Association, 1976), p. 28; also, statistics supplied by the Federal Aviation Administration.

ment malfunctions, which may have been prevented had the FAA ordered airlines to remedy certain conditions rather than recommending that those steps be taken.[46]

AIR CARGO

Air cargo represents the most rapidly growing segment of domestic aviation, with freight volume increasing at an annual rate of nearly 15 percent over the past decade. Domestic air cargo services are provided by both passenger-carrying airlines and by three all-cargo carriers, which are not permitted to conduct any passenger operations. Cargo planes are employed by both passenger lines and all-cargo lines; passenger carriers also carry cargo in the bellies of passenger aircraft. Nearly 75 percent of air freight volume is handled by the *combination carriers,* with the all-cargo lines carrying about 15 percent and supplemental carriers moving the balance of the traffic.[47] The typical air cargo shipment tends to be long distance, averaging more than 1,000 miles per shipment in recent years.[48]

The airline industry offers a variety of freight services that vary from *air freight,* which has the most attractive rates on large shipments, to *air express,* which tends to have higher rates except on quite small shipments. Air cargo movements are comparatively expensive. This is indicated by a comparison of the average revenues per ton mile in intercity service of the airlines, railroads, and class I motor carriers. The average revenue figures for 1975 were 29.61, 2.04, and 9.70 cents, respectively.[49] Once again, caution must be used in comparing such average figures due to their lack of market specificity; but it can safely be said that air freight rates tend to be considerably higher than the rates of surface carriers in most markets. However, as discussed in Chapter 2, the prospective shipper must weigh these transportation cost differences against such factors as the relative speed of the competitive modes, reliability of service, packaging requirements, and susceptibility to loss and damage. The bulk of air cargo volume consists of high-valued manufactured items; most of this traffic moves from the East and North to the West and South, creating a serious imbalance of traffic. The airlines and all-cargo carriers have attempted to alleviate this imbalance with incentive rates applied to traffic moving in the opposite direction.

Throughout the years, the shipping public has tended to view air cargo as emergency service, and until recently the air carriers did little to change that image. However, the carriers and many shippers have come to realize that in certain instances air cargo movements can become an integral part of a company's distribution system. To attract additional traffic volume, some airlines and all-cargo carriers have experimented with reduced air cargo rates in limited markets. It appears likely that the potential growth of air cargo traffic will stimulate the addition of considerable cargo-carrying capacity in the industry. The introduction of such planes as the Boeing 747 into all-cargo service may well exert a downward influence on air cargo rates in the future. If this occurs, air cargo carriers may be far more competitive with long-haul truckers for high-valued commodity movements. A parallel situation occurred in the 1930s, involving intercity motor carriers and their inroads into what was once captive rail traffic. Although airlines do not, and will not, have the potential capacity to divert as much traffic from motor carriage as motor carriage diverted from the rails, the competitive threat does pose a challenge to the long-haul motor carrier. In recognition of this possibility, a number of long-haul motor carriers, including Consolidated Freightways and Pacific Intermountain Express, have been certified as air freight forwarders by the CAB. Even though certain traffic may ultimately be diverted to the airlines for the line-haul movement, these motor carriers may still share in this traffic in a freight forwarding capacity. The role of these companies and other air freight forwarders in promoting the further development of air cargo is discussed in detail in Chapter 7.

Nearly 25 percent of air cargo volume now moves in containers that are packed by shippers at their own facilities.[50] Airline containers are smaller than those used by surface carriers and are made of light-weight materials. Each major jet freighter aircraft has tremendous capacity for containers on the lower cargo deck. Some combination carriers have introduced rates that consist of a flat charge for carrying containers which hold between 3,000 and 6,000 pounds of cargo. These rates, which are as low as 5 to 10 cents per pound for trips of up to 2,000 miles, are often lower than prevailing less-than-truckload rates.[51] Additional charges are generally levied for pickup and delivery services.

INTERNATIONAL AIR CARRIAGE

The airlines of the United States play an extensive role in international aviation, providing linkages to more than 120 other countries. In these markets, passenger services are provided by trunk lines and supplemental operators; cargo services are provided not only by these carriers, but by all-cargo lines as well.

To participate in international operations, U.S. carriers must be certified by the CAB (as well as by the foreign countries involved). Similarly, the CAB issues permits to foreign airlines that wish to serve U.S. cities. In discussing this segment of transportation, the Department of Transportation has commented that

> international air transportation operates in a complex and changing regime of laws and politics involving few multilateral treaties, many bilateral arrangements and a wide collection of national laws, regulations, and policies.[52]

The process by which international air fare levels are determined is somewhat unusual. The International Air Transport Association (IATA) is a voluntary international organization that represents scheduled airlines engaged in international operations. Representatives of the member airlines meet annually to determine the schedule of fares for the upcoming year. This fare structure is then subject to ratification by individual nations. In the United States, IATA's fare proposals must be approved by the CAB before they are implemented. Given the collective nature of these pricing decisions, it is not surprising that the fares of the scheduled carriers serving the same international route tend to be quite similar.

However, nonscheduled supplemental air carriers constitute a major competitive force in international markets. These charter operators have historically established a fare structure considerably lower than that of the scheduled carriers. The supplemental carriers, which are under no regulatory obligation to serve noncompensatory markets, have been quite successful in their competition with scheduled carriers, capturing approximately 25 percent of the North Atlantic passenger market.[53] A long-standing controversy has existed between the scheduled carriers and supplemental operators. The scheduled carriers contend that the supplementals are eroding their traffic base by diverting passengers who would normally fly at the higher scheduled fares. The scheduled carriers further argue that these higher fares are necessary if they are to internally cross-subsidize operations that are noncompensatory. The supplemental carriers disagree, and claim that they have attracted additional travelers who would not have flown at the scheduled fares. In any event, the CAB has recently liberalized its restrictions over supplemental operations, thereby allowing them greater market access. This is likely to expand the market served by supplementals, while leading scheduled carriers to engage in charter-like activities. This matter is discussed more extensively in Chapter 13.

International Passenger Market

The volume of international passenger traffic handled by U.S. carriers grew at an annual rate of 15 to 20 percent during the mid-1960s, but that growth rate was not sustained during the 1970s. In fact, U.S. carriers experienced a decline in international passenger volume in 1974 and 1975. At the same time, fuel costs increased dramatically. These factors combined to cause severe financial difficulties for several major airlines, as indicated by the 2.2 percent rate of return on investment generated by U.S. carriers serving international routes in 1975.[54] These problems prompted both Pan American World Airways and Trans World Airlines, the two largest U.S. international operators, to petition the CAB for operating subsidies to prevent financial collapse.[55] The board had not extended subsidies to trunk lines since 1962, and refused these requests. However, the carriers renegotiated financial arrangements with several financial institutions and at least temporarily avoided financial disaster. The situation raised serious questions concerning the future of U.S. carriers serving international routes, the relative role of scheduled versus charter operations, and the IATA system of rate determination. These matters are explored further in Chapters 13 and 18.

International Air Cargo

In international as well as domestic markets, air cargo has been the most rapidly expanding segment of air transportation. The combination carriers serving international markets experienced a doubling of freight volume between 1965 and 1975; however, the volume carried by the all-cargo lines increased by more than 600 percent during that period. Among the factors contributing to the traffic surge were the growing expansion of U.S. firms into multinational operations, increasing use of larger-capacity jet freighters, and growing adoption of the *total system* approach to international distribution, which weighs the higher air cargo costs against the slower, less secure cargo ship operations.

GENERAL AVIATION

The term general aviation is applied to a heterogeneous group of aircraft types and uses. It includes instruction and personal flying, and a variety of commercial operations, such as crop dusting and surveying, and business travel in corporate planes. In 1974, the 164,981 aircraft utilized in general aviation accounted for more than 98 percent of the civil aviation fleet.[56] During the same year it also accounted for nearly 75 percent of aircraft operations at airports with Federal Aviation Administration control towers.[57] Among the various classes of general aviation, business use is predominant with respect to hours and miles flown. This reflects the growth of corporate fleets and the flexibility of general aviation in serving communities with airports that do not receive regularly scheduled service by commercial carriers.

The sheer number of aircraft in general aviation causes problems in terms of compatibility with other users of the aviation system, particularly at higher altitudes and within terminal airspace. The management of airspace and the physical constraints of the domestic aviation system pose sizable challenges to the federal government in the years ahead.

SUPERSONIC TRANSPORT

One of the most controversial issues of modern commercial aviation is the desirability of introducing equipment capable of traveling at supersonic speeds. In the late 1960s, projects to develop supersonic aircraft for long-distance passenger service were initiated in the United States and the Soviet Union. A similar venture was jointly undertaken by the British and French governments.

The U.S. project relied heavily upon congressional funding. As development progressed in the United States, a variety of questions arose concerning the environmental impact of supersonic transport (SST). Although the speed advantages of the aircraft were obvious, serious questions were raised about SST noise levels and its possible contribution to atmospheric pollution. Other parties questioned the absolute cost of the project versus the rather limited market applicability of the aircraft. After extensive debate on the merits and costs of the SST in mid-1971, Congress voted to terminate the U.S. SST project, leaving future development efforts to the Russian and British–French interests.

SST service has since become a reality in international markets, with the British–French Concorde initiating service between Paris and South American cities in early 1976. The Russian SST has also instituted commercial operations. As these services were initiated, pressures grew for the United States to permit the Concorde to service some U.S. cities with transatlantic flights. Once again, this prompted extensive debate in Congress. It was decided that the Department of Transportation would make the final determination in this matter. In February 1976, Secretary of Transportation Coleman announced that the Concorde would be permitted to land at Kennedy International Airport and Dulles International Airport on an experimental basis. While Concorde operations into Dulles commenced in May 1976, opposition of the Port of New York Authority delayed the initiation of SST service into Kennedy. The DOT decision to permit the Concorde to land in the United States was strongly influenced by political considerations. The British and French governments had invested heavily in the SST development project, and potential markets for SST service were quite limited without landing rights in North America. The decision to allow SST landings in the United States also gave indications that the United States might consider re-entry into supersonic development efforts, having legitimized the concept with the DOT decision.

SUMMARY

The airline industry has emerged as the dominant form of for-hire intercity passenger carriage in the United States, accounting for nearly 75 percent of such traffic. The speed of air transportation allows it to dominate long-distance for-hire passenger carriage, particularly with respect to business travelers. Although the airlines still account for less than 1 percent of intercity freight ton mileage, cargo tonnage has grown at an annual rate exceeding 10 percent over the past decade. United States carriers have expanded the scope of their international operations in recent years, and now provide links between the United States and 120 foreign countries.

The airport–airway network of the United States is the most extensive domestic system in the world. However, the network faces significant physical capacity problems in the years ahead. The airlines are also confronted with a number of problems, including chronic overcapacity, enormous capital requirements related to fleet modernization, and a steadily rising cost spiral. These matters will necessarily demand close management scrutiny. At the same time, Congress and the CAB must address a number of important issues. These issues include the desirability of regulatory modification, the role of scheduled versus supplemental carriers, and the desirability of continued subsidies to local service air carriers.

NOTES

1. U.S. Department of Commerce, Bureau of Air Commerce, Aeronautics Bulletin No. 1, *Civil Aeronautics in the United States* (1937), p. 3, as cited by D. Philip Locklin, *Economics of Transportation,* 7th ed. (Homewood, Ill.: Richard D. Irwin, Inc., 1972), p. 770.

2. Roy J. Sampson and Martin T. Farris, *Domestic Transportation: Practice, Theory, and Policy,* 3rd ed. (Boston: Houghton Mifflin Company, 1975), p. 33.

3. For an excellent discussion of the early airline subsidy programs, see John H. Frederick, *Commercial Air Transportation,* 4th ed. (Homewood, Ill.: Richard D. Irwin, Inc., 1955), pp. 79–86.

4. U.S. Department of Transportation, Office of the Secretary, *1974 National Transportation Report* (Washington, D.C.: U.S. Government Printing Office, 1975), p. 280.

5. Ibid., p. 312.

6. Ibid.

7. Air Transport Association, *Air Transport, 1976* (Washington, D.C.: the Association, 1976), p. 1.

8. Ibid., p. 17.

9. Ibid.

10. Additional CAB classifications include two intra-Hawaiian carriers, four intra-Alaskan carriers, and three helicopter operators.

11. Charles F. Phillips, *The Economics of Regulation,* rev. ed. (Homewood, Ill.: Richard D. Irwin, Inc., 1969), p. 493.

12. Air Transport Association, *The U.S. Scheduled Airline Industry: An Economic Overview* (Washington, D.C.: the Association, 1970), p. 13.

13. U.S. Department of Transportation, op. cit., p. 310.

14. U.S. Department of Transportation, Office of the Secretary, "Commuter Air Carriers," unpublished staff study (Washington, D.C.: the Department, May 1972), p. 6. (Mimeographed)

15. U.S. Department of Transportation, *1974 National Transportation Report,* p. 315.

16. Ibid.

17. U.S. Civil Aeronautics Board, *Report to Congress, Fiscal Year, 1974* (Washington, D.C.: U.S. Government Printing Office, 1975), p. 11.

18. For a discussion of the regulatory reform proposals, see Leon N. Moses, ed., *Regulatory Reform and the Federal Aviation Act of 1975,* report of the Fifth Workshop on National Transportation Problems (Washington, D.C.: Department of Transportation, 1976).

19. D. Philip Locklin, *Economics of Transportation,* 7th ed. (Homewood, Ill.: Richard D. Irwin, Inc., 1972), p. 41.

20. Ibid., p. 808.

21. Association of American Railroads, *Government Expenditures for Highway, Waterway, and Air Facilities and Private Expenditures for Railroad Facilities* (Washington, D.C.: the Association, 1975), p. 5.

22. Hugh S. Norton, *Modern Transportation Economics,* 2nd ed. (Columbus, Ohio: Charles E. Merrill Publishing Company, 1971), p. 51.

23. Ibid., p. 46.

24. Air Transport Association, *Air Transport, 1976,* p. 24.

25. Air Transport Association, *The U.S. Scheduled Airline Industry: An Economic Overview,* p. 5.

26. Locklin, op. cit., pp. 830–31.

27. Ibid., p. 794.

28. Trunk-line air carriers have pointed out that there is no subsidy element contained in their current airmail contracts. In fact, they note that they carry mail at a lower rate of profit than normal air freight. See Air Transport Association, *Economics of Air Transport: An Economic Overview* (Washington, D.C.: the Association, 1972), p. 8.

29. Sampson and Farris, op. cit., p. 79.

30. Air Transport Association, *Air Transport, 1976,* p. 6.

31. Ibid.

32. Ibid.

33. Ibid., p. 4.

34. Air Transport Association, *Air Transport, 1972* (Washington, D.C.: the Association, 1972), p. 11.

35. Norton, op. cit., p. 46.

36. Ibid.

37. Air Transport Association, *Economics of Air Transport: An Economic Overview,* p. 9.

38. "Insanity Comes to Air Fares—Again," *Business Week,* April 21, 1975, pp. 126–29.

39. Air Transport Association, *Air Transport, 1972,* p. 4.

40. Air Transport Association, *Air Transport, 1976,* p. 13.

41. Air Transport Association, *Economics of Air Transport: An Overview,* p. 6.

42. Ibid., p. 9.
43. Norton, op. cit., p. 51.
44. "Airlines' Joint Flight-Reduction Pacts Shouldn't Be Continued, CAB Aide Rules," *Wall Street Journal,* New York, November 18, 1974, p. 8.
45. Air Transport Association, *Air Transport, 1975* (Washington, D.C.: the Association, 1975), p. 7.
46. "Homing in on Air Safety," *Business Week,* February 10, 1975, pp. 70–1.
47. Locklin, op. cit., p. 788.
48. Transportation Association of America, *Transportation Facts and Trends* (Washington, D.C.: the Association, 1976), p. 14.
49. Air Transport Association, *Air Transport, 1976,* p. 27.
50. Air Transport Association, *Air Transport, 1975,* p. 4.
51. Paul T. McElhiney, *Transportation for Marketing and Business Students* (Totowa, N.J.: Littlefield, Adams & Company, 1975), p. 113.
52. U.S. Department of Transportation, Office of the Secretary, *A Statement of National Transportation Policy* (Washington, D.C.: U.S. Government Printing Office, 1975), p. 44.
53. Air Transport Association, *The U.S. Scheduled Airline Industry: An Economic Overview,* p. 13.
54. Air Transport Association, *Air Transport, 1976,* p. 23.
55. "Subsidies for Pan Am and TWA Rejected, but CAB Will Study Pan Am Situation," *Wall Street Journal,* New York, September 19, 1974, p. 4.
56. U.S. Department of Transportation, *1974 National Transportation Report,* pp. 315–16.
57. Air Transport Association, *Air Transport, 1976,* p. 30.

SELECTED REFERENCES

Air Transport Association. *Air Transport, 1976.* Washington, D.C.: the Association, 1976.

Air Transport Association. *Economics of Air Transport: An Overview.* Washington, D.C.: the Association, 1971.

Air Transport Association. *The U.S. Scheduled Airline Industry: An Economic Overview.* Washington, D.C.: the Association, 1970.

Cassell, Eddie C. "The Financial Policy of Domestic Trunk Airlines Concerning Ownership Versus Leasing of Flight Equipment." *Transportation Journal,* X, No. 4 (Summer, 1971), pp. 23–36.

Cover, Virgil D. "The Rise of Third Level Air Carriers." *Transportation Journal,* XI, No. 1 (Fall, 1971), pp. 45–51.

Fruhan, William E. *The Fight for Competitive Advantage: A Study of the United States Domestic Trunk Air Carriers.* Boston: Division of Research, Graduate School of Business Administration, Harvard University, 1972.

Kane, Robert M., and Allan D. Voss. *Air Transportation,* 2nd ed. Dubuque, Iowa: William C. Brown Company, 1969.

Locklin, D. Philip. *Economics of Transportation,* 7th ed. Homewood, Ill.: Richard D. Irwin, Inc., 1972.
Chapter 33. "Air Transportation," pp. 770–96.
Chapter 34. "Development of Air Transport Regulation," pp. 797–810.
Chapter 35. "Problems and Policies in Air Transport Regulation," pp. 811–43.

McElhiney, Paul T. *Transportation for Marketing and Business Students.* Totowa, N.J.: Littlefield, Adams & Co., 1975.
Chapter 7. "Water, Air, and Pipeline Transport," pp. 95–116.

Norton, Hugh S. *Modern Transportation Economics,* 2nd ed. Columbus, Ohio: Charles E. Merrill Publishing Company, 1971.
Chapter 2. "Railroads, Motor Carriers, and Air Carriers," pp. 18–55.

Pegrum, Dudley F. *Transportation: Economics and Public Policy,* 3rd ed. Homewood, Ill.: Richard D. Irwin, Inc., 1973.
Chapter 2. "Elements of a Modern Transport System," pp. 22–45.

Sampson, Roy J., and Martin T. Farris. *Domestic Transportation: Practice, Theory and Policy,* 3rd ed. Boston: Houghton Mifflin Company, 1975.
Chapter 5. "Water, Air, and Other Forms of Carriage," pp. 71–87.

Schneider, Lewis M. "The Future of the United States Domestic Air Freight Industry: A Summary Report," in *Proceedings of the Thirteenth Annual Meeting of the Transportation Research Forum.* Oxford, Ind.: Richard B. Cross Company, 1972, pp. 305–20.

Scott, Ronald D., and Martin T. Farris. "Airline Subsidies in the United States." *Transportation Journal,* XIII, No. 4 (Summer, 1974), pp. 25–33.

Strazheim, Manlon R. *The International Airline Industry.* Washington, D.C.: Brookings Institution, 1969.

U.S. Civil Aeronautics Board. *Subsidy for United States Certified Air Carriers.* Washington, D.C.: the Board, 1971.

U.S. Department of Transportation, Office of the Secretary. "Commuter Air Carriers." Unpublished staff study. Washington, D.C.: the Department, May, 1972. (Mimeographed)

U.S. Department of Transportation, Office of the Secretary. *1974 National Transportation Report.* Washington, D.C.: U.S. Government Printing Office, 1975.
Chapter 4. "Trends in Intercity Transportation," especially pp. 309–18.
Chapter 9. "Airport Plans, Programs, and Alternatives," pp. 389–418.

The Airline Industry

DISCUSSION QUESTIONS

1. Distinguish between the local service, supplemental, and air taxi segments of the aviation industry.
2. Why hasn't the domestic airline industry succeeded in attracting a much higher percentage of intercity freight ton mileage?
3. Why have subsidies historically been extended to local service airlines?
4. Differentiate between the roles of the Civil Aeronautics Board and the Federal Aviation Administration in domestic air carriage.

CHAPTER
7

Freight Forwarding
and Intermodal Carriage

This chapter, which concludes Part Two, examines not only the freight forwarding component of the transportation industries, but also explores the concept of intermodal transportation. To the layman, freight forwarding is probably the least obvious activity in the domestic transportation marketplace. Forwarders do not provide intercity line-haul services, but rather function as transportation middlemen in arranging such movements. Since their basic role consists of linking shippers and line-haul carriers, forwarders are considered to be *indirect* carriers. In contrast to forwarders, railroads and other modes of intercity carriage are often referred to as *direct* carriers.

Each mode of intercity carriage has distinct performance features. Because of this, in many instances the cost and/or service characteristics of a particular shipment may be improved by using two or more modes of carriage as the shipment moves between origin and destination. The most familiar form of intermodal transportation is trailer on flatcar (TOFC), also known as piggybacking, which involves moving highway trailers or containers on railroad flatcars. This chapter also examines the potential and application of such intermodal relationships.

NATURE OF FREIGHT FORWARDING

The primary activity of freight forwarders involves the gathering of small shipments that are to move in consolidated form over intercity routes. Forwarders are permitted to use motor vehicles to gather these shipments within the terminal areas or commercial zones of the cities that they serve. These shipments are taken to the forwarder's local terminal, where they are sorted according to destination cities. However, transportation law prohibits freight forwarders from providing intercity line-haul movements. Therefore, the forwarder must arrange for a direct carrier, such as a railroad or trucker, to move the consolidated shipments to the various destination cities. If the forwarder maintains a terminal in the destination city, the shipment may be delivered to that facility, where it is disaggregated in a *break bulk* operation for final local delivery by the forwarder. If the forwarder does not have a terminal in the destination city, the break bulk and delivery functions may be provided by the line-haul carrier or by a local cartage company.

The freight forwarder issues a bill of lading to each shipper that he serves, and thereby becomes legally responsible for the shipment. In turn, the forwarder tenders consolidated shipments to line-haul carriers. Thus the forwarder is perceived as a carrier by the shipper and as a shipper by the line-haul carrier.

Forwarder Services and Rates

Freight forwarders function as common carriers and hold themselves out to serve the general public. In dealing with a forwarder the shipper pays no more, and sometimes less, for the movement than if he dealt directly with the line-haul carrier. Additionally, he may receive better pickup and delivery services and a faster line-haul movement. Forwarders also relieve shippers of a number of tasks related to billing, transfer, and tracing of shipments.

The profit margin of freight forwarders is a function of the transportation rate structure. Generally, as shipment volume increases, freight rates tend to decline on a per unit of weight basis. That is, there is a decided taper in the freight rate structure to encourage larger-volume shipments, which give line-haul carriers better equipment utilization. Thus the forwarder will likely charge individual shippers rates that are similar to prevailing less-than-truckload or less-than-carload rates, and will in turn pay the proportionately lower truckload or carload rate on the consolidated shipment he tenders to the line-haul carrier. The spread between these rates therefore provides the forwarder margin. Nearly 75 percent of freight forwarder revenues are paid out to line-haul carriers for services rendered.[1]

SURFACE FREIGHT FORWARDING

Surface freight forwarders, which are regulated as common carriers by the ICC, are restricted to the use of surface modes for the line-haul portion of their business. Thus they generally deal with motor carriers, railroads, and water carriers in arranging intercity movements. However, the Civil Aeronautics Board has permitted a number of surface freight forwarders to expand into air freight forwarding; consequently, those forwarders may also use airlines for line-haul movements.[2] Although surface forwarders have generally been associated with consolidation of small shipments, several ICC decisions in the early 1960s have permitted forwarders to handle large-volume shipments under various piggybacking plans.[3]

Development and Regulation

Surface freight forwarding originated shortly after the turn of the century when some shippers in New York and Chicago discovered that they could pool their LCL shipments, buy transportation on a carload basis, and move their shipments more rapidly than they could in dealing with the railroads on an individual basis.[4] In the years preceding World War II, surface forwarders were primarily railroad oriented. They used rail boxcars to move the vast majority of their freight between concentration and break bulk points, and their rates were generally competitive with railroad LCL rates.[5] As might be expected, the primary competitor of the forwarders was the railroad industry, which also conducted extensive LCL operations. However, in the early 1930s the railroads deemphasized their LCL services, and the bulk of small-shipment traffic shifted to intercity motor carriers. Consequently, the major competitor of the forwarders soon became the line-haul motor carriers. This relationship continues to the present, and forwarder rates tend to be quite similar to less-than-truckload rates.[6]

In the intensely competitive years of the Depression, forwarder rates became quite unstable and illegal rebates were often used as competitive tools. By 1930 the rather chaotic conditions that prevailed in forwarding led the ICC to call upon Congress to regulate surface freight forwarding.[7] However, it was not until 1942 that Congress regulated these indirect carriers. The regulatory pattern established was quite similar to that which had earlier been applied to the railroad and trucking industries. Controls were established over entry and rates, and regulations further stipulated that surface freight forwarders could not own or control direct carriers. However, forwarders could be owned or controlled by direct carriers.

Surface freight forwarders generally pay the published rates of the direct carriers, but the ICC has allowed the establishment of contracts between forwarders and common carrier truckers, which specify that the forwarders can receive a reduced rate for shipments of less than 450 miles between concentration and break bulk points.[8]

In handling more than 20 million shipments annually, surface freight forwarders account for approximately 5 percent of the small-shipment volume handled by line-haul surface modes.[9]

Industrial and Financial Structure

The number of class A surface freight forwarders (those earning more than $100,000 in annual operating revenues) rose from 61 to 119 between 1965 and 1974.[10] Because these companies do not maintain intercity vehicle fleets, their capital requirements are considerably more modest than those of the direct modes. The major investment elements of surface forwarding are the pickup and delivery fleets used in terminal areas and the consolidation and break bulk facilities. The net investment in surface freight forwarding exceeded $68 million in 1974 (see Table 7–1). Although the return on net investment generated by these carriers is rather erratic, it tends to be considerably higher than the return generated by the more capital intensive line-haul modes. The proportionately smaller capital burden of the surface forwarders is illustrated by the fact that these

Table 7–1

Investment and Operating Statistics, Surface Freight Forwarders, 1965–1974

Year	No. of Class A Forwarders	Net Investment[a] (000)	Return on Net Investment (%)
1965	59	$19,818	93.21
1966	61	28,294	80.50
1967	63	29,701	59.90
1968	64	30,687	53.61
1969	65	36,751	23.92
1970	65	32,530	9.04
1971	73	38,712	21.81
1972	91	48,507	22.89
1973	110	68,619	23.77
1974	119	68,230	35.56

[a] Net investment in transportation property plus working capital.

SOURCE: U.S. Interstate Commerce Commission, *89th Annual Report to Congress* (Washington, D.C.: U.S. Government Printing Office, 1975), p. 129, and earlier ICC annual reports.

relatively higher rates of return on net investment are generated while the forwarders' collective operating ratio tends to be in the low nineties.[11]

The majority of surface freight forwarders are engaged in regional operations; however, six forwarders operate on a national basis. There is a significant degree of concentration in this mode; three companies, Acme Fast Freight, Universal Carloading and Distributing Company, and National Carloading Corporation, handle nearly one half of all surface forwarder volume.[12]

Forwarders have moved heavily into piggyback traffic. In 1974, surface forwarders originated 265,000 piggyback trailers and containers. This marked an increase of 63 percent over the decade.[13] The shift toward piggyback utilization has led to a decrease in the number of shipments handled by surface forwarders, but it has also led to a continued increase in the average weight per shipment handled.

AIR FREIGHT FORWARDING

The activities of domestic air freight forwarders are similar to those of surface forwarders; the most significant difference is that air forwarders are restricted to the use of air carriers for the line-haul portion of their traffic movement. These companies possess a competitive advantage over direct air carriers in that they can handle all the traffic of a particular shipper regardless of the cargo's destination. Individual direct carriers are restricted as to points served, but the air forwarder may handle shipments to all points served by domestic airlines. On an annual basis, air forwarders generate approximately 40 percent of all air carrier freight revenues, with the remainder being generated by the direct air carriers themselves.[14]

Development and Regulation

At the time of the passage of the Civil Aeronautics Act of 1938, only the Railway Express Agency (REA), which was jointly owned by a number of railroads, provided services similar to those of today's air freight forwarder. Agreements between REA and the airlines provided for the division of revenues generated by REA's solicitation of express traffic. Independent air freight services offered by direct air carriers had not yet been developed. Under those circumstances, it is not surprising that the Civil Aeronautics Act did not contain specific provisions related to air freight forwarding.

However, in a 1941 case that concerned the nature of air freight forwarding, the CAB declared such operations to be *indirect* air carriage.[15]

This decision effectively established CAB jurisdiction over air freight forwarding.

Increased business activity following World War II and the institution of independent air freight operations by a number of direct air carriers created growing interest in air freight forwarding. In response to a growing number of parties interested in entering air freight forwarding, the CAB ruled that applicants were required to apply to the board to institute new services.[16] However, since that time the CAB has permitted relatively free entry into the industry.[17] It should be noted that the CAB did not welcome applications of long-haul motor carriers or railroads until 1967. At that time the board concluded that the participation of such surface carriers, with their extensive route coverage and capital backing, might stimulate the future growth of air cargo.[18] Since that time, the CAB has allowed major surface carriers, such as the Burlington Northern and Southern Pacific railroads and Consolidated Freightways and Navajo Freight Lines (motor carriers), to enter air freight forwarding on a *monitored entry* basis. This policy permitted a five-year experimental period, after which the CAB would review the performance of the surface modes to determine if they deserved permanent authorization. In 1975 a CAB administrative law judge found that these carriers had exerted a positive influence on air cargo development, and he recommended that they be permanently authorized as air freight forwarders.[19]

Industrial and Financial Structure

The relatively free entry policy of the CAB and the potential growth of air cargo have led to a major increase in the number of authorized air freight forwarders (see Table 7–2). Nearly one fourth of the authorized air forwarders are affiliated with surface carriers.[20]

As is the case in surface freight forwarding, there is a significant degree of concentration in air freight forwarding. Three companies, Emery Air Freight Corporation, Airborne Freight Corporation, and United Parcel Service Company, annually account for approximately one half of all domestic air forwarding revenues.[21] Emery is the largest single air forwarder, and the company annually generates nearly one fourth of all air forwarding revenues.[22]

Pickup and delivery fleets and terminal facilities comprise the bulk of the investment of air freight forwarders. Although there is considerable variation in the size of air freight forwarding firms, the typical air forwarder is a small business with assets per firm averaging slightly more than $2 million.[23]

The volume of traffic handled by domestic air freight forwarders has in-

Table 7–2

Authorized Air Freight Forwarders and Their Operating Profits, 1964–1973

Year	No. of Companies	Operating Profit[a] (000)
1964	100	$ 3,183
1965	108	6,069
1966	137	2,922
1967	145	3,954
1968	171	4,540
1969	195	4,266
1970	212	9,816
1971	240	−1,419
1972	249	10,226
1973	318[b]	16,250

[a] Before taxes.
[b] Of these, 236 companies hold both domestic and international forwarding operating authorizations from CAB. The balance of the authorized forwarders are restricted to either domestic or international forwarding activities.

SOURCE: U.S. Civil Aeronautics Board, *Report to Congress, Fiscal Year, 1974* (Washington, D.C.: U.S. Government Printing Office, 1975), p. 11.

creased dramatically in recent years. Between 1965 and 1975 the number of shipments handled by air forwarders increased by more than 600 percent, and the tonnage handled grew by more than 500 percent.[24]

SHIPPERS' COOPERATIVES

It is appropriate at this point to devote some attention to nonprofit shippers' cooperatives. Cooperatives are not carriers, but rather are organizations of shippers who act collectively in consolidating their shipments that are to be tendered to line-haul carriers. By doing this, they qualify for low-cost volume rates. In this capacity, shippers' cooperatives act very much like private freight forwarders. Their services are only offered to cooperative members. These organizations may be concerned only with the movement of one product type, such as agricultural goods, or they may handle a variety of goods, such as retail merchandise.

Cooperatives arrange for the line-haul movement of consolidated shipments and local delivery in destination cities. Each cooperative member then pays a proportionate share of total freight bills based upon the percentage weight of his shipments to the total.

139

SPECIALIZED SMALL-SHIPMENT CARRIERS

In addition to the basic intercity modes already discussed, a specialized group of carriers is primarily involved in small-shipment movement. Included in this grouping are the U.S. Post Office Department, United Parcel Service (UPS), and bus express operations. Prior to its declaration of bankruptcy and subsequent liquidation in 1975–1976, Railway Express Agency (REA) also participated extensively in this parcel market.[25]

Post Office Parcel Post

In its parcel post operations the Post Office Department handles shipments weighing up to 20 pounds, regardless of their domestic destination. Prices are based on weight and distance; charges are determined by shipment weight and the origin–destination zones of the movement. Many large companies use parcel post extensively. In certain instances in which a shipper generates a steadily large volume of parcel post traffic, the Post Office Department has established operating units on the shipper's property.[26]

United Parcel Service

United Parcel Service, which was established in 1907 as a local delivery service, now provides intercity services that are directly competitive with parcel post, but on a more limited geographical basis. Not all states or geographic areas are served by UPS. The company is limited to handling parcels weighing less than 50 pounds, and shippers are allowed to ship up to a maximum of 100 pounds per day to a given consignee.[27]

In many large cities UPS offers local delivery services to department and specialty stores on a contract carriage basis. However, the bulk of its volume is now generated in intercity freight movements, which the company services as a common carrier. In that capacity UPS is used extensively by mail-order firms and other manufacturers and distributors.

The company has expanded rapidly since the early 1960s, and now generates considerably more parcel tonnage than the Post Office Department.[28] United Parcel's pricing structure compares quite favorably with parcel post, and the company has a distinct advantage over parcel post in that it offers regular pickup and delivery services for a small weekly fee.

Bus Express

Express services were initiated by intercity bus operators who wished to utilize unused baggage space on buses. Bus express volume has grown steadily and now exceeds 250,000 tons annually.[29] Shippers using such service are limited to five packages per shipment, but each package may weigh up to 100 pounds.

The extensive route structure served by intercity bus operators gives good geographical coverage to bus express. Greyhound's Package Express is probably the best known of bus express services, and the company now quotes same-day delivery to most points up to 350 miles away.[30] Overnight service is offered in markets up to 700 miles away. Rates are very competitive with other package services.[31]

Railway Express Agency

Railway Express Agency (REA) was established in 1929, and was jointly owned by a number of railroads. Its early operations primarily consisted of consolidating less-than-carload traffic for the railroads, but it later obtained authority to provide combined rail, motor carrier, and air service for small-package distribution. The company not only attached its cars to fast intercity trains, but also made extensive use of its own trucking fleet. It also had authority to use the line-haul services of other modes when appropriate. Given this variety of service offerings, REA was competitive to varying degrees with parcel post, UPS, and intercity truckers.

In the late-1960s the company became independent of railroad ownership. In subsequent years REA experienced a series of operational and financial problems, which caused extreme cash shortages and refinancing difficulties. Finally, in February 1975 the company declared bankruptcy. A reorganization was attempted, but it became apparent that it could not be accomplished within a reasonable period. The court overseeing the reorganization ruled that the company should be liquidated. Consequently, the liquidation process was initiated in late 1975.[32]

INTERMODAL TRANSPORTATION

One of the most widely discussed concepts in transportation is intermodal carriage. Because of the different cost and performance characteristics of the various modes of transportation, it is frequently economically desirable to transfer a shipment from one mode to another while it moves from origin to destination. Freight transfers of this nature may be referred to as *intermodal carriage*. These transfers provide a means of utilizing the inherent advantages of the various modes of transportation in combination to reduce the total cost and/or improve the service on a particular shipment.

Intermodal movements may involve either the physical transfer of individual items from one mode to another or the transfer of a loaded transport vehicle or container from one mode to another for continuation of the journey. Trailer on flatcar (TOFC), which is also referred to as piggybacking, and other container-type movements are examples of the latter form of intermodal exchange.

Benefits of Intermodal Transportation

Intermodal movements rely upon participating modes to perform those functions for which they are economically best suited. For example, TOFC movements combine the pickup and delivery flexibility of motor carriage with the line-haul efficiency of rail carriage.

Coordination of the modes can be beneficial to shippers and carriers alike. Blending the varying modal capabilities often results in a lower cost for the total movement. Cost savings may be passed on to shippers in the form of lower prices. Coordinated movements may also promote service improvements by utilizing the differences in speed, dependability, frequency, capacity, and availability that are associated with the different modes. The possibility of coordinated movements also effectively increases the options available to shippers, and improves their ability to arrange specific shipments according to current needs. By substituting a more efficient form of carriage for a segment of a particular movement, carriers may reduce the total cost of providing service and therefore improve profit margins.[33] The ability to make such substitutions may also assist carriers in improving their market positions. The development of TOFC, for example, has provided the railroads with a means of recapturing a substantial amount of traffic that had been lost to motor carriage.

Intermodal Applications

Not all transportation tasks are well suited to intermodal movements. Intermodal movements are economically justified only when the savings in line-haul costs exceed the costs of transferring the traffic, or when the additional costs above single-mode transportation provide an improved service that is desired by a customer.

Short-haul distribution activities and many bulk commodity shipments are better suited for single-carrier handling.[34] However, many medium- to long-haul movements, particularly those involving high-valued freight, seem well suited to intermodal movements. TOFC is one important form of coordination that has wide applicability. One study of TOFC concluded that "excluding very short hauls, TOFC offers lower cost than straight truck movements."[35] The study also concluded that the superior quality of TOFC service, in most cases, offsets any advantage that straight railroad boxcar movement might possess.[36] A variety of TOFC plans are available to shippers (see Table 7–3). Each plan involves slightly different service

142

and cost considerations. Once again this illustrates the range of service choices that is available to shippers in most major markets.

TOFC has exhibited a solid long-term growth rate and is the most widely utilized and discussed form of intermodal transportation. However, in a number of instances other intermodal arrangements such as air–truck, rail–water, and water–truck are also capable of promoting cost and service improvements.

Table 7–3

TOFC Plans and Related Statistics

Plan I	Railroad movement of trailers or containers owned by motor carriers, with shipment moving on one bill of lading, and billing being done by motor carriers. This plan accounted for 7.6 percent of a total of 2,568,309 trailers–containers handled by the railroads as originated traffic in 1974 according to ICC statistics.
Plan II	Door-to-door service by railroads, using own trailers or containers and making pickup and deliveries. Rates similar to those of motor carriers. Accounted for 13.2 percent of rail-originated trailers–container traffic in 1974.
Plan II½	Traffic moving in railroad-owned trailers and containers with shippers—including freight forwarders or motor carriers—performing either pickup or delivery service or both. This is the most popular of the various plans, accounting for 54.2 percent of total railroad originations in 1974.
Plan III	Ramp-to-ramp rates based on a flat charge, regardless of contents of trailers or containers provided by shippers. No pickup or delivery performed by railroads. This plan accounted for 8.8 percent of 1974 rail originations. Rates encourage mixing of different commodities in the load, and no commodity can make up more than 60 percent of the total weight.
Plan IV	This plan requires the shipper or forwarder to provide either an owned or leased trailer or container-loaded flatcar. Railroads make flat charge for loaded or empty car movements and furnish only power and rails. This plan accounted for 7.1 percent of 1974 TOFC traffic. Mixed loads are again encouraged by state structure.
Plan V	Traffic moves under joint rail–motor rates or other arrangements of coordinated rail–motor services. Either mode may solicit traffic for through movements. Accounted for 2.5 percent of 1974 TOFC traffic.[a]

[a] Various other plans accounted for 6.6 percent of 1974 TOFC traffic.

SOURCE: Association of American Railroads, *Update on Piggybacking* (Washington, D.C.: the Association, 1975), pp. 5–6.

Intermodal operations frequently offer the potential of achieving a cost or service level that is superior to single-mode carriage. If this potential is not realized, there is a misallocation of transportation resources.

Technology and Intermodalism

The technology necessary to provide a variety of forms of intermodal service does exist. Flat cars and ships have been equipped to handle loaded trailers; container fittings have been placed on rail cars, ships, and planes; interchange facilities have been established between a number of carriers engaged in different forms of transportation.

Such technology has existed for many years. As early as 1843, sectionalized canal boats were being transported by rail in Pennsylvania, and by 1926 loaded trailers were being carried by the Chicago North Shore and Milwaukee Railroad.[37] However, the existence of technology does not guarantee that the potential of such services will be realized. The regulatory environment has a decided impact on the extent of intermodal transportation. This environment is determined by congressional policy and regulatory agency interpretation of this policy.

Means of Accomplishing Intermodal Transportation

Within the framework of government regulation of transportation, several policy alternatives are available to the federal government in attempting to promote intermodal transportation. First, the government might choose to create a regulatory environment in which regulatory barriers limit intermodal ownership, that is, ownership of several modes of carriage by a single company. In such an environment, the government would depend upon voluntary agreements between carriers in different modes to provide intermodal movements. Second, in a somewhat similar environment, the government might make intermodal coordination mandatory. Such a policy would require carriers to establish agreements with carriers engaged in other modes of carriage that would provide shippers with intermodal services. A third policy alternative available to the government would be the development of regulations that would permit individual companies to establish operations in several different modes. Such companies might individually offer integrated services to the public.

Congress has chosen to encourage intermodal transportation by relying primarily upon voluntary cooperation of carriers engaged in different modes of carriage.[38] Such voluntary agreements are subject to regulatory agency approval. At the same time, Congress has chosen to significantly limit the extent of intermodal or common ownership.[39] Whether this policy will suffice to promote adequate growth of intermodal service offerings is a matter of debate. The possibility of making intermodal arrangements compulsory has been proposed.[40] However, this suggestion has not been warmly welcomed by the carriers involved. The third policy alternative, which entails permitting formation of multimodal transportation companies, has also been subject to considerable discussion. If anything, this proposal has been more hotly debated than the previously mentioned alternative. The formation of multimodal transportation companies would substantially alter the structure of the domestic transportation system. This policy alternative and its ramifications are discussed in depth in Chapter 16.

SUMMARY

Freight forwarders play a valuable role in intercity transportation by linking shippers and line-haul carriers. The number of surface freight forwarders has increased considerably in recent years; they have expanded the scope of their operations to include not only consolidation of small shipments, but also handling of volume shipments under various piggybacking plans. The CAB's relatively free entry policy in air forwarding has led to a tripling of the number of air forwarders over the past decade, and their volume has increased dramatically. Air freight forwarders now account for more than 40 percent of all air carrier freight revenues.

A variety of specialized small-shipment services is offered in the transportation marketplace. The Post Office Department (parcel post), United Parcel, and a number of intercity bus companies offer such services. Prior to its bankruptcy and subsequent liquidation, REA also participated extensively in this field.

In many instances, intermodal transportation, which relies upon two or more modes of carriage as a shipment moves between origin and destination, offers service or cost improvements to shippers. Coordinated service offerings have expanded steadily, but much of the potential of intermodal transportation has yet to be realized.

NOTES

1. Roy J. Sampson and Martin T. Farris, *Domestic Transportation: Practice, Theory, and Policy,* 3rd ed. (Boston: Houghton Mifflin Company, 1975), p. 82.
2. D. Philip Locklin, *Economics of Transportation,* 7th ed. (Homewood, Ill.: Richard D. Irwin, Inc., 1972), p. 892.

3. Forwarder Volume Commodity Rates, Chicago and New York, 310 ICC 199 (1960); and *Eastern Central Motor Carriers Assn., Inc.* v. *Baltimore and Ohio Railroad Co.,* 314 ICC 5 (1961).

4. Paul T. McElhiney, *Transportation for Marketing and Business Students* (Totowa, N.J.: Littlefield, Adams & Co., 1975), p. 73.

5. Terrence A. Brown, "Freight Forwarder–Motor Carrier Relations," *Transportation Journal*, XII, No. 2 (Winter, 1972), pp. 28–29.

6. McElhiney, op. cit., p. 73.

7. U.S. Interstate Commerce Commission, *44th Annual Report to Congress* (Washington, D.C.: U.S. Government Printing Office, 1930), p. 81.

8. Dudley F. Pegrum, *Transportation: Economics and Public Policy*, 3rd ed. (Homewood, Ill.: Richard D. Irwin, Inc.), p. 105.

9. U.S. Interstate Commerce Commission, *89th Annual Report to Congress* (Washington, D.C.: U.S. Government Printing Office, 1975), p. 45.

10. Ibid.

11. Ibid., p. 129.

12. Hugh S. Norton, *Modern Transportation Economics*, 2nd ed. (Columbus, Ohio: Charles E. Merrill Publishing Company, 1971), p. 68.

13. Association of American Railroads, *Update on Piggybacking* (Washington, D.C.: the Association, 1975), pp. 4–5.

14. Frederick J. Stephenson, "The Right of Domestic Air Freight Forwarders to Charter Aircraft," in *Proceedings of the Seventh Annual Meeting,* Canadian Transportation Research Forum, XVI, No. 1 (Oxford, Ind.: Richard B. Cross Company, 1975), p. 169.

15. *Railway Express Agency, Inc., Grandfather Certificates,* 2 CAB 531 (1941).

16. Robert C. Lieb, *Freight Transportation: A Study of Federal Intermodal Ownership Policy* (New York: Praeger Publishers, Inc., 1972), p. 88.

17. Frederick J. Stephenson, "Deregulation—The Air Freight Forwarder Experience," *ICC Practitioners' Journal*, XLIII, No. 1 (November–December, 1975), p. 40.

18. Stephenson, "The Right of Domestic Air Freight Forwarders to Charter Aircraft," p. 169.

19. "Aeronautics Board Judge Would End Monitored Entry Rule in Forwarding," *Traffic World*, CLXIV, No. 5 (November 3, 1975), pp. 71–72.

20. Lieb, op. cit., p. 124.

21. Civil Aeronautics Board Forms 244 (Schedules P and T-1) filed by air freight forwarders.

22. Ibid.

23. Civil Aeronautics Board Forms 244 (Schedules B and P) filed by air freight forwarders.

24. U.S. Civil Aeronautics Board, *Air Freight Forwarding: The Decade 1963–*

1972 (Washington, D.C.: the Board, 1973), p. 129; also, Civil Aeronautics Board Forms 244 (Schedules T-1) filed by air freight forwarders.

25. Interstate Commerce Commission, *89th Annual Report,* pp. 48–49.

26. Donald J. Bowerson, Edward W. Smykay, and Bernard J. Lalonde, *Physical Distribution Management,* rev. ed. (New York: Macmillan Publishing Co., Inc., 1968), p. 132.

27. McElhiney, op. cit., p. 93.

28. Sampson and Farris, op. cit., p. 84.

29. McElhiney, op. cit., p. 93.

30. Ibid.

31. Ibid.

32. "Auction of REA Assets," *Transportation and Distribution Management,* XVI, No. 1 (January–February, 1976), p. 15.

33. Lieb, op. cit., p. 16.

34. Ibid., p. 17.

35. Merrill J. Roberts and Associates, *Intermodal Freight Transportation Co-ordination: Problems and Potential* (Washington, D.C.: U.S. Government Printing Office, 1967), p. 106.

36. Ibid.

37. Josephine Ayre, *History and Regulation of Trailer on Flatcar Movement* (Washington, D.C.: Department of Commerce, 1966), pp. 3–4.

38. The ICC can compel rail and water carriers to establish intermodal through routes and joint rates. This is the only instance in which a regulatory agency has the power to require such intermodal relationships.

39. U.S. Interstate Commerce Commission, *Report on Basic Policy Matters Under Consideration by the Interstate Commerce Commission* (Washington, D.C.: the Commission, 1969), p. 95.

40. Rupert L. Murphy, Commissioner, Interstate Commerce Commission, "Is Voluntary Intermodal Coordination Possible?" an address delivered at the 7th Annual Convention of the National Association of Railroad and Utilities Commissioners, Atlanta, Ga., November 1, 1967, p. 12. (Mimeographed)

SELECTED REFERENCES

Baker, Harry M., and Richard J. Riddick. "The Role of the Forwarder in Efficient Transportation," in *Transportation and Tomorrow,* Karl M. Ruppenthal (ed.). Stanford, Calif.: Graduate School of Business, Stanford University, 1966, pp. 120–30.

Brown, Terrence A. "Freight Forwarder–Motor Carrier Relations." *Transportation Journal,* XII, No. 2 (Winter 1972), pp. 28–32.

Brown, Terrence A. "Forwarder–Motor Contract Rates." *Transportation Journal,* XIII, No. 4 (Summer 1974), pp. 19–24.

Lieb, Robert C. *Freight Transportation: A Study of Federal Intermodal Ownership Policy.* New York: Praeger Publishers, Inc., 1972.
Chapter 4. "Federal Regulation of Intermodal Ownership: Air Carriage and Indirect Carriage," pp. 72–103.

McElhiney, Paul T. *Transportation for Marketing and Business Students.* Totowa, N.J.: Littlefield, Adams & Company, 1975.
Chapter 5. "Railroads and Related Services," pp. 55–75.

Norton, Hugh S. *Modern Transportation Economics,* 2nd ed. Columbus, Ohio: Charles E. Merrill Publishing Company, 1971.
Chapter 3. "Water Carriers, Pipelines, and Indirect Carriers," pp. 56–82.

Roberts, Merrill J., and Associates. *Intermodal Freight Transportation Coordination: Problems and Potential.* Washington, D.C.: Department of Commerce, 1967.

Stephenson, Frederick J. "Deregulation—The Air Freight Forwarder Experience." *ICC Practitioners' Journal,* XLIII, No. 1 (November–December, 1975), pp. 39–55.

Stephenson, Frederick J. "The Right of Domestic Air Freight Forwarders to Charter Aircraft." *Proceedings of the Seventh Annual Meeting,* Canadian Transportation Research Forum, XVI, No. 1. Oxford, Ind.: Richard B. Cross Company, 1975, pp. 169–74.

DISCUSSION QUESTIONS

1. Discuss the significance of the services provided by freight forwarders in the transportation marketplace.
2. Trace the movement of a small shipment handled by a freight forwarder as it moves from the shipper to the receiver of the shipment.
3. Explain the CAB's concept of *monitored entry*.
4. What are the factors considered by shippers in assessing the various TOFC–COFC plans?

Cost, Demand, and
Rate-making Procedures

8

Cost and Demand in Intercity Transportation

Rate-making activities of carriers are quite important in determining both the carrier's long-term survival and its relative role in the transportation marketplace. In the aggregate, rates must be high enough to allow the carriers to generate a reasonable rate of return on invested capital to assure the long-term continuance of carrier services. However, the rate structure must also be low enough to foster the movement of traffic.

In approaching the critical and complex pricing process, the carrier must necessarily consider not only the costs of providing the services, but also the demand characteristics of the various markets and customers that it serves.

This chapter examines the nature of cost and demand in intercity transportation, and prepares the reader for a detailed discussion of the pricing process, which follows in Chapter 9.

TRANSPORTATION COSTS

Comprehension of the rate-making process in transportation requires an understanding of several basic cost concepts and cost relationships. These matters are examined in the following discussion.

Cost and Demand in Intercity Transportation

Fixed and Variable Costs

As is the case in any industry, an intercity carrier's cost structure consists of fixed and variable cost components. Fixed costs are those not related to output in a direct fashion. They remain independent of output regardless of output changes. Such costs include depreciation on buildings, equipment, and rights-of-way caused by time or weather rather than usage; interest on bonds; executive salaries; property taxes; and long-term leases. Fixed costs must be calculated for a particular time period, because in the long run all costs are variable.

In contrast to such fixed costs, certain costs fluctuate directly with a company's rate of output during a particular time period. These costs are known as variable costs and include outlays for materials, operating supplies, and direct labor. In a transportation context, variable costs might include outlays for fuel, crew salaries (although part of this might be considered to be fixed in nature), tolls, and depreciation related to usage, such as deterioration of engines on power units. In the short run, variable costs constitute the controllable portion of the cost of production; they can be decreased by reducing output or increased by increasing output. When the rate of output is increased, total variable cost increases. Conversely, when the rate of output declines, total variable cost decreases.

The relationship between fixed and variable cost elements is depicted in Figure 8–1.

As long as the scale or size of the company is constant, fixed costs will remain the same for the period. However, during the period, average fixed cost per unit will decline as output increases.

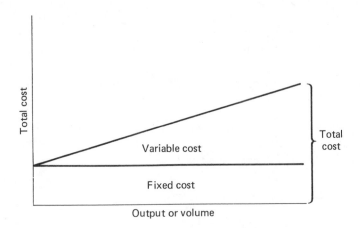

Figure 8–1

Illustration of Fixed and Variable Cost Relationships

As discussed in Chapters 3 through 7, there are significant differences in the relative proportions of fixed and variable costs experienced in the different modes of transportation. At one end of the spectrum, railroad and pipeline companies incur proportionately higher fixed costs and, consequently, realize declining average total costs over broader ranges of output as fixed cost per unit declines. Truckers, water carriers, and forwarders, with proportionately higher variable costs, experience declining per unit costs over substantially smaller ranges of output.

Figure 8–2 illustrates the unit cost behavior of a typical transportation firm. It is assumed that the size of the firm is fixed. As unit costs increase or decrease over a range of output, the cost of adding one unit to the previous output will differ from average unit costs. When the cost of an additional unit is less than the average cost of units that have been previously produced, unit costs are falling. In contrast, when the cost of an additional unit exceeds average cost, unit cost will rise. The cost of producing this additional unit is typically referred to as *marginal* cost.

Figure 8–2 also illustrates that the marginal cost curve intersects the average total cost curve from below at its minimum point. In a perfectly competitive industry, which is in equilibrium, all firms will operate at an output level that coincides with the intersection of marginal cost and average total cost. This will lead to disposal of output at a price equal to that level of cost and will produce normal profits.[1] However, such conditions do not exist in transportation. The realities of the transportation pricing process are discussed in subsequent chapters.

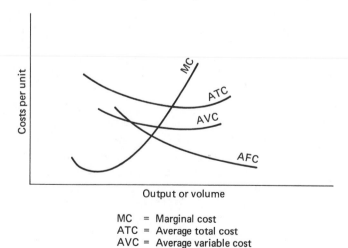

Output or volume

MC = Marginal cost
ATC = Average total cost
AVC = Average variable cost
AFC = Average fixed cost

Figure 8–2

Cost Curves—Typical Transportation Company

Cost and Demand in Intercity Transportation

Cost Traceability

Although some costs are related to the rate of output and others are independent of it, certain costs are attributable to specific units of output while others are not. In the transportation industries, services are often performed under conditions of *common* cost. That is, some productive unit generates several distinct services, and a portion of the costs of this process cannot be directly traced to individual output units. For example, passenger trains and freight trains may share the same rights-of-way under common-cost conditions. Similarly, passengers, cargo, and mail may be carried in a single plane. In these two illustrations, and many similar situations in transportation, some costs are common to several services and can only be allocated to particular services on an arbitrary basis. Similar allocation problems also arise with respect to *joint* costs, which are found when two or more services are necessarily produced together in fixed proportions. One of these services may be said to be the by-product of the other. The most common illustration of joint-cost behavior is provided by the back-haul situation.[2] Return capacity is a by-product of the loaded trip to the original destination. The bulk of the return trip costs will be generated whether or not any return traffic is obtained. However, if such return traffic is solicited, this will necessitate apportioning of joint expenses between the primary and back-haul movements. Once again, the allocation will be arbitrary.

Economies of Utilization

Having defined broad cost categories, let us now consider the impact of utilization on the per unit cost of transportation output. Throughout the years there has been some controversy concerning the most appropriate unit for defining transportation output.[3] However, for the purposes of this book, output will be expressed in terms of ton miles (one ton of freight carried one mile) and passenger miles (one passenger carried one mile).

While the scale of an enterprise remains constant, average unit costs tend to decline as output volume increases over a specific output range. Because of the sizable fixed investment incurred in several modes of carriage, and due to the cost behavior illustrated in Figure 8–2, it is quite advantageous for a carrier to use its facilities to full physical capacity, since fixed costs must be met regardless of the traffic volume handled. Therefore, carriers of freight seek heavier and more frequent loads coupled with rapid equipment turn around, and passenger carriers seek to intensively utilize facilities by attempting to generate higher load factors.

However, there are limitations to utilization economies. Pushing equipment and employees beyond their effective limits can lead to increasing equipment failure and operating problems. At this point, per unit cost rises as marginal cost exceeds average unit cost, and the carrier is better off reducing volume. The carrier may also consider scale expansion in the coming period if the traffic currently being handled appears to offer stable potential in the future.

Economies of Scale

As implied in the preceding discussion, average unit costs in transportation may also be influenced by the scale or size of the carrier. In certain industries the scale of operation is an important determinant of production costs; larger firms tend to realize lower per unit output costs compared to smaller firms.

A brief discussion of the principle of returns to scale should clarify the concept of economies of scale. The principle of returns to scale involves three stages of company activity. In the first stage, which is referred to as increasing returns to scale, output increases more than proportionately to the increase in all factor inputs. As a result, long-run average cost per unit of output declines. The forces that lead to increased productivity in response to increased scale may be referred to as *economies of scale*.[4] The second phase, constant returns to scale, occurs when output expands in direct proportion to the increase in the factors of production. Average unit cost is constant within this range. Studies of returns to scale indicate that a long phase of constant returns to scale is typical.[5] The final stage, decreasing returns to scale, occurs when output increases less than proportionately to the increase in input factors. The forces that lead to this rise in long-run average cost per unit of output might be referred to as *diseconomies* of scale. Public utilities tend to experience such economies of scale. The incidence of scale economies in the telephone, gas, and electric industries has influenced regulatory policy toward promotion of regional monopolies in hopes of realizing lower average unit production costs, and hence lower prices to consumers.[6]

In the long run a company might seek to lower average unit costs by expanding the scale of existing operations so as to realize scale economies of scale.

Causes of Economies of Scale

Several factors may lead to realization of economies of scale. First, as the scale of an operation is increased, the possibility of division and specialization of labor also increases. By performing fewer diverse tasks, workers may become more adept in completing a narrower range of·jobs and consequently become more productive. Also, the time sacrificed as a worker transfers from one job to another may be eliminated. Such oppor-

155

tunities of specialization are not limited to production workers. In fact, potential specialization in management may be far more important. The ability of management to concentrate in specific functional areas, such as personnel, traffic, finance, and marketing, may also lead to increased productivity. Machine specialization may also be of significance in lowering long-run unit costs as company scale expands.[7]

Closely related to machine specialization is the element of *factor indivisibility*. Input units may not be completely divisible. Certain types of capital goods will not perform their functions properly if they are built on too small a scale, since weight is important in their operation.[8] Division of size may lead to lower levels of productivity. Therefore, larger machines (purchased as firm scale expands) may be cheaper to obtain per unit of output capacity than similar machines of a smaller scale. Indivisibilities may also exist in a variety of managerial areas, such as advertising, research work, and financing. Advertising on a small scale tends to be relatively less effective than large-scale advertising, and research activities cannot be carried on effectively on a small scale. In the financial area, the cost of floating a bond issue is, to a large extent, independent of the size of the issue. Thus this method of financing is expensive to a firm until it has expanded beyond a certain size.[9]

Any of these factors may be of significance in realizing increasing returns to scale. However, such improvements cannot indefinitely continue to lower long-run average cost. Once the company has attained a size that is sufficient to realize all scale economies, there may be a wide range of company sizes for which returns to scale are constant. Expansion beyond this range of company size may lead to diseconomies of scale.

Causes of Diseconomies of Scale

If expansion continues, firm size may eventually increase to a point at which operations become somewhat unmanageable. The increased size of the labor force causes supervision and coordination problems that management may be unable to cope with. Similarly, employees may be overworked at such output levels. Top management finds it increasingly difficult to coordinate the efforts of various operating units of the firm.[10] Overexpansion may similarly cause the company's communications network to fail. As a result of these factors, productivity is likely to decrease, and average unit costs will rise, thereby incurring diseconomies of scale.

Instances of Economies of Scale

There is considerable difference of opinion in economic circles concerning both the importance and the incidence of economies of scale. Nevertheless, there are indications that such economies do exist in certain industries,[11] such as automobile manufacturing, natural gas distribution, telephone and telegraph services in long-distance markets, and the generation, transmission, and distribution of electric power.[12] More importantly, from the standpoint of this book, the existence of economies of scale appears to vary considerably across the modes of carriage.

Rail Carriage.   Several studies have indicated that there are economies of scale in the railroad industry. In addition to the economies that might arise through equipment and managerial specialization, and through use of large-size vehicles, there are also indications that railroads are subject to the types of indivisibilities discussed earlier in this chapter.[13]

The only major study of economies of scale in rail transportation concluded that consolidations that transformed low-density systems into a single system with higher traffic density would yield scale economies. However, the study further concluded that, where density is already high, enlargement of scale above a level of 10,000 employees would most likely be accompanied by real diseconomies.[14]

These findings are interesting in view of the recent financial problems experienced by several large railroads, particularly the Penn Central, which employed more than 90,000 workers. However, in all fairness, it should be noted that other large railroads in the western and southern sections of the country have fared much better. Also, as discussed in Chapter 3, a variety of factors, many of them unrelated to company scale, led to the collapse of the Penn Central and other Northeast railroads.

Pipelines.   The movement of petroleum products through pipelines seems to be subject to considerable economies of scale. This is particularly true with regard to pipeline diameter. As discussed in Chapter 5, studies have indicated that the unit cost of crude oil pipeline transportation declines rapidly with increases in throughput and diameter of the pipeline.[15]

Motor Carriage.   Several studies of the trucking industry have addressed the issue of scale economies in motor carriage. One such study, which related annual intercity revenues to cost per vehicle mile, average haul, and cost per ton mile, concluded that there were no significant economies of scale in the industry.[16] Similar conclusions were reached in several other studies.[17] However, due to the limited scope of these studies and the methodologies employed, the findings have been criticized as being inconclusive.[18]

Air Carriage.   Studies of air transportation have concluded that once moderate size has been attained by individual airlines, there do not appear to be any significant economies of scale. Prior to achievement of moderate size, economies appear to stem from a decline in operating costs per available seat mile, or ton mile, as the size of the plane increases.[19]

Relevance of Scale Studies

Studies of economies of scale in transportation are far from being definitive. Typically, the studies have been quite limited in coverage. Also, there is considerable debate concerning how scale economies should be measured. Therefore, caution must be used in attempting to employ the findings of such studies as the basis for transportation policy formulation. This issue is discussed further in Chapter 16, which examines federal policy related to carrier mergers and consolidations.

Other Major Cost-Influencing Factors

Many factors influence the costs of providing various transportation services. Understanding of these factors is important because of the role they play in the pricing process. As a prelude to the detailed pricing discussion contained in Chapter 9, attention now shifts to several other major factors that influence the costs incurred by carriers in offering specific services. These factors may be separated into commodity and route characteristics.

Commodity Characteristics

Some characteristics of a particular commodity that influence the costs of moving the commodity are loading characteristics, susceptibility to loss and damage, volume and regularity of movement, and the nature of the equipment required to move it.

Loading Characteristics. The loading characteristics of products vary widely. For example, some bulk and liquid products, like grain, sand, and petroleum products, are loaded through automated processes with little labor input. Other commodities, such as manufactured items, are typically loaded through more labor intensive processes. If items are packaged in standardized units, it may be possible to load and unload them using equipment such as wooden pallets that hold multiple units. In contrast, other items that are odd-shaped must be handled individually, possibly by hand. The more labor intensive the handling process, the more time consuming and costly the process is, and the greater the likelihood of damage to the shipment.

Another important loading characteristic of a particular commodity is its use of the cubic capacity of the vehicle. If the product is light but bulky, it will tend to use up the cubic capacity of the vehicle without approaching the vehicle's weight-carrying potential. Under such circumstances, it is quite common for the carrier's rate to reflect this by assessing higher charges per unit of weight to light-loading commodities.

One final loading consideration in terms of cost generation is who actually does the loading and unloading of the vehicle. This varies from mode to mode and by commodity grouping. In rail carriage (with the exception of limited amounts of LCL traffic), loading and unloading are typically handled by shippers and consignees. Consequently, this cost factor is more meaningful to shippers and consignees than it is to the rail carrier, because the costs are not borne directly by the carrier. The loading and unloading pattern is rather different in motor carriage. Drivers frequently assist in the loading and unloading process, thereby generating carrier costs that are necessarily reflected in rates.

Susceptibility to Loss and Damage. An additional unit cost-influencing factor in the provision of transportation service is the commodity's susceptibility to loss and damage, which varies quite widely across commodity groupings. Certain products, such as glassware and electronic equipment, are quite fragile and require special carrier treatment. In contrast, movement of many bulk commodities, such as sand and gravel, do not require special handling efforts and consequently generate lower costs. Other products, like agricultural goods, are perishable. This may necessitate use of special refrigerated trailers or rail cars, and this generates additional costs.

Certain products are quite vulnerable to pilferage, particularly items that are small and valuable, such as pocket calculators and cameras. Because of the high incidence of pilferage in certain product categories, and due to the resulting high cost of claims, at various times certain carriers have unofficially attempted to embargo carriage of such items. However, a carrier cannot legally do that, and such action can be stopped by the regulatory agencies.

Some pilferage occurs in carrier terminal areas; this has led to a variety of cargo security measures, ranging from placement of security guards on carrier docks to installation of surveillance cameras.

Pilferage in transportation is not limited to small-scale theft. Hijacking is still a problem in the trucking industry, particularly involving truckloads of such commodities as cigarettes, razor blades, or pharmaceuticals. Hijacking is so serious a problem in certain cities that some motor carriers now number the tops of trailers so that stolen trailers might be spotted by police helicopters. Such extraordinary security efforts naturally generate additional costs in serving certain commodity groupings that are highly susceptible to theft.

Cost and Demand in Intercity Transportation

Loss and damage considerations provided a major stimulus in the movement toward containerization of both domestic and international traffic. Placement of items in sealed containers not only facilitates ease of handling, but also provides additional cargo security.

The costs generated by loss and damage are not limited to the amount of loss and damage claims; they also include the costs of claim investigation and payment processing.

Nature of Equipment Required. As discussed earlier in this chapter, some cargo can be handled by general-purpose equipment such as straight trailers or boxcars, but other cargo types necessitate carrier purchase and operation of more costly specialized equipment. Due to the nature of the commodities carried, some transportation vehicles may have to be specially cushioned, refrigerated, or equipped to handle liquid commodities. Naturally, these equipment modifications add to the costs incurred by the carrier.

Traffic Volume and Regularity. The volume in which a commodity moves also influences the per unit cost of providing the service. Any unit of transportation output is burdened with some arbitrary overhead allocation. As shipment size increases, these fixed costs are spread over greater traffic volume, and average costs per unit of output tend to taper off. This phenomenon is reflected in the rate structure, which generally assesses lower transportation charges per unit of traffic handled as shipment size increases.

Also, as shipment size increases, the likelihood of application of labor-saving devices such as palletization also increases. Potentially, this can lower handling costs per unit. This situation tends to lead to considerable differences in the costs of handling truckload versus less-than-truckload (LTL) freight. The smaller average shipment size of LTL traffic tends to generate considerably more manual handling, and hence higher costs.

The regularity with which specific traffic types are handled also tends to influence the cost of the movement. Frequent movement, particularly of commodities that necessitate use of specialized equipment, facilitates improvements in scheduling and equipment utilization.

Route Characteristics

The characteristics of the route over which traffic moves also influence the costs of providing the service. Foremost among these cost-influencing factors are route distance, operating conditions, and traffic density.

Distance. The distance over which traffic moves between origin and destination naturally influences the carrier's costs. Total cost rises as distance increases, but the cost per mile tends to decline. Certain rather fixed costs, such as those associated with moving the transportation vehicle through terminal facilities, are spread over longer distances. The following example illustrates this concept. Assume that it costs $75 to move a loaded rail car through a rail yard and terminal facility. If the car moves 100 miles to its destination, the *recovery rate* on these terminal costs is 75 cents per mile. In contrast, if the shipment moves 1,000 miles, the *recovery rate* becomes 7.5 cents per mile. This spreading out of terminal expenses is reflected in the rate structure, which tends to assess tapering rates as shipment distance increases. That is, total transportation charges do not tend to increase proportionately with shipment distance.

The distance a shipment travels between origin and destination may vary considerably across the modes due to the circuity of the routes traveled by certain carriers. For example, quite often water carrier distance between two cities is considerably greater than that of their railroad competitors due to the limitations of the natural waterway system. Regulatory policies can also influence the distance a carrier travels between origin and destination by restricting the routes a carrier might use. For example, the ICC has often granted motor carrier applicants operating rights that are rather circuitous to protect the operating authority of more established motor carriers that offer direct service.[20] However, in recent years a combination of deregulation pressures and energy considerations have led the regulatory agencies to take steps to substantially reduce certificate circuity.[21]

Operating Conditions.   Costs are also influenced by the operating conditions that prevail over specific routes. The route's topography is important in that regard. Negotiation of grades and curves generates higher costs than operation over rather flat routes. In the railroad industry, grade crossings force reduction in speed, which tends to raise operating costs. Consequently, it is generally more expensive to operate in heavily populated areas. In the trucking industry the nature of the highway system to be traveled is important. Stop-and-go operation over unlimited access highways not only tends to be more time consuming, but also more costly in terms of fuel consumption than operation over Interstate highways.

Traffic Density.   A final route characteristic that has a major influence on carrier costs per unit of traffic handled is the traffic density of the route. Traffic density may be defined as the amount of traffic that a carrier handles per mile over a given route. Earlier in this chapter the impact of increasing shipment size on average cost was discussed. The same basic principles applies to a given route as volume or density increases over the route. The fixed-cost burden of each unit of traffic moving over the route lessens as density increases.

Often traffic density over a particular route is lower in one direction than the other. As a result (ignoring topographical considerations), costs per unit of traffic carried tend to be higher in the lighter traffic direction. In response to this situation, carriers often establish lower incentive rates in the lighter density direction to stimulate additional traffic.

TRANSPORTATION DEMAND

Whereas cost considerations tend to establish a lower limit in transportation pricing decisions, demand considerations set the effective pricing ceiling. Understanding the demand characteristics of potential customers is important to carriers, because these characteristics, in the aggregate, determine the quantity of carrier services that will be consumed at a particular price at a given time.

Transportation demand analysis and forecasting are not nearly as refined as carriers and government officials would like them to be. Nevertheless, the pricing decisions of carriers are at least partially based on an evaluation of customer demand schedules. Carriers are constantly faced with such questions as how responsive will passenger demand be if air coach fares between New York and Miami are lowered from $150 to $130, or how will demand react to a 5 percent increase in the rate charged for moving wheat from Minneapolis to Chicago? As discussed later in this chapter, the ultimate answer to questions like these is based on the elasticity of demand for those services.

The demand for transportation services is derived in nature. That is, the level of transportation demand is dependent upon societal demands for other goods and services. This is particularly true with respect to freight services. People do not purchase ton miles solely for the sake of consuming them. Ton miles of transportation service are purchased because they add value or place utility to the commodity that is to be moved. For example, raw materials and finished products generally must be moved from their point of production to potential markets to realize an increase in value. Hence transportation services create additional value by providing place utility.

Similarly, in a passenger context, people do not generally purchase passenger miles because they enjoy consuming them. Rather, there is some specific trip purpose, such as increasing individual place utility for either personal or business reasons through travel.

Because of the derived demand nature of transportation, particularly in the area of freight movements, carriers must be sensitive to conditions that

162

prevail in the markets for final products to accurately forecast their demand picture and to plan marketing strategies.

Determinants of Demand

The demand for transportation services, at any level of aggregation, is a function of many factors, including economic, social, and political considerations. Let us first examine transportation demand from the macro level by looking at national freight and passenger demand in totality. This is often referred to as *aggregate* demand. The level of aggregate demand for transportation services in a country is closely related to the general level of economic activity in the country. Because of this close relationship, car loadings and truck loadings have long been viewed as indexes of national business activity.[22]

During periods of rising business activity, aggregate demand for freight services tends to increase as the volume of raw materials and finished goods consumed in the economy rises. As disposable personal income rises, people tend to spend more on transportation, particularly on pleasure travel.[23]

As business activity slows, the situation is reversed with respect to freight volume, and personal expenditures for pleasure travel tend to be reduced. Even the business portion of passenger demand is affected by economic slowdowns. During such periods, many firms reduce employee travel and rely upon other less expensive forms of communications.

The proportion of Gross National Product (GNP) devoted to freight movements tends to remain stable or decline as an economy matures. Movement from an extractive, raw material orientation generally witnesses a growth in service-oriented industries. The service share of GNP increases, but services require less movement of goods than mining or manufacturing.[24] As a result, the freight transportation proportion of GNP declines. Somewhat offsetting this trend, however, in terms of aggregate transportation demand, is the fact that the demand for passenger movement tends to increase as the economy matures and discretionary income rises.

Modal Demand

The aggregate transportation demand of an economy is divided among the several modes and between for-hire and private carriage. The relative national market share of each form of carriage (modal split) is a function of many factors. In the freight sector, the most important mode-determining factors are the composition of the traffic moved, availability of alternative modes, service characteristics, prices of alternative modes, the geographical dispersion of economic activity, and the regulatory environment.

As industrialization expands in a country, transportation alternatives tend to increase, and growing emphasis is placed on faster, more expensive modes for movement of manufactured goods.[25] In many instances this has reduced the market share of railroads and water carriers, which had dominated bulk commodity movements in the earlier stages of economic growth. This pattern has been visible in the United States over the past 40 years, with the steady shift of high-valued commodities from rail to motor and air carriage. Technological and regulatory changes, coupled with aggressive marketing behavior, may contribute to shifts in the aggregate freight modal split, but such shifts tend to be rather gradual.

The aggregate modal split of passenger carriage is also influenced by a variety of factors. Predominant among these factors are the availability of alternatives, comparative prices, and numerous service considerations, including speed, convenience, comfort, dependability, and safety. In intercity markets, the U.S. public has clearly demonstrated a preference for the automobile; nearly 87 percent of intercity passenger miles are registered in automobiles. It is clear that the convenience of the private automobile outweighs other choice variables for most intercity travels. The modal choice of passengers is explored further in Chapter 19, which examines urban travel.

Specific Demand

At the micro level, the shipper generally weighs a number of variables in making carrier selection decisions. Assuming that the shipper does not engage in private carriage, he must choose among the modes (if he is fortunate enough to have alternatives available), and then select a particular carrier within the mode chosen. The shipper ordinarily weighs a variety of price–service considerations in assessing possible trade offs. His decision may be guided by company policies that call for certain customer service standards. In this case his concern is realization of these standards while minimizing transportation outlays. In negotiations with carriers, the shipper often attempts to play one carrier, or mode, off against the other. Depending on the volume of freight that he controls, the shipper may influence carrier price levels and service offerings.

In soliciting traffic, the carrier is faced with many potential customers, each being unique in its needs. Consequently, to be effective the carrier must develop some understanding of these needs while realizing his own capabilities. The carrier naturally would like to carry nothing but high-density, high-rated traffic that has limited susceptibility to loss and damage. Unfortunately for the carrier, the transportation market-place in which it operates does not generally conform with this ideal. Consequently, the carrier will attempt to cultivate the more desirable traffic while tolerating other accounts.

The factors that affect the demand for specific passenger services vary somewhat between business and nonbusiness travelers. The business traveler, often traveling on an expense account, tends to be somewhat less concerned with the price differences of his alternatives and somewhat more concerned with the value of his time. Consequently, the business traveler is likely to be influenced in his carrier selection by such factors as service frequency, speed of service, his past experience with the companies serving the market, and the total package of amenities offered by the competitors. To a certain extent, long-distance business travel is somewhat captive to the airline industry; as a result, the traveler's choice tends to be limited to selection of one of several airlines serving the cities he is moving between. In shorter-distance markets, rail and bus alternatives become available, as does the automobile, and the carrier selection process becomes more complex.

The nonbusiness traveler is likely to be somewhat more concerned with the comparative costs of modal alternatives than his business counterpart, because direct costs will come from the nonbusiness traveler's personal budget. Nevertheless, even though considerable evidence has been compiled which suggests that for-hire modes are less expensive than the private automobile for many intercity trips, the automobile continues to dominate such private travel.

Elasticity of Demand

The supplier of any transportation service is naturally concerned with the responsiveness of customer demand to price changes, which is usually referred to as the *price elasticity of demand*. If total revenues vary inversely with price changes, demand is said to be elastic. In contrast, if revenues vary directly with price changes, demand is said to be inelastic. An illustration should serve to clarify this concept. If an airline lowered its coach fare between New York and Miami from $150 to $130 and total market revenues rose (due to an increase in market demand), demand would be considered to be elastic. Conversely, if revenues fell following the price reduction, demand would be considered to be inelastic. In that case, even though passenger demand may have risen, its growth was not sufficient to offset the $20 per passenger revenue reduction related to the price cut.

Naturally, the management of carrier operations would be considerably simplified if a data base existed that documented demand elasticity by

165

market and service. Unfortunately, such a data base is lacking in most instances. As documented earlier, price experimentation has not been widely employed in transportation. Even when experimentation has occurred, a number of intervening variables, such as changes in economic conditions, tend to cloud the results. Consequently, much transportation pricing represents sophisticated guesswork, and the results are not always favorable. At least two highly touted price reduction programs were rescinded by carriers in 1975 due to the failure of additional demand to offset per unit revenue reductions. In late 1975, National Airlines announced curtailment of its *No Frills* New York to Miami service, which had offered approximately a 30 percent fare reduction.[26] Earlier in the year, Boston's MBTA system scrapped its *Dime Time* program of off-peak fare reductions due to lagging revenues.[27] Fortunately, not all carrier price reduction efforts have resulted in such performance. Much of the recent success of the railroad industry in attracting high-value commodity movements has been related to selective price reductions, particularly through trailer-on-flatcar offerings. Similarly, the promotional fare programs of the charter airlines have stimulated substantial increases in ridership and revenues.

The aggregate demand for transportation services tends to be rather price inelastic in the short run. However, over longer periods, aggregate demand has demonstrated a responsiveness to changing price levels.[28] As might be expected, modal demand tends to be more price elastic than aggregate demand. At the specific carrier–shipper level, the relative elasticity or inelasticity of demand for particular services is determined to a great extent by what competitors charge for their services and the availability of such services. Furthermore, it might be reasonably expected that services for which there are adequate substitutes will show higher elasticities than services for which there is little or no competition. Also of importance is the ability of the purchaser of transportation service to pass along price increases to other members of the production–consumption channel. If the rate increase does not have to be absorbed by the party paying the transportation bill, demand for the specific service is not likely to be impaired. However, the ability to pass such increases along the channel is a function of the demand situation faced by the commodity in final markets.

Value of Service

As implied in the preceding discussion, different commodities and passenger groups exhibit different demand elasticities. That is, various customer groups tend to react differently to price modifications. These differences are reflected in the concept of *value of service* in transportation. The value of a specific transportation service might be said to be the upper limit of the freight or passenger charge. Essentially, this is the highest price that can be assessed for that particular service without diverting the traffic to another carrier or stopping its movement altogether.

Carrier and regulatory agency assessment of value of service plays a major role in transportation pricing. Although cost certainly plays a role in price setting in transportation, the most important reason for differences in prevailing rates on low- and high-value commodities is the greater ability of the valuable articles to stand higher rates.[29] These differences in ability to pay are consequently reflected in the transportation pricing structure, which, as discussed in Chapter 9, discriminates among various classes of passenger service and among commodity types according to value.

This philosophy of pricing leads to charging what the traffic will bear: carriers will strive to charge the rate on each commodity or significant traffic movement that, when the volume of traffic is considered, will make the largest total contribution to fixed expenses.

SUMMARY

The cost characteristics of the several modes of intercity carriage differ significantly. These differences involve not only fixed–variable cost proportions, but also include differences in the incidence of economies of scale. Numerous factors influence the costs incurred by a company in providing transportation services. Among the most important cost-influencing factors in freight movements are the loading characteristics of the commodity being shipped, the equipment used, the volume in which it moves, and the route over which it travels. In passenger movements, costs are highly influenced by the density of passenger volume, the equipment employed, and regulatory guidelines.

Basically, the demand for transportation services is derived in nature. The level of aggregate transportation demand tends to be closely related to the level of economic activity in a particular country. Modal demand is a function of many factors, including the range of available alternatives and price–service relationships. The demand for service at the specific shipper–carrier level is similarly influenced by a multitude of considerations.

The demand for transportation services may be discussed in terms of elasticity, or responsiveness to price changes. Different commodities and passenger groups exhibit varying demand elasticities. This has led to a heavy reliance upon value-of-service considerations in transportation pricing.

The blending of such cost and demand considerations in the transportation pricing process is discussed in Chapter 9.

NOTES

1. Marvin L. Fair and Ernest W. Williams, *Economics of Transportation and Logistics* (Dallas, Tex.: Business Publications, Inc., 1975), p. 148.

2. Ibid.

3. For a summary of this controversy, see Hugh S. Norton, *Modern Transportation Economics*, 2nd ed. (Columbus, Ohio: Charles E. Merrill Publishing Company, 1971), pp. 99–101.

4. Richard H. Leftwich, *The Price System and Resource Allocation,* 3rd ed. (New York: Holt, Rinehart and Winston, 1966), p. 144.

5. John F. Due and Robert W. Clower, *Intermediate Economic Analysis,* 5th ed. (Homewood, Ill.: Richard D. Irwin, Inc., 1966), p. 111.

6. Charles F. Phillips, *The Economics of Regulation,* rev. ed. (Homewood, Ill.: Richard D. Irwin, Inc., 1969), pp. 22–23.

7. Joe S. Bain, *Industrial Organization,* 2nd ed. (New York: John Wiley & Sons, Inc., 1968), p. 166.

8. Due and Clower, op. cit., p. 108.

9. Ibid., p. 109.

10. Dudley F. Pegrum, *Transportation: Economics and Public Policy,* rev. ed. (Homewood, Ill.: Richard D. Irwin, Inc., 1968), p. 130.

11. John B. Lansing, *Transportation and Economic Policy* (New York: Free Press, 1966), p. 16. For a discussion of the lack of agreement concerning the existence of scale economies, see Richard D. Low, *Modern Economic Organization* (Homewood, Ill.: Richard D. Irwin, Inc., 1970), pp. 147–80.

12. Phillips, op. cit., p. 23; and Lansing, op. cit., p. 14.

13. Due and Clower, op. cit., p. 108.

14. Kent T. Healy, *The Effects of Scale in the Railroad Industry* (New Haven, Conn.: Committee on Transportation, Yale University, 1961).

15. Leslie Cookenboo, Jr., "Costs of Operating Crude Oil Pipe Lines," *Rice Institute Bulletin* (April, 1954), as cited by Charles F. Phillips, op. cit., p. 23.

16. Robert A. Nelson, "The Economic Structure of the Highway Carrier Industry in New England," *Motor Freight Transport in New England* (Boston: New England Governors' Committee on Public Transportation, 1956), pp. 34–35.

17. Merrill J. Roberts, "Some Aspects of Motor Carrier Costs: Firm Size, Efficiency, and Financial Health," *Land Economics,* XXXII (August 1956), pp. 228–38; also, Edward Smykay, "An Appraisal of the Economies of Scale in the Motor Carrier Industry," *Land Economics,* XXXIV (May 1958), p. 146.

18. Smykay, op. cit., p. 148.

19. Richard E. Caves, *Air Transport and Its Regulators* (Cambridge, Mass.: Harvard University Press, 1962), pp. 57–61.

20. James C. Johnson, *Trucking Mergers: A Regulatory Viewpoint* (Lexington, Mass.: D.C. Heath & Company, 1973), pp. 73 and 144.

21. U.S. Interstate Commerce Commission, *The Regulatory Issues of Today* (Washington, D.C.: the Commission, 1975), pp. 21–26.

22. Norton, op. cit., p. 123.

23. Martin T. Farris and Forrest E. Harding, *Passenger Transportation* (Englewood Cliffs, N.J.: Prentice-Hall, Inc., 1976), pp. 22–23.

24. Norton, op. cit., p. 122.

25. Wilfred Owen, "Transport and Technology," in *Transport Investment and Economic Development,* Gary Fromm (ed.) (Washington, D.C.: Brookings Institution, 1965), p. 72.

26. "National Airlines to End 'No-Frills' Fare at End of April," *Wall Street Journal,* New York, March 22, 1976, p. 2.

27. "MBTA Report: Dime Time Fails, Zone Fares Likely," *Boston Globe,* July 12, 1976, p. 3.

28. Roy J. Sampson and Martin T. Farris, *Domestic Transportation: Practice, Theory, and Policy* (Boston: Houghton Mifflin Company, 1975), pp. 162–63.

29. D. Philip Locklin, *Economics of Transportation,* 7th ed. (Homewood, Ill.: Richard D. Irwin, Inc., 1972), p. 159.

SELECTED REFERENCES

Fair, Marvin L., and Ernest W. Williams. *Economics of Transportation and Logistics.* Dallas, Tex.: Business Publications, Inc., 1975.
Chapter 9. "Costs and Cost Finding in Transport and Distribution," pp. 143–62.

Healy, Kent T. *The Effects of Scale in the Railroad Industry.* New Haven, Conn.: Committee on Transportation, Yale University, 1961.

Meyer, John R., Merton J. Peck, John Stenason, and Charles Zwick. *The Economics of Competition in the Transportation Industries.* Cambridge, Mass.: Harvard University Press, 1964.
Chapter 7. "Transportation Rates and Demand Characteristics of the Transportation Market," pp. 168–202.

Milne, A. M., and J. C. Laight, *The Economics of Inland Transport,* 2nd ed. London: Sir Isaac Pitman & Sons, Ltd., 1963.
Chapter 4. "Cost of Transport (I)," pp. 76–104.
Chapter 5. "Cost of Transport (II)," pp. 105–44.

Nelson, Robert A. "The Economic Structure of the Highway Carrier Industry in New England," in *Motor Freight Transport in New England*. Boston: New England Governors' Committee on Public Transportation, 1956, pp. 22–43.

Norton, Hugh S. *Modern Transportation Economics*, 2nd ed. Columbus, Ohio: Charles E. Merrill Publishing Company, 1971.
Chapter 5. "The Cost of Producing Transport Services," pp. 99–119.
Chapter 6. "The Demand for Transport Services," pp. 120–33.

Pegrum, Dudley F. *Transportation: Economics and Public Policy*, 3rd ed. Homewood, Ill.: Richard D. Irwin, Inc., 1973.
Chapter 6. "The Economic Structure of Transport," pp. 121–40.
Chapter 7. "The Theory of Pricing," pp. 141–63.
Chapter 8. "Theory of Pricing for Transport," pp. 164–85.

Phillips, Charles F. *The Economics of Regulation*, rev. ed. Homewood, Ill.: Richard D. Irwin, Inc., 1969.
Chapter 14. "Public Policy and the Transportation Industries," pp. 483–536.

Roberts, Merrill J. "Some Aspects of Motor Carrier Costs: Firm Size, Efficiency, and Financial Health." *Land Economics*, XXXII (August 1956), pp. 228–38.

Sampson, Roy J., and Martin T. Farris. *Domestic Transportation: Practice, Theory, and Policy*, 3rd ed. Boston: Houghton Mifflin Company, 1975.
Chapter 10. "The Economic and Legal Basis of Rates," pp. 153–71.

Wilson, George W. *Essays on Some Unsettled Issues in the Economics of Transportation*. Bloomington, Ind.: Foundation for Economic and Business Studies, Indiana University, 1963.

DISCUSSION QUESTIONS

1. Discuss the long-standing controversy concerning the propriety of fully distributed cost versus variable cost pricing of transportation services.
2. What are scale economies and what are their significance from a regulatory standpoint?
3. Explain the importance of the concept of value-of-service pricing to carriers in determining the rates to be charged for various transportation services.

9

Rate-making Procedures

The pricing of transportation services takes place in two quite different environments. As discussed in earlier chapters, for operations that are exempt from regulation, rates are freely determined through the interaction of carriers and shippers, and rates tend to vary significantly over rather short time periods. In contrast, regulated carriers must price their services in a rather constrained environment in which regulation significantly influences pricing decisions. This chapter examines the pricing process in transportation and gives attention not only to carrier procedures, but also to the interaction among carriers, shippers, and regulatory agencies. Distinctions are made between the procedures employed in establishing freight rates and passenger fares.

RATE BUREAUS

One unique feature of domestic transportation is its heavy reliance upon collective pricing by carriers in a particular mode of transportation. Such behavior is generally illegal according to our nation's antitrust laws, but carrier rate bureaus have been granted antitrust exemptions. The bureaus are nonprofit, carrier-maintained organizations that are legally permitted to initiate joint carrier pricing action. Such collective pricing in transportation is often referred to as the *conference method* of rate making. It must be stressed, however, that, although these organizations initiate rate changes, such pricing modifications are typically subject to possible regulatory agency review.

Development

Due to the relatively small geographical scale of most early railroads, carriers necessarily conferred on the establishment of through routes, which covered the movement of traffic from the lines of the originating carrier to a destination on the lines of another carrier, and on the joint rates that applied to such traffic. When the Act to Regulate Commerce (Interstate Commerce Act) was passed in 1887, it empowered the ICC to require railroads to establish agreements of that nature to better serve the shipping public. The ICC also sought to reduce predatory pricing behavior through such collective rate making.

However, the passage of the Sherman Act of 1890 made collective pricing illegal.[1] The courts ruled that collective railroad pricing was in violation of that statute.[2] Nevertheless, the Justice Department permitted continuance of these practices as long as the ICC had final control over rates, and carriers had the right to take independent action, that is, establish rates which differed from those of the bureau.[3]

Subsequently, the practice came to be generally accepted in railroading, and it was later adopted by the trucking industry following passage of the Motor Carrier Act of 1935. That statute gave the ICC regulatory control over interstate motor carriage, and required that motor carrier rates had to be filed with the ICC and published. Similar arrangements were established in domestic water carriage following its regulation in 1940.

However, the legal status of rate bureaus was still questionable, and in 1944–1945 legal actions were initiated by the Justice Department and the state of Georgia against collective pricing practices in both rail and motor carriage.[4] In the Georgia case, the Supreme Court ruled that the railroads were indeed subject to antitrust pricing statutes and that Congress had not given the ICC power to exempt collective carrier pricing from antitrust laws.[5] Following that ruling, Congress held extensive hearings on the matter and found strong support for collective pricing from carriers and shippers alike. In response to this investigation, Congress passed the Reed–Bulwinkle Act of 1948.[6] The statute added Section 5(a) to the Interstate Commerce Act, which exempts from the antitrust laws any regulated carrier agreement on rates and charges which has been approved by the ICC. One major modification of the exemption was made by the Railroad Revitalization and Regulatory Reform Act of 1976. The statute specified that railroad bureaus were no longer permitted to allow agreement or voting on single line rates, and that only carriers that could practicably participate in the movement could vote on joint line rates.[7]

Bureau Structure and Functions

Rate bureaus are generally organized on a regional basis, and inter-regional rates are established between each territory. The membership of a particular bureau is limited to carriers within a single mode. That is, railroads cannot be members of motor carrier bureaus, and vice versa. Because the operating rights of a particular carrier may encompass a broad geographical region, the carrier may be a member of more than one bureau.

Membership in a particular bureau is typically open to all carriers (in that mode) that serve the bureau's region. However, some motor carrier bureaus have restricted their membership to common carriers.[8] The members of a bureau usually grant the bureau powers of attorney, which allow the bureau to commit the carriers to various rate agreements. Rate bureau operations are primarily supported by member contributions, which are usually assessed as a percentage of each member's gross operating revenues. Additional bureau income is often generated through sale of bureau publications to carriers and shippers.

There are 10 railroad rate bureaus, and 11 major rate bureaus in the trucking industry.[9] Additionally, there are several domestic water carrier bureaus. Airlines, pipeline operators, bus companies, and freight forwarders do not belong to collective price-setting organizations. However, international airlines do rely upon such an organization, the International Air Transport Association (IATA), to establish international fares. The role of the IATA in setting international passenger fares is discussed later in this chapter.

In addition to providing a mechanism for collective rate making, rate bureaus perform several other useful functions. Among these are the dissemination of information concerning such matters as regulatory changes, the provision of a forum to discuss problems of mutual concern, and publication of rates in tariffs, which are the equivalent of transportation price lists.

Bureau Procedures

Although procedures may vary somewhat from bureau to bureau, a general procedural pattern is followed by most bureaus in handling rate proposals. This pattern (and an emergency procedure) is illustrated in Figure 9–1.

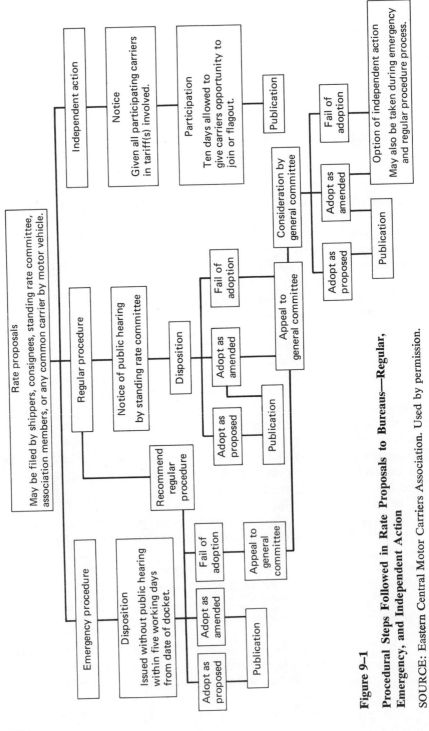

Figure 9–1

Procedural Steps Followed in Rate Proposals to Bureaus—Regular, Emergency, and Independent Action

SOURCE: Eastern Central Motor Carriers Association. Used by permission.

As illustrated, a rate proposal may be filed with a bureau by a shipper, consignee (one who receives freight), bureau member, other carriers, or by the bureau's standing rate committee. This committee consists of full-time bureau employees; its role is discussed in the following paragraphs.

Once a proposal has been filed with the bureau, the standing rate committee dockets, or schedules, consideration of the matter. If any interested party requests it, a public hearing will be held after adequate notice (30 to 60 days) is given to those with some interest in the proceeding. This is usually accomplished through announcement in industry publications or through weekly docket bulletins published by bureaus and subscribed to by carriers and shippers.

At the hearings conducted by the standing rate committee, all interested parties are given the opportunity to make their views known, and cost and traffic volume data are usually presented. Those involved in the proceeding often attempt to forecast the competitive impact of the rate modification. Following the hearings, the standing rate committee considers the evidence and makes public its decision on the proposal. If no objections are registered, the bureau will file the rate change with the ICC, or with the proper state agency if the rate applies to intrastate movements.

However, the decisions of the standing rate committee are generally subject to appeal to the bureau's general rate committee, which is composed of traffic executives of member carriers. If the general rate committee upholds the earlier finding of the standing rate committee, it files the rate change with the appropriate regulatory agency.

If the general rate committee denies the proposal, the carrier or carriers seeking the rate change may choose to take independent action. If such action is taken, all carriers that participate in the bureau tariffs involved must be notified and given 10 days to join in the rate change or to *flag out*. The independent rate is then published and filed with the regulatory agency.

Procedures before rate bureaus are quite time consuming. Motor carrier bureaus have generally disposed of rate proposals within 50 to 100 days from submission, but railroad bureaus historically tended to average six months or more on such matters.[10] The relative slowness of railroad bureau procedures came under increasing attack in the early 1970s, and Congress addressed the matter in the Railroad Revitalization and Regulatory Reform Act of 1976. The statute required railroad bureaus to reach final disposition of all cases within 120 days of docketing.

It has generally been contended that independent actions are far more common in motor carrier bureaus than railroad bureaus.[11] However, one recent study found that the rate of independent filings did not differ significantly between the railroad and motor carrier bureaus studied.[12]

RATE MAKING AND THE
INTERSTATE COMMERCE COMMISSION

The rate-making process does not end with the rate bureau procedures. Rate changes initiated by bureaus or individual carriers must be filed with the ICC 30 days prior to their effective date. Any interested party, including the ICC itself, may protest a rate change that has been filed with the commission. However, less than 1 percent of the rate changes filed with the ICC are suspended for commission investigation.[13]

Rate Change Protests

Normally, if a rate filed with the ICC is protested, the commission will suspend the rate proposal to allow itself sufficient time to study the proposal. Rate proposals may be legally suspended by the ICC for up to seven months, and in certain complex cases, the ICC may request that the filing carrier grant a time extension. An exception to these basic guidelines was established by the Railroad Revitalization and Regulatory Reform Act of 1976, which required the ICC to reach a decision within six months on any proposed rate that involved a capital investment of $1 million or more by a carrier, shipper, or receiver.

During the rate suspension period, hearings may be held before an administrative law judge who has been appointed by the ICC. At the conclusion of the hearings, the administrative law judge renders a decision on the case. If his finding is acceptable to all parties, it becomes an ICC order. However, appeals to a division of the commission (which consists of three ICC commissioners) and even to the full commission are possible if the case has general transportation significance. Finally, the orders of the ICC may be appealed on legal grounds in the courts.

This process can be extremely time consuming and expensive for parties involved in controversial rate cases. Many rate cases take months (some even years) to move through the entire process. The ICC has been widely criticized because of the slowness of the process, and it has responded by modifying some of its procedures.[14] However, the desirability of rapid ICC action in such cases must be weighed against the desirability of allowing all interested parties to present their views both before the ICC and in courts of law.

Testimony Before the ICC

As noted, in rate suspension cases, the ICC generally schedules hearings before an administrative law judge. The range of possible hearing participants is quite broad. For example, if the case involves a rate decrease,

176

competitive carriers from the same or a different mode may testify against the proposal. They may argue that the proposed rates are unreasonably low, and that they would not only divert traffic from them, but would also impair overall carrier health.

Certain shippers such as company A, which might benefit from the rate cut, will testify on behalf of the proposal, citing their need for the lower rate and its projected impact on their business. In contrast, company B, which is a competitor of company A, may protest the rate modification. It might argue that it is located in another region and therefore does not have access to the proposed lower rate; consequently, the reduction will give its competitor an unfair market advantage in markets that they both serve. The chamber of commerce of the town in which company B operates may also testify that the company's loss of business would cause the town to suffer undue economic hardship, and that therefore the rate change should not be granted. Testimony may also be given by other government agencies and consumer groups.

In defending the rate change proposal, the sponsoring carrier is likely to present cost data to justify the change. Although the cost data may be based on the proposing carrier's actual cost figures, they may be restructured according to ICC cost formulas. Such formulas have been developed by the commission for railroads, motor carriers of general freight, and domestic water carriers. The formulas generate broad average territorial costs. They are published regularly by the ICC, and are periodically updated according to appropriate price indexes.

Commission reliance upon these cost-generating formulas has led to considerable controversy throughout the years. Critics have attacked the reliance of the formulas upon historical rather than replacement costs, formula allocation of costs to specific cost categories (i.e., fixed versus variable), and formula generation of broad geographical average costs that deemphasize the particular carrier's cost structure.[15] However, use of the formulas by a carrier in an ICC proceeding may offer an advantage to the carrier, because formula-produced data are not ordinarily challenged, whereas individual carrier data often are subject to challenges.[16]

In addition to presenting relevant cost data, the sponsoring carrier may choose to present additional information concerning a variety of factors, such as market demand and its own equipment utilization and revenue needs.

Commission Considerations

In judging the merits of a specific rate proposal that has been protested, the ICC must consider many factors. Naturally, the cost and demand data presented will be evaluated. Additionally, the ICC must ultimately decide if the proposed rates are reasonable, and it must determine that they are not unduly discriminatory. In terms of reasonableness, the rates must at the same time be low enough to facilitate traffic movement, yet high enough to generate adequate carrier revenues. It must also be established that the rates are not unduly discriminatory against particular persons, firms, or places. The meanings of both *reasonable* and *unduly discriminatory* are somewhat vague and, consequently, subject to ICC interpretation. The origin of each term and the development of their applications are discussed in subsequent chapters.

While evaluating these factors, the ICC must also be sensitive to the potential impact of the rate change on shippers and carriers.

General Rate Increases

To this point, the rate-making discussion has been placed in the context of a rate proposal to change a specific rate, such as the rate charged for moving steel ingots from Pittsburgh to Steelton, Kentucky. However, in certain instances, carriers may seek general freight rate increases in which rates are raised on all commodities carried. Usually, such increases are expressed in percentage terms, for example, freight rates being increased 4 percent across the board. Naturally, rate proposals of this scope must be filed with the governing regulatory agency.

Petitions for general rate increases may be prompted by rising costs, depressed carrier earnings, or a combination of the two. If granted, general rate increases tend to ignore the specifics of a particular freight market, and they have frequently resulted in substantial traffic diversion.[17] For this reason, carriers in certain regions may be reluctant to join in general rate increases at the national level, or they may choose to apply rate increases only to selective traffic groups. This has occurred in the railroad industry several times during the past decade, when more prosperous western and southern railroads have refused to join in general rate increase proposals initiated by revenue-starved eastern railroads.

In reviewing general rate-increase proposals, regulatory agencies typically consider cost, revenue, employment, and productivity data submitted by the sponsoring carriers; they weigh this information against the possible negative impact of the increases on the national economy as well as specific shipping interests.

Soaring costs and depressed revenue levels have led to a number of general rate increases in recent years. In 1975 alone, the nation's railroads received ICC permission to implement three general increases that ultimately amounted to a 13 percent increase on the average shipment.[18] Trunk-line air carriers, faced with sluggish demand and the aftermath of rapidly rising fuel costs, implemented two separate 3 percent general increases between November 1975, and April 1976.[19] Similarly, most inter-city motor rate bureaus were granted a 6.3 percent general increase in response to settlement of the national Teamster contract in April 1976.[20]

Contract Carrier Rates

Contract carriers in both motor and water carriage do not hold themselves out to provide service to the general shipping public, but rather establish individual contracts with one or more shippers. Rates are agreed upon through negotiation between shippers and the contract carrier. Consequently, the collective pricing activities of rate bureaus do not apply to the contract carriage rate-making process.

The actual rates charged by contract carriers must be filed with the ICC, and these rate schedules are open to public inspection. Contract carrier rates may also be challenged by interested parties before the ICC.

ICC Rate Policies

Thus far, this chapter has focused on the procedural aspects of carrier rate making. However, as noted at the beginning of this chapter, the actual rates established by carriers are subject to considerable regulatory agency influence. In turn, the agencies themselves are influenced by a myriad of transportation laws and government policies that relate to carrier pricing. These statutes and policies, and their implementation by the ICC, influence such matters as establishment of relevant costs in rate-making proceedings and the degree of competitive intensity between carriers.

At this point, an attempt might be made to synthesize ICC rate policies. However, these matters might be treated in a more meaningful manner by examining them while tracing the development of transportation regulation. This takes place in Chapters 11 through 13.

Criticisms of Rate Bureaus

The collective pricing activities of carrier rate bureaus have been widely criticized during the past several years. It has been charged that these organizations stifle intramodal competition to the detriment of the shipping public.[21] It has been further alleged that bureaus not only protect inefficient carriers through collective pricing, but also effectively preclude significant independent actions on the behalf of member carriers.[22]

One of the most vocal attackers of the conference method of rate making has been the federal Department of Transportation. Beginning in 1971, the DOT submitted several legislative proposals to Congress that sought to limit the scope of bureau influence. DOT criticisms of collective pricing in transportation brought considerable public attention to the issue, and several subsequent steps have been taken to reduce bureau power. In 1975, the ICC issued an order which ultimately prohibited motor carrier bureaus from opposing independent filings by member carriers that were published in bureau tariffs.[23] Also, as discussed earlier in this chapter, the following year Congress prohibited railroad bureaus from permitting agreement or voting on single-line rail rates. It also limited bureau voting on joint-line rates to those carriers that might practicably participate in the movement involved.[24]

It appears likely that the near future will witness continued attacks on the conference method of rate making. Similarly, the movement toward greater carrier pricing freedom will probably lead to a further reduction in the influence of rate bureaus in transportation pricing. However, bureaus are likely to survive and will continue to play an important role in such matters as interline agreements and tariff publication and filing.

ESTABLISHMENT OF PASSENGER FARES

The procedures employed in establishing interstate passenger fares differ somewhat from those used in setting freight rates. The procedures that are used in efforts to modify airline, bus, and rail fares are examined in the following discussion.

Airlines

Rather than formulating fare proposals collectively, the domestic airlines file individual proposals with CAB. It should be noted, however, that carriers flying the same route often choose to follow the fare action taken by a competitor, and file similar fares with the CAB.

Fares must be filed with the CAB 30 days before they are to become effective. This allows time for possible protests to be filed with the board. Once the CAB receives an airline fare proposal, it may approve, reject, or suspend the fare for further study. Hearings may be held on certain fare proposals, and all interested parties may present their views. Having considered the evidence presented as well as regulatory and promotional goals, the CAB renders a decision, which may be appealed on legal grounds in the courts.

Proposals for general fare changes may be filed simultaneously by carriers. Such general rate level proposals are subject to similar CAB procedures.

United States air carriers that fly international routes are members of the International Air Transport Association (IATA) which is a nongovernmental organization primarily concerned with the commercial and economic aspects of international air transportation. Membership is open to all the airlines of the world, and the vast majority have joined.

Although IATA plays a variety of roles in such matters as settling interline accounts and solving problems related to air law and liability, its major role pertains to fare and rate establishment. Carrier representatives attend biannual traffic conferences and negotiate the fare agreements that will prevail on specific international routes. These agreements are voluntary, but after lengthy negotiations carriers reach agreements that member carriers will honor. IATA fares are then subject to approval by each nation involved in a given fare.[25]

Bus Companies

The National Bus Traffic Association acts as the coordinating agent for interstate bus operators in filing fares with the ICC. The organization files not only charges pertaining to specific routes and individual carriers, but it also files general rate-level proposals that pertain to many carriers. The procedures before the ICC are similar to those previously described related to freight rate proposals.

Amtrak

When the National Rail Passenger Corporation (Amtrak) was created in 1970, it was granted pricing freedom, and its fares are not subject to ICC review or suspension. However, those rail carriers that continue to provide intercity passenger service outside the Amtrak system are still bound by the earlier procedures that applied to fare changes in rail passenger service. Rates must be filed 30 days prior to their effective date, and they are subject to possible ICC suspension, review, and denial.

SUMMARY

With the exception of exempt operations, transportation pricing takes place in a rather constrained environment in which regulatory agencies play a major role in pricing decisions. Nevertheless, transportation is unique in that it relies heavily upon the collective pricing behavior of carriers in a particular mode.

Rate bureaus, which have been granted an exemption from antitrust pricing guidelines, provide the vehicle for collective pricing action. Other bureau functions include dissemination of information to member carriers, provision of a forum for discussion of common problems, and filing of carrier or bureau tariffs with regulatory agencies.

Even though carriers may be members of rate bureaus, they maintain the right of independent action, which allows them to file rates that differ with those of the bureau. In most instances, rates filed by carriers or bureaus may be protested before the regulatory agencies. In certain instances, rate-change proposals are suspended and hearings are held. In such proceedings the ICC and CAB consider not only the cost and demand data presented by carriers and shippers, but also the relationship of the proposal to a variety of statutes and government policies pertaining to transportation. The decisions of the regulatory agencies in such cases are then subject to possible challenge in the courts.

NOTES

1. 25 Stat. 209, Chap. 647 (1890); 15 U.S.C.A. 1.

2. *United States* v. *Trans-Missouri Freight Association,* 166 U.S. 290 (1897).

3. Dudley F. Pegrum, *Transportation: Economics and Public Policy,* 3rd ed. (Homewood, Ill.: Richard D. Irwin, Inc., 1973), p. 234.

4. *State of Georgia* v. *Pennsylvania Railroad Company,* 324 U.S. 439 (1945); *United States* v. *Association of American Railroads,* U.S. District Court, Lincoln, Neb., 4 F.R.D. 510 (filed in 1944).

5. 324 U.S. 439 (1945).

6. 62 Stat. 472 (1948).

7. Association of American Railroads, *Basic Provisions of Railroad Revitalization and Regulatory Reform Act of 1976* (Washington, D.C.: the Association, 1976), p. 1.

8. Charles A. Taff, *Commercial Motor Transportation,* 4th ed. (Homewood, Ill.: Richard D. Irwin, Inc., 1969), p. 351.

9. Grant M. Davis, Martin T. Farris, and Jack J. Holder, *Management of Transportation Carriers,* 3rd ed. (Praeger Publishers, Inc., 1975), p. 102.

10. Marvin L. Fair and Ernest W. Williams, *Economics of Transportation and Logistics* (Dallas, Tex.: Business Publications, Inc., 1975), p. 366.

11. Hugh S. Norton, *Modern Transportation Economics,* 2nd ed. (Columbus, Ohio: Charles E. Merrill Publishing Company, 1971), p. 273.

12. Charles S. Sherwood, "The Operational Reality of Independent Rate Making: Some Empirical Findings," *Transportation Journal,* XV, No. 2 (Winter, 1975), p. 8.

13. U.S. Interstate Commerce Commission, *Regulatory Issues of Today* (Washington, D.C.: the Commission, 1975), p. 7.

14. "Will Politics Change Transportation?" *Traffic Management*, XV, No. 1 (January, 1976), p. 32.

15. Fair and Williams, op cit., p. 153.

16. Ibid., p. 155.

17. D. Philip Locklin, *Economics of Transportation*, 7th ed. (Homewood, Ill.: Richard D. Irwin, Inc., 1972), pp. 63–65.

18. Association of American Railroads, *Yearbook of Railroad Facts* (Washington, D.C.: the Association, 1976), p. 3.

19. Information supplied by the Civil Aeronautics Board.

20. Transportation Association of America, "What's Happening in Transportation," April 20, 1976, p. 2. (Newsletter)

21. Robert C. Fellmeth, *The Interstate Commerce Omission* (New York: Grossman Publishers, Inc., 1970), p. 141.

22. See U.S. Department of Transportation, Office of the Secretary, *Executive Briefing: Transportation Regulatory Modernization and Assistance Legislation* (Washington, D.C.: the Department, 1972), pp. 5–21, 45–50.

23. *Ex-Parte 297*, 349 ICC 859 (1975).

24. Association of American Railroads, *Basic Provisions of Railroad Revitalization and Regulatory Reform Act of 1976*, p. 1.

25. By mid-1976, serious questions had been raised about the future viability of IATA. A controversy had arisen between the United States and Britain concerning the desirability of maintaining existing route and fare agreements. For a discussion of the controversy, see "The Perils of No Policy on International Aviation," *Business Week* (August 16, 1976), pp. 104–108.

SELECTED REFERENCES

Davis, Grant M., Martin T. Farris, and Jack J. Holder. *Management of Transportation Carriers*. New York: Praeger Publishers, Inc., 1975.
Chapter 6. "Pricing and Rate Making," pp. 90–110.

Davis, Grant M., and Charles S. Sherwood. *Rate Bureaus and Antitrust Conflicts in Transportation*. New York: Praeger Publishers, Inc., 1975.

Fair, Marvin L., and Ernest W. Williams. *Economics of Transportation and Logistics*. Dallas, Tex.: Business Publications, Inc., 1975.
Chapter 17. "Rate Making in Practice," pp. 308–41.

Farris, Martin T., and Forrest E. Harding. *Passenger Transportation*. Englewood Cliffs, N.J.: Prentice-Hall, Inc., 1976.
Chapter 3. "Pricing Systems," pp. 63–102.

Lowe, G. E. *Practice and Procedure Before Rate Making Associations*. Washington, D.C.: Traffic Service Corporation, 1967.

Rate-making Procedures

McElhiney, Paul T. *Transportation for Marketing and Business Students.* Totowa, N.J.: Littlefield, Adams & Company, 1975.
Chapter 10. "Freight Rates and Tariffs," pp. 163–91.

Moore, Thomas G. *Freight Transportation Regulation: Surface Freight and the Interstate Commerce Commission.* Washington, D.C.: American Enterprise Institute for Public Policy Research, 1972.
Chapter 4. "Regulatory Practices," pp. 41–70.

Norton, Hugh S. *Modern Transportation Economics,* 2nd ed. Columbus, Ohio: Charles E. Merrill Publishing Company, 1971.
Chapter 8. "Transportation Rates and the Pricing Process," pp. 151–64.

Sampson, Roy J., and Martin T. Farris. *Domestic Transportation: Practice, Theory, and Policy.* Boston: Houghton Mifflin Company, 1975.
Chapter 11. "Freight Classifications and Tariffs: Their Preparation and Use," pp. 172–87.

Sherwood, Charles S. "The Operational Reality of Independent Rate Making: Some Empirical Findings." *Transportation Journal,* XV, No. 2 (Winter 1975), pp. 5–12.

Taff, Charles A. *Commercial Motor Transportation,* 4th ed. Homewood, Ill.: Richard D. Irwin, Inc., 1969.
Chapter 15. "Rates," pp. 327–64.

DISCUSSION QUESTIONS

1. As an industrial traffic manager who utilizes a large for-hire motor carrier on a regular basis, you wish to have the existing rate lowered on the commodity that you ship. Trace the steps involved in getting such a rate changed.

2. In a rate-making context, what is an independent action, and what is its importance to you as a shipper?

3. Do you believe that carrier rate bureaus should be allowed to maintain their antitrust exemption? Be specific and discuss the reasoning behind your answer.

10

Freight Classification Systems and Rate Terminology

One seemingly simple but rather complex and important process in transportation is the quotation of rates to shippers. The complexity becomes obvious when one considers not only the millions of different commodities that are shipped, but also the multitude of origins and destinations between which these commodities might move. Further complicating this situation are the many routes that might be used in moving traffic between any specific origin–destination combination. Rather than quoting an individual rate on each commodity moving between every possible origin–destination combination over every possible route, carriers have long attempted to simplify rate quotation through freight classification systems. These systems group commodities into a limited number of classes according to their transportation characteristics, and then prescribe rates on the various classes.

This chapter examines the development and operation of freight classification systems. It also introduces some important rate terminology and discusses the relationship between rates and such factors as distance moved and shipment size.

UNDERSTANDING CLASSIFICATION SYSTEMS

Basic understanding of freight classification systems is important to employees of carriers and shippers alike. To the carrier the classification system is an important component of the rate quotation process. Knowledge of the system may be useful in developing prices for new commodity movements and in presenting cases before regulatory agencies. Understanding of classification systems and their role in carrier pricing also enhances the ability of carrier employees, regardless of line or staff backgrounds, to communicate with each other on important issues.

As viewed by the shipper, classification systems are integral parts of the pricing system. Understanding of such systems may be useful in attempts to gain lower classifications for existing products and in getting new commodities classified. Communications with carrier representatives are also improved if both parties have a common frame of reference.

Although the shipper can request rate quotes from carriers, it is impractical to do so in many instances. This is particularly true if the company is conducting research, such as market analysis that involves estimation of delivered prices (including freight charges) into many areas. Similarly, forecasts of expected transportation costs in markets presently served are simplified if shipper employees have a working knowledge of such classification systems. Finally, as discussed in Chapter 2, the shipper may want to audit a carrier's freight bills. Due to the complexity of the pricing process, mistakes are common. For example, one source has estimated that mistakes are made on 5 to 6 percent of the freight bills sent to shippers by the motor carrier industry.[1] Such freight bill auditing may be conducted internally if employees are familiar with carrier pricing systems. If not, freight bill audits would have to be conducted by outside auditors.

DEVELOPMENT OF THE RAIL CLASSIFICATION SYSTEM

Development of freight classification systems is usually thought of in the railroad context, but such efforts actually predated the railroads. To simplify their pricing systems, early barge and wagon operators established limited numbers of freight classes and grouped commodities into these classes for rate quotation purposes.[2] For similar reasons, the railroads soon developed far more elaborate classification systems. However, as many railroads adopted individual classifications, different classification systems abounded. This caused problems in quoting rates on traffic that moved over the lines of more than one railroad.

Classification differences were quite cumbersome, and, following its creation in 1887, the ICC prodded the railroads to streamline the classification system.[3] Regional classification systems emerged before 1900, but it was not until 1956 that the Uniform Freight Classification system, which had been developed by the railroads, was extended to the entire country. Adoption of this system meant that the same commodity moving by rail anywhere in the United States would be placed in the same class.[4]

The rail industry maintains the Uniform Classification Committee, which handles classification of new commodities and applications for reclassification of commodities. In many instances, the committee holds hearings and takes testimony from carriers and shippers on such classification matters.

The Uniform Freight Classification contains 31 classes, 8 above class 100 and 22 below. Class 100 serves as the base class; other classes are stated as percentages of class 100. The highest is class 400; the lowest is class 13. Although these class numbers have no inherent meaning in terms of specific transportation charges, the higher the class number, the higher the related rate. This matter is explained in greater detail later in this chapter.

CLASSIFICATION SYSTEMS OF OTHER MODES

The motor carrier industry has also developed several freight classification systems. Most motor carriers outside New England adopted the National Motor Freight Classification following passage of the Motor Carrier Act of 1935. The act required motor carriers to file rates with the ICC, and, rather than undertaking development of a completely new classification system, the motor carriers simply followed the rail classification. Consequently, most entries in the original National Motor Freight Classification had descriptions that were identical to those in the rail classification.[5] In fact, many entries are still identical due to rail–motor competition.

In 1952 the National Motor Freight Classification was modified to provide a single set of national ratings. A National Classification Board is now maintained by the industry and it functions in a parallel capacity to that of the Uniform Classification Committee of the railroads.

New England truckers developed a separate classification system, which is known as the Coordinated Motor Freight Classification. The system groups all commodities into five classes based on a density or weight per cubic foot formula. The ratings in that classification are designed to produce approximately the same revenue per truckload on all commodities carried.[6]

The other modes of intercity carriage have not developed similar national classification systems. Domestic water carriers often use the rail or motor classification systems. Freight forwarders also rely upon rail and motor classifications, depending upon the mode of carriage being used for the line-haul movement. The air freight industry has not yet developed a national classification system.

FACTORS CONSIDERED IN RATING FREIGHT

Many factors are likely to be considered in establishing a classification *rating* for a particular commodity. Generally, these factors include the following:

1. Shipping weight per cubic foot.
2. Liability for damage.
3. Liability for damage to other commodities with which it is transported.
4. Perishability.
5. Liability for spontaneous combustion or explosion.
6. Susceptibility to theft.
7. Value per pound in comparison with other articles.
8. Ease or difficulty in loading or unloading.
9. Stowability.
10. Excessive weight.
11. Excessive length.
12. Care or attention necessary in loading and transporting.
13. Trade conditions.
14. Value of service.
15. Competition with other commodities transported.
16. Quantity offered as a single consignment.[7]

As might be expected, the importance assigned to each of these considerations is likely to vary from item to item.

Many commodities, particularly new commodities for which a rating has not yet been established, are classified by comparison with other commodities possessing similar transportation characteristics. This is often referred to as classification by *analogy*. In fact, pending establishment of a specific rating for his traffic, a shipper may use such an analogy to determine the applicable rate on his shipments.[8] Such applications may, however, be appealed by carriers.

Shippers may use similar logic in protesting to a classification committee that the rating on an existing commodity is too high (and hence related rates are too high). Carriers may also use such comparisons in attempting to get the ratings of specific commodities raised, thereby leading to higher rates on the traffic.

It must be remembered that determination of the rating of a specific commodity is just the first step in determining the applicable rate. The following discussion illustrates the rate-determination process from beginning to end.

USE OF A CLASSIFICATION SYSTEM

As illustrated in Figure 10–1, which is a page from the Uniform Freight Classification of the railroad industry, items are listed alphabetically in classifications, and item descriptions are quite detailed. Consequently, the first step involved in using a freight classification is determination of the proper item description for the product being shipped. Once this definition is established and the item is located in the classification, the user must next determine the applicable item rating. Figure 10–1 also shows that rail classifications typically specify less-than-carload (LCL) and carload (CL) ratings for a particular item. In motor carrier classifications, less-than-truckload (LTL) and truckload (TL) ratings are generally provided. It should be noted that there tends to be considerable absolute differences in the LCL and CL ratings. Remember, these are not rates, but the larger the rating, the higher the related rate. Also notice that the classification specifies a carload minimum (TL minimum in the motor carrier classifications); this establishes the minimum shipment size that qualifies for the lower CL rating. As discussed later in this chapter, in some instances shippers will send a lower quantity than the minimum CL shipment size *as the carload minimum* to qualify for the lower CL rating.

Shipping Illustration

Assume that you are shipping 10,000 pounds of elevator cars (item 16310 in Figure 10–1) from Boston to Chicago. This quantity is less than the necessary volume to qualify for the carload rating. Consequently, the relevant LCL rating for your shipment is 85.

At this point, you have only established the *rating* of the commodity being shipped. To obtain the related rate, you must now refer to a class tariff, a separate publication that is the equivalent of a transportation price list. This is no simple task, because there are literally thousands of tariffs, some issued by bureaus and some by individual carriers. Fortunately, due to the limited number of commodities shipped and destinations involved, most shippers generally use only a few tariffs on a regular basis. Consequently, the tariff-search process tends to be streamlined with more frequent use. However, shipments to new points tend to cause varying degrees of shipper trauma in determining the appropriate tariff to be used. In some

Item	Articles	Less carload ratings	Carload minimum (pounds)	Carload ratings
	BUILDING OR PAVING MATERIALS, MISCELLANEOUS (Subject to Item 15860)— Continued:			
16180	Doors, folding, metal or wood and fabric or plastic combined in boxes, crates or Packages 226 or 1286..	85	24,000R	55
16190	Doors, garage or industrial building, overhead or sliding, other than rolling, aluminum or aluminum and steel or wood combined, see Rule 33 and Notes 4 and 20, Items 16191 and 16821, LCL, in packages; also CL, loose..	100	12,000R 24,000R	85 55
16191	NOTE 4. —Ratings include door hangers, hanger rails, tracks, hooks, springs, pulleys, chains, brackets, locking rods, handles, lock rod guides locks, rollers, lift handles or other fittings for installation.			
16200	Doors, mine, with frames and fixtures, automatic, KD, loose or in packages	85	24,000	45
16210	Doors, revolving, with frames, KD, in boxes or crates............................	85	24,000	55
16220	Doors or grilles, rolling, curtain type, see Note 8, Item 16261, aluminum and iron or steel combined, in packages; also CL, loose......................	85	24,000	55
16230	Doors, smoke house, or smoke house firing, with frames, steel, loose or in packages..	85	24,000	45
16235	Doors, swinging, impact opening, self-closing, metal and plastic or rubber, in boxes or crates......	70	24,000R	45
16240	Doors with service cabinet compartments, with or without metal ventilators, in boxes or crates..	100	24,000R	55
16250	Doors or door sections, garage or industrial building, overhead or sliding, wooden, with or without hardware applied, see Note 6, Item 16251, in packages; also CL, loose..	70	30,000	35
16251	NOTE 6. —Carload ratings include hardware and fittings necessary for installation with or without operating mechanism for the doors which they accompany.			
16255	Doors or door sections, garage or industrial building, overhead, reinforced plastic and aluminum combined, with or without door track, in packages; also CL, loose..........	85	24,000R	55
16260	Doors or door sections or grilles, garage or industrial building, overhead, sliding, rolling or curtain type, iron or steel, see Note 8, Item 16261, in packages; also CL, loose..	70	30,000	$37\frac{1}{2}$
16261	NOTE 8. —Ratings include hardware and fittings necessary for installation with or without operating mechanism for the doors or grilles which they accompany.			
16275	Doors or partitions, folding, wood slat, with or without hardware, track or fixtures necessary for installation, in packages.................................	$92\frac{1}{2}$	24,000R	55
16280	Doors or windows, insulated, cold storage, not glazed, with or without frames or fixtures or power-operated door control mechanism, LCL, in boxes or crates; CL, loose or in packages..	70	24,000R	40
16290	Doors, partitions or shutters, rolling, curtain type, wooden, see Note 10, Item 16291, in packages; also CL, loose.....................................	70	36,000	$37\frac{1}{2}$
16291	NOTE 10. —Ratings include door hangers, hanger rails, tracks, hooks, springs, chains, brackets, locking rods, handles, lock rod guides, locks, rollers, lift handles or other fittings for installation.			
16300	Elevator car platforms, loose or in packages..	85	24,000	45
16310	Elevator cars, freight or passenger, KD, loose or in packages.................	85	24,000	45
16320	Elevator crossheads, loose or in packages...	50	40,000	35
16330	Elevator gates, wooden:			
	SU, in packages..	85	30,000	35
	KD, or collapsed, in packages...	70	30,000	35
16340	Elevator guide clips, iron, in packages..	50	40,000	35
16350	Elevator guide or weight posts, wooden, loose or in packages.................	70	36,000	35
16360	Elevator guides, iron, loose or in packages...	50	40,000	35
16370	Elevator guides, wooden, loose or in packages..	70	36,000	35
16380	Elevator plungers, steel, in boxes or crates, or enclosed in steel casing.....	70	30,000	40
16390	Elevator weights, iron, loose or in packages..	50	40,000	35
16400	Expansion fillers, building construction, corrugated lead, in packages......	85	36,000	55
16410	Fire escapes, steel, chute, tubular or spiral, in SU sections, loose or in packages..	150	15,000R	70
16420	Fire escapes, steel, noibn, loose or in packages......................................	70	36,000	$37\frac{1}{2}$
16430	Fireplaces and mantels combined, cast stone, without hearth or with hearth detached, in boxes or crates; also CL, braced and racked in car	$77\frac{1}{2}$ 70	30,000 30,000	45 40
16450	Forms and gaskets, sewer pipe joint, steel, nested, in boxes....................	100	24,000R	55
16460	Gutters or downspouts, plastic, with or without fittings, in boxes..........	85	24,000	55
16480	Ironing boards, folding, wooden, in metal cabinets, in boxes or crates.....			
16490	Ironing boards, folding, steel, in cabinets, steel, wooden, or synthetic plastic, separate or combined, in packages...	85	24,000R	55
16500	Lathing, copper, expanded, in packages..	$77\frac{1}{2}$	30,000	50
16510	Lathing, steel and paper combined, in packages.......................................	70	36,000	$37\frac{1}{2}$
16520	Lathing, zinc, expanded, in packages; also CL, loose..............................	$77\frac{1}{2}$	36,000	$45\frac{1}{2}$
16525	Light frames (frames for containing glass bricks or blocks), LCL in barrels, boxes or crates; also CL, loose or in packages:			
	Aluminum..	300	10,000R	85
	Steel or concrete..	60	36,000	35

Courtesy: Uniform Freight Classification Committee.

Figure 10–1

Sample Page from Uniform Freight Classification 12

190

cases, several tariffs must be used if the shipment moves between regions.

Assume that you have determined the appropriate tariff. It is now necessary to relate your shipment to a specific origin and destination. Tariffs list origin and destination combinations and assign them *rate base numbers*. In many instances, groupings of origins or destinations are assigned a common rate base number. Figure 10–2 presents a rate base listing from a railroad class tariff. As noted earlier, your shipment is moving between Boston and Chicago. This origin–destination combination is represented by the rate base number 973 in the illustration.

Thus far you have determined the rating, which specifies what is moving, and the rate base number, which indicates the origin–destination combination. The final step in actually determining the rate is the cross referencing of these two numbers in the tariff section, which specifies *rates in cents per 100 pounds shipped*. Figure 10–3 illustrates such a tariff section. Read down the rate base column to the fourth entry, which includes rate base number 973, and then read across the class listing to 85. This yields the class rate in cents per 100 pounds shipped. Multiplication of that rate, $4.03, times the 100-pound equivalents in your shipment (100) gives $403 in total transportation charges.

As mentioned earlier, due to the significant differences in LCL and CL rates (and LTL and TL rates), it is often possible to save transportation dollars by sending a shipment that weighs less than the carload minimum listed in the classification as if it met the carload minimum weight. In the illustration just completed, the rate base of the LCL shipment is $4.03 per hundredweight. As illustrated in Figure 10–3, the class rate for the carload rating of 45 is $2.13 per hundredweight. To determine when a shipment should be sent *as the carload minimum weight* instead of at its actual weight, the following simple formula can be used:

$$\text{CL rate} \times \text{CL minimum weight} = \text{LCL rate} \times Y$$
$$\$2.13 \times 24{,}000 = \$4.03Y$$
$$51{,}120 = 4.03Y$$
$$12{,}685 = Y$$

Therefore, given the prevailing rates on moving elevator cars between Boston and Chicago, any shipment weighing more than 12,685 pounds should be shipped as 24,000.

According to transportation law, carriers must inform shippers of this *break-even point* for their freight and should bill the shipper accordingly. However, mistakes are sometimes made in the billing process, and this break-even formula can be useful to shippers in reviewing carrier charges.

In summary, the basic steps involved in the determination of the applicable class rate are as follows: (1) use the classification to look up the

SECTION 1 – APPLICATION OF RATE BASES

ILLINOIS

BETWEEN ☞ AND ➡ — RATE BASES APPLICABLE

Item		Carmi	Carthage	Centralia	Champaign	Chicago	Danville	Decatur	De Kalb	Dixon	East Burlington	East Clinton	East Dubuque	East Ft. Madison	East Louisiana	East St. Louis	Edgewood	Eldorado
	MASSACHUSETTS																	
2550	Boston	1107	1194	1126	1027	973	994	1068	1031	1070	1168	1111	1133	1194	1191	1174	1098	1133
2552	Fitchburg	1057	1144	1076	977	923	944	1018	981	1020	1119	1061	1083	1144	1141	1124	1038	1083
2554	Framingham	1091	1178	1110	1011	957	978	1052	1015	1054	1153	1095	1117	1178	1175	1158	1072	1117
2556	Gardner-Heywood	1042	1129	1061	962	908	929	1003	966	1005	1104	1046	1068	1129	1126	1109	1023	1068
2558	Gloucester	1128	1215	1147	1048	994	1015	1089	1052	1091	1190	1132	1154	1215	1212	1195	1109	1154
2560	Greenfield	1001	1088	1020	921	867	888	962	925	964	1063	1006	1027	1088	1085	1068	982	1027
2562	Hyannis	1178	1265	1197	1098	1044	1065	1139	1102	1141	1240	1182	1204	1265	1262	1245	1156	1204
2564	Lawrence	1101	1188	1120	1021	967	988	1062	1025	1064	1163	1105	1127	1188	1185	1168	1082	1127
2566	Newburyport	1122	1209	1141	1042	988	1009	1083	1046	964	1063	1005	1148	1209	1206	1189	1103	1148
2567	North Adams	965	1052	984	885	831	852	926	889	928	1027	969	991	1052	1049	1032	946	991
2568	Pittsfield	970	1057	989	890	836	857	931	894	933	1032	974	996	1057	1054	1037	951	996
2570	Springfield	1022	1109	1041	942	889	909	983	947	986	1084	1027	1048	1109	1106	1089	1003	1048
2572	Taunton	1123	1212	1142	1043	989	1010	1084	1047	1086	1185	1127	1149	1210	1207	1190	1104	1149
2574	Ware	1048	1135	1067	968	914	935	1009	972	1011	1110	1052	1074	1135	1132	1115	1029	1074
2576	West Townsend	1083	¶1170	1102	1003	949	970	1044	1007	1046	1145	1087	1109	1170	1167	1150	1064	1109
2578	Worcester	1068	1155	1087	988	934	955	1029	992	1031	1130	1072	1094	1155	1152	1135	1049	1094
	MICHIGAN																	
2580	Adrian	376	433	378	266	211	233	307	269	308	405	349	383	433	430	415	340	401
2582	Akron	505	523	504	382	289	359	423	348	387	487	416	437	523	533	532	466	530
2584	Alba	561	543	553	427	323	413	468	355	442	507	397	418	543	578	578	515	586
2586	Alma	480	487	472	346	253	332	387	311	340	451	353	374	487	497	497	434	505
2588	Alpena	597	615	595	475	381	450	515	440	479	579	499	520	615	624	625	558	622
2590	Ann Arbor	412	464	413	302	230	268	342	288	327	428	368	402	464	465	450	376	437
2592	Ashley	464	482	462	341	248	317	382	307	341	446	354	375	482	493	491	425	489
2594	Bad Axe	545	563	544	422	329	399	463	388	427	527	456	477	563	574	592	506	570
2596	Battle Creek	372	390	370	249	156	225	289	214	253	354	294	328	390	399	398	333	397
2598	Bellaire	585	544	576	451	324	437	485	356	385	508	395	419	544	584	591	539	610
2600	Benton Harbor	322	325	309	184	91	170	224	149	188	289	229	263	325	334	335	272	347
2602	Boyne City	585	567	577	452	347	437	492	380	408	531	421	442	567	602	603	539	611
2604	Cadillac	501	482	493	368	263	353	408	296	324	446	336	357	482	518	519	455	527
2606	Charlotte	397	416	396	275	182	251	315	240	279	380	320	354	416	425	424	358	423
2608	Cheboygan	642	624	633	508	404	494	549	625	465	588	478	499	624	658	659	596	667
2610	Clare	511	493	503	377	273	363	418	305	334	457	347	368	493	528	528	465	537
2612	Clifford	510	536	512	395	302	367	435	360	399	500	431	452	536	545	544	474	530
2614	Detroit	435	492	436	325	267	291	365	325	364	464	405	439	492	486	473	409	474
2616	Durand	448	467	447	326	233	302	366	291	330	431	367	388	467	476	475	409	474
2618	Falmouth	525	507	517	391	287	377	432	319	348	471	361	382	507	542	542	479	550
2620	Fling	465	483	464	343	250	319	383	308	347	447	383	404	483	493	492	426	491
2622	Frankfort	523	462	495	370	242	365	403	274	303	426	316	337	462	502	509	458	541
2624	Grand Jct	354	357	341	216	123	202	256	181	220	321	261	295	357	336	367	304	379
2626	Grand Rapids	404	411	395	270	177	256	310	235	264	375	277	298	411	420	421	358	429
2628	Grayling	585	576	584	461	356	439	501	388	417	540	430	451	576	611	611	546	611
2630	Greenville	441	448	432	307	214	293	347	272	301	412	313	334	448	457	458	395	466
2632	Harrisville	565	583	563	442	349	418	489	408	447	547	467	488	583	592	592	546	590
2634	Hart	455	443	443	317	223	303	358	361	287	407	297	318	443	471	470	405	480
2636	Holland	382	385	370	245	152	230	285	210	249	349	267	268	385	395	395	322	408
2638	Holly	459	487	461	346	253	316	387	312	351	451	387	408	487	496	496	423	484
2640	Howard City	438	445	429	304	211	290	344	269	297	409	310	331	445	454	455	392	463
2642	Howell	432	467	434	322	234	289	363	292	331	431	372	396	467	477	476	396	457
2644	Ionia	436	446	431	305	212	289	346	268	297	410	309	330	446	456	456	393	461
2646	Jackson	385	424	386	275	194	241	315	252	291	392	332	366	428	436	423	349	410
2648	Jonesville	360	406	362	250	173	217	291	232	271	370	311	345	406	411	399	324	385

For explanation of reference marks, see concluding page of this tariff.

Courtesy: Traffic Executive Association-Eastern Railroads.

Figure 10–2

Sample Page from Class Tariff E-1009-A

SOURCE: Traffic Executive Association—Eastern Railroads. Used by permission.

CLASS RATES IN CENTS PER 100 POUNDS																
RATE BASIS NUMBERS (Numbers inclusive)	CLASSES															
	400	300	250	200	100	$97\frac{1}{2}$	95	$92\frac{1}{2}$	90	$87\frac{1}{2}$	85	47	46	45	44	43
876 to 900...	1816	1362	1135	908	454	443	431	420	409	397	386	213	209	204	200	195
901 to 925...	1844	1383	1153	922	461	449	438	426	415	403	392	217	212	207	203	198
926 to 950...	1868	1401	1168	934	467	455	444	432	420	409	397	219	215	210	205	201
951 to 975...	1896	1422	1185	948	474	462	450	438	427	415	403	223	218	213	209	204
976 to 1000...	1928	1447	1205	964	482	470	458	446	434	422	410	227	222	217	212	207
1000 to 1025...	1956	1467	1223	978	489	477	465	452	440	428	416	230	225	220	215	210
1026 to 1050...	1980	1485	1238	990	495	483	470	458	446	433	421	233	223	223	218	213
1051 to 1075...	2012	1509	1258	1006	503	490	478	465	453	440	428	236	231	226	221	216
1076 to 1100...	2036	1527	1273	1018	509	496	484	471	458	445	433	239	234	229	224	219
1101 to 1125...	2068	1551	1293	1034	517	504	491	478	465	452	439	243	238	233	227	222
1126 to 1150...	2092	1569	1308	1046	523	510	497	484	471	458	445	246	241	235	230	225
1151 to 1175...	2120	1590	1325	1060	530	517	504	490	477	464	451	249	244	239	233	228
1176 to 1200...	2152	1614	1345	1076	538	525	511	498	484	471	457	253	247	242	236	231
1201 to 1225...	2180	1635	1363	1090	545	531	518	504	491	477	463	256	251	245	240	234
1226 to 1250...	2204	1653	1378	1102	551	537	523	510	496	482	468	259	253	248	242	237
1251 to 1275...	2236	1677	1398	1118	559	545	531	517	503	489	475	263	257	252	246	240
1276 to 1300...	2260	1695	1413	1130	565	551	537	523	509	494	480	266	260	254	249	243
1301 to 1325...	2288	1716	1430	1144	572	558	543	529	515	501	486	269	263	257	252	246
1326 to 1350...	2316	1737	1448	1158	579	565	550	536	521	507	492	272	266	261	255	249
1351 to 1375...	2340	1755	1463	1170	585	570	556	541	527	512	497	275	269	263	257	252
1376 to 1400...	2372	1779	1483	1186	593	578	563	549	534	519	504	279	273	267	261	255
1401 to 1425...	2404	1803	1503	1202	601	586	571	556	541	526	511	282	276	270	264	258
1426 to 1450...	2428	1821	1518	1214	607	592	577	561	546	531	516	285	279	273	267	261
1451 to 1475...	2452	1839	1533	1226	613	598	582	567	552	536	521	288	282	276	270	264
1476 to 1500...	2484	1863	1553	1242	621	605	590	574	559	543	528	292	286	279	273	267
1501 to 1525...	2512	1884	1570	1256	628	612	597	581	565	550	534	295	289	283	276	270
1526 to 1550...	2532	1899	1583	1266	633	617	601	586	570	554	538	298	291	285	279	272
1551 to 1575...	2568	1926	1605	1284	642	626	610	594	578	562	546	302	295	289	282	276
1576 to 1600...	2596	1947	1623	1298	649	633	617	600	584	568	552	305	299	292	286	279
1601 to 1625...	2624	1968	1640	1312	656	640	623	607	590	574	558	308	302	295	289	282
1626 to 1650...	2648	1986	1655	1324	662	645	629	612	596	579	563	311	305	298	291	285
1651 to 1675...	2676	2007	1673	1338	669	652	636	619	602	585	569	314	308	301	294	288
1676 to 1700...	2704	2028	1690	1352	676	659	642	625	608	592	575	318	311	304	297	291
1701 to 1725...	2736	2052	1710	1368	684	667	650	633	616	599	581	321	315	308	301	294
1726 to 1750...	2760	2070	1725	1380	690	673	656	638	621	604	587	324	317	311	304	297
1751 to 1775...	2792	2094	1745	1396	698	681	663	646	628	611	593	328	321	314	307	300
1776 to 1800...	2820	2115	1763	1410	705	687	670	652	635	617	599	331	324	317	310	303

Figure 10–3

Portions of Class Tariff E-1009-A

SOURCE: Traffic Executive Association—Eastern Railroads. Used by permission.

commodity being shipped and to determine its rating; (2) select the appropriate tariff and determine the rase base number that applies to the origin–destination combination of the shipment; (3) cross reference the rating and the rate base number in the section of the tariff that gives class rates in cents per 100 pounds shipped.

EXCEPTIONS AND COMMODITY RATES

Although development of freight classification systems sought to simplify the rate-quotation process, competitive conditions have compelled carriers to move much of their traffic at rates that differ from normal class rates. Rates covering such special traffic movements may be established by filing either exception ratings or commodity rates.

An *exception rating* is essentially an amendment to the classification, which is created to meet competition or to attract a particular type of traffic that the carrier believes will not be attracted by existing class rates. The exception substitutes a lower rating for the normal one. It is still a rating, however, and the class rate applicable to that rating still applies. Frequently, exceptions are published along with rates in a class rate tariff, but some separate exception tariffs do exist.

Commodity rates are often thought of as the transportation equivalent of wholesale prices. In many instances a carrier can afford to charge less than the prevailing class rate. This might be the case if the commodity involved moves in large quantities on a rather regular basis, or if the traffic is needed due to unused capacity or empty backhauls.[9] Under any of these circumstances the carrier may establish a commodity rate (subject to the normal regulatory review). Such rates generally cover specific point-to-point movements of a particular commodity. In most instances commodity rates are lower than class rates, and the shipper is legally entitled to the lowest published rate that might be applied to his traffic. That is, at any given time, only one legal rate applies to a specific shipment handled by a specific carrier.

As illustrated in Figure 10–4, commodity rates are quoted directly in a commodity tariff rather than through the medium of a freight classification. Like class tariffs, commodity tariffs often make extensive use of grouping points of origin and destination. The carload or truckload minimum of commodity rates is often higher than that which would apply under the class rate. Many important commodities, such as coal, ore, cement, brick, grain, and livestock, generally move at commodity rates.[10]

Commodity rates have come to dominate intercity freight movements in several modes. More than 80 percent of rail tonnage and the bulk of trucking tonnage now move according to commodity rates.[11] Most common carrier water traffic also moves via such rates.[12] Air freight moves according to general commodity and specific commodity rates. Unless a specific commodity rate has been established for an item, a single general commodity rate applies to all commodities that move between each set of cities.

The class, commodity, and exception tariffs discussed thus far yield rates that cover not only the line-haul movement, but also normal pickup and delivery and terminal processing expenses. However, many accessorial or additional services may be offered by carriers at additional charge. Storage, diversion in transit to an alternative destination, and multiple stops for loading or unloading are but a few of the accessorial services that may be available. The fees for such services are generally contained in

	Section 2		
	Exceptions ratings and commodity rate columns		
Item	Commodities-carloads	Exception rating	Commodity rate column
(F6) 60350	COMPUTERS, as described in Item 60350 of UFC, in straight or mixed carloads. METERS, as described in the following Items of UFC, in straight or mixed carloads: 68810 68850 68900 68820 68860 68910 68830 68870 68920 68835 68880 68930 68840 68890 68937 Min wt 24,000 lbs (See Note)..	....	532
	(a) Min wt 30,000 lbs, (not applicable on shipments provided for (b) below)..	....	546
	(b) On shipments weighing in excess of 30,000 lbs, loaded in the same car. (See Note):		
	On first 30,000 lbs.	....	546
	On weight in excess of 30,000 lbs................................	....	547
	NOTE. —Not subject to Rule 24 or exceptions thereto or Rule 34 of UFC. EXCEPTION Will not apply from or to points as described in Item 810.		
(F6) 60735	CRUSHER PARTS, iron or steel, viz: Liner plates or lifter bars. Min wt 50,000 lbs.. Min wt 80,000 lbs..	....	916 905
(F6) 61410	ENGINES, STEAM or INTERNAL COMBUSTION, noibn, as described in Item 61410 of UFC, OR IRON AND STEEL PARTS THEREOF (See Note). Min wt 24,000 lbs.. NOTE. —Rates will not apply on Passenger or Freight Automobile Internal Combustion Engines, nor on Internal Combustion Engines which form a part of Agricultural Implements, other than hand.	....	741
61440	INDUSTRIAL NOISE or PULSATION SUPPRESSORS, DISMANTLED. Min wt 30,000 lbs (not subject to Rules 24, 29 or 34 of UFC or exceptions thereto).. Rates will not apply when a single article in the shipment weighs in in excess of 40,000 lbs, nor when special type heavy-duty flat cars provided in TL-CTRTB Tariff 740-C,I.C.C. C-812 are used to transport the shipments. Rates to or from points on the Dansville and Mt. Morris Railroad to be subject to an arbitrary of five (5) cents per 100 lbs. Rates apply on Domestic Traffic only.	....	813
(F6) 61790	GARBAGE DISPOSAL UNITS (food waste or garbage disposers), SINK, HOUSEHOLD, ELECTRIC, as described in Item 61790 of UFC. Min wt 24,000R lbs (See Note and Item 201626).................... Min wt 22,000R lbs (See Note and Item 201626).................... (15) Will NOT apply where provision is made in Item 1005. (16) Will ONLY apply as provided for in Item 1005. NOTE. —Not subject to any rules authorizing the use of more than one car.	....	(15) 261 (16) 136 968
	For explanation of other reference marks, see concluding pages of this tariff.		

Figure 10–4

Sample Page from Rail Commodity Tariff E-2009-I

SOURCE: Traffic Executive Association—Eastern Railroads. Used by permission.

special-service tariffs; these fees must be added to the relevant class, commodity, or exception rates to determine the total transportation charges for a particular move that requires such special services.

OTHER RATE TERMINOLOGY

The jargon pertaining to transportation pricing is extensive. Class, commodity, and exception rates have already been discussed. However, several other significant rate terms should be explored.

Transportation rates are sometimes discussed in terms of the manner in which the line-haul journey occurs. The term *local rate* is often applied to a rate which covers a movement that takes place entirely over the lines of one carrier. For example, if a motor carrier picks up a truckload of traffic in New York and carries it to its final destination in Los Angeles, the rate that covers this movement may be referred to as a *local rate*. In contrast, if that same shipment is interlined with another trucking company on its way to Los Angeles, the rate that applies to the shipment is often referred to as a *joint rate*. In both cases, the terms *local* and *joint* refer only to how the traffic moved. The rates are still class, commodity, or exception rates and are quoted in the appropriate tariffs.

Two other terms frequently employed in transportation pricing are the *any commodity rate* or the *freight-all-kinds rate*. Such rates ignore the commodity being shipped, and instead establish flat charges for moving certain volumes between specific points. These rates deemphasize value as a pricing consideration; they are most extensively utilized in several rail piggybacking plans.

Incentive rates are rates that encourage shippers to tender very large shipments to carriers. For example, a railroad might offer a base rate that applies to the first 50,000 pounds of a commodity loaded in a rail car and a lower rate on any additional volume loaded in the same car. *Incentive rates* encourage heavier loading of equipment, and hence lead to better utilization of that equipment.

Multiple-car and *multiple-truck* rates are quoted to cover the carrying capacity of more than one transportation vehicle. Such rates are often quoted to offset the capacity advantages enjoyed by competitive forms of carriage. An illustration of such multiple-vehicle rates would be provided by a rate offered by a railroad on the movement of 1,000 tons of coal, even though the capacity of a single hopper car is closer to 100 tons.

The term *transit privilege* has been applied to an agreement in which a carrier establishes a single rate to cover not only the line-haul movement of a commodity, but also any stops en route for such treatment as milling, fabricating, or refining. Grain movements are often handled under such agreements, which permit grain to be unloaded and milled, then reloaded as flour and moved to its ultimate destination. *Transit privileges* originated in the 1870s and have been extended to such commodities as lumber, steel, and cotton.[13]

DISTANCE, WEIGHT, AND RATE RELATIONSHIPS

As might be expected, freight rates tend to increase as the distance from origin to destination increases. However, rates are only generally related to distance.

Class rates tend to be structured on a distance basis; they typically increase with distance according to *mileage blocks* rather than with each additional mile. These rates do not increase in direct proportion to distance; rather, the increase per mileage block rises gradually as total distance increases. This is known as the *tapering principle* of freight rates. The taper is caused by a variety of factors, including the spreading of terminal costs over longer distances and the perceived lowering of line haul per unit costs as distance increases.[14] The tapering distance–rate relationship is illustrated in Figure 10–5.

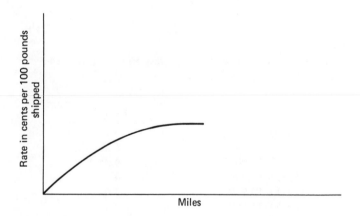

Figure 10–5

Illustration of Rate Taper with Distance

One major departure from this mileage–rate relationship is the group-rate system, which groups points of origin or destination, or both. Such systems and the related rates, which are often called *blanket rates,* take

197

two basic forms. Either all points included in the group where traffic originates are assessed the same rate for the same shipments to a specific destination, or all points in a destination group will take the same rate from a specific point of origin. *Blanket rates* tend to ignore distance, sometimes over broad geographical areas, in assessing transportation charges. In some instances such grouping of origins or destinations have been established largely for the convenience of carriers to simplify rate quotation. In other cases, the desire of shippers to be competitive in distant markets has prompted establishment of group-rate systems. One such *blanket rate* applies the same rate on lumber shipments for the Pacific Northwest to all destination points in the Northeast.[15] Another levies the same carload charges on dried fruits and vegetables from Fresno, California, to all points outside the Mountain Pacific territory except New York, which receives a lower rate.[16]

Commodity rates, which are influenced by numerous competitive factors and the desire of carriers to generate greater equipment utilization, tend to be less closely related to distance than class rates.

Freight rate levels are also influenced by shipment size. Transportation charges per unit of traffic handled tend to decline as shipment size increases. This weight–rate relationship, which encourages larger loads and better equipment utilization, is illustrated in Table 10–1, which lists a

Table 10–1

Sample Entry, Massachusetts Class Rates, Tariff 524-J (rates in cents per 100 pounds)

Pounds	Rate
0–499	$6.78
500–1,999	6.26
2,000–5,999	4.92
6,000–11,999	4.23
12,000–19,999	3.42
20,000–31,999	2.22
Minimum Weight 32,000	1.54 (TL Rate)

Courtesy: New England Motor Rate Bureau.

sample of intrastate motor carrier rates in Massachusetts according to shipment size. Such *weight breaks* lead many shippers to accumulate freight and ship in larger quantities to take advantage of the weight–rate taper.

Passenger Fares

Passenger fares tend to reflect mileage more than any other single factor. Early rail passenger fares were constructed according to a uniform mileage principle, which levied a uniform fare per mile traveled. Between 1920 and 1933 a flat fare of 3.6 cents per mile was employed by the railroads throughout most of the country.[17] However, the Depression of the 1930s led to sizable reductions in fares, and national uniformity in rail fares ended.[18] Additional charges have historically been levied for extra service, such as first-class or sleeping accommodations. Reductions have generally been given on round trips. Although Amtrak initially adopted the basic fare structure of the predecessor railroads, its attempts to increase patronage through promotional fares have led to significant departures from the early uniform mileage fares.

Intercity bus fares have tended to be considerably less uniform throughout the country, reflecting the highly competitive environment caused by widespread automobile ownership.[19] Bus fares, however, do exhibit a distance taper, with the rate per mile declining as distance increases.[20] Bus companies have also generally offered reductions on round trips.

Air fares also exhibit a taper, with passengers on longer runs being assessed lower per mile fares than passengers in shorter-haul markets. The widespread adoption of promotional fares, however, has tended to offset at least partially the strong mileage–fare relationship in the industry.

SUMMARY

The rate quotation process in transportation is quite complex. To partially cope with this complexity, carriers developed freight classification systems, which quote rates on a limited number of classes which contain many products that have been grouped according to their transportation characteristics. Because of their importance in carrier pricing, a basic understanding of such systems is important to employees of carriers and shippers alike.

Although such classification systems are still utilized, their relative significance has decreased as competitive considerations have led many carriers to initiate commodity rates on specific movements. The bulk of intercity rail, motor, and common carrier water traffic now moves under commodity rather than class rates.

Freight rates do not increase in direct proportion to distance, but rather increase gradually as distance increases. This is known as the *tapering principle* of freight rates. Passenger fares also demonstrate a similar distance

199

taper. Freight rates also tend to decline per unit of weight as shipment size increases, due to carrier price adjustments aimed at generating larger shipments.

NOTES

1. Information presented at the Yellow Freight Company's Educators Industry Program, Shawnee Mission, Kan., June, 1975.
2. D. Philip Locklin, *Economics of Transportation*, 7th ed. (Homewood, Ill.: Richard D. Irwin, Inc., 1972), p. 174.
3. Ibid., p. 175.
4. However, as discussed later in this chapter, exceptions may be filed to modify this rating.
5. Charles A. Taff, *Commercial Motor Transportation*, 4th ed. (Homewood, Ill.: Richard D. Irwin, Inc., 1969), p. 310.
6. Ibid.
7. *Motor Carrier Rates in New England*, 47 MCC 660, 661 (1948).
8. Roy J. Sampson and Martin T. Farris, *Domestic Transportation: Practice, Theory, and Policy*, 3rd ed. (Boston: Houghton Mifflin Company, 1975), p. 176.
9. Paul T. McElhiney, *Transportation for Marketing and Business Students* (Totowa, N.J.: Littlefield, Adams & Company, 1975), p. 166.
10. Locklin, op. cit., p. 178.
11. Dudley F. Pegrum, *Transportation: Economics and Public Policy*, 3rd ed. (Homewood, Ill.: Richard D. Irwin, Inc., 1973), p. 222.
12. Ibid., p. 227.
13. Marvin L. Fair and Ernest W. Williams, *Economics of Transportation and Logistics* (Dallas, Tex.: Business Publications, Inc., 1975), p. 81.
14. Sampson and Farris, op. cit., pp. 201–202.
15. Stuart Daggett and J. P. Carter, *Structure of Railroad Rates* (Berkeley, Calif.: University of California Press, 1947), as cited in Pegrum, op. cit., p. 225.
16. Sampson and Farris, op. cit., p. 211.
17. Locklin, op. cit., p. 209.
18. Ibid.
19. Pegrum, op. cit., p. 219.
20. Ibid.

SELECTED REFERENCES

Bowersox, Donald J., Edward W. Smykay, and Bernard J. Lalonde. *Physical Distribution Management: Logistics Problems of the Firm*, rev. ed. New York: Macmillan Publishing Co. Inc., 1968.
Chapter 7. "Transportation Costing," pp. 164–93.

Fair, Marvin L., and Ernest W. Williams. *Economics of Transportation and Logistics*. Dallas, Tex.: Business Publications, Inc., 1975.
Chapter 17. "Rate Making in Practice," pp. 308–41.

McElhiney, Paul T. *Transportation for Marketing and Business Students*. Totowa, N.J.: Littlefield, Adams & Company, 1975.
Chapter 10. "Freight Rates and Tariffs," pp. 163–91.

Norton, Hugh S. *Modern Transportation Economics,* 2nd ed. Columbus, Ohio: Charles E. Merrill Publishing Company, 1971.
Chapter 8. "Transportation Rates and the Pricing Process," pp. 151–64.

Pegrum, Dudley F. *Transportation: Economics and Public Policy,* 3rd ed. Homewood, Ill.: Richard D. Irwin, Inc., 1973.
Chapter 10. "Rate Making in Practice," pp. 308–41.

Sampson, Roy J., and Martin T. Farris. *Domestic Transportation: Practice, Theory, and Policy*. Boston: Houghton Mifflin Company, 1975.
Chapter 11. "Freight Classification and Tariffs: Their Preparation and Use," pp. 172–87.
Chapter 12. "Freight-Rate Structures," pp. 198–216.

Taff, Charles A. *Commercial Motor Transportation*, 4th ed. Homewood, Ill.: Richard D. Irwin, Inc., 1969.
Chapter 14. "Motor Freight Classification," pp. 309–26.

DISCUSSION QUESTIONS

1. Assume that you intend to ship 30,000 pounds of automatic mine doors with frames and fixtures (in packages) between Springfield, Massachusetts, and Decatur, Illinois. Based on the information provided in this chapter, determine the class rating, rate base number, and the rate in cents per hundred pounds that would apply to this shipment.

2. In a rate context, what is the break-even point on the shipment discussed in question 1?

3. What is the reason for the distance taper in the freight rate structure?

4. Discuss the steps involved in determining if there is a commodity rate which applies to a shipment that you are planning to make.

Transportation Regulation and Promotion

11

Theory and Development of Early Transportation Regulation

The transportation system of the United States operates in a highly regulated environment. The regulatory structure seeks not only to protect the shipping public from potential carrier abuses, but also attempts to facilitate the development of an efficient and economic transportation network that adequately serves national needs.

Understanding of the regulatory structure is important, because that structure determines the guidelines by which shipper, carrier, and governmental interaction occurs. To promote such understanding, this chapter traces the development of the common carrier concept and reviews the nature of regulation through 1920. Throughout the chapter, attention is given to the forces that led to regulation and the impact that regulation has had on the national transportation system.

HISTORICAL DEVELOPMENT OF THE COMMON CARRIER CONCEPT

Since the Middle Ages, transportation has been subjected to various regulatory controls. Such regulations have their roots in early English law, which considered those engaged in the provision of transportation services to the general public to be fulfilling a *common calling*. As a result, *common carriers* were required to serve all customers at reasonable rates and without discrimination. Carriers were also held liable for the safe delivery of goods tendered to them.

The nature and degree of early regulation were influenced by public dependency upon such service and the potential abuses inherent in the carrier–shipper relationship, particularly if the carrier operated as a market monopolist. As a result of this dependency relationship, common carriers were held to be "affected with the public interest."

State Control of Early Railroads

A philosophy of transportation regulation had evolved throughout the years, but such regulation was not applied to any great extent in the United States until the late nineteenth century. Until that time, the major public concern was expansion of transportation capabilities for developmental and defense needs. This generally led to encouragement rather than restraint of carriers. Although many early canal and railroad companies were subject to varying degrees of regulation through state charters, these regulations often were not strictly enforced, and the atmosphere remained basically supportive. Essentially, a laissez-faire attitude prevailed as the economy developed.

In the pre-Civil War period, competition among railroads, canals, riverboats, and wagons precluded the need for extensive regulation. This was to change, however, with the growing maturity of the railroad industry.

Although the bulk of the capital that financed the development of the railroads came from the private sector, state and local governments used tax concessions, loans, security guarantees, and land grants to entice the railroads to lay new track. Similarly, massive federal land grants equal to 6.8 percent of the total land area of the United States were extended to a number of railroads to facilitate a transcontinental linkage, which was ultimately completed in 1869.[1]

These financial inducements not only led to tremendous expansion of the rail network, but also provided an opportunity for financial mismanagement. Many early railroad promoters amassed sizable fortunes by swindling investors in railroad securities. Attempts were made to conceal earnings, worthless stock was issued, and fraudulent bankruptcies were filed. The behavior of the *robber barons,* who manipulated the railroad industry during that period, played a major role in turning public attitude against the railroads. Such abuses led to calls for railroad regulation.

Following the Civil War, competition in the rail industry grew in intensity. Extensive overbuilding had occurred over many routes, and excess capacity led to price wars between railroads. Price competition was extremely intense between New York and Chicago, Chicago and the West Coast, and in the South.[2]

While prices over competitive routes were depressed, rates to less densely populated areas, which were typically served by a single carrier, rose dramatically. To alleviate the cutthroat nature of competition and to stabilize prices, the railroads established traffic *pools,* which apportioned the traffic of a given route among the carriers. However, the desire of individual carriers to generate additional traffic led to rampant rebates and other collusive agreements between carriers and shippers. The net result of such behavior was the failure of most traffic pool agreements. Discriminatory pricing practices were quite common as large shippers commanded lower rates than their competitors. The railroads, due to overcapacity, were in a poor bargaining position to deal with industrial giants.

The Grange Movement

While the railroads attempted to cope with excess capacity and cutthroat competition, the agricultural sector also faced critical problems. New lands had been opened, and improved technology led to tremendous expansion of agricultural productivity. However, domestic demand declined following the Civil War, as did foreign demand for grain. As a result, farm prices plummeted while inflation increased farm costs. Furthermore, agrarians had invested heavily in the railroads, and they now found many railroad securities to be worthless. Additionally, rail service was poor, rates were high, and discrimination was widespread. In an effort to resolve their common problems (only some of which were railroad related), farmers in the Midwest relied upon a rural group known as the Grange. This organization was founded in 1867 primarily as an educational and social organization for farmers, but it soon became a vehicle for protest and political action against the railroads.[3] The Grange movement was particularly strong in Illinois, Iowa, Minnesota, and Wisconsin. Between 1871 and 1874 the legislatures of these states enacted *Granger laws,* which regulated various railroad activities.

Granger Laws

Although there were variations from state to state, the laws were generally quite similar in content. Each established maximum-rate controls. In Wisconsin and Iowa the state legislatures were empowered to prescribe maximum railroad rates; similar powers were conferred on railroad commissions that were established in Illinois and Minnesota. *Pro rata clauses,* which stipulated that rates could not be higher for shorter than longer hauls, were enacted to prohibit local discrimination. These guidelines were applied to any distance, regardless of the direction of traffic movement, and they did not distinguish between branch and main lines. Railroad consolidations were viewed as being anticompetitive in nature, and were generally forbidden by the Granger laws, as were free passes to public officials.

Granger Cases

The railroads argued that they could not effectively function in such a regulated environment, and they sought to have the state laws overturned. The carriers contended that as private businesses they could not be subjected to rate regulation. They claimed that such regulation ran counter to the Fourteenth Amendment of the Constitution, which provides that a state cannot deprive one of his property without due process of the law. Furthermore, the carriers argued that, even if they were subject to regulation, they were interstate in nature and thus only subject to federal control.

These contentions led to a series of six *Granger cases* before the Supreme Court. The most important of the cases was *Munn* v. *Illinois* (1887), which pertained to the ability of the state of Illinois to regulate grain elevator rates in Chicago.[4] In its decision, the Supreme Court ruled that grain elevators were part of the transportation process and were thus subject to the Illinois laws. More importantly, the Court ruled that the state had the right to regulate an industry "affected with the public interest," and that certain activities had fallen into that category under common law for centuries. Transportation was one such activity. This Supreme Court ruling became the basic foundation upon which transportation regulation has been structured in this country.

Two other court findings in *Munn* v. *Illinois* were quite important. First, the Court ruled that the decisions of regulatory agencies were final, and that once the right to regulate had been established the role of the courts had been exhausted. However, a short time later this ruling was reversed by the Court, and the right of judicial review was established. Second, the Court ruled that until federal legislation was enacted to regulate interstate commerce, states could regulate such activities even though state action would indirectly affect interstate commerce. This ruling was subsequently reversed by the Court in the landmark Wabash case (1886), which played a major role in establishing federal regulation of transportation.[5] The specifics of the Wabash case are discussed later in this chapter.

Experience Under the Granger Laws

Despite the judicial support accorded to the Granger laws, the success of these statutes in regulating the railroads was limited. Commissions often proved incompetent, and discrimination among various shipping points and among shippers continued.[6] Some railroads worsened the situation by taking full advantage of the maximum-rate schedules prescribed for them.[7]

208

Railroad arguments against the Granger laws were reinforced by the Panic of 1873 (a short, severe depression), which caused a number of railroad bankruptcies and led to financial problems for many other carriers. The combination of these factors led the Granger states, with the exception of Illinois, to repeal or significantly modify the Granger laws by the late 1870s.

However, the Granger laws were important in several respects. They initiated the idea of the regulatory agency, and they clearly demonstrated the ineffectiveness of highly inflexible laws. More importantly, the Granger cases established the right of the state to formulate controls over businesses that were "affected with the public interest."

MOVEMENT TOWARD FEDERAL REGULATION

While the Granger laws were creating a transportation regulatory structure at the state level, Congress was also giving increasing attention to the railroads. Monopolistic abuses were being widely publicized, and representatives of agricultural states were joined by groups representing various shipper and merchant interests in calling for federal control of the railroads. Due to the failure of the rail industry's pooling efforts to stabilize prices and earnings, the executives of many railroads also publicly supported federal regulation.[8]

In 1872 the Senate responded to a request from President Grant to investigate the railroads by creating the Windom Committee. Specifically, the committee was to study the possibility of lowering rail rates from the Midwest to the East. In its report to the Senate in 1874, the committee charged that the defects and abuses of the railroads included "insufficient facilities, unfair discriminations, and exorbitant charges."[9] The report contended that, although competition was the best regulator of rates, railroad consolidations often precluded such competition. As a result, the report concluded that effective rail competition could only be achieved through federal construction and operation of railroad lines to compete with privately owned lines. It was recommended that one or more federally owned lines be constructed and that further development of the inland waterway system be undertaken.

Congress did not act upon these recommendations. However, pressures for federal regulation of the railroads continued to mount, and the House passed bills that provided for such regulation in 1874, 1878, and 1884. However, similar action had not yet been taken in the Senate. Finally, in 1885, the Senate passed its first railroad regulation measure, but it differed significantly from its House counterpart and a deadlock resulted. The Senate then appointed another special committee, the Collum Committee, to readdress the railroad issue. In its 1886 report the committee focused on a variety of railroad abuses, and was particularly concerned about discrimination and rebates to large industrial shippers.[10] Instead of advocating federal–private competition, as the Windom Committee had done, the Collum Committee called for federal regulation of the railroads.

Also in 1886 a Supreme Court decision in the Wabash case made it apparent that effective railroad regulation would necessitate federal intervention.[11] In that case, which pertained to interstate rates charged by the Wabash, St. Louis & Pacific Railroad, the Court held that states could not regulate an interstate business regardless of the inactivity of the federal government. This decision, which reversed the Supreme Court ruling on this matter in the *Munn* v. *Illinois* case, applied to nearly three fourths of the nation's rail traffic, which was interstate in nature. Thus such operations were beyond state control. Congress responded to this ruling and the recommendations of the Collum Committee by passing the Act to Regulate Commerce, which was signed into law by President Cleveland on February 4, 1887.

INTERSTATE COMMERCE ACT

The Interstate Commerce Act, which still serves as the cornerstone for transportation regulation in the United States, became effective on April 5, 1887. Its provisions were applicable to all common carriers by railroad engaged in interstate and foreign commerce. The act did not apply to common carriers wholly by water, but did include common carriers partly by water and partly by rail when they were under common control or arrangement for continuous carriage or shipment.

Much of the substance of the act was directed at the prevention of monopoly abuses and the control of discriminatory practices. The desire of Congress to protect the shipping public from such treatment is apparent in the major sections of the act.

Reasonableness of Rates

Section 1 of the act required that all rates be just and reasonable, and stipulated that all unjust and unreasonable rates were unlawful. This marked the statutory enactment of a long-standing common law rule, which had often been applied to businesses "affected with the public interest." This section applied to both freight and passenger operations. Congress chose not to define the nature of a reasonable or just charge, and in effect entrusted the interpretation of these terms to the ICC (which the act also created) and the federal courts. The resulting vagueness of this section was later to cause continuing difficulties for the ICC.

Personal Discrimination

Section 2 prohibited personal discrimination by making it unlawful for a carrier, by any device (including rebates), to charge one person more than another for like or contemporaneous service under substantially similar circumstances and conditions. Later sections of the act did permit exceptions pertaining to transportation for federal, state, and municipal governments or for charitable purposes, and railroads were permitted to grant free passes to their employees.

By forbidding rebates, Section 2 effectively sought to stabilize carrier prices while simultaneously protecting shippers from monopolistic abuses.

Undue Preference or Prejudice

Section 3 constituted a blanket prohibition of undue or unreasonable preference or advantage of any form to any person, place, or kind of traffic. It should be noted that the section did not prohibit preferential or differential treatment, but only limited them to what might be considered just and reasonable. Once again, the directive was vague and subject to commission interpretation.

Long- and Short-Haul Clause

Section 4 of the act prohibited carriers from charging or receiving any greater compensation from transportation of passengers or property under substantially similar circumstances and conditions, for a shorter than for a longer distance over the same line, in the same direction, the shorter being included in the longer distance. This provision was far less restrictive than the *pro rata clauses* of the Granger laws, and the commission was given authority to grant exceptions to this prohibition "in special cases."

Pooling

Under the provisions of Section 5 of the act, it was unlawful for common carriers to enter into any contract, agreement, or combination for the pooling of their freight or for the division of the aggregate or net proceeds of their earnings. This reflected the prevailing view of Congress that enforced competition was the best regulator of rail rates. Inclusion of Section 5 was opposed by railroad spokesmen who believed that such agreements were necessary to prevent ruinous competition.[12] The first chairman of the ICC shared the railroad view on this matter.[13]

Publication of Rates

Section 6 stated that all rates and fares were to be published, made available for public inspection, and filed with the ICC. Railroads could no longer maintain secret rates and offer concessions to preferential customers to generate additional business. The public was to be given 10-day notice before prices were raised. In 1889 an amendment to the act provided that 3-day notice had to be given prior to rate reductions so as to protect shippers from rapid rate reductions. Such reduction might be discriminatory if some shippers were advised of the change in advance while others were not.

Creation of the Interstate Commerce Commission

The act also created the Interstate Commerce Commission to administer the new laws. The ICC was to consist of five members, each serving a six-year term. Members were to be appointed by the president, with the advice and consent of the Senate. Later the ICC was expanded to 11 members, and the terms were extended to seven years. There was, and is, no limitation on reappointment.

The act further specified that the ICC was to be bipartisan, and that no commissioner could engage in any other business, vocation, or employment while holding office. Commissioners could be removed by the president due to their inefficiency, neglect of duty, or malfeasance in office. By amendment in 1889, the ICC was ordered to report directly to Congress, thereby assuring the agency an independent status.

In administering the act, the ICC was given the power to order carriers to prepare annual reports and to prescribe a uniform system of accounts to be employed in these reports. The ICC could also conduct investigations into carrier affairs based on complaints or its own motion. Following such an investigation, the ICC could issue cease and desist orders. It was also empowered to determine awards of damages caused by carrier violations. However, there was no penalty for failure to obey an ICC order; if a carrier failed to comply with a directive, the ICC had to appeal to a federal court for enforcement.

Carriers were made liable for damages sustained by any party due to violations of the act. Nevertheless, only the courts could force payment of such damages.

EARLY EXPERIENCE WITH THE ACT

Initially, the railroads generally complied with ICC orders, and little controversy arose. However, imperfections in the act soon appeared, and the ICC began to encounter opposition to its orders.

It is important to remember that the ICC had to rely upon the courts for enforcement of its orders. Carriers were not required to obey the orders of the ICC during the period of court review, and no preference was given to ICC cases in terms of expediting their hearing in federal courts. As a result, it was not unusual for several years to elapse between the initial ICC cease and desist order and the final court ruling on the case.

In its early years the commission also encountered difficulties in getting witnesses to testify in ICC proceedings. In fact, in 1892 the Supreme Court held that witnesses could refuse to give testimony before the ICC that might be self-incriminating under the Fifth Amendment of the Constitution.[14] However, this issue was resolved the following year when Congress passed the Compulsory Testimony Act, which gave witnesses immunity with respect to their testimony.

The most severe blows to ICC authority were Supreme Court rulings in 1896 and 1897 which made it clear that the ICC did not have the power to prescribe either actual or maximum rates.[15] Prior to these rulings the ICC had often prescribed maximum rates upon finding carrier rates to be unreasonable. As a result of these decisions, even if the courts upheld an ICC ruling on the reasonableness of rates, a minor modification by the carrier could start the entire time-consuming process anew. Commission authority in rate cases was further eroded when the Supreme Court found that all differences in competitive conditions at end points and intermediate points on a given route could justify long- and short-haul clause departures.[16] Consequently, the prohibition against local discrimination was effectively invalidated, because it could generally be shown that such differences did exist.

An excellent summary of the impact of these Court decisions on the ICC is provided by Justice Harlan's dissent in the Alabama Midland case:

Taken in connection with other decisions defining the powers of the Interstate Commerce Commission, the present decision . . . goes far to make that commission a useless body, for all practical purposes, and to defeat many of the important objects designated to be accomplished by the various enactments of Congress relating to interstate commerce. The commission was established to protect the public against the improper practices of transportation companies engaged in commerce among the several states. It has been left, it is true, with power to make reports and to issue protests. But it has been shorn, by judicial interpretation, of authority to do

213

anything of an effective character. It is denied many of the powers which, in my judgment, were intended to be conferred upon it.[17]

Despite its legal setbacks, the Interstate Commerce Act did achieve some measure of success in its early years. Rates were now being published, and the more blatant forms of discrimination had been eliminated. However, it was apparent that, if the ICC was to play an important role in regulating the railroads, additional congressional action would be necessary.

REVITALIZATION OF THE INTERSTATE COMMERCE COMMISSION

Congress responded to the plight of the ICC and to growing national sentiment for stronger federal control of business in general by enacting several important pieces of transportation legislation between 1903 and 1910. The major provisions of these statutes are reviewed in the following discussion.

To partially reduce the time lag involved in processing of ICC cases in the federal court system, the Expediting Act of 1903 gave ICC cases priority over other cases when the attorney general certified that the case was of public importance. In the same year, the Elkins Act sought to reduce personal discrimination, which had become widespread with the ineffectiveness of the Interstate Commerce Act. The Elkins Act, which was originally written by the legal staff of the Pennsylvania Railroad, declared every departure from a published tariff to be a misdemeanor. Such departures were to be considered prima facie evidence of discrimination. The ICC was empowered to levy fines on both the giver and receiver of rebates. Furthermore, while the act eliminated imprisonment for rebating, it increased the maximum fine for such offenses to $20,000, thereby reducing the incentive of large shippers to press railroads for rebates.

Further shipper agitation for tighter railroad regulation led to passage of the Hepburn Act of 1906. Commission jurisdiction was expanded to include regulation of express companies, sleeping car companies, and oil pipelines, thus establishing ICC controls beyond the railroad industry. Commission authority in rate cases was significantly improved in that the ICC was given the power to prescribe maximum rates once the agency had determined that a rate was unjust and unreasonable. The railroads did not oppose this action, as they likely saw it as a means of promoting further rate stability. The act did not, however, give the ICC the ability to prescribe either actual or minimum rates. Also with respect to rates, the ICC was given the power to establish through routes when carriers refused to do so, and it could prescribe the maximum joint rates and carrier divisions in such instances. To allow more time for shippers, carriers, and the ICC to respond to rate proposals, the act required carriers to give 30-day notice on all rate changes.

Another provision of the Hepburn Act, which is often referred to as the *commodities clause,* made it illegal for railroads to haul goods that they produced, with the exception of lumber and goods produced for their own consumption. Prior to this act, many carriers had been actively engaged in nonrailroad enterprises. For example, a number of coal-hauling railroads also had substantial coal interests. Congress feared that either directly or indirectly the railroads could gain an unfair competitive advantage over other producers under such circumstances. The commodities clause thus led to substantial railroad divestiture of nonrailroad interests. This matter was to become topical again in the 1960s as many railroads used a loophole in the law to diversify into nonrailroad businesses. This issue and its implications to national transportation policy are discussed further in Chapter 16.

The last major legislative initiative of this period aimed at strengthening the ICC was the Mann–Elkins Act of 1910. One major provision of the statute, which had strong shipper support, permitted the ICC to suspend rate change proposals for up to 120 days while it addressed the reasonableness of the proposal. An additional six-month suspension period was permitted if the original period proved inadequate for complete review of the rate proposal. Prior to the passage of this act, the ICC could not act until the rate became effective. The Mann–Elkins Act also shifted the burden of proof in rate increase cases to the railroads, forcing them to justify their increases if their rates were challenged. The statute also revitalized the long- and short-haul clause by removing the words "under substantially similar circumstances and conditions" from Section 4 of the Interstate Commerce Act. As a result, regardless of the conditions that prevailed, carriers were forbidden to charge more for a short haul than a long haul over the same route unless they were given permission to do so by the ICC. Other significant provisions of the act gave the ICC power over railroad freight classification, and empowered shippers to designate the route over which their traffic would move.

RAIL REGULATION, 1910–1920

The statutes that strengthened the ICC led to its emergence as a formidable regulatory body. Given its expanded authority, the ICC actively sought to protect shipper interests in the years immediately preceding World War I. However, the philosophy and actions of the ICC during that period have often been classified as negative. While the agency sought to eliminate railroad abuses, it showed little concern with protection of carrier interests. Congress had long contended that enforced competition would provide adequate carrier earnings, and the ICC appeared to share this view. However, such a position ignores the basic cost structure of the industry, which initially led to regulation.

Armed with its broader authority over carrier rate making, the ICC proceeded to suspend, then deny, most railroad rate increase proposals between 1911 and the beginning of World War I.[18] At the same time, the railroads faced rapidly escalating wage and material costs due to inflation.

ICC restraint of railroad rate increases intensified the problems faced by many carriers that were overcapitalized from the earlier expansion period. Financial difficulties caused many railroads to reduce maintenance and equipment outlays, and rail service began to deteriorate. The financial plight of the railroads is illustrated by the fact that by 1916 nearly 10 percent of the industry's trackage was in receivership.[19]

World War I and Nationalization

Traffic expansion following the entrance of the United States into World War I in April 1917 placed heavy demands on the already troubled railroads. Although many railroad executives worked hard to promote effective coordination among the railroads, by the fall of 1917 it was apparent that the railroads were unable to cope with growing national demands. As a result, the railroads were taken over by proclamation of President Wilson on December 28, 1917.

Congress created a United States Railroad Administration to facilitate federal coordination. During the period of federal control, each railroad was guaranteed profits equal to the average of the three previous years.

Government efforts were primarily concerned with the rapid movement of troops and supplies, and profitability was a secondary consideration. Federal control and operation of the railroads lasted until March 1, 1920. While under federal control the national railroad system incurred a deficit of $1.5 billion, nearly $2 million per day.

While controlling the railroads, the federal government sought both to halt an inflationary spiral and to promote the movement of needed commodities by holding down rail rates.[20] This was a major cause of the rail system deficit. Despite these measures, inflation continued and railroad wages rose, thereby creating problems that were to plague the railroads following their return to the private sector. Furthermore, although during federal control the government spent more for maintenance than the railroads had during a similar prewar period, inflation led to a decline in actual maintenance work.[21] As a result, the physical plant deteriorated even further during government control.

The rigors of the war effort left many railroads in poor financial condition. Railroad revenues were barely meeting operating expenses, and labor, encouraged by active government promotion of organization efforts during the war, pressed for still higher wages. The possibility of widespread railroad bankruptcies seemed likely, and Congress hesitated to return the railroads to the private sector. Although Congress gave some attention to the concept of permanent railroad nationalization, this alternative was deemed undesirable, and the railroads were returned to the private sector in March 1920. Short-term income guarantees and loans were extended by the federal government to assist the railroads in meeting immediate requirements. However, Congress realized that fundamental problems existed in the regulatory structure, and that revitalization of the railroads would necessitate a more positive approach that gave greater attention to the financial needs of the railroads. Congress attempted to rectify the regulatory imbalance toward negative regulation with passage of the Transportation Act of 1920.

TRANSPORTATION ACT OF 1920

As Congress pondered the plight of the railroads in extensive hearings during 1919 and 1920, it became obvious that, although regulation of the railroads was far from complete, the existing regulation did not appear to be working particularly well. The ICC had not yet been given authority over such important railroad matters as the issuance of securities, minimum rates, abandonments or line extensions. At the same time, the dominant philosophy of enforced competition appeared to give too little attention to development of a healthy carrier environment. Consequently, the Transportation Act of 1920, which served as transitional legislation in the transfer of the railroads back to the private sector, both broadened the scope of ICC controls over the railroads and shifted the regulatory philosophy to a more positive approach. Review of the major provisions of the 1920 legislation illustrates this changing regulatory philosophy.

Control of Rates

With the passage of the Transportation Act of 1920, ICC control over railroad rates expanded greatly. The act gave the ICC authority over minimum and actual rates, strengthened its role in intrastate rate making, and clarified its approach to aggregate industry rate making.

217

Rule of Rate Making

The legislation added Section 15(a) to the Interstate Commerce Act. This provision directed the ICC, in exercising its control over rates, to endeavor to allow the railroads as a whole, or in groups, to earn a fair return on the fair value of their transportation properties. The wording of the provision had originated in an 1898 Supreme Court decision in *Smyth v. Ames,* which prescribed a general level of compensation for regulated enterprises.[22]

Designation of a fair return and fair value was left to the ICC, but for the first two years following enactment Congress specified a 5.5 percent target return (the ICC could add 0.5 percent for improvements). At the end of the two-year period, Congress raised the suggested return to 5.75 percent.

The target return was not a guarantee, but rather a goal. It was not to be applied to individual railroads, but rather to the railroads as a whole or in groups. However, due to the variance in traffic and operating conditions from carrier to carrier, a rate level that might yield a fair return to carriers as a whole might also generate inadequate revenues for some carriers while producing excess profits for others. To cope with such possible discrepancies and to strengthen particularly weak railroads, Congress incorporated a *recapture clause* in the legislation. The clause specified that any carrier which earned more than the target return in a given year would give one half of the excess to the ICC. With these funds, the commission would establish a contingency fund to make loans to weaker carriers for the purpose of capital outlays or refunding of debt. Such loans would carry a 6 percent interest rate. The other one half of excess earnings could be kept by the carrier and placed in a reserve fund for such purposes as making interest or dividend payments during periods of depressed earnings. The 1920 act also specified that, if the reserve fund reached 5 percent of the carrier's valuation, it could be used for any purpose.

Minimum Rate Control

Congressional desire to prevent ruinous rate competition and to stabilize carrier earnings was also reflected in a provision of the act that gave the ICC control over railroad minimum rates. The commission had been actively seeking such control since 1893.[23] This marked a decided reversal of earlier policies, which had fostered such rate-cutting behavior. Congress further broadened ICC rate authority by giving the commission the power to prescribe actual rates once a rate had been found to be unjust or unreasonable. Commission control over rail rates was now complete.

Intrastate Rate Control

Throughout the years, a series of federal–state confrontations concerning state control over intrastate rates had affected interstate commerce. A Supreme Court decision in the 1914 Shreveport case held that the power of a state to prescribe intrastate rates could not be exercised in such a way as to inhibit legitimate exercise of federal control over interstate commerce, but the ruling had not been given statutory status.[24] The 1920 act unquestionably gave the ICC the authority to require intrastate rates to be raised if it considered them to be too low and thus burdensome to interstate commerce.

Control over Entry and Abandonment

During its formative years the railroad industry had suffered from overexpansion and duplication of investment. The federal regulatory philosophy of enforced competition was at least partially responsible for those developments. To reduce the likelihood of imprudent expansion in the future, while also affording some degree of market protection to existing carriers, the 1920 act conferred authority over new railroad construction upon the ICC. Railroads seeking line extensions in the future would have to obtain a certificate of public convenience and necessity from the ICC before undertaking such projects. At the same time, the ICC was granted authority over rail abandonments. Prior to that time, state authorities had often required railroads to maintain unprofitable branch lines, and these lines constituted a sizable financial burden for the industry. The ICC was given final authority over abandonment applications; this power would later prove both useful and controversial in efforts to rationalize the industry.

Regulation of Rail Securities

As outlined earlier in this chapter, financial abuses were widespread in the early years of the railroad industry. However, even though the ICC had advocated federal control of railroad security issues as early as 1907, and despite the endorsement of such control by Presidents Roosevelt and Taft, Congress had not acted on this matter prior to 1920.[25] Some state control did exist, but the guidelines varied from state to state and only served to confuse an already complex matter. In recognition of this regulatory gap, and undoubtedly influenced by the impaired ability of many railroads to sell securities in the capital markets, Congress gave the ICC exclusive control over issuance of new railroad securities. It did not, however, receive control over securities that had already been issued.

Railroad Consolidations

Railroad consolidation activity had been slowed considerably after 1900 by Supreme Court interpretation of the Sherman and Clayton acts, which had established antitrust controls for U.S. industry. However, in drafting the Transportation Act of 1920, Congress sought to create an environment in which rail duplication might be reduced through consolidation of carriers. This was accomplished through inclusion of a provision in the act that permitted the ICC to withdraw any railroad consolidation from operation of the antitrust statutes. This procedure allowed the ICC to approve consolidations that might result in a lessening of competition among rail carriers. This also marked a significant shift in federal policy from enforced intramodal competition to active promotion of rail consolidations that might reduce such competition.

The act also directed the ICC to develop a consolidation plan that would combine weak and strong lines into a limited number of systems of approximately equal earning power. The plan was to preserve competition as fully as possible while maintaining existing routes and channels of trade whenever possible. All future rail consolidations were required to conform to the plan, which the ICC was to formulate. However, carrier participation in this plan was to be strictly voluntary.

Due to a variety of difficulties, no such plan was ever implemented. The specific problems encountered by the ICC in this effort and later development of consolidation policy are discussed further in Chapter 16.

Other Significant Provisions

The Transportation Act of 1920 also addressed several other major issues, including railroad service, labor relations, intercorporate relationships, and the size of the ICC.

To facilitate improvement in railroad services, the ICC was granted control over car service rules, and was given broad powers related to utilization of rail equipment in times of emergency. The ICC was also empowered to compel carriers that owned terminal facilities to share those facilities with other carriers if the ICC believed such arrangements were in the public interest. Carriers using terminal facilities of other railroads would be required to pay adequate compensation to the owners. Specifically, this provision sought to promote better use of existing facilities while preventing unnecessary duplication of expensive terminal facilities.

Several earlier congressional enactments had dealt with railroad labor relations, but none of these had produced an adequate machinery for resolving labor–management disputes. The industry had a long history of labor–management confrontations, and pressures were mounting as unions agitated for higher wages upon return to the private sector. To improve this situation, Congress created a nine-member Railroad Labor Board to intervene in such disputes. Board membership consisted of representatives of management, labor, and the general public. The act did not contain an anti-strike provision, and the decisions of the board were nonbinding.

Additionally, the Transportation Act of 1920 prohibited interlocking directorates, permitted pooling if it could be shown that such agreements were in the public interest, and expanded the ICC to 11 members to deal with the commission's increased responsibilities.

Experience with the 1920 Act

The results of the Transportation Act of 1920 were mixed. Railroad earnings improved following the enactment, and in 7 of the next 10 years the aggregate railroad rate of return exceeded 5 percent.[26] Twice it reached the ICC's 5.75 percent standard.[27] Railroad credit also rebounded with ICC control over securities, and service improved with the stabilization of carrier earnings.

Other provisions of the act were not as successful. The rule of rate making was the subject of considerable interpretational difficulty, and this led to a series of court cases. It was subsequently modified during the Depression. The master consolidation plan, despite many years of ICC effort, failed to gain industry endorsement as profitable carriers demonstrated little interest in absorbing weaker lines. The plan was ultimately abolished in 1940. The Railroad Labor Board created by the act proved ineffective, and continued labor difficulties led to abolition of the board with the passage of the Railway Labor Act of 1926. The provisions of that statute, which still govern railroad labor relations, are examined in Chapter 15, which specifically addresses labor in the transportation industries.

However, despite the failure of several major provisions of the 1920 act, it did mark a dramatic change in federal regulatory philosophy in its shift toward positive regulation. Public concern with the financial viability of the railroads was to increase in the ensuing years, which witnessed both the emergence of competitive modes of carriage and the economic chaos of the Depression.

SUMMARY

Although regulation of transportation originated in the Middle Ages, such controls were not broadly applied in this country until the late nineteenth century. Prior to that time, an attitude of laissez faire prevailed, and government was generally supportive of transportation expansion.

However, as railroads came to dominate the transportation marketplace, financial abuses and discrimination became widespread. These conditions led to the passage of the Granger laws in several Midwestern states, and eventually necessitated enactment of the Interstate Commerce Act to govern interstate transportation.

Early railroad regulation was primarily concerned with enforcing competition and preventing monopoly abuses. Little concern was given to the financial well-being of the carriers. These negative regulatory controls contributed to financial problems in the industry, which led to passage of the Transportation Act of 1920. That statute sought to create a more balanced approach to regulation that considered both the needs of the shipping public and the carriers. Although the act improved carrier earnings and credit, it did not deal with the major structural changes that were taking place in the national transportation system.

NOTES

1. John F. Stover, *American Railroads* (Chicago: University of Chicago Press, 1961), p. 88.

2. Charles F. Phillips, *The Economics of Regulation,* rev. ed. (Homewood, Ill.: Richard D. Irwin, Inc., 1969), p. 445.

3. Hugh S. Norton, *Modern Transportation Economics,* 2nd ed. (Columbus, Ohio: Charles E. Merrill Publishing Company, 1971), p. 225.

4. *Munn* v. *Illinois,* 94 U.S. 113 (1877).

5. *Wabash, St. Louis & Pacific Railway Co.* v. *Illinois,* 118 U.S. 557 (1886).

6. Phillips, op. cit., p. 447.

7. Dudley F. Pegrum, *Transportation: Economics and Public Policy,* 3rd ed. (Homewood, Ill.: Richard D. Irwin, Inc., 1973), p. 270.

8. Thomas G. Moore, *Freight Transportation Regulation: Surface Freight and the Interstate Commerce Commission* (Washington, D.C.: American Enterprise Institute for Public Policy Research, 1972), p. 5.

9. *Report of Senate Select Committee on Transportation Routes to the Seaboard,* 1873–1874, 43rd Cong., 1st Sess., Senate Report No. 307 (1874).

10. 49th Cong., 1st Sess., Senate Report no. 46 (1886).

11. 118 U.S. 557 (1886).

12. Moore, op. cit., p. 12.

13. Ibid.

14. *Counselman* v. *Hitchcock,* 142 U.S. 547 (1892).

15. *Cincinnati, New Orleans and Texas Pacific Railway Company* v. *Interstate Commerce Commission*, 162 U.S. 116 (1896); and *Interstate Commerce Commission* v. *Cincinnati, New Orleans and Texas Pacific Railway Company*, 167 U.S. 479 (1897).

16. *Interstate Commerce Commission* v. *Alabama Midland Railway Company*, 168 U.S. 144 (1897).

17. *Interstate Commerce Commission* v. *Alabama Midland Railway Company*, dissenting opinion, p. 176.

18. Marvin L. Fair and Ernest W. Williams, *Economics of Transportation and Logistics* (Dallas, Tex.: Business Publications, Inc., 1975), p. 388.

19. Moore, op. cit., p. 18.

20. Walter W. Splawn, *Government Ownership and Operation of Railroads* (New York: Macmillan Publishing Co., Inc., 1928), pp. 375–382.

21. Ibid., p. 381.

22. *Smyth* v. *Ames*, 169 U.S. 466 (1898).

23. Moore, op. cit., p. 22.

24. 234 U.S. 342 (1914).

25. D. Philip Locklin, *Economics of Transportation*, 7th ed. (Homewood, Ill.: Richard D. Irwin, Inc., 1972), p. 241.

26. Phillips, op. cit., p. 454.

27. Ibid.

SELECTED REFERENCES

Fair, Marvin L., and John Guandola. *Transportation Regulation,* 7th ed. Dubuque, Iowa: William C. Brown Company, 1972.
Chapter 1. "Bases of Regulation," pp. 1–23.

Fair, Marvin L., and Ernest W. Williams. *Economics of Transportation and Logistics.* Dallas, Tex.: Business Publications, Inc., 1975.
Chapter 20. "Regulation of Transportation: Origin and Scope," pp. 337–404.

Fogel, Robert W. *Railways and American Economic Growth: Essays in Econometric History.* Baltimore, Md.: Johns Hopkins Press, 1964.

Friedlaender, Ann F. *The Dilemma of Freight Transport Regulation.* Washington, D.C.: Brookings Institution, 1969.
Chapter 2. "The Rationale of Regulation," pp. 7–27.

Grodinsky, J. *The Iowa Pool: A Study in Railroad Competition, 1870–1884.* Chicago: University of Chicago Press, 1950.

Kahn, Alfred E. *The Economics of Regulation: Principles and Institutions,* vol. I. New York: John Wiley & Sons, Inc., 1970.

Theory and Development of Early Transportation Regulation

Chapter 1. "Introduction: The Rationale of Regulation and the Proper Role of Economics," pp. 1–19.

Kolko, Gabriel. *Railroads and Regulation, 1887–1916*. Princeton, N.J.: Princeton University Press, 1965.

Lansing, John B. *Transportation and Economic Policy*. New York: Free Press, 1966.
Chapter 7. "Transportation in the Economic Development of the United States in the Nineteenth Century," pp. 91–111.

Locklin, D. Philip. *Economics of Transportation*, 7th ed. Homewood, Ill.: Richard D. Irwin, Inc., 1972.
Chapter 9. "Beginning of Railroad Regulation," pp. 211–21.
Chapter 10. "Federal Legislation, 1887–1920," pp. 222–39.
Chapter 11. "The Transportation Act of 1920," pp. 240–54.

MacAvoy, Paul W. *The Economic Effects of Regulation: The Trunk Line Railroad Cartels and the Interstate Commerce Before 1900*. Cambridge, Mass.: The MIT Press, 1965.

Norton, Hugh S. *Modern Transportation Economics*, 2nd ed. Columbus, Ohio: Charles E. Merrill Publishing Company, 1971.
Chapter 11. "Development of Regulation, 1887–1920," pp. 221–33.

Pegrum, Dudley F. *Transportation: Economics and Public Policy*, 3rd ed. Homewood, Ill.: Richard D. Irwin, Inc., 1973.
Chapter 12. "The Fundamentals of Transport Regulation," pp. 268–89.
Chapter 13. "Railroad Regulation Since World War I," pp. 290–309.

Phillips, Charles F. *The Economics of Regulation*, rev. ed. Homewood, Ill.: Richard D. Irwin, Inc., 1969.
Chapter 13. "Regulation of the Transportation Industries," pp. 441–82.

Sampson, Roy J., and Martin T. Farris. *Domestic Transportation: Practice, Theory, and Policy*, 3rd ed. Boston: Houghton Mifflin Company, 1975.
Chapter 20. "The Regulation of Transportation Monopoly," pp. 315–36.

Splawn, Walter W. *Government Ownership and Operation of Railroads*. New York: Macmillan Publishing Co., Inc., 1928.

DISCUSSION QUESTIONS

1. What were the reasons for the enactment of the Interstate Commerce Act in 1887?
2. Why was the ICC relatively ineffective during its early years?
3. What were the reasons for the failure of the early railroad traffic *pools?*
4. Compare and contrast federal regulation of the railroads prior to and following the passage of the Transportation Act of 1920.

224

CHAPTER

12

Intermodal Competition and the Expansion of Federal Regulation

Conditions changed rapidly in the transportation marketplace during the 1920s. Government spending increased and technological changes led to a new era of intermodal competition. However, the Depression rocked the basic foundation of the transportation industries, and the related financial difficulties of many carriers led to calls for expanded federal regulatory controls in transportation. Ultimately, federal controls were extended to motor and air carriage during the 1930s and to water carriage and freight forwarding during the early 1940s.

This chapter focuses on the emergence of intermodal competition during that period. It examines the factors that led to each of the regulatory statutes, and traces the development and nature of the resulting regulatory structure through the early 1940s.

THE 1920s AND THE DEPRESSION

Railroad earnings improved during the 1920s, but not all railroads shared the prosperity. Economic fluctuations were frequent and sharp, and they were particularly burdensome on some railroad systems. Other sectors of the economy were also troubled during the decade. In particular, the agricultural sector continued to be plagued with overproduction and price softness.

Intermodal Competition and the Expansion of Federal Regulation

Hoch–Smith Resolution

In response to the problems of agriculture, Congress passed the Hoch–Smith Resolution in 1925.[1] The directive called upon the ICC to consider the conditions that prevailed in various industries that originated freight when determining minimum rates. Furthermore, the ICC was directed to establish the lowest possible lawful rates for products of agriculture, including livestock, in view of the problems of that economic sector.

The 1925 resolution was important in two respects. By passing the resolution, Congress effectively gave its approval to the long-standing railroad policy of value-of-service pricing. As discussed in Chapter 9, that policy bases prices on the relative price elasticities of various commodities. It generally leads to higher transportation prices on manufactured items and other items of relatively high market value, while assessing lower prices on items with lower market values. Some argue that value-of-service pricing promotes an indirect cross subsidy from shippers of high-value items to other shippers. However, it might also be contended that, if the rates on low-value items failed to reflect their price elasticities, the items might either shift modes or fail to move. This would increase the overhead burden of the high-value goods that continue to move, and could lead to higher rather than lower transportation prices for such goods.[2]

Value-of-service pricing has continued to be a major source of controversy in transportation. Recent legislation has sought to promote greater reliance upon cost as a price determinant.[3] This issue is discussed again later in this chapter.

The second element of significance in congressional enactment of the Hoch–Smith Resolution was its impact on the rates assessed to nonagricultural traffic. The artificially depressed agricultural rates had to be offset elsewhere in the railroad pricing structure by higher than normal rates on other items if the pricing structure was to be viable. The railroads believed that this strategy was sound. However, the pricing policies of truckers during the late 1920s and early 1930s, which sought to attract high-rated goods, left the railroads primarily with low-rated bulk commodities and serious financial problems.

Intermodal Competition and the Depression

The 1920s were marked by increasing federal government promotion of other forms of intercity carriage. Expenditures accelerated in highway building, waterway development, and expansion of the airway system. At the same time, the bulk of airline revenues was being provided by federal airmail contracts. This expanded federal support, coupled with growing

226

state outlays, was to play a major role in the emergence of a truly competitive intermodal transportation network in the 1930s.

With the onset of the Depression, the financial condition of the railroad industry, which was already precarious, deteriorated rapidly. Gross operating revenues fell from $6.3 billion in 1929 to $3.1 billion in 1933; railroad employment contracted from 1.66 million to 952,000 during the same period.[4] The industry's rate of return on net investment, which had declined steadily from 5.3 percent in 1929, plummeted to 1.4 percent by 1933.[5] Industry cost-cutting programs and freight rate increases failed to increase industry profitability; by 1933, seventy-five class I railroads were in the hands of receivers.[6] Numerous other railroad bankruptcies were averted by loans to railroads through the Reconstruction Finance Corporation. However, loans were not the long-run solution to the problems of the railroads. Congress sought to provide the solution by amending the Bankruptcy Act and passing the Emergency Transportation Act of 1933.

1933 Rail Legislation

Because of public dependency upon continued railroad service, the federal government could not simply allow the Depression to liquidate a major component of the railroad industry. Instead, individual railroad reorganizations were governed by the rather cumbersome procedures of the Bankruptcy Act of 1898. Under the provisions of that statute, railroad reorganizations often involved several courts, and all creditors had to agree to the reorganization. To simplify and accelerate railroad reorganizations, Congress amended the Bankruptcy Act in 1933 by giving only one court jurisdiction over such proceedings. Also, the ICC was empowered to approve reorganization plans and court-appointed trustees. The amendments further stipulated that only two thirds of any creditor class had to agree to the reorganization. These provisions considerably shortened the reorganization process, and simplified the process of revitalizing individual railroads.

Emergency Transportation Act of 1933

The Emergency Transportation Act of 1933 had several significant components. First, it created a temporary Office of the Federal Coordinator of Transportation. The coordinator, who was appointed by the president, was to plan national railroad improvements, aid the railroads in reorganization attempts, and attempt to reduce unnecessary railroad duplication. These goals were to be achieved through voluntary cooperation. However, union lobbying efforts led Congress to include job protection provisions in the act, and it was difficult to promote major efficiencies without layoffs.[7]

Further complicating the coordinator's task was the failure of railroad management to agree on project priorities. Consequently, the success of the coordinator in realizing these goals was limited, and the office was abolished in 1936. However, several studies released by the office were useful in legislative efforts.

The 1933 act also repealed the *recapture clause*. During the life of the program, little money was actually paid to the ICC by the railroads. However, to promote financial relief, the 1933 legislation returned those funds that had been transferred, and abolished any outstanding railroad obligations under the program.

Probably the most significant provision of the Emergency Transportation Act of 1933 was its modification of the rule of rate making. Given the economic pressures of the period and Supreme Court refusal to accept ICC attempts to establish an acceptable fair value for the industry, the 1920 rule of rate making did not generate the returns envisioned by Congress.[8] Furthermore, it had been enacted in a railroad-dominated environment, which no longer prevailed in the early 1930s. The competitive behavior of other modes of intercity carriage was having a very dramatic impact on railroad earnings, and the ICC as yet had no control over such modes.

The amended rule of rate making directed the ICC, in prescribing just and reasonable rates, to consider among other factors

> the effect of rates on the movement of traffic; to the need, in the public interest, of adequate and efficient railway transportation service at the lowest cost consistent with furnishing of such service; and to the need of revenues sufficient to enable the carriers . . . to provide such service.

Although the ICC was no longer required to establish a fixed return for the railroads, it was nevertheless required to consider numerous factors in rate cases. In attempting to stabilize railroad finances, the ICC was to reject railroad rate applications if it thought the proposed rates would divert traffic to other modes. Interpretation of this rule led to a long series of railroad–ICC disputes, and the rule was later amended in 1940 and again in 1958.

REGULATION OF MOTOR CARRIAGE

During the 1920s, truck and bus operations emerged as strong competitors for previously captive railroad business. Capital requirements were limited and the number of motor carrier operations expanded rapidly. Most operations were of small scale, but the sizable profits generated soon led to the emergence of the first large motor carriers. The profit potential attracted numerous operators into motor carriage. Competition was vigorous, but so was economic activity.

Development of State Regulation

As the number of motor vehicles increased and as more truck and bus companies established for-hire operations, there was an increasing outcry for some form of government regulation. Proponents advocated regulation of motor carriage for such diverse reasons as governance of highway use, protection of shippers and passengers from carrier irresponsibility, and protection of the railroads from the inroads of new competitors.

Initial regulation of motor carriage occurred at the state level. Early state regulations were primarily directed at promotion of safety and control of the use of state highways. Individual states established regulatory standards that governed such factors as vehicle speeds, weights, lengths, braking and lighting systems, and driver qualifications. Later many states enacted regulations that also governed the economic aspects of the industry. Typically, the economic controls provided a state certification process for common carriers, which required a demonstration that the applicant was fit, willing, and able to provide the service and that the service was consistent with the public interest. Rates were also generally regulated, and carriers were required to publish prevailing rates. By 1932, transportation of passengers by motor vehicle was regulated by all states except Delaware, and 39 states had established regulatory controls related to motor carriers of property.[9]

The evolution of state regulation of motor carriage was not without controversy. One major conflict involved the tendency of states to regulate all motor carriers as common carriers. Early railroad experience had established the right of government to regulate common carriers, but it was unclear if all motor carriers could be compelled to act as common carriers. Contract carriage had emerged, and in 1923 the Michigan legislature passed a statute which stipulated that any person engaged in the for-hire transportation of goods over public highways was a common carrier. Two years later, the law was declared unconstitutional by the Supreme Court, which ruled that a state could not transform a contract carrier into a common carrier simply by passing a law.[10] After several similar state efforts had been rebuffed by the Supreme Court, Texas enacted legislation in 1931 requiring any party wishing to institute contract carrier operations to apply to a state commission for a permit. The law also granted the state commission extensive controls over such matters as contract carrier minimum rates.[11] In 1932 the Supreme Court upheld the Texas law, and thereby approved public regulation of contract carriage.[12]

Another major controversy concerned the relative role to be played in motor carrier regulation by federal and state agencies. In 1925 a regulatory commission in Michigan refused to issue a permit to an interstate carrier. Subsequently, the Supreme Court overruled the commission, holding that a state could not regulate interstate commerce, and that it therefore could not deny a permit to an interstate carrier.[13] That same year, the Court ruled in the *Buck* v. *Kuykendall* case that a state could not refuse an interstate bus operator a certificate of public convenience and necessity on the grounds that adequate service by rail and bus already existed.[14] These two decisions were consistent with the Court finding in the 1886 Wabash case, which held that states could not regulate interstate commerce either directly or indirectly.

Pressures for Federal Regulation

The financial collapse of the economy during the Depression and the related economic slowdown brought about great changes in transportation. Excess capacity arose in all forms of carriage. This was particularly true in the trucking industry. The industry was overcrowded, and the desire to capture any traffic led to destructive competition among motor carriers and with the railroads.[15] Discriminatory pricing and deteriorating service were typical of the trucking industry, and intensified intermodal competition threatened the solvency of the competitors.[16]

These problems intensified the need for federal regulation of the trucking industry, as state regulations were unable to cope with the chaotic conditions that existed. The railroads and a number of the larger motor carriers, as well as many shippers, alarmed at the rapidly worsening conditions, petitioned Congress to enact legislation that would lead to the regulation of interstate motor carriage.[17] Such requests, however, were not new. As early as 1925, bills that sought federal regulation of trucking had been introduced into Congress. Similarly, the ICC had requested such legislation on a number of occasions.[18] The federal coordinator of transportation also supported such regulation.

Motor Carrier Act

In 1935, after a total of 37 bills requesting motor carrier regulation had been introduced in Congress, the Motor Carrier Act was passed. The act established ICC control over interstate motor carriage, and was subsequently incorporated into the Interstate Commerce Act as Part II. Many of the regulatory controls established in 1935 have remained unchanged to the present time.

In passing this legislation, Congress declared that the Motor Carrier Act had been passed "to recognize and preserve the inherent advantages of, and foster sound economic conditions in motor transportation and among motor carriers."[19]

The Motor Carrier Act created a comprehensive system of federal controls over motor carriers engaged in carrying passengers and property in interstate and foreign commerce. However, intrastate common carriers were permitted to transport passengers and property moving in interstate commerce between points within that state without obtaining ICC permission, if they operated lawfully under jurisdiction of a state regulatory agency.

The federal regulatory structure applied to motor carriage was closely patterned after earlier rail regulation. This similarity has long been a source of controversy. It has often been argued that the rail pattern of regulation was directed at preventing monopoly abuses, which often arise in industries that have natural monopoly characteristics, and that motor carriage is far more competitive and should be less stringently regulated.[20] Such views have led to numerous proposals for modification of motor carrier regulation. These proposals and their implications are discussed further in Chapter 18.

Due to the diversity of motor carrier operations, it was clear that a single set of regulations could not be applied to all forms of motor carriage. Consequently, the Motor Carrier Act divided intercity motor carriage into common, contract, exempt, and private carriage, and established a fifth grouping, which consisted of truck brokers. The composition of each grouping and the provisions of the act that applied to each are discussed next.

Common Carriers

Motor carriers who hold themselves out to serve the general public are classified as common carriers. The 1935 act established regulation of common carrier entry, rate making, consolidations, security issuances, and safety.

Entry. Common carriers that had been engaged in bona fide interstate operations on June 1, 1935, were permitted to continue their operations. Inclusion of this *grandfather clause* in the act was a congressional attempt to protect the operating rights of those who were legitimately operating prior to the passage of the Motor Carrier Act. Under the grandfather provisions, carriers were required to file applications with the ICC to legalize their existing operations. The commission received more than 89,000 grandfather applications and did not complete processing them until 1941.[21]

As provided by the 1935 statute, anyone wishing to establish new common carrier operations or to extend existing operations is required to apply to the ICC for a certificate of public convenience and necessity. To obtain a certificate, the applicant is required to demonstrate that he is fit, willing, and able to provide the service, and that the service is required by present and future public necessity. Obtaining such a certificate is by no means simple. The certification process is often drawn out and expensive in terms of legal fees. In such proceedings before the ICC, other carriers who serve the markets in question may argue that they adequately serve these points and that additional competition will only erode carrier finances. The ICC has often been criticized as being too protective of existing carriers in dealing with applications for new operating rights, and several legislative attempts have been made to ease entry into motor carriage. To date, these attempts have been unsuccessful.[22]

The certificate obtained by a common carrier specifies the geographical operating authority, routes to be followed, and commodities to be carried. In contrast to the strict abandonment controls applied to rail carriage, the ICC was not granted authority over motor carrier abandonment. The competitive nature of the industry and the relatively low financial entry barriers influenced congressional thinking in this matter.

Rates. The Motor Carrier Act closely followed the railroad pattern of regulation with respect to ICC control over common carrier rate making. Rates and fares must be just and reasonable. Unjust and unreasonable preference or prejudice to persons, places, or commodities is forbidden. Rates must be published and adhered to. Rate modifications must be preceded by 30-day notice, and the ICC may suspend and investigate such proposals for up to seven months. Upon finding that a rate is unreasonable or unjust, the ICC can prescribe the maximum, minimum, or actual rate.

Due to the large number of carriers and the competitive conditions that prevailed in most major markets, Congress did not include a long- and short-haul clause in the Motor Carrier Act. To discriminate effectively, a carrier needs a considerable degree of monopoly power. Congress believed that the extent of competition in motor carriage thus limited the likelihood of long- and short-haul abuses. Similarly, Congress chose not to give the ICC the power to prescribe through routes and joint rates in motor carriage, but rather preferred carriers to initiate such services in response to market demand.

Consolidation. The provisions of the Interstate Commerce Act that applied to railroad consolidations were extended to motor carriage by the 1935 act. The ICC was given authority over such consolidations and instructed to determine that applications were consistent with the public interest before approving them. ICC approval was not necessary if the consolidation involved fewer than 20 vehicles. In 1965 this provision was modified to exempt consolidations if the combined operating revenues of the applicants did not exceed $300,000.

Security Issuances. Security issuances of motor carriers are subjected to the same provisions of the Interstate Commerce Act that applied to railroads. However, ICC approval is unnecessary if the par value of securities outstanding and to be issued does not exceed $1 million. Furthermore, notes and debentures with a maturity period of two years or less can be issued without ICC approval if they do not exceed $200,000.

Other Coverage. Common carriers are also required to maintain liability insurance and insurance on the goods that they carry. The ICC is empowered to prescribe a uniform system of accounts for common carriers. The 1935 act similarly charged the ICC with development of rules to govern the maximum hours of operator service, equipment safety standards, and related safety matters. These powers were subsequently transferred to the Department of Transportation following its creation in 1966.

Contract Carriage

The second category of carriers recognized by the 1935 enactment was contract carriage. Contract carriers transport passengers and property under special and individual contracts or agreements. They generally serve a limited number of accounts and do not hold themselves out to the general public.

The grandfather clause of the Motor Carrier Act also applied to contract carriage. However, any party wishing to initiate new contract carrier operations and/or wishing to expand existing operations must demonstrate that he is fit, willing, and able, and that the operation is consistent with the public interest. It is generally believed that this is a less significant burden than is the proof of public convenience and necessity required in common carrier certificate cases.

Originally, the act did not require contract carriers to publish their actual rates, but rather required publication of their minimum rates or charges. However, continuing complaints from common carriers that this lack of information put them at a disadvantage in competing with contract carriers led Congress to amend the act in 1957. Contract carriers are now required to publish their actual rates and to adhere to them.

Rates filed with the ICC by contract carriers may be suspended and investigated. Following investigation, the ICC may prescribe the minimum rates of contract carriers, but it cannot prescribe their actual rates. Thus competition from common carriers is relied upon to provide effective maximum rate control.

Contract carriers are subject to the same statutory guidelines as common carriers in such areas as consolidations, security issues, accounts and reports, maximum hours of service for employees, and other safety standards. However, although the act requires contract carriers to have liability insurance, it does not require them to insure the goods that they carry. It is assumed that the shipper will protect himself through his arrangements with the carrier.

It should be noted that except under extreme circumstances the ICC does not permit a single company to conduct *dual operations* as both a common and contract carrier. Congress feared that such operations would provide the opportunity for a carrier to discriminate by hauling goods for favored shippers under lower contract rates.

Exempt Carriers

The Motor Carrier Act also contained numerous exemptions, which excluded 11 classes of for-hire motor vehicles from ICC economic control. Several of these exemptions are quite significant.

One exemption excludes from ICC control the transfer, collection, or delivery services conducted in terminal areas by railroads, water carriers, and freight forwarders. These services were seen as incidental to the line-haul services of other modes. A 1938 amendment to the act also exempted motor vehicles used exclusively in the transportation of passengers or property when incidental to movement by aircraft.

A variety of local motor carrier operations is also excluded from ICC control, including school buses, taxicabs, hotel buses, trolley buses, and motor vehicles under the control of the secretary of the interior.

However, by far the most significant exemption contained in the act is the agricultural commodity exemption. Prior to the passage of the Motor Carrier Act, agricultural interests lobbied intensely against the regulation of motor carrier movement of agricultural goods. They contended that trucking rates would rise rather than fall following regulation. In response to these concerns, Congress exempted vehicles owned and operated by farmers that carry products of farms and supplies (essentially private carriage) and motor vehicles controlled and operated by cooperative associations. More importantly, the act also exempted all motor vehicles carrying livestock, fish, or agricultural commodities. In 1952, horticultural products were included in the agricultural exemption. As a result of these exemptions, some agricultural trucking is handled by regulated motor carriers as back-haul traffic, and their rates on such movements are beyond ICC control.

As might be expected, the agricultural exemption has long been the subject of dispute. Rail interests have argued that either the exemption should be abolished or extended to the railroads to put them on an equal competitive footing with truckers. Farm interests have continued to support the exemptions.[23] There have also been periodic questions concerning the items to be included on the agricultural exempt list. The ICC's exempt list now includes slightly more than 100 agricultural commodities.

It must be remembered that, although exempt carriers are not bound by economic regulations, they are still subject to prevailing safety guidelines.

Brokers and Private Carriers

During the early days of trucking a number of enterprises emerged that sold or arranged for transportation by truck. These truck *brokers* were independent of both shippers and carriers and served as intermediaries. Brokers were particularly important to relatively small motor carriers that had limited sales forces. The Motor Carrier Act recognized brokerage as a legitimate and important function in the industry, and stipulated that brokers must be licensed by the ICC. Brokers are required to conform to the same ICC rules concerning accounts and reports as direct motor carriers. Additionally, they must furnish bonds or other security to insure their financial responsibility for the services that they perform. To the present, brokers are particularly important in the household goods sector of interstate trucking; they also play a major role in exempt trucking.

The act also dealt with private motor carriers that transported goods in interstate commerce for themselves and not for-hire. Private motor carriers comprise the largest group of motor carriers of property. The rationale behind private carriage and the problems inherent in these operations were discussed in Chapter 4.

Private carriers must abide by safety regulations, but they are not subject to the economic controls of the ICC. However, the commission attempts to prevent private carriers from expanding into for-hire-type operations that might infringe on the operations of regulated carriers. In the ICC's view, private carriage must be specialized to meet the needs of the company that controls it. In this regard, the ICC uses a *primary business test* in determining if a company is primarily engaged in transportation, or if such transportation is supplemental to the company's other endeavors. For this reason, a subsidiary company used by a parent company for transportation is not considered to be engaged in private carriage.[24] Commission restrictions of private carriage have led to criticism of ICC policies as energy concerns have grown. Pressures have been mounting for the ICC to allow private carriers to serve as for-hire carriers on back hauls to promote greater energy efficiency and better equipment utilization. The ICC has given serious consideration to this alternative, but has not yet permitted the expansion of private carriage into for-hire operations.[25] It must be remembered that such action would create additional competition for common and contract carriers, and this might lead to poorer utilization of their equipment. Once again the ICC is faced with a regulatory trade-off that has both costs and benefits associated with each alternative.

Federal–State Relationships

The Motor Carrier Act of 1935 did not totally displace state regulatory controls. Specifically, the act did not give the ICC jurisdiction over intrastate motor carrier rates, provided that the carrier is operating legally under the jurisdiction of a state regulatory agency. Thus the *Shreveport principle,* which had been applied in rail carriage, was not extended to trucking.

The act also provided for the establishment of *joint boards* to consider certain types of applications and complaints involving no more than three states. At its own discretion the ICC may refer cases involving more than three states to joint boards. Members of the joint boards are appointed by the ICC; they are usually members of state regulatory commissions or nominees submitted by the governors of the states involved.

The decisions in cases referred to joint boards are final if no exceptions are filed within 20 days of the decision, and if the ICC chooses not to review the decision. If an exception is filed, the ICC must review the decision of the joint board.

The relative significance of joint boards is illustrated by the fact that between one third and one half of all motor carrier case decisions are initially issued by joint boards.[26] The existence of these procedures serves not only to reduce the ICC's workload, but also fosters decentralized administration of the act by promoting decision making by those governmental units closest to the situation involved.[27]

REGULATION OF AIR CARRIAGE

The next major mode of intercity carriage to be regulated by the federal government in the 1930s was air transportation. Although federal involvement in air transportation dated to the early days of aviation, it accelerated following World War I because of the potential commercial and military applications of aircraft.

Development of Federal Regulation and Promotion

By 1925 the feasibility of airmail service had been demonstrated, and Congress passed the Kelly Act, which permitted the Post Office Department to award airmail contracts to private companies on a competitive-bid basis. These contracts provided a much needed source of steady income for many early airlines, and played a major role in promoting the further development of the industry.

Federal involvement in aviation expanded significantly in 1926 with the passage of the Air Commerce Act. The statute established the Bureau of Air Commerce within the Department of Commerce, and directed it to develop, operate, and maintain all necessary air navigation facilities except airports. The act also conferred upon the Department of Commerce the ability to regulate private and commercial operations with respect to safety. With the precedent set for federal regulation of air safety, the department proceeded to require registration of aircraft, examination of pilots, and establishment of a variety of minimum safety standards.

Even though the airmail contracts provided a steady source of income for the industry, many mail contractors continued to lose money. Passenger fares were too low to be compensatory, but price increases led to reduction in demand.[28] To help stabilize and unify the industry, Congress enacted the McNary–Watres Act of 1930. The statute specified that the postmaster general could award airmail contracts without competitive bidding.[29] The Post Office Department was also granted power to certify routes, control carrier consolidations and extensions, and prescribe a system of accounts for carriers. Thus the precedent for federal economic regulation of the airlines was set.

Early in 1934 a special committee headed by Senator Hugo Black sought and obtained cancellation of all domestic airmail contracts because of suspected collusion between air carriers and Post Office officials.[30] These cancellations resulted in the loss of substantial revenues for the airlines and initiated a difficult period in which the army carried the mail.

Congress sought not only to prevent further deterioration of the financial condition of the industry, but also to establish tighter regulatory controls in passing the Air Mail Act of 1934. Under the act and its 1935 amendments, the Post Office Department was empowered to award airmail contracts and to enforce airmail regulations. The ICC was given authority to set *fair and reasonable* airmail rates and was to review these rates periodically. The act also charged the Bureau of Air Commerce with responsibility for air safety and the development and maintenance of the airway system. The statute also called for creation of a committee to study and make recommendations regarding airline regulation. The final report of the committee, which was released in 1935, later served as the basis of the Civil Aeronautics Act of 1938.

Despite congressional action, airline problems persisted. A series of accidents in the winter of 1936–1937 eroded public confidence in the industry, and the general business slowdown of early 1938 caused serious financial problems for many airlines. Conditions in the industry during that period have been summarized by John Frederick:

> By the middle of 1938, the entire industry was in a chaotic state, with several major carriers facing bankruptcy, half of the original investment in the airlines lost forever, and new capital so backward as to be practically unobtainable.[31]

In an effort to at least partially remedy these conditions, the airline industry itself sponsored the Civil Aeronautics Act, which established federal control of the industry. The act was passed in June 1938. In the act, Congress directed the Civil Aeronautics Authority to "recognize and preserve" the inherent advantages of air transportation, and to promote "adequate, economical and efficient" air service adapted to the "present and future needs" of foreign and domestic commerce.

Coverage of the Act

To administer the economic regulations contained in the 1938 act, Congress created the Civil Aeronautics Authority (renamed the Civil Aeronautics Board in 1940). The five members of the board are appointed by the president with the advice and consent of the Senate; they serve six-year terms. There had been considerable debate prior to the enactment of the statute as to whether air regulation should be administered by the ICC. President Roosevelt originally favored extension of ICC authority, but Congress believed that the differences in the industries and the breadth of the ICC's already existing responsibilities necessitated creation of a new agency. However, Congress borrowed liberally from the regulatory structure that it had created for rail and motor carriage in designing airline regulations.

Policy Statement

The Civil Aeronautics Act of 1938 contained a policy statement that directed the newly created regulatory agency to encourage and develop the national air transportation system to meet the present and future needs of our country. No mention was given to other modes of carriage, and Congress clearly intended the CAB to regulate air transportation independently and without regard to the impact of its decisions and policies on other modes. It was also clear from the policy statement that Congress intended air transportation regulation to be promotional as well as remedial. The policy statement still serves as the preamble for the body of regulations that govern air carriage.

Entry

As had been the case in the Motor Carrier Act, the Civil Aeronautics Act contained a grandfather clause. Air carriers engaged in bona fide operations on May 17, 1938, were automatically granted the right to continue those services. However, as established in 1938, new entry or extension of existing operations can only be obtained by demonstrating to the CAB that the applicant is fit, willing, and able, and that there is a public need for the service.

The industry structure inherited by the CAB was much simpler than that of motor carriage, and it involved far fewer carriers. Consequently, through its entry and consolidation decisions, the CAB has been able to play a major role in determining the industry structure that eventually emerged.

Air carriers must also obtain CAB approval before abandoning a route that they have been awarded. Congress had not included such abandonment controls in motor carriage in 1935. However, Congress was convinced that the greater risk factor of air carriage and its more substantial financial entry barriers dictated inclusion of such public protection standards.

Rates

The degree of control over carrier rates and fares accorded to the CAB is quite similar to those of the ICC over rail and trucking rates. Airline charges are to be just and reasonable. Undue discrimination is prohibited, and rates are to be published and observed. A 30-day notice is required on all rate and fare changes, and the CAB can suspend and investigate rate proposals for up to 180 days. Following its investigation in rate cases, the CAB can prescribe the maximum, minimum, or actual charges. In doing so, the board is to consider, among other things

1) The effect of such rates upon the movement of traffic; 2) the need in the public interest of adequate and efficient transportation of persons and property by air carriers at the lowest cost consistent with the furnishing of such services; 3) such standards respecting the character and quality of service to be rendered by air carriers as may be prescribed by or pursuant

239

to law; 4) the inherent advantages of transportation by aircraft; and 5) the need of each air carrier for revenue sufficient to enable such air carrier, under honest, economical, and efficient management, to provide adequate and efficient air carrier service.

Miscellaneous Controls

CAB authority is not limited to entry, abandonment, and rate making. It also includes control over consolidations, mergers, and acquisition of control. Additionally, the CAB is empowered to prescribe a uniform system of accounts for carriers, and it can require periodic reports from carriers. It was not, however, granted authority over the security issues of carriers.

The act also gives the CAB the power to exempt any air carrier or class of carriers from economic regulation if it believes that such regulation would place an undue burden on the carriers involved. As discussed in Chapter 5, the CAB has chosen to exempt third-level carriers from regulation for that reason.

A mechanism for creation of joint boards involving ICC and CAB personnel was also included in the act to deal with such matters as intermodal through routes and joint rates.

The board also plays a role in international aviation through the issuance of permits to domestic and foreign carriers to engage in international air carriage when the continental United States is involved. However, as discussed in Chapter 14, the president maintains ultimate control over such matters, and on a number of occasions, CAB decisions have been overruled by the president.

Safety

From the time of its creation in 1926 until 1938, the Bureau of Air Commerce administered the airway system and enforced safety regulations pertaining to air transportation. The Civil Aeronautics Act, as amended in 1940, provided for centralized safety regulation and airway operation and regulation under the Civil Aeronautics Administration. Both the administration and the CAB were placed within the Department of Commerce for budgeting and accounting purposes under a 1940 reorganization plan sponsored by President Roosevelt.

Until 1958 the Civil Aeronautics Administration remained the dominant federal agency involved in the promotion of air safety. However, several serious accidents in 1958 raised questions concerning the effectiveness of the agency and prompted congressional passage of the Federal Aviation Act of 1958. The statute created the Federal Aviation Agency (FAA) to assume the function of the Civil Aeronautics Administration. The act outlined the following responsibilities for the FAA:

1) The regulation of air commerce in such a manner as to best promote its development and safety and fulfill the requirements of national defense. 2) The promotion, encouragement, and development of civil aeronautics. 3) The control of the use of the navigable airspace of the United States and the regulation of both civil and military operations in such airspace in the interest of the safety and efficiency of both. 4) The consolidation of research and development with respect to air navigation facilities as well as the installation and operation thereof. 5) The development and operation of a common system of air traffic control and navigation for both military and civil aircraft.

Thus the FAA was accorded comprehensive authority over air safety and control over air space. The agency was renamed the Federal Aviation Administration and was included in the Department of Transportation upon its creation in 1966. In the same legislation, Congress established an independent agency, the National Transportation Safety Board, to investigate accidents and make related recommendations to government agencies and carriers. A major task of the agency since its creation has been investigation of airline crashes. Its relative role and relationship to other federal agencies are discussed in Chapter 14.

TRANSPORTATION ACT OF 1940

During 1938 and 1939, Congress held extensive hearings on the status of the domestic transportation system. The hearings identified several major areas of concern. Domestic water carriage, particularly the coastal and intercoastal segments, was troubled by rate instability and discriminatory pricing practices.[32] Destructive competition had surfaced. Also, water carriage had become a more effective competitor for previously captive railroad traffic. As a result, congressional concerns about the deteriorating conditions in water carriage were reinforced by railroad calls for regulation of water transportation. The railroads had not completely rebounded from the effects of the Depression. Contributing to the precarious financial position of many railroads were technological advances in the other modes and increased public spending on highways, waterways, and airport–airway development.

It was obvious that the national transportation system was rapidly becoming truly intermodal in nature, and competition among the modes was increasing in intensity. Therefore, Congress sought to draft legislation that would strengthen and stabilize the several modes, while restricting the intensity of intermodal competition. The result was the Transportation Act of 1940. The statute not only established ICC control over domestic water carriage, but also contained a statement of national transportation policy to guide ICC regulation of the several modes. Additionally, the act modified several facets of railroad regulation.

Water Carrier Regulation

Although several earlier statutes had regulated various aspects of domestic water carriage, prior to 1940 water carrier operation over inland rivers and canals was not regulated. Similarly, contract carriage was unregulated except over intercoastal routes. The 1940 act superseded the previous statutes and vested regulatory powers in the ICC.

As originally conceived, the 1940 act was envisioned as a bill to bring all domestic water carriage under ICC control. However, shippers of bulk and liquid commodities and agricultural interests lobbied against the legislation because they feared that it might lead to higher rates. These pressures led to inclusion of several major exemptions in the act that still prevail.

Exemptions

The most important exemption contained in the act is the *bulk commodity exemption,* which specifies that common carriers whose cargo consists of not more than three bulk commodities in the cargo space of a vessel (or tow) are exempt from the economic controls of the ICC. Liquid commodities carried in bulk in tank vessels are similarly exempted, as are contract carriers that have both specialized vessels and cargo and that do not compete with common carriers. The exemptions also include all private carriers, small craft of less than 100 tons, and water carriers used by rail and motor carriers in their normal operations. As a result of these exemptions, nearly 90 percent of total intercity ton miles moved by water carriage is exempt from ICC economic controls.[33] Although the 1940 act did permit regulated carriers to haul exempt commodities as a back haul to regulated movements, it did not permit regulated carriers to mix regulated and exempt commodities in a single vessel or tow. However, as noted in Chapter 5, in 1973 Congress abolished the no mixing rule, thereby allowing regulated and exempt commodities to be hauled simultaneously by regulated carriers.[34]

For those carriers subject to ICC controls under the 1940 act, Congress again relied upon a regulatory pattern similar to that which had been applied to other ICC-regulated modes. Regulations pertaining to water carriage became Part III of the Interstate Commerce Act.

Entry

Grandfather rights were extended to common carriers engaged in bona fide operations on January 1, 1940. Since that time any party wishing to enter the industry or extend its operations has been required to secure certificates from the ICC by proving that it is fit, willing, and able to perform the service and that it would serve the public convenience. Contract carriers are required to obtain permits from the ICC before initiating or extending operations. Dual operation as both a common and a contract carrier is forbidden, but the ICC is permitted to grant exceptions to that stipulation.

Rates

Water carrier rates must be just and reasonable, and they cannot be unduly discriminatory. Common carrier rates must be published and observed. Thirty-day notice must precede changes in common carrier rates, and these rates may be suspended and investigated by the ICC. Upon finding a common carrier rate unreasonable, the ICC can prescribe the maximum, minimum, or actual rates of the carrier.

Contract carriers in water transportation are required to file only their minimum rates, and these can be suspended and investigated by the ICC. The rates must also meet the standards of reasonableness and discrimination that are applied to common carrier rates.

Miscellaneous Controls

The ICC was also given control over consolidations, mergers, and acquisition of control of common and contract carriers by water. The commission may also prescribe accounting procedures to be followed by these carriers and can require periodic reports. Additionally, through route and joint rate arrangements between water carriers may be required by the ICC.

Although the act extended the long- and short-haul clause to water carriage, due to the limited importance of intrastate water carriage, it did not apply the Shreveport principle to such operations. Because of the relative ease of entry into water carriage and the competitive conditions that prevailed at the time of the enactment, Congress did not establish ICC control over water carrier abandonments. Security issuances by water carriers are also beyond ICC control.

Policy Statement

In the Transportation Act of 1940, Congress attempted, for the first time, to express the national transportation policy of the United States in a simplified format. It was to serve, and still does, as the preamble to the Interstate Commerce Act. The statement outlines a broad range of considerations to be observed by the ICC in regulating the various modes subject to its jurisdiction. It does not apply to air carriage. The statement of policy reads as follows:

> It is hereby declared to be the national transportation policy of the Congress to provide for fair and impartial regulation of all modes of transportation subject to the provisions of the act, so administered as to recognize and preserve the inherent advantages of each; to promote safe, adequate, economical and efficient service and foster sound economic conditions in transportation and among the several carriers; to encourage the establishment and maintenance of reasonable charges for transportation services, without unjust discriminations, undue preferences, or advantages, or unfair or destructive competitive practices; to cooperate with the several States, and the duly authorized officials thereof; and to encourage fair wages and equitable working conditions—all to the end of developing, coordinating, and preserving a national transportation system by water, highway, and rail as well as other means, adequate to meet the needs of the commerce of the United States, of the Postal Service, and of the national defense. All of the provisions of this act shall be administered and enforced with a view to carrying out the above declaration of policy.

Controversy has surrounded the policy statement since its writing. It has been argued that many of the goals of the policy statement are mutually exclusive and that it is an unworkable directive.[35] Some of the difficulties encountered by the ICC in attempting to reflect the goals of the policy statement in specific regulatory decisions are discussed in Chapter 13.

Changes in Railroad Regulation

Several provisions of the Transportation Act of 1940 sought to modify existing railroad regulations. These provisions concerned railroad consolidations, the rule of rate making, the burden of proof in rate-reduction cases, and land grant rates.

The Transportation Act of 1920 had directed the ICC to develop a master consolidation plan to reduce the number of railroad systems in the United States. However, despite considerable effort, the ICC was unable to develop a plan that met with industry approval. Consequently, the 1940 statute stipulated that future railroad consolidations would not have to conform to an ICC master plan. However, the act specified a range of factors to be considered by the ICC in consolidation cases. The guidelines still serve to direct ICC decision making in railroad consolidation cases. The specifics of these consolidation guidelines are considered in Chapter 16.

The rule of rate making, as modified in 1933, declared that the ICC was to give due consideration in railroad rate cases to the "effects on the movement of the traffic." This was modified in 1940 to restrict consideration to the movement of traffic by "the carrier or carriers for which the rates are prescribed." By making this change, Congress sought to prevent the ICC from prescribing railroad rates that were designed to protect the traffic of other modes. Although this directive appears rather clear, its consideration in view of the many goals of national transportation policy has led to continuing disputes over the meaning of the rule. This controversy is discussed further in Chapter 13.

The act also placed the burden of proof upon the railroads in any rate case. Prior to that time there was no such burden on the carriers in rate-reduction cases. However, this change was generally viewed as a step to strengthen ICC control over competitive intermodal pricing reductions.

The act also released the land grant railroads from their obligation to carry government property and mail at reduced rates. The land grant rates had originated with the federal land grants to the railroads between 1850 and 1871. However, railroad obligation to carry military troops at reduced rates was not ended until 1945. At the present, governmental units are free to negotiate rates with carriers under section 22 of the Interstate Commerce Act. This provision often results in the federal government paying lower transportation charges than other shippers who receive similar services. The Department of Transportation has advocated abolition of section 22 rates, but Congress has chosen not to eliminate that provision of the Interstate Commerce Act.[36]

REGULATION OF FREIGHT FORWARDING

Following passage of the Transportation Act of 1940, the only major mode of intercity carriage that had not come under federal regulation was freight forwarding. As early as 1930 the ICC had requested that Congress bring freight forwarders under the ICC's jurisdiction. In its annual report of that year, the ICC stated that a previously conducted investigation of forwarding activities had indicated that forwarders were routinely departing from published rates, and that rates were quite unstable.[37] Furthermore, rebating practices had been uncovered by the ICC. The report also noted that the business of forwarding companies was in a general state of chaos, and the agency argued that legislation was needed to prevent the practices that had depleted carrier revenues and led to unequal and unjustly discriminatory treatment of shippers.[38]

However, this ICC request and a number of subsequent petitions brought little response from Congress. Nevertheless, the ICC continued to call for legislative action. Finally, in 1939, the Senate authorized a study of surface forwarding to be conducted by the Senate Committee on Interstate Commerce.[39] In response to the findings of that investigation, Congress passed the Freight Forwarder Act in May 1942. The statute established ICC jurisdiction over surface forwarders. The forwarder regulations became Part IV of the Interstate Commerce Act.

Coverage of the Act

The Freight Forwarder Act covered freight forwarders using surface modes in interstate commerce. A grandfather clause allowed continuation of existing forwarding operations. However, as specified by the act, entry into forwarding or extension of existing operations requires an ICC permit. Such permits are issued to applicants who demonstrate that they are fit, willing, and able to provide the proposed service, and that the service is consistent with the public interest.

Rate regulation of freight forwarders is similar to that of common carriers in other modes. Rates must be just, reasonable, and not unduly discriminatory. The rates must be published and followed. A 30-day notice must be given in advance of any rate change, and forwarder rates can be suspended and investigated. The ICC may prescribe the maximum, minimum, or actual charges of forwarders.

Forwarders are not permitted to own or control carriers subject to Part I, II, or III of the Interstate Commerce Act. However, railroads, motor carriers, or water carriers may own or control freight forwarders.

Although freight forwarders operate as intermediates between carriers and shippers, they were declared to be common carriers in a 1950 amendment to the Interstate Commerce Act.

SUMMARY

Between 1935 and 1942 federal regulatory controls were extended to motor, air, water carriage, and freight forwarding. In each instance, passage of the governing statute was at least partially the result of chaotic conditions that had emerged in each particular mode of carriage. Congress was increasingly concerned with regulation of intermodal competition.

In regulating these modes of carriage, Congress relied quite heavily upon the regulatory format that had earlier been applied to rail carriage.

Although there have been some modifications of these regulations since that time, the regulatory framework that they established has not been substantially changed.

Recent years have witnessed widespread questioning of the propriety of a number of these regulatory guidelines, and many parties have advocated regulatory modification. These developments and structural changes in the framework of transportation regulation and promotion are the subjects of Chapter 13.

NOTES

1. 43 Stat. 801 (1925).
2. For an interesting discussion of this topic, see Roy J. Sampson, "The Case for Full Cost Ratemaking," *ICC Practitioners' Journal*, XXXIII, No. 1 (March 1966), pp. 490–95.
3. The Railroad Revitalization and Regulatory Reform Act of 1976, Public Law 94–210, promoted greater pricing freedom for the railroads and will eventually permit the railroads to lower prices to variable cost at their own discretion. This issue is discussed further in Chapter 13.
4. Charles F. Phillips, *The Economics of Regulation*, rev. ed. (Homewood, Ill.: Richard D. Irwin, Inc., 1969), p. 455.
5. Ibid.
6. Ibid.
7. Ibid.
8. Dudley F. Pegrum, *Transportation: Economics and Public Policy*, 3rd ed. (Homewood, Ill.: Richard D. Irwin, Inc., 1973), p. 298.
9. Thomas G. Moore, *Freight Transportation Regulation: Surface Freight and the Interstate Commerce Commission* (Washington, D.C.: American Enterprise Institute for Public Policy Research, 1972), p. 25.
10. *Michigan Public Utilities Commission v. Duke*, 266 U.S. 570 (1925).
11. Pegrum, op. cit., pp. 311–12.
12. *Stephenson v. Binford*, 287 U.S. 251 (1932).
13. *Michigan Public Utilities v. Duke* (1925).
14. *Buck v. Kuykendall*, 276 U.S. 307 (1925).
15. William J. Hudson and James A. Constantin, *Motor Transportation: Principles and Practices* (New York: Ronald Press Company, 1958), p. 463.
16. Ibid.
17. Ibid., p. 465.

18. *Motor Bus and Motor Truck Operations,* 140 ICC 685 (1928); also *Coordination of Motor Transportation,* 182 ICC 263 (1932).

19. 49 Stat. 543 Sec. 202(a) (1935).

20. For an extensive discussion of this issue, see James C. Nelson, "The Effects of Entry Control in Surface Transport," in *Transportation Economics* (New York: National Bureau of Economic Research, 1965), pp. 382–422.

21. Moore, op. cit., p. 27.

22. Several times between 1971 and 1977 the Department of Transportation submitted legislation to Congress that sought to ease entry into motor carriage. In each instance the legislation was found to be unacceptable by Congress.

23. Richard N. Farmer, "The Case for Unregulated Truck Transportation," *Journal of Farm Economics,* XLVI, No. 2 (May 1964), pp. 398–409.

24. *Keller Industries, Inc.,* 103 MCC 520 (1966) and 107 MCC 75 (1968).

25. Interstate Commerce Commission, *The Regulatory Issues of Today* (Washington, D.C.: the Commission, 1975), pp. 16–25.

26. Charles A. Taff, *Commercial Motor Transportation,* 4th ed. (Homewood, Ill.: Richard D. Irwin, Inc., 1969), p. 382.

27. D. Philip Locklin, *Economics of Transportation,* 7th ed. (Homewood, Ill.: Richard D. Irwin, 1972), p. 682.

28. John H. Frederick, *Commercial Air Transportation,* 4th ed. (Homewood, Ill.: Richard D. Irwin, Inc., 1955), p. 81.

29. Ibid.

30. Marvin L. Fair and Ernest W. Williams, *Economics of Transportation,* rev. ed. (New York: Harper & Row, Inc., 1959), p. 139.

31. Frederick, op. cit., p. 85.

32. Pegrum, op. cit., p. 361.

33. Moore, op. cit., p. 32.

34. For a discussion of this issue, see U.S. Department of Transportation, Office of the Secretary, *Implementing Transportation Policy* (Washington, D.C.: the Department, 1973), pp. 8–9.

35. Martin T. Farris, "National Transportation Policy: Fact or Fiction?" *Quarterly Review of Economics and Business,* X, No. 2 (Summer 1970), pp. 7–14.

36. U.S. Department of Transportation, Office of the Secretary, *Executive Briefing: Transportation Regulatory Modernization and Assistance Legislation* (Washington, D.C.: the Department, 1972), pp. 31–32.

37. U.S. Interstate Commerce Commission, *44th Annual Report of the Interstate Commerce Commission* (Washington, D.C.: U.S. Government Printing Office, 1930), p. 81.

38. Ibid., p. 82.

39. U.S. Interstate Commerce Commission, *53rd Annual Report of the Inter-*

state Commerce Commission (Washington, D.C.: U.S. Government Printing Office, 1939), p. 35.

SELECTED REFERENCES

Caves, Richard E. *Air Transport and Its Regulators.* Cambridge, Mass.: Harvard University Press, 1962.

Fair, Marvin L., and John Guandolo. *Transportation Regulation.* Dubuque, Iowa: William C. Brown Company, 1972.

Fair, Marvin L., and Ernest W. Williams. *Economics of Transportation and Logistics.* Dallas, Tex.: Business Publications, Inc., 1975.
Chapter 20. "Regulation of Transportation: Origin and Scope," pp. 377–404.

Farris, Martin T. "National Transportation Policy: Fact or Fiction?" *Quarterly Review of Economics and Business,* X, No. 2 (Summer 1970), pp. 7–14.

Frederick, John H. *Commercial Air Transportation,* 5th ed. Homewood, Ill.: Richard D. Irwin, Inc., 1965.
Chapter 4. "Regulatory Legislation," pp. 107–25.

Fulda, Carl H. *Competition in the Regulated Industries: Transportation.* Boston: Little, Brown and Company, 1961.
Chapter 2. "The Regulatory Acts: Their History and Purposes," pp. 7–23.

Hudson, William J., and James A. Constantin. *Motor Transportation: Principles and Practices.* New York: Ronald Press Company, 1958.

Locklin, D. Philip. *Economics of Transportation,* 7th ed. Homewood, Ill.: Richard D. Irwin, Inc., 1972.
Chapter 29. "Development of Motor-Carrier Regulation," pp. 666–84.
Chapter 32. "Regulation of Water Transportation," pp. 745–69.
Chapter 34. "Development of Air Transport Regulation," pp. 797–810.

Moore, Thomas G. *Freight Transportation Regulation: Surface Freight and the Interstate Commerce Commission.* Washington, D.C.: American Enterprise Institute for Public Policy Research, 1972.
Chapter 3. "Development of Multi Modal Regulation," pp. 25–40.

Pegrum, Dudley F. *Transportation: Economics and Public Policy,* 3rd ed. Homewood, Ill.: Richard D. Irwin, Inc., 1973.
Chapter 13. "Railroad Regulation Since World War I," pp. 290–309.
Chapter 14. "Regulation of Motor Transport," pp. 310–35.
Chapter 15. "Regulation of Air, Water, and Pipeline Transportation," pp. 336–68.

Phillips, Charles F. *The Economics of Regulation,* rev. ed. Homewood, Ill.: Richard D. Irwin, Inc., 1969.
Chapter 13. "Regulation of the Transportation Industries," pp. 441–82.

Sampson, Roy J., and Martin T. Farris. *Domestic Transportation: Practice, Theory, and Policy,* Boston: Houghton Mifflin Company, 1975.
Chapter 22. "Regulation of Transportation Competition: Evolution," pp. 352–67.

Spychalski, John C. "On the Non-Utility of Domestic Water Transport Regulation." *ICC Practitioners' Journal,* XXXVIII, No. 1 (November–December, 1969), pp. 7–20.

Taff, Charles A. *Commercial Motor Transportation,* 4th ed. Homewood, Ill.: Richard D. Irwin, Inc., 1969.
Chapter 17. "Regulation of Motor Carriers," pp. 377–401.

U.S. Interstate Commerce Commission. *The Regulatory Issues of Today.* Washington, D.C.: the Commission, 1975.

DISCUSSION QUESTIONS

1. Discuss the significance of the 1925 Hoch–Smith Resolution.
2. In your opinion, what role should regulation play in determining the rate of return on investment generated by regulated carriers?
3. Why were grandfather clauses included in the Motor Carrier Act of 1935 and the Civil Aeronautics Act of 1938?

13

Evolution of Federal Regulation and Promotion Since World War II

The years preceding World War II were marked by a substantial expansion of regulatory controls in intercity transportation, but the postwar period has witnessed growing concern about the propriety of existing regulation. This concern has been motivated by the continuing financial problems experienced by many intercity carriers and the national need for a viable, efficient transportation system. In an effort to facilitate improvements in the transportation network, the federal government has substantially increased its involvement in promotional activities.

This chapter focuses on both the reevaluation of regulatory policies and the major structural and regulatory changes that have taken place since World War II. The growing federal role in the promotion of intercity transportation development is also examined. Federal involvement in urban transportation has also expanded dramatically in recent years; discussion of this development is deferred to Chapters 19 and 20.

TRANSPORTATION SYSTEM: WORLD WAR II TO 1958

During World War II, intercity traffic volume rose and for-hire carriers generally experienced higher earnings. The railroads were not nationalized during the conflict, as they had been during World War I, and they carried the great bulk of wartime freight.

Evolution of Federal Regulation and Promotion Since World War II

Two wartime developments had a decided impact on the national transportation system following the war. First, in 1944 Congress approved in principle the construction of the Interstate Highway System. Approval of this high-speed highway network to link all major metropolitan areas in this country was primarily motivated by military considerations. However, following its funding in 1956, the interstate network was to take on major economic significance in the transportation setting. The system allowed higher effective speeds between cities and lower operating costs to trucks, buses, and private automobiles. As a result, the highway modes were to become even more competitive for freight and passenger movements in intercity markets. Second, the massive movement of military personnel by air during the war clearly demonstrated the passenger-carrying capability of that mode to the general public, and commercial patronage rose rapidly in the postwar years. This development was a contributing factor to the further decline of intercity rail passenger service.

Traffic volume in intercity carriage normalized following the conflict. Economic activity was brisk, and the period into the early 1950s bore little resemblance to the chaotic conditions of the 1930s. Little congressional action of regulatory significance occurred during this period. The only exception was the passage of the Reed–Bulwinkle Act of 1948, which granted an antitrust exemption to the collective rate-making activities of ICC-regulated carriers.[1]

Although railroad earnings improved from the late 1940s into the early 1950s, the market share of intercity traffic handled by the railroads declined steadily. Intermodal competition had intensified, and the other modes continued to erode the railroad traffic base. In addition to more intense competition from for-hire carriers, the railroads also faced rapid expansion of private carriage in freight markets and steady growth of the private automobile fleet, which reduced rail passenger volume.

Further complicating matters was the fact that the traffic volume which the railroads maintained tended to be low value and, consequently, generated relatively low revenues. This is illustrated by the fact that in 1956 trucks carried only 24 percent of all rail and truck ton miles, but earned 64 percent of the corresponding revenues on such traffic.[2] At the same time, the railroad passenger deficit rose dramatically in the postwar period, and regularly absorbed more than 35 percent of the net operating revenues generated in railroad freight operations.[3]

The aggregate rate of return on net investment of the railroads plummeted between 1955 and 1958, reaching 2.76 percent in 1958.[4] The physical plant of many railroads deteriorated during that period, and refinancing became increasingly difficult. Many class I railroads faced the threat of bankruptcy.

The deterioration of the railroads had not gone unnoticed at the federal level. Numerous federal studies of the "railroad problem" were conducted during the early 1950s. These studies generally recommended a lessening of railroad regulation and a greater reliance upon market forces in transportation.[5] However, none of the studies prompted congressional action.

Finally, prodded by railroad interests, Congress held extensive hearings on the problems of the railroads in early 1958. As a result of these hearings, Congress enacted the Transportation Act of 1958.[6]

TRANSPORTATION ACT OF 1958

The basic goal of the 1958 statute was to strengthen the financial position of the nation's railroads. In attempting to accomplish that goal, the act included several distinct components. With respect to railroad regulation, the act granted the ICC control over railroad passenger train discontinuances, broadened ICC controls over intrastate rail rates, and revised the rule of rate making. It also extended loan guarantees to the railroads, and made several amendments to the Motor Carrier Act (Part II of the Interstate Commerce Act).

Passenger Train Discontinuances

The passenger service losses being incurred by the railroads were a major concern of Congress. In 1957 those losses exceeded $700 million on a fully distributed cost basis. The losses absorbed approximately 44 percent of the net operating revenues which the industry generated in moving freight during that year.[7]

The ICC was sensitive to the railroad passenger problem, but had never been granted authority over rail passenger service. Consequently, the railroads were generally at the mercy of state regulatory agencies in passenger train discontinuance proceedings. Often the state agencies were unreceptive to such railroad petitions.

To remedy this situation, Congress granted the ICC authority over passenger train service. According to the 1958 act, the railroads could issue a 30-day notice of discontinuance on any passenger run that crossed state lines and was subject to any state law or agency. The notice was to be filed with the ICC, and discontinuance would be permitted unless the ICC ruled otherwise. The act also covered passenger operations that were strictly intrastate. A railroad wishing to abandon such an operation was required to apply to the appropriate state agency. However, if the application was denied by the state agency, the decision could be appealed to the ICC.

The ICC would then hold hearings in the state involved, and could permit abandonment if it found that continuance of the service would place an unjust or undue burden on the interstate operations of the carrier.

The passenger train discontinuance provisions of the 1958 statute were quite significant, and between 1958 and 1970 the ICC permitted discontinuance of many intercity passenger trains.[8] These discontinuances partially alleviated the railroad passenger problem, but passenger deficits persisted. In fact, between 1958 and 1970, when Amtrak was established, the aggregate passenger service deficit of the railroads ranged between $394 million and $480 million annually.[9]

Intrastate Rates

An amendment to the Transportation Act of 1920 had given the ICC the power, under Section 13 of the Interstate Commerce Act, to raise intrastate rail rates when necessary to remove discrimination against interstate commerce. However, two Supreme Court rulings in 1958 raised serious questions about the viability of this ICC power.

In one case the Court ruled that the ICC had to demonstrate that the out-of-pocket loss on low intrastate commutation fares was not offset by revenues from other intrastate passenger and freight operations.[10] In the second case, the Court held that lower intrastate rates than applied on interstate commerce could not be found to cause an undue burden on interstate commerce, unless the ICC could provide evidence that the relative costs of moving intrastate traffic were as high as the costs of moving interstate traffic.[11]

It was obvious that these two decisions would make ICC administration of Section 13 difficult. In responding to this problem, Congress stipulated in the 1958 act that the ICC could hold low intrastate rates to be unduly burdensome on interstate commerce *without* showing that the intrastate losses were not offset by other intrastate operations, and *without* separating interstate and intrastate property, revenues, and expenditures.

Loan Guarantees

The continuing financial problems of the railroads caused capital access difficulties for the carriers. In many instances, conventional refinancing channels were blocked due to depressed carrier earnings. To partially alleviate this problem, the Transportation Act of 1958 created a loan guarantee program. Under the provisions of the program, the ICC was authorized to guarantee loans by financial institutions to the railroads for the purpose of financing capital outlays or maintenance work. The aggregate amount of ICC loan guarantees outstanding to the railroads at any given time was limited to $500 million by the act. The ICC was only to guarantee such loans if it found that the applicants could not obtain needed funds without the guarantee, and if it further found that there was a reasonable assurance of carrier repayment.

The program, which was originally to expire in March 1961, was later extended to June 1963. During the life of the program nearly $240 million in loan guarantees was authorized by the ICC.[12]

The 1958 loan guarantee program cannot readily be classified as a success.[13] Critics of the program have claimed that it merely postponed bankruptcies. This is borne out by the experience under the act. The five major recipients of the guarantees provided by the act, the Lehigh Valley, the Central of New Jersey, the New Haven, the New York Central, and the Reading, all subsequently declared bankruptcy. These five lines received nearly one half of the loan guarantee total granted under the act. Several railroad executives contended that the basic problem of the railroads was not obtaining loans, but rather repaying existing debt obligations.[14] Furthermore, they argued that loan programs failed to address the problems that caused the railroads to have difficulty in meeting outstanding obligations.[15] Loan guarantees were later used in the early 1970s following the collapse of the Penn Central. However, it has become apparent that such programs must be coupled with other substantive changes if they are to do more than simply buy additional time.

Rule of Rate Making

As discussed in Chapter 12, the 1940 amendment to the rule of rate making sought to prevent the ICC from holding up the rates of one mode to protect the traffic of another. However, subsequent ICC rulings in intermodal rate cases were rather inconsistent, and it was obvious that there had been disagreements among ICC members concerning interpretation of the revised rate-making rule. The railroads accused the ICC of continued *umbrella rate-making* practices, and in the hearings that preceded the passage of the 1958 statute the railroads requested further congressional clarification of the 1940 amendment. Congress believed that the ICC had not consistently adhered to the 1940 rate-making directive, and that it had often prevented the railroads from making competitive rate adjustments. The ICC was accused of promoting a *fair sharing* of traffic by holding up railroad rates.

Therefore, Congress modified Section 15(a) of the Interstate Commerce Act by adding the following paragraph:

In a proceeding involving competition between carriers of different modes of transportation subject to this Act, the Commission, in determining whether a rate is lower than a reasonable minimum rate, shall consider the facts and circumstances attending the movement of the traffic by the carrier or carriers for which the rate is applicable. Rates of a carrier shall not be held up to a particular level to protect the traffic of any other mode of transportation, giving due consideration to the objectives of the national transportation policy declared in this Act.

The wording of the final sentence of the amendment should be noted carefully. It directs the ICC to give "due consideration to the objectives of national transportation policy" in dealing with rate cases. The policy statement disapproves of "unfair and destructive competitive practices." The question that naturally arises is at what point do competitive rate reductions become "unfair and destructive competitive practices"? Thus the final congressional qualification of this amendment gave the ICC considerable room for interpretation in future intermodal rate cases. The directive was ambiguous enough that both the railroads and their motor and water carrier opponents believed that their views had prevailed in revising the rule of rate making.[16] Interpretation of the revised rule awaited ICC cases and court actions.

In the first major court test of the amendment, the ICC was reversed by the Supreme Court in the Pan Atlantic Steamship case.[17] The Court ruled that railroad rates could not be declared unlawful simply because they would divert traffic from others. Furthermore, the Court stated that "something more than even hard competition must be shown before a particular rate can be declared unfair or destructive."[18]

That Court decision, however, did not address the issue of the propriety of various cost standards to be used by the ICC in determining the inherent advantages of carriers in intermodal rate cases. That issue had long been a matter of controversy. The railroads contended that out-of-pocket or variable costs were the only relevant costs in such proceedings; water and motor interests argued that fully distributed costs should set the pricing floor in intermodal rate cases. This dispute was to become the focal point of the now famous Ingot Molds case.[19] In that case the Louisville & Nashville Railroad and the Pennsylvania Railroad filed a rate on the movement of steel ingots that was above their out-of-pocket cost, yet below the related fully distributed cost. The rate was equal to the joint barge-truck rate that prevailed over the route. Division 2 of the ICC ruled that the rate was lawful, but was reversed by the full commission. The majority ruled that fully distributed cost was the only appropriate basis for measuring inherent advantages in the context of national transportation policy. The ICC also contended that if the proposed rail rates were implemented practically all the traffic in question would shift to rail movement.

The case was eventually appealed to the Supreme Court after a lower court had set aside the ICC's ruling. The Court ruled that the 1958 rule of rate making amendment had delegated jurisdiction to the ICC to choose its own criteria in such cases, and that fully distributed cost was reasonable as such a standard.[20] Effectively, this ruling held that the ICC was free to choose whatever cost standard it believed appropriate in such matters. One author has described this decision as a massive reversal of the trend toward greater pricing flexibility.[21]

It should be noted that, although the ICC tended to adhere to the fully distributed cost standard in determining the low-cost carrier in such proceedings, it did not extend protection from variable-cost rate making to unregulated carriers, even though they might have been the low-cost carriers in certain instances. The ICC's primary concern was with the impact on regulated carriers.[22]

By far the most significant development in intermodal rate making since 1958 was the enactment of the Railroad Revitalization and Regulatory Reform Act of 1976.[23] The act, which is discussed in detail later in this chapter, initiated a program of gradual pricing flexibility, and acknowledged congressional acceptance of variable cost as an appropriate rate-making standard in cases of intermodal competition.

Motor Carrier Provisions

The Transportation Act of 1958 also made several significant amendments to Part II of the Interstate Commerce Act, which governs motor carriage. The most important of these amendments were aimed at preventing further diversion of traffic from regulated to nonregulated carriers.

Judicial interpretation of the exemptions contained in the Motor Carrier Act had led to a growing list of exempt commodities. In the 1958 act, Congress sought to place limits on such judicial interpretation by ending several specific exemptions, including those on frozen fruits, frozen vegetables, and frozen berries. Exemptions on several agricultural commodities that were not domestically produced were also ended. Congress was also concerned with the growing problem of for-hire carriers that represented themselves as being engaged in private carriage. Such companies often engaged in *buy and sell* activities; they took title to goods and then sold them to a consignee for a price equal to the price paid by the carrier plus transportation charges. To prevent such activity, the ICC had developed the *primary business test,* which required that private carriage be related to the primary business of the truck owner. However, this principle was inconsistently applied in the courts.[24] As a result, Congress wrote the *primary business test* into the Interstate Commerce Act through an amendment contained in the 1958 statute.

257

PRESIDENTIAL MESSAGES AND CREATION OF THE DEPARTMENT OF TRANSPORTATION

The passage of the Transportation Act of 1958 was a significant step toward regulatory reform, but it did not end federal concern with the problems of the transportation sector. As discussed in Chapter 12, that same year the Federal Aviation Act created the Federal Aviation Agency (FAA) to replace the Civil Aeronautics Administration and to assume its functions. The new agency was also granted powers to establish air safety regulations. These powers had previously been vested in CAB. The FAA was later to become a component of the Department of Transportation (DOT). The Federal Aviation Act also reenacted the economic regulatory structure that had been included in the 1938 act, and permitted continuation of CAB control over economic regulation.

The existing regulatory structure continued to be criticized in many circles. In 1961 and 1962 seven major studies of transportation and its regulation were released by various federal agencies and study groups.[25] Although the recommendations of these studies varied, they generally supported relaxation of federal regulations and greater reliance upon market forces.

The Kennedy Transportation Message

In response to the continuing problems of the U.S. transportation system, President Kennedy delivered a special transportation message to Congress on April 5, 1962.[26] In that address, Kennedy criticized the existing regulatory structure as being inconsistent and outdated, and recommended a number of federal regulatory and promotional changes. He proposed more flexible carrier rate making and suggested that minimum rate regulation should be eliminated on bulk and agricultural movements involving common carriers. He also recommended extension of the agricultural and fishery exemptions to all carriers. His message stressed what he perceived to be inconsistencies in policies of taxation and user charges in transportation. To remedy this situation, he urged repeal of the 10 percent tax on railroad and bus transportation while simultaneously calling for an increase in user charges in air transportation. He also suggested implementation of a waterway user-charge program to recover federal outlays in that area. Additionally, President Kennedy sought to promote more evenhanded treatment of intercity modes by reducing CAB subsidies to local service carriers while abolishing such subsidies to trunk lines.

Obviously, President Kennedy believed that the future viability of the national transportation system required major regulatory and promotional changes in the various modes. His suggestions were subsequently incorporated into legislation and submitted to Congress. As might be expected, in the hearings that followed, many of his recommendations met with strong resistance from those modal interests that were somehow threatened by the proposals. The opposition was strong enough to kill the legislation in committee. Nevertheless, several of President Kennedy's recommendations, particularly those related to expansion of the user-charge concept, were reflected in subsequent statutes.

The Johnson Transportation Message

In 1966, President Johnson also chose to deliver a special transportation message to Congress. Departing from the economic regulatory theme of the Kennedy message, President Johnson instead focused more on the need for coordination of the national transportation system, reorganization of transportation planning activities, and active promotion of safety.[27]

In his address President Johnson contended that the U.S. transportation system lacked true coordination and that this resulted in system inefficiency. He advocated creation of a federal Department of Transportation to promote coordination of existing federal programs and to act as a focal point for future research and development efforts in transportation. The new agency would also become actively involved in transportation policy review and critique, but the economic regulatory functions of the ICC, CAB, and the Federal Maritime Commission were to be unaffected. This was not a new proposal. In fact, a cabinet-level transportation agency had first been proposed in 1870.[28]

Another major focus of President Johnson's remarks was transportation safety. He suggested creation of a National Transportation Safety Board to investigate major accidents and to make related recommendations to the appropriate federal bodies. The board was to be placed under the secretary of transportation, yet was to remain independent of DOT operating units. In another safety matter, President Johnson called for establishment of a new highway safety program to be administered by the DOT.

Other recommendations contained in the Johnson message dealt with a broad range of topics, including development of supersonic aircraft, control of aircraft noise, and research and development involving high-speed ground transportation.

Creation of the Department of Transportation

Congressional hearings were held on several bills involving most of President Johnson's recommendations. Although some opposition was expressed to specific proposals, there was general support for creation of the Department of Transportation. The legislation creating the agency was approved in October 1966.[29] The DOT commenced operations on April 1, 1967; Alan S. Boyd was appointed the first secretary of transportation. Specifics concerning the DOT structure and its activities are examined in Chapter 14.

EXPANSION OF FEDERAL PROMOTIONAL ACTIVITIES

Although federal involvement in transportation promotion dates to the early days of our country, it expanded significantly during the 1970s. The promotional expansion was at least partially due to the financial problems incurred by several modes, but it was also motivated by a congressional desire to broaden the capabilities of the national transportation system.

In 1970 the Airport and Airway Development Act established an Airport and Airway Trust Fund, which was to be administered by the secretary of transportation through the Federal Aviation Administration.[30] The fund accumulates revenues from a variety of user charges, ranging from an excise tax on airline passenger tickets and freight bills to registration fees on aircraft. In expanding federal funding of airport–airway development and operation, the 1970 act sought to place the program on a self-financing basis, with users bearing the costs of the system. This same pattern had been applied to building the Interstate Highway System through creation of the Highway Trust Fund in 1956.

Federal funding of urban transportation also expanded dramatically in 1970 with passage of the Urban Mass Transportation Assistance Act.[31] That statute, which was passed in response to congressional concerns with the decline of mass transit and the deterioration of air quality in many cities, created a $12 billion funding program for urban transportation projects. The funds were to be administered by the DOT's Urban Mass Transportation Administration (UMTA). This urban funding program was later extended by the $11.8 billion National Mass Transportation Assistance Act of 1974.[32] These urban funding programs and their role in the federal effort to revitalize urban transit are examined in detail in Chapters 19 and 20.

The maritime industry also benefited from the expansion of federal promotional programs during the 1970s. In 1969, President Nixon delivered a special address to Congress in which he recommended expansion of maritime promotional efforts to stabilize the faltering U.S. merchant marine fleet. In response to this request, Congress passed the Merchant Marine Act of 1970.[33] The program, which is administered by the Maritime Administration, increased federal operating and construction subsidies, provided additional tax incentives for ship owners, and guaranteed up to $3 billion in construction and mortgage loans.

As a result of the passage of these several statutes, the federal government played a greatly expanded promotional role in transportation in the 1970s. The federal funding involvement was to become even more extensive due to the serious financial problems of the railroads, which led to creation of Amtrak in 1970 and reorganization of the Northeast railroads in 1973.

AMTRAK

As noted previously, railroad passenger service losses placed a substantial financial burden on U.S. railroads following World War II. Although the situation improved somewhat following the passage of the Transportation Act of 1958, which gave the ICC authority to grant passenger train discontinuances, sizable deficits persisted.

Continuing passenger service losses coupled with the June 1970 bankruptcy of the Penn Central, which annually absorbed nearly one third of the national rail passenger service loss, led to passage of the Rail Passenger Service Act in October 1970.[34] The act established a quasi-public corporation, Amtrak, to manage the national intercity rail passenger service network. Amtrak initiated service in May 1971. Congress provided grants of $40 million and loan guarantees of $100 million to the new organization; the railroads paid $197 million in entry fees to become affiliated with Amtrak.

Performance of the System

Amtrak was originally envisioned by Congress as eventually becoming a for-profit corporation, but since its inception Amtrak has given little promise of approaching the break-even point. The annual deficits, which are offset by congressional appropriations, soared from $153.5 million in fiscal 1972 to more than $300 million in fiscal 1975.[35] During that period, Congress also expanded the loan guarantees available to Amtrak to $900 million. By early 1975 it had become apparent to Congress that Amtrak would be unable to repay the more than $860 million government-backed loans that it had already received.[36] Therefore, Congress reclassified those funds as outright federal grants. Furthermore, Amtrak's voracious appetite for federal monies has shown little sign of abatement. A report released by the Government Accounting Office in May 1976 estimated that Amtrak would require $6.2 billion in additional federal funds over the ensuing five years.[37]

Financially, Amtrak has been a disaster. Since its inception Amtrak has incurred annual deficits of more than 5 cents per passenger mile.[38] However, Amtrak is not solely to blame for this development. Congress has annually made continued Amtrak funding dependent upon Amtrak's commitment to continue existing runs while adding experimental runs. Scheduled service actually increased by more than 25 percent between 1972 and 1976.[39]

Although rail passenger service has improved since Amtrak's creation and ridership has risen, there are serious questions concerning Amtrak's future. Many of the routes included in the system offer little hope of economic viability; clearly they serve political purposes. Paul Reistrup, elected president of Amtrak in early 1975, argued that Amtrak should give greater emphasis to short-haul corridor-type markets in the future while rationalizing the scope of the system.[40] Reistrup was joined by the Department of Transportation in calling for a reduction in the number of routes served by the system.

The role of Amtrak in the U.S. transportation system must be viewed in terms of social and environmental considerations as well as economic standards. Clearly, there is some societal value associated with the stand-by capability of a national rail passenger system should energy problems intensify. Nevertheless, the continued commitment of massive amounts of federal monies to a system that generates approximately 1 percent of intercity passenger miles seems unwarranted at the present. In many instances modal alternatives exist that are capable of providing comparable service. Clearly, the challenge rests with Congress to end its *pork barrel* approach to Amtrak and to develop standards by which a rational rail passenger network might be developed.

NORTHEAST RAILROAD REORGANIZATION

One of the most significant transportation developments of this century was the Northeast railroad reorganization. Chapter 3 contained a discussion of the factors that led to the collapse of the railroad system of the region in the early 1970s. However, the significance of that crisis and the related reorganization deserves further attention at this point.

The Regional Rail Reorganization Act of 1973 was signed into law by President Ford in January 1974.[41] The bill initiated a transportation planning effort that was unprecedented in scope and complexity. Following the planning process, which lasted nearly two and one-half years, Conrail initiated operations on April 1, 1976. By the time service began nearly 3,000 miles of lightly used branch lines had been pared from the system, and several thousand additional miles of track were operated under a three-year joint federal–state subsidy program. In total, the Conrail system included approximately 17,000 miles of track.

During the early months of operation Conrail was widely praised for the quality of its operations, and its cash flow position was better than expected.[42] At that time Conrail projected profitable operations by 1980. Many observers have questioned the reasonableness of these projections, but it is vitally important than Conrail achieve economic self-sufficiency as soon as possible. The longer Conrail relies upon congressional funding for its financial well-being, the greater the risk of another Amtrak-like experience, only on a far greater scale.

The reorganization and rationalization of the Northeast railroads was late in coming. Congress again awaited the emergence of crisis conditions before acting on the problems of the railroads. Earlier congressional action could have precluded at least partially the ultimate deterioration in both the service provided and the financial condition of the railroads.

The collapse of the railroads in the Northeast was not without positive aspects. The reorganization led to substantial reduction in duplicate rail facilities, while moving strongly toward a philosophy that requires those who directly benefit from a particular transportation service to bear its true cost. Furthermore, the collapse focused national attention on the economic significance of the railroads, and led to examination of many of the problems that threatened the future viability of the mode. It is far too early to evaluate the success of the reorganization. However, the significance of the reorganization should not be underestimated. It may well determine whether or not railroad nationalization will become inevitable in the Northeast.

REGULATORY REFORM MOVEMENT

There had long been calls for regulatory reform in transportation, and the continuing problems of common carriers and concern for the quality of for-hire service intensified the reform movement in the 1970s. Critics contended that economic regulation protected inefficient operators, promoted unreasonably high rates, and generally fostered a misallocation of transportation resources.[43] Attacks were made on the regulatory structure of each major mode of intercity carriage.

Among the leading advocates of regulatory reform during the 1970s were the president's Council of Economic Advisers and the federal Department of Transportation. Both called for substantial relaxation of federal economic regulation and a greater reliance upon competitive forces. The views of the DOT were summarized in the agency's Statement of National Transportation Policy, which was issued in September 1975. In part the report stated:

263

Carriers, shippers and passengers frequently face a web of restrictive government regulations which stifle competition, discourage innovation and foster inefficiency. The present regulatory structure is in many respects outdated, inequitable, inefficient, uneconomical and frequently irrational. It often misplaces incentive and disincentive, distorts competitive advantage, protects inefficient carriers from effective competition, overrestricts market entry, artificially inflates rates and misallocates our Nation's resources . . . . The inflexibility of these outmoded regulations impedes the development of lower cost, more efficient national transportation.[44]

The DOT had taken this position for a number of years in its role of critiquing national transportation policy. Beginning in 1971, the DOT annually submitted legislation to Congress to promote substantial changes in the economic regulation of railroads, motor carriers, and airlines. However, although DOT's initiatives attracted some shipper and consumer group support, none of the bills was enacted.

The department's legislative efforts were more successful in 1975. Examination of the problems of the railroads during the Northeast railroad reorganization made it apparent to Congress that at least some of those problems were a function of regulation. Under intense pressure to modify its procedures, the ICC also somewhat reluctantly agreed that some regulatory modification was probably necessary. After conducting extensive hearings on the 1975 DOT railroad proposals, Congress passed the Railroad Revitalization and Regulatory Reform Act, which was signed into law in early 1976.[45]

Railroad Revitalization and Regulatory Reform Act

The statute provided some of the most significant changes in transportation regulation in nearly 40 years. It also made additional federal funding available to revitalize the U.S. railroad system.

Rate Making

The most important regulatory changes contained in the act pertained to railroad rate making. The ICC was given new standards to be applied to railroad rate proposals in determining if the rates were just and reasonable. Rates equal to or exceeding variable cost were not to be found unjust or unreasonable on the basis that they were too low. This provision was a major victory for the railroads, which had advocated the acceptance of variable-cost (or out-of-pocket cost) rate making for many years. Furthermore, the act provided that no rate was to be declared unjust or unreasonable on the basis that it was too high unless the ICC first determined that the carrier had *market dominance* over the traffic involved. The ICC was also charged with development of market dominance standards.

The 1976 statute also reaffirmed congressional disapproval of umbrella rate making. It declared that rates should not be held up to a particular level to protect the traffic of any other carrier or mode unless the ICC found that the proposed rates would reduce the going-concern value of the company charging the rates. To further clarify this issue, the act stated that any rate equaling or exceeding variable cost should be considered to be contributing to a company's going-concern value. Once again, the railroad position in intermodal rate making appeared to be strengthened.

Some regulatory reform advocates had called for total pricing freedom, but the 1976 act took a more moderate stance, and sought to create a gradually expanding zone in which carriers would have pricing freedom. Under the provisions of the act, during the following two years the railroads were free to raise or lower specific rates by as much as 7 percent annually from the level of rates in effect at the beginning of each year, and these rates could not be suspended on the basis of their reasonableness. The ICC retained the power to suspend any other rate proposal for up to seven months, with a possible three-month extension. The burden of proof in such rate cases was shifted to the complaining party, which had to prove that the rate could cause injury and that it should be found unlawful.

In other rate-related matters, the ICC was given time guidelines to be observed in rate cases involving major capital outlays by carriers, shippers, or receivers, and it was charged with development of standards to produce adequate carrier revenues.

The rate-making activities of rate bureaus were also addressed by the act. To accelerate bureau processing of rate proposals, the act required bureaus to reach final decisions on all docketed cases within 120 days. Furthermore, bureaus were not permitted to allow agreement or voting on single line rates, and only those carriers participating in the movement were to be permitted to vote on joint line rates.

Other Changes in ICC Duties

Other ICC responsibilities were also modified by the Railroad Revitalization and Regulatory Reform Act of 1976. The ICC was granted the authority to exempt certain railroad activities from regulation if it believed that such regulations were not required by the public interest. It may be recalled that similar authority had been granted to the CAB in the Civil Aeronautics Act of 1938, and it has been used to exempt third-level air carriers from economic regulation.

The act also sought to streamline ICC procedures for handling railroad

265

merger and consolidation proposals. Following enactment, the ICC was to rule on any merger and consolidation proposal within two years of its submission to the ICC. In the past the commission had often taken much longer than that to rule on such matters.

Concern with the relative role of federal and state government in intrastate rate making again surfaced in the 1976 act. It gave the ICC exclusive jurisdiction over intrastate rates when state agencies have failed to rule on such rates within 120 days of carrier filing.

Additionally, the ICC was charged to propose modernization and revisions in the Interstate Commerce Act within two years.

Railroad Funding

Financing of railroad improvements was also a major aim of the 1976 act. Several of its provisions dealt specifically with that issue. To complete the restructuring of the bankrupt railroads in the Northeast and Midwest, $2.1 billion was made available to Conrail. Funding was generated by granting the new organization authority to issue bonds and stock to the United States Railway Association (the planning and financing agency created by the Regional Rail Reorganization Act of 1973). Additionally, a $600 million government loan program was established to finance railroad rehabilitation of plant and equipment. Loan guarantees of up to $1 billion were also provided for railroad purchases of plant and equipment, and the act also provided $1.75 billion for upgrading rail passenger service in the Northeast corridor.

Other Provisions

Several other major issues were also addressed by the Railroad Revitalization and Regulatory Reform Act of 1976. These included subsidies to railroad branch lines, discriminatory state taxation of railroads, and special studies to be conducted by the ICC.

With respect to the branch-line issue, the act provided $360 million over five years to subsidize unprofitable branch lines. Under the program the federal share of branch-line deficits was set at 100 percent the first year, 90 percent the second, 80 percent the third, and 70 percent for the next two years. At that time further subsidization was to become a local issue. This provision sought to transfer the economic burden of such operations to state and local government on a gradual basis, thereby allowing these governmental units sufficient time to assess their needs and options.

For many years approximately 20 states had maintained property tax systems that were blatantly discriminatory against the railroads.[46] This issue had come before Congress several times, but no action had been taken. Under the 1976 act, states were barred from such practices, and the railroads were permitted to seek relief from state tax discrimination in federal courts. States were also barred from imposing other taxes in lieu of discriminatory property taxes.

The ICC was also directed to conduct studies into a variety of transportation issues. Among these were the impact of the conglomerate movement in transportation (see Chapter 16), the impact of federal aid to the various modes, and the projected effects of light-density-line abandonment outside the Northeast and Midwest.

Reform Proposals in Air and Motor Carriage

The movement toward regulatory reform in transportation has not been limited to rail regulation. During the 1970s numerous bills were submitted to Congress that sought to reduce the degree of regulation of the economic aspects of air and motor carriage.

Air Carrier Proposals

During the early 1970s the airline industry encountered a number of serious problems. These included chronic overcapacity, enormous capital requirements related to fleet modernization, and a steadily rising cost spiral. The financial position of several major airlines deteriorated to the brink of insolvency. As this was occurring, the industry was also confronted with proposals for regulatory change. Among the critics of existing airline regulation were consumer groups, a Senate subcommittee headed by Senator Edward Kennedy, a staff group within the Civil Aeronautics Board, and the Department of Transportation. The position of the DOT was summarized by Secretary of Transportation William T. Coleman in a presentation to the Aviation Subcommittee of the Senate Commerce Committee in April 1976. His remarks pertained to the DOT's Aviation Act of 1975. In part Coleman stated:

> The existing [airline] regulatory system has denied the American consumer the benefits of open competition. Regulation once intended to benefit the public now serves primarily to protect established firms from competitive market forces. Regulation has prevented management from adjusting to market conditions and responding effectively to market opportunities. It has also prevented airlines from achieving the cost efficiencies that are possible in a modern air transportation system. As a result, we believe, air fares are higher than they should be.[47]

The Aviation Act of 1975 sought a major overhaul of the economic regulatory structure of air carriage. Under the act, entry controls were to be liberalized, as were controls over carrier pricing. The act also sought to facilitate abandonment of noncompensatory services. Furthermore, it called for removal of many restrictions from charter operations to make them more directly competitive with the scheduled airlines.

The regularly scheduled airlines generally opposed the legislation. They contended that such changes would lead to chaos in the industry, and that the airlines and the consuming public would ultimately be harmed by such changes. Many communities that were threatened with the potential loss of local service runs also registered opposition to these measures. Congressional hearings were held on the bill during 1976, but Congress did not enact the legislation.

Motor Carrier Proposals

The regulation of motor carriage has been subjected to criticism since its inception in 1935. Critics have contended that entry and pricing controls are too rigid, that rate bureaus are too powerful, and that ICC operating restrictions have hindered competition while promoting inefficiency. Among those advocating changes in motor carrier regulation in the 1970s were some consumer and shipper groups, the Council of Economic Advisers, and the Department of Transportation. Although several earlier efforts aimed at regulatory changes in motor carriage had been rebuffed by Congress, the DOT again submitted a trucking bill in 1975.

The bill concerned several major aspects of the regulatory structure of motor carriage. It called for more liberalized entry into motor carriage and less restrictive control of routes served and commodities carried. Considerably greater rate and fare freedom for truck and bus companies was also requested. Additionally, the bill sought to remove some of the ICC's ability to grant antitrust immunity to motor carrier rate bureaus.[48]

The trucking bill was not greeted with widespread endorsement. The American Trucking Association, an organization that represents trucking interests, called the proposal "the ultimate in government irresponsibility."[49] Strong opposition to the regulatory changes was also voiced by motor carriers, and some shippers who feared a potential deterioration of service. The DOT bill was considered by the 95th Congress, but Congress did not enact the legislation. This matter is discussed further in Chapter 18.

SUMMARY

Since World War II a number of important transportation developments have occurred. In the Transportation Act of 1958, Congress attempted to revitalize the national railroad system. Although several provisions of the act brought some relief to the industry, the financial and competitive problems of the railroads persisted.

In 1967 the federal Department of Transportation was established to centralize federal planning and promotion of transportation. The agency was granted considerable power in safety regulation, but its role in economic regulation was basically limited to policy review and critique. Nevertheless, in recent years the agency has become a leading advocate of regulatory change.

The financial drain of rail passenger service losses and the bankruptcy of the Penn Central led to the creation of Amtrak to operate the intercity rail passenger service network. Since starting operations in 1971, Amtrak has improved service and ridership, but the annual deficits have risen dramatically. This development has led to serious questions concerning the future role of Amtrak in the national passenger network.

In 1973, Congress enacted the Regional Rail Reorganization Act, which led to the collective reorganization of seven bankrupt railroads in the Northeast and Midwest. The reorganization was unparalleled in both scope and complexity. The operating body that the act created, Conrail, initiated operations in April 1976, and its early operations were widely praised. However, it is far too soon to assess the organization's ability to revitalize rail services in the region.

The problems experienced by railroads, motor carriers, and airlines in the early 1970s led to a strong movement toward regulatory reform in transportation. The most significant development related to that movement was passage of the Railroad Revitalization and Regulatory Reform Act of 1976, which modified several major aspects of railroad regulation while increasing federal funding of railroad improvements. Similar proposals for regulatory reform in air and motor carriage have been submitted to Congress, but they have faced strong and effective opposition.

This chapter has emphasized regulatory and promotional developments; the next chapter focuses on the interaction and structure of the federal agencies that develop, administer, and critique national transportation policy.

NOTES

1. See Chapter 9 for a complete discussion of the Reed-Bulwinkle Act.

2. George W. Hilton, *The Transportation Act of 1958: A Decade of Experience* (Bloomington, Ind.: Indiana University Press, 1969), p. 11.

3. Ibid., p. 13.

4. Association of American Railroads, *Yearbook of Railroad Facts* (Washington, D.C.: the Association, 1968), p. 24.

5. For an excellent summary of the major transportation studies of that period, see Charles F. Phillips, *The Economics of Regulation*, rev. ed. (Homewood, Ill.: Richard D. Irwin, Inc., 1969), Appendix, Chapter 14, "Selected Bibliography of Postwar Studies of National Transportation Policy," pp. 534–36.

6. Public Law 85–625 (1958).

7. Hilton, op. cit., p. 36.

8. Ibid., pp. 107–16.

9. Association of American Railroads, *Yearbook of Railroad Facts* (Washington, D.C.: the Association, 1975), p. 21, and several earlier association reports.

10. *Chicago, Milwaukee, St. Paul & Pacific R.R. Co. v. Illinois*, 355 U.S. 300 (1958).

11. *Public Service Commission of Utah v. United States*, 356 U.S. 421 (1958).

12. U.S. Interstate Commerce Commission, *83rd Annual Report of the Interstate Commerce Commission* (Washington, D.C.: U.S. Government Printing Office, 1969), p. 80.

13. For an extensive analysis of these guarantees, see Hilton, op. cit., pp. 97–154.

14. Statement of George W. Hilton before the Senate Commerce Committee, July 30, 1970, p. 5. (Mimeographed)

15. Ibid.

16. Marvin L. Fair and Ernest W. Williams, *Economics of Transportation and Logistics* (Dallas, Tex.: Business Publications, Inc., 1975), pp. 465–66.

17. For the ICC ruling, see *Commodities-Pan Atlantic S.S. Corp.*, 309 ICC 587; also, 313 IC 23 (1960).

18. *ICC v. New York, New Haven & Hartford R.R.*, 372 U.S. 744, 759 (1963).

19. See *Ingot Molds, Pennsylvania to Steelton, Ky.*, 323 ICC 758 (1965); also, *Ingot Molds, Pennsylvania to Steelton, Ky.*, 326 ICC 77, 85 (1965).

20. *American Commercial Lines, Inc., et al. v. Louisville & Nashville R.R. Co., et al.*, 392 U.S. 571 (1968).

21. Hilton, op. cit., p. 74.

22. Ibid., p. 76.

23. Public Law 94–210 (1976).

24. Hliton, op. cit., p. 41.

25. Roy J. Sampson and Martin T. Farris, *Domestic Transportation: Practice, Theory, and Policy*, 3rd ed. (Boston: Houghton Mifflin Company, 1975), p. 486.

26. *The Transportation System of Our Nation,* message from the president of the United States, April 5, 1962, House of Representatives, Doc. No. 384, 87th Cong., 2nd Sess. (Washington, D.C.: U.S. Government Printing Office, 1962).

27. *Creating a Department of Transportation,* Hearings, Subcommittee on Government Operations, House of Representatives, 89th Cong., 2nd Sess. (Washington, D.C.: U.S. Government Printing Office, 1966), pp. 36–49.

28. Sampson and Farris, op. cit., p. 372.

29. Public Law 89-670 (1966).

30. Public Law 91-258; 84 Stat. 219 (1970).

31. Public Law 91-453 (1970).

32. Public Law 93-503 (1974).

33. For a discussion of the act, see Gerald R. Jantscher, *Bread upon the Waters: Federal Aids to the Maritime Industries* (Washington, D.C.: Brookings Institution, 1975), pp. 42–44.

34. Public Law 91-518; 84 Stat. 1327 (1970).

35. Continental Trailways, Inc., *Amtrak Yesterday, Today and Tomorrow* (Dallas, Tex.: Continental Trailways, Inc., 1976), p. 12.

36. "Aid for Amtrak of $1.1 Billion Is Voted in House," *Wall Street Journal,* New York, March 17, 1975, p. 5.

37. Transportation Association of America, *What's Happening in Transportation,* May 4, 1976, p. 2.

38. Continental Trailways, op. cit., p. 12.

39. "Amtrak Campaigns to Run Its Own Show," *Business Week* (February 23, 1976), p. 32.

40. Lewis M. Phelps, "Amtrak Seen Stressing Short-Haul Runs Under Leadership of Its New President," *Wall Street Journal,* New York, January 30, 1975, p. 11.

41. Public Law 93-236; 45 U.S.C (1973).

42. Association of American Railroads, "Conrail Operations Drawing Praise," *Information Letter,* No. 2193 (May 26, 1976), p. 1.

43. For two critical evaluations of federal regulatory policies in transportation, see Thomas G. Moore, *Freight Transportation Regulation: Surface Freight and the Interstate Commerce Commission* (Washington, D.C.: American Enterprise Institute for Public Policy Research, 1972); also U.S. Senate, Committee on the Judiciary, Subcommittee on Administrative Practice and Procedure, *Civil Aeronautics Board Practices and Procedures,* 94th Cong., 1st Sess., 1975 (Washington, D.C.: U.S. Government Printing Office, 1975).

44. U.S. Department of Transportation, Office of the Secretary, *A Statement of National Transportation Policy* (Washington, D.C.: U.S. Government Printing Office, 1975), p. 13.

45. Public Law 94-210 (1976).

46. U.S. Senate, Committee on Interstate and Foreign Commerce, Special Study Group on Transportation Policies in the United States, *National Transportation Policy* (Doyle Report), 87th Cong., 1st Sess., 1960 (Washington, D.C.: U.S. Government Printing Office, 1961), p. 451.

47. U.S. Department of Transportation, Office of the Secretary, *Statement of U.S. Secretary of Transportation William T. Coleman, Jr. to the Aviation Subcommittee of the Senate Committee on Commerce Regarding the Aviation Act of 1975,* presented April 7, 1976 (Washington, D.C.: the Department, 1976), p. 3.

48. For a summary of DOT views concerning motor carrier regulation, see U.S. Department of Transportation, *Statement of John W. Snow, Administrator, National Highway Traffic Safety Administration Before the House Committee on Public Works and Transportation, Subcommittee on Surface Transportation, on Motor Carrier Regulatory Reform,* presented September 14, 1976 (Washington, D.C.: the Department, 1976).

49. "Ford Unveils Bill Curbing ICC Authority over Motor Carriers; Truckers Score Plan," *Wall Street Journal,* New York, November 14, 1975, p. 6.

SELECTED REFERENCES

Allen, Bruce W. "ICC Behavior in Rail Abandonments." *ICC Practitioners' Journal,* XLI, No. 5 (July–August, 1974), pp. 553–71.

Douglas, George W., and James C. Miller. "The CAB's Domestic Passenger Fare Investigation." *Bell Journal of Economics,* V. No. 1 (Spring, 1974), pp. 205–22.

Fellmeth, Robert. *The Interstate Commerce Omission.* New York: Grossman Publishers, 1970.

Harbeson, Robert W. "Some Policy Implications of Northeastern Railroad Problems." *Transportation Journal,* XIV, No. 1 (Fall, 1974), pp. 5–12.

Harbeson, Robert W. "Toward a More Compensatory Rail Rate Structure." *ICC Practitioners' Journal,* XL, No. 2 (January–February, 1973), pp. 145–63.

Hilton, George W. *The Transportation Act of 1958: A Decade of Experience.* Bloomington, Ind.: Indiana University Press, 1969.

Hynes, Cecil. "Small Business and Deregulation of the Motor Common Carriers." *Transportation Journal,* XV, No. 3 (Spring 1976), pp. 74–86.

Kahn, Fritz. "The Reformation of Railroad Regulation." *ICC Practitioners' Journal*, XLIII, No. 4 (May–June, 1976), pp. 509–17.

Lieb, Robert C. "Relaxing Motor Carrier Regulation—The Massachusetts Attempt." *Logistics and Transportation Review*, XI, No. 2 (Fall, 1975), pp. 193–201.

Moore, Thomas G. *Freight Transportation Regulation: Surface Freight and the Interstate Commerce Commission*. Washington, D.C.: American Enterprise Institute for Public Policy Research, 1972.
Chapter 3. "Development of Multi Modal Regulation," pp. 25–40.

Sampson, Roy J., and Martin T. Farris. *Domestic Transportation: Practice, Theory, and Policy*, 3rd ed. Boston: Houghton Mifflin Company, 1975.
Chapter 22. "Regulation of Transportation Competition: Evolution," pp. 352–67.
Chapter 23. "National Transportation Planning: A New Era," pp. 368–83.

Spychalski, John C. "Criticisms of Regulated Freight Transport: Do Economists' Perceptions Conform with Institutional Realities?" *Transportation Journal*, XIV, No. 3 (Spring 1975), pp. 5–17.

Spychalski, John C. "Imperfections in Railway Line Abandonment Regulation and Suggestions for Their Corrections." *ICC Practitioners' Journal*, XL, No. 4 (May–June, 1973), pp. 454–69.

Task Force on Railroad Productivity. *Improving Railroad Productivity*. Final Report to the National Commission on Productivity and the Council of Economic Advisers. Washington, D.C.: Task Force on Railroad Productivity, 1973.
Chapter 6. "Regulatory Modernization," pp. 187–209.

U.S. Congress, Senate, Committee on Interstate and Foreign Commerce, Special Study Group on Transportation Policies in the United States. *National Transportation Policy* (Doyle Report). 87th Cong., 1st Sess., 1960. Washington, D.C.: U.S. Government Printing Office, 1961.

U.S. Congress, Senate, Committee on the Judiciary, Subcommittee on Administrative Practice and Procedure. *Civil Aeronautics Board Practices and Procedures*. 94th Cong., 1st Sess., 1975. Washington, D.C.: U.S. Government Printing Office, 1975.

U.S. Department of Transportation, Office of the Secretary. *A Statement of National Transportation Policy*. Washington, D.C.: U.S. Government Printing Office, 1975.

U.S. Department of Transportation, Office of the Secretary. *The Northeastern Railroad Problem*. A report to Congress. Washington, D.C.: the Department, 1973.

Wilson, George W. "Regulation, Public Policy, and Efficient Provision of Freight Transportation." *Transportation Journal*, XV, No. 1 (Fall, 1975), pp. 5–20.

DISCUSSION QUESTIONS

1. What are government loan guarantees and how do they differ from direct loans?
2. What were the major differences in the transportation messages delivered to Congress by Presidents Kennedy and Johnson?
3. Why has so much attention been devoted to the topic of regulatory reform in transportation during the 1970s?
4. Discuss the significance of the changes in railroad pricing regulations that were contained in the Railroad Revitalization and Regulatory Reform Act of 1976.

CHAPTER

14

Federal Regulatory Agencies: Their Structure and Activities

A complex institutional structure has evolved at the federal level to facilitate the formulation and administration of transportation policy. This chapter. examines the structure and activities of the institutions involved. Included is a discussion of the federal regulatory agencies and their interaction with the legislative, executive, and judicial branches of government in the development and administration of regulatory policy. Attention is also given to the multifaceted role played by the Department of Transportation in this process and to the structure of state agencies involved in regulation of intrastate transportation.

DEVELOPMENT OF THE REGULATORY AGENCY CONCEPT

As discussed in Chapter 11, the earliest regulatory controls applied to domestic transportation were administered at the state level by legislative bodies and the courts. However, typically these processes were slow, rather inflexible, and quite negative in nature. The difficulties inherent in these regulatory patterns led to the emergence of the early state railroad commissions in the pre-Civil War period. Basically, the commissions were fact-finding and advisory bodies, which reported to the state legislatures. The direct regulatory powers of the commissions were generally quite limited.

The Grange movement of the early 1870s fostered creation of state commissions, which were granted broad regulatory powers by the state legislatures. The Granger laws, and the commissions that administered them, established structural and jurisdictional patterns that were later applied to regulatory agencies at both the federal and state levels. A federal regulatory framework for transportation was ultimately initiated with the establishment of the ICC in 1887, and was later extended with the creation of CAB in 1938.

Role and Status of the Federal Agencies

The ICC and CAB are expert bodies primarily involved in administration of the regulatory statutes. They were created by Congress, and their authority has been broadly prescribed by statute. As discussed later in this chapter, the regulatory agencies are integrally related to the legislative, executive, and judicial branches of the federal government in the development and administration of transportation policy.

An important feature of the regulatory agencies is their independent status. This independence from the other branches of the federal government minimizes the likelihood of political interference in their activities. ICC commissioners and CAB board members are appointed by the president, with the advice and consent of the Senate, but the agencies report directly to Congress. The appointments of the regulators expire in a staggered fashion so that a single-term president cannot, except under unusual circumstances, appoint a majority of ICC or CAB members. No more than a simple majority of the members of the ICC or CAB may be from one political party, and they can only be removed from office due to inefficiency, neglect of duty, or malfeasance in office.

The ICC and CAB have been given broad transportation policy guidelines by Congress, and they are charged with the development of specific regulations and procedures within these limits. As a result, the agencies not only serve in an administrative capacity, but also act to formulate policies in those areas in which the related statutes are nonspecific.

The actions of the regulatory agencies have been characterized as being both quasi-legislative and quasi-judicial. In rule-making proceedings the agencies act in a legislative capacity; when interpreting the laws and issuing orders for compliance with established guidelines, the agencies act in a judicial manner.

The promotional role of the regulatory agencies should also be stressed. The CAB is specifically charged with promotion as well as regulation of air carriage; the ICC has no such mandate. However, in attempting to foster sound economic conditions within the modes it regulates, the ICC necessarily must concern itself with carrier welfare. Thus its decisions in such

276

matters as proposals for general rate increases or carrier consolidations are necessarily influenced by promotional considerations.

The federal regulatory agencies also act as fact-finding bodies that compile carrier statistics and conduct research into various transportation policy issues. Carrier statistics are routinely made public, and the agencies periodically release reports that outline agency opinions on policy matters. One such report, "The Regulatory Issues of Today," was released by the ICC in January 1975.[1] At the time the ICC was confronted with widespread attacks on the regulatory structure; the report summarized the views and decisions of the ICC on such matters as rate regulation, abandonment of service, and entry controls in trucking. During the same year the ICC also released a study that was quite critical of the impact of the conglomerate movement in the railroad industry, and the CAB released a staff study that called for substantial economic deregulation of air carriage.[2] Such agency research is often used to document the views of the agencies in presentations before congressional committees that are considering regulatory modifications.

INTERSTATE COMMERCE COMMISSION

As discussed in previous chapters, the ICC is the federal regulatory agency that controls many of the economic aspects of interstate surface carriage. With some exceptions, the interstate operations of railroads, motor carriers, oil pipelines, water carriers, surface freight forwarders, and brokers are included in the agency's domain. In carrying out its statutory responsibilities, the ICC is actively involved in such matters as control of entry, abandonment of service, rate making, consolidations, mergers and acquisition of control, and carrier security issues.

The ICC consists of 11 members appointed by the president with the advice and consent of the Senate. The commissioners serve seven-year terms and may be reappointed. The terms of office are staggered to provide continuity and to limit possible interference from the president through the appointment process. No more than six commissioners may be from one political party.

Prior to 1970 the commissioners annually elected a chairman to oversee and coordinate ICC activities. The position was generally rotated among ICC members on a yearly basis. However, under a reorganization plan approved by Congress in 1969, the president was given authority to designate the chairman of the ICC. The commissioners then select a vice-chairman to assist the chairman in carrying out his administrative responsibilities.

The reorganization sought to provide a greater degree of stability and continuity in the position of chairman while improving communications between the executive branch and the ICC. A reorganization had been proposed several times prior to 1969, but was defeated each time due to congressional concern that allowing the president to select the ICC chairman would jeopardize the independence of the agency.

Structure

The ICC has developed a rather complex structure to carry out its broad regulatory responsibilities. As illustrated in Figure 14–1, the agency is organized on a divisional basis, with each division having specific responsibilities under the Interstate Commerce Act.

Division 1 of the ICC, Operating Rights, has jurisdiction over the issuance of certificates and permits to motor carriers, water carriers, freight forwarders, and brokers. Division 2, Rates, Tariffs, and Valuation, is concerned with rates, charges, and the valuation of railroad and pipeline property for rate-setting purposes. Division 3, Finance and Service, oversees security issuances, consolidations and mergers, and discontinuance of service proposals. Three commissioners are assigned to each division, while one commissioner serves as chairman and another serves as vice-chairman.

Procedures

Many of the matters that come before the ICC are not reviewed directly by 11 commissioners. Cases that do not involve issues of "general transportation significance" are handled by one of 16 employee boards maintained by the ICC. The jurisdiction of each employee board coincides with different sections of the Interstate Commerce Act. Many informal proceedings, which do not involve holding public hearings or taking testimony, are processed by employee boards. The boards were created in the 1960s to free the commissioners from unnecessary administrative work so that they might concentrate on issues of greater significance.[3]

A different procedure is used by the ICC in handling formal cases involving presentation of evidence at public hearings. Such cases are usually initially handled by administrative law judges of the ICC. These agency employees hold hearings and compile evidence on the case, and ultimately render a decision on the matter. If the decision of the administrative law judge is acceptable to all parties, it becomes an official ICC order.

Appeal of the administrative law judge's decision to the appropriate division is possible. The case will then be reviewed, and the division will render a decision. The divisions do not always uphold the decisions of the administrative law judges. In fact, one study indicated that during a two-year period approximately 20 percent of those decisions were overturned by the divisions or the full commission.[4]

Interstate Commerce Commission

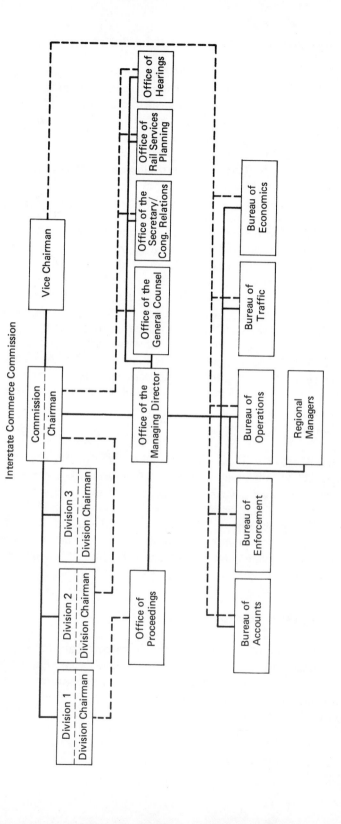

Figure 14–1

Structure of the Interstate Commerce Commission

SOURCE: U.S. Interstate Commerce Commission, *89th Annual Report to Congress* (Washington, D.C.: U.S. Government Printing Office, 1975), p. 99.

If a case reviewed by a division of the ICC does not have "general transportation significance," the order of the division is final. However, if the case does have such significance, it may be appealed to the full commission. In some instances, such as the previously discussed Ingot Molds case, the full commission has reversed the decisions of the divisions.[5]

In any event, the final ICC decision on a given case may be appealed on certain grounds in the courts. The appeals procedure and the grounds for appeal are discussed later in this chapter.

Pursuing a case before the ICC can be both time consuming and expensive. One study found that the least expensive case argued before the ICC will cost about $3,000; more complicated cases often cost the applicants hundreds of thousands of dollars in fees.[6] It must be remembered that there is no guarantee that the ICC will rule in favor of the applicant in such cases. Undoubtedly, the potential cost and risk associated with such proceedings influences the thinking of carriers and shippers contemplating action before the ICC.

Several procedural changes have been implemented by the ICC in recent years, but it is unclear how streamlined the regulatory process might become. It has often been said that one man's red tape is another man's due process. Expediency at the cost of justice is undesirable; this must be considered in future attempts to accelerate ICC deliberations in complex cases.

Workload and Budget

Given its broad range of regulatory responsibilities, the ICC has a quite sizable workload. While employing a staff of 2,098 in 1975, the agency handled 8,315 cases during the year.[7] The majority of the cases involved rates, operating rights, and finance proceedings. Additionally, the ICC was involved in 14,821 informal cases.[8] That year 150 of the ICC's decisions were challenged in the federal court system, and the agency made 21 appearances before congressional committees.[9] The ICC's budget for the year was approximately $47 million.

CIVIL AERONAUTICS BOARD

The regulatory jurisdiction of the CAB is far more narrow than that of the ICC. Its primary concern is the economic regulation and promotion of air carriage. To a great extent, the structure and operating procedures of the CAB were patterned after those of the ICC.

The board consists of five members who serve staggered six-year terms.

They are appointed by the president with the advice and consent of the Senate. Members may be reappointed. No more than three CAB members may be from one political party.

The president designates the chairman and the vice-chairman of the CAB on an annual basis. This presidential power has stimulated controversy in recent years, particularly in 1975 when White House pressures forced the resignation of the chairman of the CAB, who strongly opposed deregulation. President Ford then replaced the resigning CAB member with an ex-DOT official who strongly favored deregulation. The new CAB member was designated chairman of the CAB and became an agency advocate of airline deregulation.[10] This political maneuver raised serious questions concerning the degree of independence that is realistically maintained by the regulatory agencies. A continuation of such practices would constitute a strong argument for a reduction of presidential power in this area.

In administering the regulatory statutes, the CAB plays the same type of quasi-legislative and quasi-judicial role that the ICC does. As outlined in earlier chapters, the jurisdiction of the agency includes such matters as entry into markets, control over abandonment of service, rate making, consolidations and mergers, and numerous other economic aspects of domestic air carriage. The CAB also certifies U.S. carriers to fly international routes and grants permits to foreign airlines to allow them to serve U.S. cities. In addition to its regulatory role, the CAB also plays an active promotional role in aviation, which it is directed to do by the Declaration of Policy in the Federal Aviation Act. This concern for promotion of the industry not only plays a role in cases that come before the CAB, but is also reinforced by CAB administration of subsidies to local service airlines. The dual role of regulation and direct promotion is an uncomfortable one for the CAB to play; it has often been criticized as being overly concerned about carrier welfare while giving inadequate attention to the needs of the traveling public.

Structure and Procedures

The internal structure of the CAB is illustrated in Figure 14–2. Although CAB procedures are generally similar to those employed by the ICC, there are two important differences. First, the CAB makes far greater use of informal procedures in handling cases than does the ICC. More than 80 percent of the cases handled by the CAB rely upon such informal procedures.[11] Second, the CAB does not utilize employee boards to deal with cases that do not involve "general transportation significance."[12] These two procedural differences are possible because the CAB deals with far

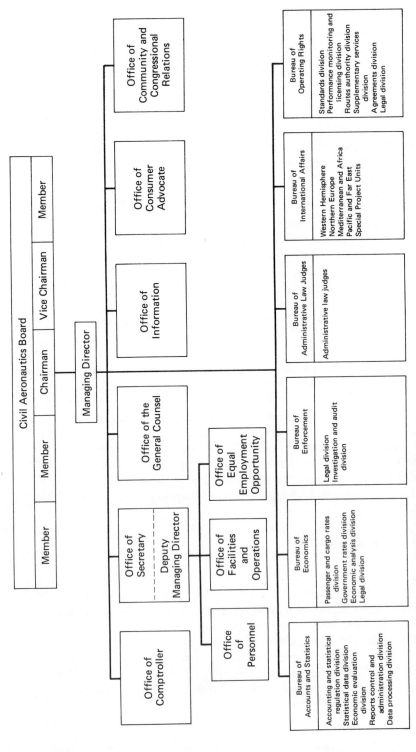

Figure 14–2 Structure of the Civil Aeronautics Board

SOURCE: U.S. Civil Aeronautics Board, *Reports to Congress* (Washington, D.C.: U.S. Government Printing Office, 1975), p. iv.

fewer carriers and a far lighter case load than the ICC. Route awards and fare proposals comprise the bulk of the CAB's case load. The CAB employed 688 people in 1974, and had an operating budget of more than $15 million during that year.[13]

AGENCY RELATIONSHIP WITH THE LEGISLATIVE BRANCH

Despite the organizational independence of the federal regulatory agencies in transportation, a very strong relationship exists between the agencies and Congress. The legislative branch not only established the regulatory agencies, but it also formulates the basic statutory transportation policy that they administer. Additionally, Congress controls agency appropriations and reviews presidential appointments to the ICC and CAB.

Formulation of Transportation Policy

Given its power to enact regulatory guidelines by statute, Congress is the dominant force in the formulation of national transportation policy. Congress relies quite heavily upon several major committees that review regulatory proposals. The most important of these committees are the House and Senate Committees on Interstate and Foreign Commerce. These committees and their subcommittees conduct hearings on specific proposals and take the testimony of interested parties. Often regulatory agency personnel testify in congressional hearings, as do representatives of other government agencies, shippers, carriers, and consumer groups.

The influence of industrial associations, such as the American Trucking Association, the Air Transport Association, and the Association of American Railroads, in such proceedings should not be underestimated. These industry-supported organizations, which represent carrier interests, are generally well prepared on regulatory issues and are well mobilized. They respond rapidly and effectively to legislative proposals that may run counter to the interests of their members. Throughout such proceedings, carrier associations and other interest groups conduct *lobbying* efforts with influential congressmen. In recent years the term "lobbying" has tended to take on a rather shady, semi-legal connotation. However, the information-conveying function of these efforts is legitimate and important. In fact, government agencies conduct similar lobbying efforts through officials often known as *congressional liaisons*. However, the coupling of industrial lobbying efforts with political contributions and other favors raise important ethical considerations and may constitute undue political influence.

To support the analysis that accompanies review of regulatory change proposals, Congress has funded numerous studies of transportation policy issues. In some instances the task force created to conduct the study has included regulatory agency personnel. These studies can ultimately influence the statutory guidelines given to the regulatory agencies by Congress.

Most regulatory change proposals die in committee. However, those which are reported favorably out of committee in both the House and the Senate have taken a major step toward enactment. Following floor action, if differences exist in the House and Senate versions of the legislation, these discrepancies may be resolved in joint House–Senate compromise committees before final enactment. The president must then decide whether to sign the final bill into law.

Through formulation of regulatory policy by statute, Congress strongly influences the activities of the regulatory agencies, which must operate within the statutory guidelines. As noted earlier, the terminology of these statutes is often somewhat vague in referring to such concepts as "reasonableness" and "consistency with the public interest." To a certain extent, this imprecise wording is both necessary and desirable. Congress cannot possibly anticipate the numerous factors and circumstances which might apply in a given case that comes before a regulatory agency. Consequently, the regulatory agencies are typically given a degree of interpretational latitude in the regulatory statutes. Also, conditions change over time, and flexible statutory guidelines permit the agencies to modify regulatory standards. However, in certain instances the wording of the regulatory statutes is so vague that it provides little insight into congressional intent. This has often caused administrative problems for the ICC and CAB, and Congress has frequently failed to respond to the requests of the agencies for further direction.

Budgetary Control and Agency Appointments

The regulatory agencies report directly to Congress and are dependent upon Congress for their annual appropriations. Final congressional budgetary decisions can therefore affect agency staffing and research activities. In turn, this can influence the performance of the agencies. Although the annual budgets of the ICC and CAB have grown steadily in recent years, both agencies have generally contended that they are underfunded, given their workloads.

As noted earlier in this chapter, presidential appointments to the regulatory agencies must be approved by the Senate. Generally, the confirmation hearings have proceeded smoothly, and few appointments have failed to win Senate approval.

284

AGENCY RELATIONSHIP WITH THE EXECUTIVE BRANCH

The ICC and CAB also have considerable interaction with the executive branch of the federal government. Through his powers to appoint agency personnel and to select the chairmen of the ICC and CAB, the president can play a major role in shaping the regulatory philosophies of the regulatory agencies. This is particularly true if the president serves two terms, or if some regulatory agency appointees resign before their terms expire. Furthermore, realistically there are a variety of political means available to a president that can be employed to make a regulatory agency appointee uncomfortable enough to resign. The combination of these factors, therefore, can have a quite significant impact on the regulatory process if the president is so inclined.

The president can also attempt to influence the annual appropriations made available to the ICC and CAB. Agency budget requests are submitted to the Office of Management and Budget (OMB), which is part of the executive office of the president. In formulating the final budget requests to be sent to Congress, the OMB might choose to delete funds for certain agency activities, which could constrain agency performance. However, Congress ultimately approves the appropriations, and such cuts could be restored by Congress if they appeared unjustified.

The president also possesses some direct regulatory power in the realm of international transportation. Due to the foreign policy implications of international airline operations, the president has been given final authority over international route awards granted to the airlines. Although the authority has been exercised infrequently, in certain instances presidential intervention has been quite significant. An example occurred in December 1976 when President Ford overruled the CAB in a series of trans-Atlantic route awards.[14]

The president may also play a role in transportation policy formulation through recommendations to Congress. In the years prior to the creation of the Department of Transportation, Presidents Kennedy and Johnson delivered transportation messages directly to Congress. However, since the establishment of the cabinet-level DOT, that executive agency has tended to represent the views of the administration before Congress.

Enforcement and Defense of Agency Orders

The orders of the ICC and CAB are binding unless set aside by the courts, but the agencies must rely upon the Department of Justice to seek enforcement of their rulings in cases of noncompliance. Furthermore, when the regulatory agencies are challenged in court, they cannot directly

285

defend themselves, but must rely upon the defense of the attorney general. The agencies have long argued that this places them at a disadvantage, and that they should be permitted to provide their own defense. Complicating this situation is the fact that in some instances the relationship of the regulatory agencies with the Department of Justice has been tenuous. There have been cases in which the department has refused to defend a regulatory agency decision in court because it did not agree with the agency's decision in the case.[15] Such occurrences illustrate the cumbersome nature of this relationship and raise serious questions about its viability.

Intervention in Agency Cases

Executive branch agencies, such as the DOT and the Department of Justice, are also permitted to intervene in the proceedings of the ICC and CAB. Although these agencies cannot directly determine regulatory policy, they have sought to influence regulatory decisions, particularly in cases in which the statutory guidelines are unclear. In recent years, the DOT has intervened in a number of rate cases before the ICC and the CAB, and the Department of Justice has appeared before the regulatory bodies in several merger and consolidation cases.

AGENCY RELATIONSHIP WITH THE JUDICIAL BRANCH

In administering the federal regulatory statutes, the ICC and CAB also have frequent contact with the federal judicial system. These contacts involve occasional court review of regulatory agency decisions, enforcement of agency orders, and court review of agency damage and reparation awards.

Review of Agency Decisions

The federal courts act to limit the powers of the regulatory agencies by assuring that their decisions do not violate constitutional guarantees or overextend their statutory authority. The possibility of judicial review protects the public against arbitrary or capricious action on the behalf of the agencies.

Several levels of appeals may be pursued by parties who are dissatisfied with a regulatory agency ruling. Decisions may be appealed to (1) a federal district court, (2) a federal circuit court of appeals, and (3) the Supreme Court. Relatively few cases proceed completely through the appeals process. Besides the expense and time involved in such appeals, the Supreme Court limits its considerations of transportation-related cases to those which have national transportation significance. Among the transportation cases that have reached the Supreme Court over the past decade have been the previously discussed Ingot Molds case, and the appeal of the ICC decision to permit the Penn Central consolidation.[16] In both cases the Court upheld the earlier ICC decisions.

As discussed in Chapter 11, from the time of its establishment in 1887 until 1910 the ICC was hampered by continuous court review of its decisions. Generally, the courts insisted upon rehearing the entire case, and they did not accept the ICC's fact finding in the case. Rather, the courts compiled their own record. This court treatment of ICC cases contributed to the relative ineffectiveness of the commission during its early years.

However, in a decision issued in 1910 the Supreme Court ruled that future court review of ICC decisions was to be restricted to consideration of purely legal and constitutional matters.[17] In subsequent years the courts have therefore accepted the fact-finding credibility of the ICC and CAB, and have limited their review of agency cases to matters of law.

There are a number of specific circumstances under which regulatory agency decisions may be set aside by the courts. The primary grounds for reversal are as follows. The decision may be set aside if the statute under which the order was issued was unconstitutional. The ruling may also be overturned if it violates the rights prescribed by the Constitution; such cases usually involve claims that the decision violates the 5th or 14th amendments to the Constitution, which prohibit the taking of private property without due process. The courts may reverse the decision of the regulatory agency if the agency has misinterpreted the intention of the governing statute or if it has failed to abide by proper procedures. Similarly, the courts may rule in favor of the complainant if the agency has made the decision without evidence or contrary to the evidence involved.[18]

Enforcement and Review of Agency Awards

The regulatory agencies can issue orders, but only the courts can force compliance with these orders. Therefore, the agencies authorize the courts to issue injunctions to prevent violation of their directives.

The courts may also play a role in cases involving agency awards of damages or reparations. If the carrier fails to comply with the order, the injured party must bring suit in court to collect. In reviewing cases in which the agencies have ruled that injury has been sustained and have awarded damages, the courts are not bound to accept the agencies' judgment in terms of either the injury involved or the propriety of the damages awarded.

PROBLEMS OF AGENCY ADMINISTRATION

Reliance upon regulatory agencies to administer congressional guidelines and formulate transportation policy where appropriate is not without problems. Among these are staffing difficulties, threats to the independence of the agencies, the possibility of the agencies coming under the control of the industries that they regulate, and regulatory lag.

Staffing

Periodically, questions have been raised concerning the qualifications of regulatory agency appointees. One study of appointments to the ICC contended that the most important qualification tended to be political contacts and alliances.[19] There can be no denying that political patronage plays at least a limited role in agency appointments. However, in recent years most appointees have also had some prior experience in either transportation or public regulation of business. The Senate must necessarily be concerned with the qualifications of the candidates that they consider for regulatory agency positions. A congressional posture that simply rubber stamps presidential appointments to the agencies could seriously hinder the performance of the agencies.

One author has suggested that there are difficulties in attracting qualified young people for agency positions because the relatively low profile of agency commissioners holds little appeal for younger people with political aspirations.[20] It was further suggested that agency positions are, however, appealing to older candidates who are seeking a comfortable spot to spend their declining years of public service.[21]

Maintenance of Independence

The ICC and CAB have historically been confronted with numerous threats to their independence. Realistically, the maintenance of this independence is quite difficult, given the close interaction of the agencies with the legislative, executive, and judicial branches of the federal government. Yet some degree of independence is necessary if the agencies are to impartially administer regulatory standards. To protect this independence, Congress should continuously monitor the relationship between the agencies and the president. The presidential powers of both appointment and designation of agency chairmen pose a significant threat to agency independence.

Industry Dominance

There has been growing concern in recent years that the ICC and CAB have fallen under the control of the industries that they regulate. Critics have contended that the agencies are overly concerned with protection of carrier interests, and that they give inadequate attention to consumer welfare.[22] It has also often been noted that, following expiration of their terms with the regulatory agencies, many former regulators assume executive positions in the industries that they previously regulated.[23] However, such developments cannot necessarily be assumed to constitute payment for previously rendered services. Given the understanding of the regulatory process that these people develop during their tenure with the agencies, they can provide quite valuable insight to carrier organizations. Consequently, it is only natural that carriers recruit such people. At the same time, it is unrealistic to expect the ex-regulator to ignore transportation in assessing future career options.

The task faced by the regulatory agencies in balancing consumer and carrier interests, while striving to achieve the goals of U.S. transportation policy, is quite difficult. The regulatory bodies must necessarily be concerned with the financial well-being of the carriers if the transportation system is to remain operational. In attempting to promote stability and a financially sound carrier structure, the agencies will often take actions that might easily be interpreted as pro-carrier by consumer interests. However, such decisions must be placed in proper perspective by relating them to the multifaceted goals of the agencies. A review of the recent financial performance of many regulated carriers would lead one to conclude that, if the agencies have been overly concerned with carrier well-being, they have been relatively ineffective in pursuing that end.

Regulatory Lag

In transportation there has often been a substantial time lapse between changes in industrial conditions and related changes in regulatory policies. It has frequently been asserted that the regulatory agencies are responsible for this *regulatory lag*. Although the agencies have never been noted for rapid response to industrial changes, these charges must be kept in perspective. In many instances the actions of the agencies are circumscribed by the governing statutes. In such cases, unless Congress acts to modify the statutes, the agencies are not free to change related policies. However, many regulatory statutes are imprecise and permit considerable interpretational latitude on the behalf of the agencies. In interpreting these guidelines the regulatory agencies have tended to be quite conservative, and have generally relied heavily upon earlier agency interpretations.

It should be realized that the workload of the regulatory agencies has historically been quite substantial, and that their administrative responsibilities have undoubtedly limited the time available for long-range policy analysis. Consequently, in the absence of increased direct congressional action, there is little to suggest that the regulatory lag is likely to be substantially reduced.

REORGANIZATION PROPOSALS

Periodically, there have been suggestions that the regulatory agency concept employed in domestic transportation should be modified. One such proposal sought to make the agencies more responsive to the executive branch by placing them under the control of the president.[24] Such a reorganization would seriously jeopardize the independence (to the degree that it exists) of the regulatory agencies. Agency independence is important. This was illustrated by the 1973 disagreement between the ICC and the DOT on the basic features to be incorporated into the Northeast railroad reorganization.[25] The DOT originally took a quite extreme position on the reorganization, calling for private sector financing of the reorganization, massive cutbacks in service, and no job protection or allowances for affected workers. In contrast, the ICC called for active federal participation in financing the reorganization, a more moderate reduction in service, and a concerted federal effort to minimize the negative impact of the changes on the workforce. The ICC's position was far more practical given the political realities of the situation. Congress, being quite concerned with the impact on both shippers and organized labor, was not about to accept the DOT proposals. Nevertheless, the differences that existed between the ICC and DOT stimulated extensive congressional debate on the issues and strongly influenced the final composition of the legislation. If the DOT and the ICC had both been housed in the executive branch, it is quite likely that the secretary of transportation and the chairman of the ICC would both have maintained the party line on these matters. This would have tended to make the analysis too one sided. The continued independence of the regulatory agencies will tend to facilitate a more broadly based examination of important transportation policy issues.

At various times it has also been suggested that the ICC and CAB (and possibly the Federal Maritime Commission) should be consolidated into a single regulatory agency.[26] Clearly, the establishment of a single regulatory agency with control over all forms of interstate transportation would assist in the development of integrated transportation policies. Such structural changes, however, would also necessitate substantial modification of the regulatory statutes and the related policy statements. However, it is also possible that the span of control of such an agency would be so extensive that it might preclude effective administration of its responsibilities. A thorough assessment of such a structural reorganization and its many ramifications is clearly beyond the scope of this book. However, if legislative steps are taken to substantially reduce economic regulation, and hence cut agency workloads, Congress should seriously consider structural alternatives.

DEPARTMENT OF TRANSPORTATION

The federal DOT was established in 1967. The objectives that Congress set for the organization were stated in the act that created the DOT:

> To assure the coordinated, effective administration of the transportation programs of the Federal Government; to facilitate the development and improvement of coordinated transportation service, to be provided by private enterprise to the maximum extent feasible; to encourage cooperation of Federal, State, and local governments, carriers, labor, and other interested parties toward the achievement of national transportation objectives; to stimulate technological advances in transportation; to provide general leadership; to develop and recommend to the President and Congress for approval national transportation policies and programs to accomplish these objectives with full and appropriate consideration of the needs of the public, users, carriers, industry, labor, and the national defense.[27]

The secretary of transportation is a cabinet member appointed by the president with the advice and consent of the Senate. He reports directly to Congress.

Figure 14–3 illustrates the organization and responsibilities of the DOT and its main components. As documented in Figure 14–4, many major structural components of the DOT were housed in other federal agencies prior to the creation of the DOT. The department has more than 70,000 full-time permanent employees and maintains in excess of 3,000 field offices in the United States and foreign countries.[28]

Role in Transportation Regulation

The DOT's role in direct regulation of transportation is basically limited to the realm of safety. Figure 14–3 also describes the roles played in transportation safety by such DOT units as the Federal Aviation Administration, the Federal Railroad Administration, and the Federal Highway

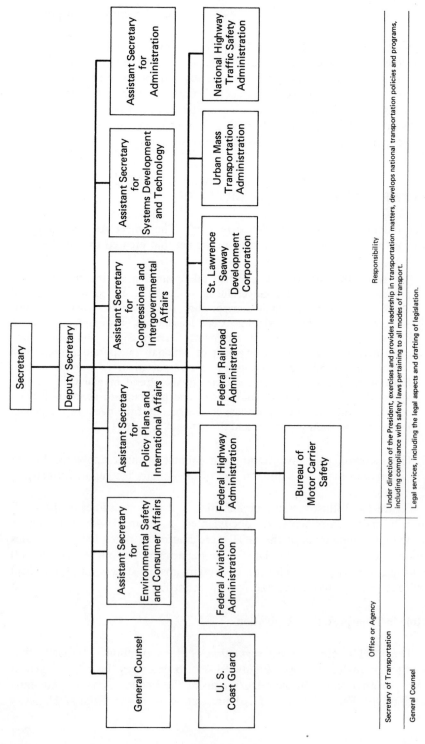

Secretary

Deputy Secretary

General Counsel

Assistant Secretary for Environmental Safety and Consumer Affairs

Assistant Secretary for Policy Plans and International Affairs

Assistant Secretary for Congressional and Intergovernmental Affairs

Assistant Secretary for Systems Development and Technology

Assistant Secretary for Administration

U. S. Coast Guard

Federal Aviation Administration

Federal Highway Administration

Federal Railroad Administration

St. Lawrence Seaway Development Corporation

Urban Mass Transportation Administration

National Highway Traffic Safety Administration

Bureau of Motor Carrier Safety

Office or Agency	Responsibility
Secretary of Transportation	Under direction of the President, exercises and provides leadership in transportation matters, develops national transportation policies and programs, including compliance with safety laws pertaining to all modes of transport.
General Counsel	Legal services, including the legal aspects and drafting of legislation.

292

Office or Agency	Responsibility
Asst. Secy. for Environmental Safety and Consumer Affairs	Coordination of regulations: on safety in movements of hazardous materials, on gas and oil pipeline safety; of policies, programs, and resources of DOT transport programs with public and private efforts to solve environmental problems having impact on transportation. To represent the public viewpoint in the Department.
Asst. Secy. for Policy Plans and International Affairs	Economic and systems analysis; policy review; transport data; international transport facilitation; and, technical assistance.
Asst. Secy. for Congressional and Intergovernmental Affairs	Coordination of DOT policy and planning with the Congress and with State and Local government bodies.
Asst. Secy. for Systems Development and Technology	Scientific and technologic research and development relating to the speed, safety and economy of transportation; noise abatement; and, transportation information planning.
Asst. Secy. for Administration	Organization, budgeting, staffing, personnel management, logistics and procurement policy, management systems and other administrative support for the Department.
U. S. Coast Guard	Provides navigational aids to inland and offshore water and trans-oceanic air commerce; enforces federal maritime safety, including approval of plans for vessel construction and repair. Administers Great Lakes Pilotage Act of 1960. Has responsibility for water vessel anchorages, drawbridge operation, and locations and clearances of bridges over navigable water (Previously under the Corps of Engineers).
Federal Aviation Administration	Promotes civil aviation generally, including research and promulgation and enforcement of safety regulations. Develops and operates the airways, including facilities. Administers the federal airport program.
Federal Highway Administration	Responsible for implementation of the Federal-Aid Highway Program; National Traffic and Motor Vehicle Safety Act of 1966; and the Highway Safety Act of 1966. Responsibility for reasonableness of tolls on bridges over navigable waters (previously under the Corps of Engineers). Administers federal highway construction, research planning, safety programs, and Federal-Aid highway funds (formerly under Bureau of Public Roads).
Federal Railroad Administration	Responsible for the operation of the Alaska Railroad; administration of the High-Speed Ground Transportation Program; implementation of railroad safety laws; and advises the Secretary on matters pertaining to national railroad policy developments.
St. Lawrence Seaway Dev. Corp.	Administers operation and maintenance of the U. S. portion of the St. Lawrence Seaway, including toll rates.
Urban Mass Transportation Administration	Responsible for developing comprehensive coordinated mass transport systems for metropolitan and urban areas, including R & D and demonstration projects; aid for technical studies, planning, engineering, and designing; financial aid and grants to public bodies for modernization, equipment, and training of personnel.
National Highway Traffic Safety Administration	Formulation and promulgation of programs for use by the States in driver performance; development of uniform standards for keeping accident records and investigation of accident causes; vehicle registration and inspection and the safety aspects of highway design and maintenance. Planning, development and enforcement of federal motor vehicle safety standards relating to the manufacturing of motor vehicles.
Bureau of Motor Carrier Safety	Administers and enforces motor carrier safety regulations (formerly under the ICC) and the regulations governing the transportation of hazardous materials.

Figure 14-3

Department of Transportation—Organization and Responsibilities

SOURCE: Transportation Association of America, *Transportation Facts and Trends* (Washington, D.C.: Transportation Association of America, 1976), p. 35.

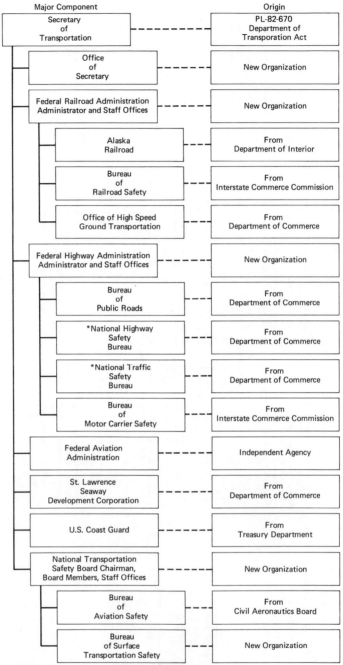

Major Component	Origin
Secretary of Transportation	PL-82-670 Department of Transporation Act
Office of Secretary	New Organization
Federal Railroad Administration Administrator and Staff Offices	New Organization
Alaska Railroad	From Department of Interior
Bureau of Railroad Safety	From Interstate Commerce Commission
Office of High Speed Ground Transportation	From Department of Commerce
Federal Highway Administration Administrator and Staff Offices	New Organization
Bureau of Public Roads	From Department of Commerce
*National Highway Safety Bureau	From Department of Commerce
*National Traffic Safety Bureau	From Department of Commerce
Bureau of Motor Carrier Safety	From Interstate Commerce Commission
Federal Aviation Administration	Independent Agency
St. Lawrence Seaway Development Corporation	From Department of Commerce
U.S. Coast Guard	From Treasury Department
National Transportation Safety Board Chairman, Board Members, Staff Offices	New Organization
Bureau of Aviation Safety	From Civil Aeronautics Board
Bureau of Surface Transportation Safety	New Organization

*Combined June 4, 1967 into the National Highway Safety Bureau

Figure 14–4 Origin of Major DOT Components

SOURCE: U.S. Department of Transportation, *Annual Report, Fiscal Year, 1967* (Washington, D.C.: U.S. Government Printing Office, 1967), p. 9.

294

Administration. Many of the present DOT safety responsibilities were administered by other federal agencies prior to 1967. The subject of transportation safety and its enforcement is pursued further in Chapter 17.

In terms of economic regulation, the DOT's role is primarily limited to policy review, critique, and recommendation. Since its inception, the DOT has been an advocate of regulatory change in transportation. However, the early regulatory initiatives of the DOT suffered from the fact that they were too ambitious, and it is clear that Congress will not respond favorably to proposals that seek extensive regulatory changes in a relatively short period.[29] As a result, the DOT had little success in selling its regulatory change proposals to Congress. It also took the DOT several years to establish its credibility with Congress. In its early experiences before Congress, the DOT was clearly overmatched by carrier lobbies.

Congressional enactment of the Railroad Revitalization and Regulatory Reform Act of 1976 marked a major victory for the DOT in its efforts to promote regulatory reform. The department subsequently submitted to Congress regulatory change proposals related to air carriage and trucking, and it might well be expected to play a similar advocacy role in the near future. It has also sought to influence economic regulatory policy through intervention in an increasing number of ICC and CAB cases.

Promotional Role

The DOT also plays an important role in financing specific transportation projects and funding research and development efforts involving the several modes. In dispensing federal monies for transportation projects, the DOT has a major influence on the nature of the transportation marketplace. These outlays have a cumulative effect on the relative position of the modes. Consequently, there is an indirect linkage between the DOT's promotional and research outlays and the administration of the regulatory statutes, which involves regulatory agency consideration of the status and needs of the several modes.

In acting as the major federal administrator of transportation funding, with a budget authority of more than $12 billion during fiscal year 1976, the DOT has sought to maintain a multimodal orientation while "minimizing the inequitable distortions of government intervention."[30]

STATE REGULATORY COMMISSIONS

Although this chapter is primarily concerned with the federal institutional structure in transportation, some mention should be given to such organization at the state level. All 50 states plus the District of Columbia have established commissions that are in some way involved in the regulation of intrastate transportation.[31]

Many state-level commissions or boards also regulate a broad range of businesses, including public utilities, that are affected with the public interest. The typical state regulatory commission has between three and five members; the commissioners are generally appointed by the governor with the approval of the state legislature.[32] Terms of office tend to be staggered to promote continuity and political independence.

There has been a decided movement toward establishment of state-level departments of transportation. By 1972 such organizations had been created in 15 states.[33] In most instances these state agencies have been created to coordinate state transportation planning and funding of transportation projects. However, the state DOTs have not generally been granted economic regulatory authority. These powers have remained vested in the state regulatory agencies. The degree of regulatory control exercised at the state level varies both by state and mode.

SUMMARY

The ICC and CAB not only administer the regulatory statutes in transportation, but also formulate policy within the broad legislative guidelines set by Congress. In carrying out their responsibilities the agencies often play quasi-legislative and quasi-judicial roles.

Although the regulatory agencies are organizationally independent of the other branches of the federal government, they still interact extensively with the legislative, executive, and judicial branches. These interactions have a major impact on the regulatory philosophy that prevails at any given time.

As the basic formulator of national transportation policy, Congress provides the regulatory agencies with statutory guidelines and authorizes annual appropriations for the agencies. The president not only appoints the regulatory commissioners, subject to the advice and consent of the Senate, but also designates the chairmen of the agencies. He may also seek to influence the agencies' annual appropriations through the Office of Management and Budget. Further interaction with the executive branch is necessitated by the fact that the agencies must rely upon the Department of Justice both to seek enforcement of their rulings in cases of noncompliance and to defend agency decisions that are challenged in the courts. Furthermore, through advocacy of regulatory changes and through intervention in agency cases, the DOT may also seek to influence the activities of the agencies. Interaction with the judicial branch involves occasional court reviews of regulatory agency decisions, enforcement of agency orders, and court review of agency damage and reparation awards.

NOTES

1. U.S. Interstate Commerce Commission, *Regulatory Issues of Today* (Washington, D.C.: the Commission, 1975).
2. See Association of American Railroads, "Commission Raps Trend Toward Conglomerates," *Information Letter,* No. 2174 (September 3, 1975), p. 1; also "Plan to Deregulate Airlines May Reach Congress This Week," *Wall Street Journal,* New York, September 8, 1975, p. 4.
3. D. Philip Locklin, *Economics of Transportation,* 7th ed. (Homewood, Ill.: Richard D. Irwin, Inc., 1972), pp. 307–308.
4. Unspecified study cited by Lyman A. Keith and Carlo E. Gubellini, *Introduction to Business Enterprise,* 4th ed. (New York: McGraw-Hill Book Company, 1975), p. 83.
5. *American Commercial Lines, Inc., et al.* v. *Louisville & Nashville R.R. Co., et al.,* 392 U.S. 571 (1968).
6. Robert Fellmeth, *The Interstate Commerce Omission* (New York: Grossman Publishers, 1970), p. 11.
7. U.S. Interstate Commerce Commission, *89th Annual Report* (Washington, D.C.: U.S. Government Printing Office, 1975), p. v.
8. Ibid.
9. Ibid.
10. "CAB Member Timm Resigns from Board Under Pressure from the White House," *Wall Street Journal,* New York, December 11, 1975, p. 24.
11. Roy J. Sampson and Martin T. Farris, *Domestic Transportation: Practice, Theory, and Policy,* 3rd ed. (Boston: Houghton Mifflin Company, 1975), p. 391.
12. Ibid.
13. U.S. Civil Aeronautics Board, *Reports to Congress* (Washington, D.C.: U.S. Government Printing Office, 1974), p. 81.
14. "Ford Sends Back Case Involving North Atlantic Routes," *Wall Street Journal,* New York, December 29, 1976, p. 2.
15. Locklin, op. cit., p. 302.
16. See *American Commercial Lines, Inc., et al.* v. *Louisville & Nashville R.R. Co., et al.,* 392 U.S. 571 (1968); also, *Penn Central Merger Cases,* 389 U.S. 486, 498–502 (1968).

17. *Interstate Commerce Commission* v. *Illinois Central Railroad Co.,* 215 U.S. 452, 470 (1910).

18. For an extensive review of these issues, see Locklin, op. cit., pp. 295–99.

19. Fellmeth, op. cit., p. 4; also, for an interesting discussion of the backgrounds of a number of ICC commissioners, see Dan Cordtz, "Its Time to Unload the Regulators," *Fortune,* LXXXIV, No. 1 (July, 1971), pp. 64–67, 143–45.

20. Hugh S. Norton, *Modern Transportation Economics,* 2nd ed. (Columbus, Ohio: Charles E. Merrill Publishing Company, 1971), p. 316.

21. Ibid.

22. George W. Hilton, "The Basic Behavior of Regulatory Commissions," a paper presented at the American Economic Association Meeting, New Orleans, December, 1971, cited by Grant M. Davis, "The Basic Behavior of Regulatory Commissions—A Comment," *Transportation Journal,* XII, No. 1 (Fall, 1972), p. 36.

23. Ibid.

24. *Reorganization of the Executive Departments,* 75th Cong., 1st Sess., Senate Doc. No. 8 (1937), pp. 67–71.

25. For summaries of the initial positions of the ICC and DOT concerning the Northeast Railroad Reorganization, see U.S. Interstate Commerce Commission, *Ex Parte No. 293, Northeastern Railroad Investigation,* a report to Congress (Washington, D.C.: Interstate Commerce Commission, 1973); also U.S. Department of Transportation, Office of the Secretary, *The Northeastern Railroad Problem,* a report to Congress (Washington, D.C.: the Department, 1973).

26. For a discussion of this issue, see Grant M. Davis, "An Evaluation of the Propriety of Establishing One Consolidated Transportation Regulatory Commission," *ICC Practitioners' Journal,* XXXVIII, No. 5 (July–August, 1971), pp. 726–45.

27. Public Law 89-670, Section 2 (1970).

28. U.S. Department of Transportation, *Budget Status Report* (Washington, D.C.: the Department, March, 1976), p. 2.

29. For a discussion of this issue, see Robert C. Lieb, "Promoting Change in Transportation Regulation," *Business Horizons,* XVIII, No. 3 (June, 1975), pp. 91–94.

30. U.S. Department of Transportation, Office of the Secretary, *A Statement of National Transportation Policy* (Washington, D.C.: U.S. Government Printing Office, 1975), p. 3.

31. Charles F. Phillips, *The Economics of Regulation,* rev. ed. (Homewood, Ill.: Richard D. Irwin, Inc., 1969), p. 89.

32. Ibid., p. 91.

33. James W. Bennett and William J. Dewitt, "The Development of State

Departments of Transportation—A Recent Organizational Phenomena,"
Transportation Journal, XII, No. 1 (Fall, 1972), p. 12.

SELECTED REFERENCES

"A Case for Grounding the CAB." *Fortune,* LXXXIV, No. 1 (July, 1971), pp. 66, 145–47.

Baldwin, John R. *The Regulatory Agency and the Public Corporation: The Canadian Air Transportation Industry.* Cambridge, Mass.: Ballinger Publishing Company, 1975.

Cordtz, Dan. "Its Time to Unload the Regulators." *Fortune,* LXXXIV, No. 1 (July, 1971), pp. 64–67, 143–45.

Davis, Grant M. "An Evaluation of the Propriety of Establishing One Consolidated Transportation Regulatory Commission." *ICC Practitioners' Journal,* XXXVIII, No. 5 (July–August, 1971), pp. 726–45.

Davis, Grant M. "The Basic Behavior of Regulatory Commissions—A Comment." *Transportation Journal,* XII, No. 1 (Fall, 1972), pp. 36–39.

Davis, Grant M. *The Department of Transportation.* Lexington, Mass.: D.C. Heath & Company, 1970.

Fair, Marvin L., and John Guandolo. *Transportation Regulation,* 7th ed. Dubuque, Iowa: William C. Brown Company, 1972.
Chapter 9. "Practice and Procedure," pp. 295–391.
Chapter 10. "Judicial Review and Court Action," pp. 392–408.

Fellmeth, Robert. *The Interstate Commerce Omission.* New York: Grossman Publishers, 1970.
Chapter 1. "The Commission," pp. 1–39.

Handberg, Roger. "The ICC Before the Supreme Court: 1950–1975." *ICC Practitioners' Journal,* XLIII, No. 2 (January–February, 1976), pp. 204–06.

Kohlmeier, Louis M. *The Regulators.* New York: Harper & Row, Inc., 1969.

Lieb, Robert C. "Promoting Change in Transportation Regulation." *Business Horizons,* XVIII, No. 3 (June, 1975), pp. 91–94.

Locklin, D. Philip. *Economics of Transportation,* 7th ed. Homewood, Ill.: Richard D. Irwin, Inc., 1969.
Chapter 13. "The Agencies of Control," pp. 282–310.

Norton, Hugh S. *Modern Transportation Economics,* 2nd ed. Columbus, Ohio: Charles E. Merrill Publishing Company, 1971.
Chapter 17. "The Administrative Agencies of Control and Their Policy Making Role," pp. 303–30.

Pegrum, Dudley F. *Transportation: Economics and Public Policy,* 3rd ed. Homewood, Ill.: Richard D. Irwin, Inc., 1973.
Chapter 11. "The Agencies of Regulation," pp. 241–67.

Phillips, Charles F. *The Economics of Regulation,* rev. ed. Homewood, Ill.: Richard D. Irwin, Inc., 1969.
Chapter 4. "The Independent Regulatory Commissions," pp. 83–122.

Sampson, Roy J., and Martin T. Farris. *Domestic Transportation: Practice, Theory, and Policy,* 3rd ed. Boston: Houghton Mifflin Company, 1975.
Chapter 24. "Regulatory Institutions," pp. 384–402.

Spychalski, John C. "An Evaluation of Messrs. Hilton's and Sampson's Proposed Cures for Regulatory Defects." *Transportation Journal,* XII, No. 1 (Fall, 1972), pp. 22–35.

DISCUSSION QUESTIONS

1. As a staff assistant to the chairman of the Senate Subcommittee on Surface Transportation, you have been asked to respond to a memo concerning the ICC. A number of congressmen are calling for abolition of the agency, and the chairman of the subcommittee has asked for your opinions concerning the establishment of standards to measure the performance of the agency. Do you believe that establishment of such standards is justified? How might the agency's performance be measured? Can you suggest any standards? If so, give both their significance and your rationale in suggesting them.

2. In your opinion, what qualifications should candidates for positions on the ICC and CAB have?

3. Explain the relationship that exists between the divisions of the ICC and the full commission.

4. Would you favor any institutional changes in transportation regulation (e.g., formation of a single regulatory agency with jurisdiction over all modes), or do you favor the status quo? Outline the reasons for your response.

Management Problems and Policy Issues in Transportation

CHAPTER
15

Labor in the Transportation Industries

One highly publicized and quite important element of the national transportation system is the labor component. We have all read or heard about airline and railroad strikes, and we are periodically apprised by the media of contract negotiations involving U.S. truckers or longshoremen. The attention devoted to such labor–management interaction in transportation is quite understandable. Labor compensation is one of the major cost elements of the intercity carriers and, therefore, a primary determinant of carrier pricing.

When we read that the Teamsters have received a sizable wage increase, it is not superfluous news, because the settlement will result in price increases in many of the commodities that we consume. Other transportation labor contract provisions, such as those related to work rules, are similarly important because they influence the efficiency and health of the transportation industries. Also, transportation strikes can play havoc with the economy not only by retarding the flow of commerce, but also by increasing unemployment among workers in industries that are heavily dependent upon for-hire carriage.

This chapter attempts to provide insight into the nature of existing labor–management relationships in the various modes of intercity carriage.[1] It examines such matters as trends in employment, compensation, and worker productivity. Additionally, it reviews industry bargaining patterns and federal mechanisms for dealing with carrier labor disputes.

Labor in the Transportation Industries

EMPLOYMENT

Employment in the transportation industries comprises approximately 13 percent of the total workforce in the United States.[2] Total carrier employment has been influenced by several factors. In many instances technological progress has resulted in the substitution of capital for labor. For example, this has occurred in both the railroad and airline industries with development of equipment with greater load capacities. Another important development that has influenced personnel requirements has been the reduction in service offerings in several modes. Reduction in rail passenger service, and airline flight cutbacks aimed at improving load factors provide illustrations of this development. Also, as discussed later in this chapter and in Chapter 16, mergers and consolidations of carriers have eliminated many duplicate positions. These workforce reductions have generally taken place gradually due to job protection provisions, which are often contained in transportation labor agreements.

Two factors have combined to at least partially offset these job-reducing developments. First, as the national economy has grown, the aggregate demand for transportation services has also increased. Second, although many operating positions have been eliminated, the need for managerial talent in the transportation industries has expanded. As the size and market complexity of carriers has increased, there has been a corresponding growth in the need for managerial specialists in many functional areas, such as finance, marketing, and labor relations.

Many carriers, realizing that their past operating orientation may be inadequate to cope with the future environment, have become active recruiters on college campuses. Similarly, formal management-development programs for training new employees have become common. Further, many companies now encourage managers to pursue part-time continuing education programs. Typically, the companies reimburse their employees for tuition outlays related to such educational pursuits.

These and other management-development efforts in transportation are important and long overdue. For many years the development of managerial talent in transportation lagged, due to both limited recruiting efforts and the failure of transportation companies to convince talented young people that there were excellent career opportunities in transportation.

A new wave of professionally trained managers in transportation, armed with modern managerial techniques, could make a significant contribution to revitalization of the industry.

The employment needs of the several modes have varied widely in recent years. The factors that have led to these variations are identified in the following discussion.

Rail Carriage

The railroad workforce declined from 780,494 in 1960 to 525,177 in 1974 (see Table 15–1). This marked an extension of the downward trend

Table 15–1

Average Number of Employees, Intercity Modes, 1960–1974 (in 000)

Mode	1960	1965	1970	1974
Railroads	780.5	640.0	566.3	525.2
Motor Carriers[a]	326.6	375.4	500.4	492.4
Airlines	166.2	210.8	297.4	303.3
Oil Pipelines	21.3	15.6	15.0	15.2
Water Carriers[b]	14.3	10.3	8.3	8.1

[a] Only class I motor carriers of property.
[b] Only classes A and B water carriers on inland and coastal waterways.

SOURCE: Selected annual reports of the Association of American Railroads, the Air Transport Association, and the Interstate Commerce Commission.

in railroad employment that began following World War II. Some factors leading to the decline have been the changing technology of the industry, reductions in passenger and branch-line operations, consolidations, and changes in work rules.[3] Also, the Northeast Railroad Reorganization, which led to abandonment of nearly 3,000 miles of branch-line track in the region and the call for similar abandonments in other regions, has exerted downward pressure on the workforce. Because long-term employees in the railroad industry have historically been granted substantial job protection, most reductions have been accomplished through a process of attrition. Under such an agreement, long-term employees are given job protection, and the workforce is reduced by not refilling positions when workers retire or voluntarily leave jobs for other reasons.

Motor Carriage

Although there have been some short-term fluctuations, the intercity motor carrier industry has experienced a steady increase in employment throughout the years. Reflecting this trend, the workforce of class I motor carriers rose from 326,600 in 1960 to 492,400 in 1974, an increase of 51 percent. These figures considerably understate motor carrier employment because they fail to include class II and class III common carriers, as well

305

as numerous exempt, local service, and private carriers who are beyond the regulatory jurisdiction of the ICC.

Major reasons for the growth of trucking employment include the expansion of the U.S. highway system (particularly the Interstate), the success of the industry in attracting an increasing percentage of intercity ton mileage, and the emergence of the truck as the dominant form of carriage in short-haul markets.

Air Carriage

Until the early 1970s, expansion of CAB route awards and the steady growth of airline demand led to growth in airline employment. Between 1960 and 1969 the airline workforce grew from 166,235 to its all-time high of 311,922. However, the softening of demand in the early 1970s coupled with the fuel shortages during the Arab oil embargo led to sizable cutbacks in both flights and employment. By the mid-1970s this downturn had been reversed as the country recovered from recessionary pressures. But the growing use of wide-body planes in major markets and the continuing pressures to reduce airline costs by dropping unprofitable runs will likely exert downward influence on airline employment in the near future.

Water Carriage

Domestic water carrier employment has declined significantly in recent years despite the fact that the traffic volume of that mode has risen. Employment declined from 14,338 in 1960 to 8,075 in 1974. Although traffic volume increased, the introduction of more powerful towboats and the development of barges with greater capacity reduced employee requirements. Also contributing to the employment decline was the implementation of the *barge mixing rule* in 1962 (see Chapter 6), which permitted regulated and exempt commodities to be carried in a single tow. This reduced the number of tows necessary to handle a given volume of traffic. The employment figures contained in Table 15–1 also understate total employment in domestic water carriage. The figures reflect the employment base of approximately 70 companies that possess common carrier authority from the ICC; they do not account for the manpower of the approximately 1,150 exempt and 400 private carriers that serve the same routes. One source has estimated that total employment on the inland waterway system alone is approximately 160,000.[4]

In international water carriage, maritime employment in both seafaring and longshoring job categories has declined substantially in recent years. The most important job-reducing factors have been the growing use of containerships in international operations and the application of automated loading and unloading techniques to such operations.

Oil Pipelines

Employment in the oil pipeline industry declined from 21,231 in 1960 to 15,222 in 1974. This decline primarily resulted from the growing automation of the industry; this trend may continue as more powerful pumping equipment and larger-diameter pipelines become operational.[5] However, if experiments involving movement of other commodities, such as coal slurry, through pipelines prove economically feasible, they would likely have a positive impact on future industry employment.

COMPENSATION

The significance of worker compensation in transportation is illustrated by the fact that in one recent year employee compensation equaled 61 percent of the total operating expenses in the railroad industry, 41 percent in the trucking industry, and 24 percent in the water carrier industry.[6] Consequently, carrier management must be constantly concerned with the efficient utilization of manpower.

In comparison with U.S. workers in other occupational categories, the transportation workforce is generally well paid. The average worker in U.S. industry earned approximately $11,000 in 1974; the average annual earnings of workers in the three major modes of intercity carriage were as follows: airlines, $18,000; intercity trucking, $17,000; and railroads, $14,000.[7] However, it must be realized that the skill requirements and responsibilities of transportation workers are often greater than those of workers in other occupational categories, and thus some differential may well be justified.

There is a strong linkage between carrier wage levels and consumer prices. In most cases the signing of new labor agreements calling for increased wages is automatically followed by carrier requests to the regulatory agencies for rate increases. In turn, these additional transportation costs are generally reflected in the prices of consumer goods.

Industries that incur heavy labor expenses tend to automate whenever possible, and the transportation industries are no exception. Therefore, it is not surprising that activities such as control over pipeline movements, handling of containers, and movement of rail cars through classification yards have been automated. Although further automation appears likely, it may be expected that such changes will occur gradually, and that they will have limited short-run impact on carrier labor requirements.

LABOR PRODUCTIVITY

Because the cost of providing transportation services is so substantial, and due to the direct relationship between such costs and prices, there is naturally concern with the measurement of productivity in transportation. These measurement efforts attempt to determine if the resources devoted to the provision of transportation services are being utilized efficiently.

Simply stated, productivity expresses the relationship between the quantity of labor, capital, land, energy, and other inputs employed and the output of goods and services generated by those inputs. Most parties would agree with this simplified definition of productivity, but this is generally where agreement between management and labor concerning the most appropriate means of measuring labor productivity ends. Similarly, there is little agreement among economists concerning not only how this elusive concept might best be measured, but also the significance of these measurements once they are calculated.

Resolution of these conflicts is beyond the scope of this book. However, it is still possible to comment on productivity trends in several modes of carriage. One of the most frequently used measurements of worker productivity is *output per employee*. This measurement, which is calculated annually for more than 90 industries by the Department of Labor's Bureau of Labor Statistics (BLS), relates the output of an industry in a given year to the number of employees in that industry.[8] These measures reflect the combined effects of changes in the efficiency with which labor and capital are used, the amount of capital per employee, and the average quality of labor.[9] However, these measures do not provide insight into the relative contribution of any of the previously mentioned change factors.

Throughout the years, considerable criticism has been leveled at employment practices in transportation. It has often been charged that the transportation unions, particularly those in the railroad industry, have promoted widespread overmanning and featherbedding. However, given the measures of productivity calculated by the BLS, the transportation industries rank quite high in comparison with other industries examined by the BLS (see Table 15–2).

Rail Carriage

On the basis of BLS calculations, the railroads have significantly outpaced the overall level of productivity increase in the private sector over the past 25 years. There are a number of reasons for the railroad performance. The technology of the industry has changed substantially in

Table 15-2

Annual Average Increases in Output per Employee, Total Private Sector and Selected Transportation Industries, 1950-1974

Industry	Annual Average Increase (%)
Total Private Sector	2.8
Railroads[a]	3.7
Intercity Trucking	2.7
Airlines	6.9
Oil Pipelines	8.8

[a] This measurement reflects "car miles" as the output unit. An additional series is calculated annually for the railroads that relies upon "revenue traffic" as the output unit. Between 1950 and 1974 that output measure increased at an annual rate of 5.3 percent.

SOURCE: U.S. Department of Labor, Bureau of Labor Statistics, *Productivity Indexes for Selected Industries* (Washington, D.C.: U.S. Government Printing Office, 1976).

recent years. Also, many jobs have been eliminated, thereby realizing economies that were previously prohibited by job protection agreements. Investment per employee has risen substantially, partially due to the contraction of the workforce, and greater-capacity equipment has been introduced.[10] The establishment of Amtrak has also resulted in a major reduction of intercity rail passenger service offerings, which previously tended to depress aggregate measures of employee productivity. Further railroad productivity gains may be expected in the near future as the Northeast Railroad Reorganization both reduces employment and eliminates low-productivity branch-line operations.

Intercity Trucking

The 2.7 percent annual rate of increase in output per employee registered by intercity trucking between 1950 and 1974 lagged behind the performance of the total private sector. The mediocre performance of the industry may stem from the fact that the trucking industry continued to expand its employment between 1965 and the early 1970s, even though traffic volume increased more slowly than it did during the previous decade. Also, the primary burden of providing labor-intensive small-shipment service falls upon motor carriers. Much of that traffic, which requires considerable platform and terminal handling, has shifted from rail to motor carriage, thereby tending to reduce motor carrier productivity. This trend

309

may be partially offset in the future by the expanded use of multiple-bottom trailers on intercity runs and through increased trailer payloads.

Air Carriage

In terms of growth in output per employee, the domestic airline industry was one of the leading industries in the United States between 1950 and 1974. It registered an annual average increase of 6.9 percent during that period. Among the factors that contributed to that performance were a tremendous growth in airline demand, the dramatic expansion of air cargo volume, and improving utilization of airline equipment.[11] Continued introduction of high-capacity jets into major markets coupled with growing industry interest in abandonment of service in marginal markets is likely to stimulate further productivity gains in the industry.

Oil Pipelines

The annual average increase in output per employee of 8.8 percent registered by the oil pipeline industry between 1950 and 1974 was the highest growth rate exhibited by any industry surveyed by the BLS. As discussed earlier in this chapter, the application of automated techniques to the industry has increased significantly, and manpower requirements have fallen. While these developments have occurred, the volume handled by the industry has risen steadily.

Labor Productivity: An Overview

Although the productivity gains registered by several modes of intercity carriage between 1950 and 1974 appear impressive, they must be viewed with caution. Productivity measurement is a complex concept that involves the interaction of a number of variables. Attempts to measure and interpret productivity in transportation have often led to disputes between management and labor. Consequently, productivity figures have played a rather limited role in transportation contract negotiations. However, the energy crisis and the recessionary pressures of the early 1970s stimulated widespread interest in productivity measurement and promotion in all economic sectors. In recognition of the importance of this matter, the ICC sponsored a conference on productivity measurement in transportation, which attracted 500 participants in November 1974.[12] Such efforts may foster refinement of measurement techniques, and may permit further application of such measurements to the collective bargaining process in transportation.

UNION STRUCTURE AND BARGAINING PATTERNS

The labor force in transportation is highly unionized. Only 22.6 percent of the U.S. workforce was unionized in 1970, but the percentage was considerably higher in each major mode of carriage.[13] The degree of transportation unionization is illustrated by the fact that nearly 80 percent of the railroad workforce is unionized and 87 percent of common carrier truckers are union members.[14] This extensive unionization has had important impact on the nature of bargaining in transportation.

Union Structure

Although there has been a long-term reduction in the number of unions that represent transportation employees, there is still a proliferation of labor organizations in transportation. The sheer number of bargaining units in several modes of carriage tends to promote difficulty in reaching agreements.

The union structure in transportation tends to have a craft orientation. That is, different unions tend to represent different crafts in a given industry. The craft union orientation is changing somewhat, however, due to consolidation of unions. A number of *industrial* unions have emerged whose membership is open to all workers in a particular industry, regardless of their occupational categories. The Brotherhood of Teamsters, Chauffeurs, and Warehousemen (Teamsters) is an example of such an industrial union. It represents more than 500,000 motor carrier employees in this country.

The majority of transportation unions are affiliated with the AFL–CIO. Two major exceptions are the Teamsters and the Brotherhood of Locomotive Engineers, which maintain independent status.

Bargaining Patterns

Because of the sizable number of unions representing workers in several modes, bargaining patterns tend to be rather complex. However, there has been a decided movement toward national contracts in transportation, and this has simplified the bargaining situation. When a union, such as the Teamsters, signs a national master contract, it establishes a basic wage and benefit pattern for union members throughout the country. In some instances, local modifications concerning such matters as work rules are permitted.

National bargaining tends to strengthen the union position by presenting a unified front to management. To offset this strength, carriers in several modes have established bargaining units to collectively represent carriers in national negotiations. The National Railway Labor Conference has represented collective railroad interests in dealing with rail unions for many years; similar bargaining units have also emerged in the trucking and airline industries during the past decade. As a result of these developments, there is a tendency toward national settlements involving bargaining between *big labor* and *big management*.

Mutual Aid Agreements

As implied earlier in this chapter, due to public dependency upon continued transportation services and because of the negative economic impact of major transportation strikes, there is limited tolerance for such strikes on a national basis. As a result, there are a number of federal procedures for postponing or preventing transportation strikes that have national significance. The transportation unions have come to realize that national strikes (particularly in rail carriage) will likely prompt federal intervention; therefore, the unions have tended to rely heavily upon *selective strikes* to resolve disputes in recent years.[15] Under such strikes the unions do not strike all carriers in a particular mode, but rather limit strikes to particular carriers or particular regions. Work stoppages of that nature are not nearly as likely to lead to federal intervention. The strike is more likely to run its course, and the unions may seek to use the final settlement from the selective strike as a pattern for settlements with other carriers. This pattern of work stoppage has been used quite effectively by rail unions.

To offset union strength in such situations, carriers in the railroad and airline industries have established *mutual aid* pacts. Under these agreements the carriers that continue to operate make contributions to struck lines to assure partial coverage of fixed charges. These payments assist struck lines in maintaining a strong bargaining posture with the unions. The operation of such mutual aid agreements is illustrated by the airline industry's program. Payments to struck lines begin at 50 percent of normal operating expenses and scale down to a minimum of 35 percent as the strike continues.[16] Despite union objections, the courts have upheld the legality of mutual aid pacts among carriers.

There is little doubt that these agreements do assist the carriers in their negotiations with the unions. In fact, as mutual aid payment levels have increased in the airline industry, the average duration of strikes has increased. However, during 1974 contract negotiations, airline unions succeeded in getting several financially troubled airlines to withdraw from mutual aid pacts in return for wage and benefit concessions.[17] These developments have raised serious questions concerning the future viability of such agreements in the airline industry.

THE FEDERAL GOVERNMENT AND TRANSPORTATION LABOR DISPUTES

Because of the importance of the transportation system to the realization of national goals, the federal government has developed a variety of legislative mechanisms for dealing with labor disputes in transportation.[18] Federal concern with transportation work stoppages originated during the nineteenth century as the railroads emerged as the nation's first big business. The importance of the railroads to the economy soon became apparent, and any possibility of a work stoppage in the industry became regarded as a threat to national well-being. Therefore, throughout the latter part of the century, and into the first quarter of the twentieth century, Congress enacted several statutes that sought to improve labor relations in the railroad industry. This railroad-oriented legislation later served as a basis for labor organization and social legislation related to employer–employee relationships throughout U.S. industry.

Early Labor Legislation

The movement toward organization of railroad employees began in the 1860s. Fearing the power of the railroads, workers sought strength in unity. However, the carriers were far from enthused with the idea of *organized* labor, and sought to limit organizational efforts. Practices such as blacklisting of union organizers and the utilization of *yellow dog* contracts, under which employees, as part of their employment contract, agreed not to join a union, were quite prevalent. Employees responded to such practices in a variety of ways, many violent, and the railroads frequently reacted to strikes and slowdowns with force. Labor–management relations in the industry deteriorated in the early 1880s, and violence became quite prevalent.

In response to these conditions, Congress passed the Arbitration Act of 1884, which provided for voluntary arbitration of railroad–worker disputes. However, neither the railroads nor the unions expressed any great interest in submitting their disputes to arbitration, and it is generally held that this statute failed to improve labor relations.[19]

Congress tried again in 1898 with the passage of the Erdman Act. Whereas the statute of 1884 lacked formalized procedures for bringing management and labor together for bargaining sessions, the Erdman Act provided a format for promotion of mediation and arbitration. Under the provisions of the act, the chairman of the Interstate Commerce Commission and the commissioner of labor were to administer the law. If negotiations between the railroads and unions failed to produce a settlement, either party could ask for government assistance in resolving the deadlock. Under these circumstances, the federal officials were to suggest binding arbitration. Assuming that this was agreeable, each bargaining party was to select an arbitration representative. These two representatives were then to jointly select a neutral third party, who was to act as chairman of the three-man arbitration committee. Awards of the committee were to be binding for a period of one year.

As was the case with the Arbitration Act of 1884, neither railroad management nor unions looked favorably upon the idea of submitting their disputes to binding arbitration. The statute also placed considerable pressure on the neutral third party. As a result, the Erdman Act had limited success in fostering labor settlements.[20]

In recognition of the failure of the two earlier labor statutes, Congress passed the Newlands Act of 1913. The statute provided for establishment of a three-man Board of Mediation and Conciliation. A significant difference between the Newlands Act and previous labor legislation was the fact that the board did not have to wait for an invitation to intervene in labor disputes, but could act on its own behalf. Once again, however, if mediation failed, the board was to suggest arbitration of the dispute. If the parties agreed to arbitration, a board of arbitration was to be created. The board would then be given 30 days to reach a decision, but its recommendations were not binding on the parties.

Most labor authorities consider the Newlands Act to have been a significant improvement over previous labor legislation. The act "operated with some success until the pressure for the eight-hour day became an issue shortly before World War I."[21]

In 1916 four major railroad unions demanded an eight-hour day. Management refused, and attempts under the Newlands Act failed to resolve the dispute. Consequently, the unions threatened to strike. However, before the strike could begin, President Wilson recommended and received congressional legislation to resolve the impasse.

Congressional response to this matter was contained in the Adamson Act of 1916. It specified that all train service personnel who operated trains in interstate commerce were to be granted eight-hour days. Although the railroads initially challenged the legality of the legislation in the courts, in 1917 the carriers agreed to put the provisions of the Adamson Act into effect. During the ensuing three years, which witnessed federal control and operation of U.S. railroads, the eight-hour day became standard for all railroad employees; it established a pattern that was to be generally followed by the rest of U.S. industry.

While the railroads operated under direct federal control, the unions made considerable progress in establishing collective bargaining powers. They also gained acceptance of standardized national operating practices. The unions were aided in their efforts by active federal government promotion of the expansion of the organized labor movement in the industry.

In view of these developments, new federal mechanisms were needed to deal with railroad labor issues in the postwar period. Congress sought to provide such mechanisms in several labor-related provisions of the Transportation Act of 1920. The statute defined procedures for establishment of labor adjustment boards to intervene in cases involving grievances and working condition disputes. It also established a Railroad Labor Board, which was given exclusive jurisdiction over wage controversies. However, the law did not provide any means of enforcing the decisions of the board, nor did it include any antistrike provisions. As a result, it was not too surprising that the legislation failed to achieve its principal objectives.[22] Labor disputes continued, and several major strikes occurred during the next few years. The dissatisfaction of both labor and management with the provisions of the 1920 legislation led to their active cooperation in supporting the Railway Labor Act of 1926.

Railway Labor Act

The 1926 legislation (and the creation of the National Railway Adjustment Board in 1934) established the procedures that still govern labor disputes in the railroad industry. The act replaced all previous legislation dealing with railroad labor disputes; its provisions apply to all railroad employees. It relies heavily upon collective bargaining and conciliation or mediation as the basic means of solving labor–management disputes. If such voluntary procedures fail to generate a settlement, federal intervention may follow.

Minor Disputes

The Railway Labor Act provided that bipartisan adjustment boards were to be created through agreement between carriers and unions to settle *minor* disputes—those involving interpretation of existing contracts. However, difficulties arose in establishing the boards; as a result, the National Railroad Adjustment Board was created in 1934. The board consists of 36 members, 18 selected by carriers and 18 chosen by the unions. The board has jurisdiction over disputes arising out of grievances, or out of interpretation of agreements concerning rates of pay, rules, or working conditions. Different classes of railroad employees are covered by four divisions within the board. If the appropriate division cannot reach a decision in a particular case, a neutral referee is selected to break the deadlock. Decisions of the board are final and binding on both parties.

Major Disputes

There is no similar procedure for solving *major* disputes in the railroad industry. These disputes arise out of new contract negotiations. If collective bargaining fails to generate a mutually agreeable pact, no procedure requires binding arbitration, short of direct congressional action.

The National Mediation Board (NMB) was created in 1934 to facilitate settlement of major disputes. The board consists of three presidentially appointed members, each serving three-year terms. The board has jurisdiction over disputes involving rates of pay or changes in rules and working conditions in those instances in which the parties to an agreement have been unable to reach a settlement.

When either party to a railroad labor contract desires a major modification, they are required to issue a *Section 6 notice*. This is a written notice filed at least 30 days before intended action concerning the contract. If the desired changes cannot be settled through collective bargaining, either party may request the services of the NMB, or the board may intervene without request.

Initially, the board attempts to promote a settlement through mediation. If this fails, the board seeks to have the parties agree to binding arbitration. If arbitration is refused, the NMB notifies the parties that its mediatory efforts have failed, and for 30 days thereafter, unless the parties agree to arbitration in the interim or an emergency board is created, no change shall be made in the conditions that prevailed at the time the dispute arose. At that point, if in the NMB's opinion a strike could lead to a national emergency, it is required to notify the president, who may create an emergency board, which has 30 days to investigate the dispute. For that period, and for a 30-day period following the report of the emergency board, the parties to the dispute must maintain the status quo.

Following its study, the emergency board reports its findings to the president. The recommendations of the emergency board are not enforceable, but they have been accepted in a number of instances. However, in recent years this has seldom been the case. Faced with a potential strike due to the failure of the parties to accept the findings of the emergency board (which may lead to a national emergency), the president can either allow the strike to occur or ask Congress for emergency legislation to prevent it. The latter course of action has been taken quite frequently in recent years.

316

Air Carrier Coverage

The provisions of the Railway Labor Act were broadened in 1936 to cover employees of air carriers engaged in interstate commerce. The coverage and procedures of the act are the same for airline disputes as for similar disputes in the railroad industry. The act authorizes the creation of a National Air Transport Adjustment Board, but no such board has ever been established.[23] However, carriers and unions have formed *system boards of adjustment*, and these have been reasonably successful in settling minor disputes concerning grievances and contract interpretation.[24] The National Mediation Board functions in the same manner in airline disputes as it does in railroad conflicts.

Labor Disputes in Other Modes

Although the impact of strikes in other forms of carriage can also have quite negative effects on the U.S. economy, there are no *special* legislative procedures to prevent such strikes. Work stoppages in motor carriage, domestic water carriage, or the maritime industry are handled like disputes in any other industry (excluding rail and air carriage). Overall industry guidelines have, however, come about through enactment of the National Labor Relations Act of 1935 (the Wagner Act), the Fair Labor Standards Act of 1938, and the Labor–Management Relations Act of 1947 (better known as the Taft–Hartley Act).

The 1935 statute recognized the right of collective bargaining throughout U.S. industry, and required management to bargain with unions that were duly certified by the National Labor Relations Board. The act also gave the board the power to deal with unfair labor practices. In conjunction with this law, the Fair Labor Standards Act of 1938 provided standards for minimum wages and maximum hours in interstate commerce.

In 1947 the Taft–Hartley Act added a list of unfair employee practices to the list of unfair employer practices contained in the 1935 act. Among those practices forbidden by the law were the coercion of employers or employees and charging excessive initiation fees. The law also established a cooling-off period that could be utilized to gain additional time to settle disputes which might lead to strikes that threatened national health or safety. Accordingly, a 60-day notice must be given by a party wishing to change or terminate prevailing conditions of employment. During the following 60 days, the Federal Mediation and Conciliation Service (created by the act) attempts to bring the two parties to agreement. If an agreement has not been reached by the expiration of the 60-day period, the unions are free to strike. At that point, if the conflict has national significance, the president may appoint a board of inquiry to investigate the dispute. At the same time, if the president believes that the strike poses a threat to national well-being, he has the power to direct the attorney general to request an injunction (Taft–Hartley injunction) from a federal court. If the attorney general obtains the injunction, workers must return to work for 80 days. During the 80-day period, efforts are made to settle the disputes. However, if an agreement is not reached during that time span, the legislative procedures have been exhausted, and only direct congressional action can prevent the strike.

Another labor statute, the Labor–Management Disclosure Act of 1959, was enacted in response to conditions in the transportation industries. In particular, alleged mismanagement of Teamster pension funds by union officers led directly to passage of that statute, which made mandatory the reporting and disclosure of certain transactions of labor organizations and employers.[25]

Experience Under Federal Labor Guidelines

The procedures provided in the Railway Labor Act for handling major railroad disputes have been used frequently since their inception. Since 1926 more than 200 railroad emergency boards have been created, following the failure of the NMB to promote labor–management agreement on contract issues. However, the recommendations of the emergency boards have infrequently been accepted by the parties, and strikes have often resulted.[26] In a number of instances, direct congressional action has been required to settle the disputes. This experience has raised questions concerning the adequacy of the Railway Labor Act guidelines. It has been argued that the existence of these procedures effectively postpones the need for any hard bargaining until the emergency-board study period is nearly expired.[27] There appears to be some credibility to that argument. Only once in the history of railroad labor negotiations, in 1973, have all bargaining issues been settled in advance of the bargaining deadline.[28] It has also been argued that the NMB and its procedures are basically redundant to those of the Federal Mediation and Conciliation Service, and that railroads and airlines should be brought under the provisions of the Taft–Hartley Act.[29]

However, the application of the Taft–Hartley Act to transportation has also encountered difficulties. This has been particularly true with respect to maritime industry disputes. Taft–Hartley injunctions were only utilized 24 times between 1948 and 1975, but 10 of these involved one industry—the maritime industry.[30]

The Federal Government and Transportation Labor Disputes

Antistrike Proposals

In response to a number of major transportation strikes during his administration, President Nixon, late in 1970, sent a bill to Congress which called for permanent legislation that would promote compulsory settlement of transportation strikes. The Nixon proposals sought to extend the Taft–Hartley Act for handling transportation disputes:

1. The president would be given power to add up to 30 more days to the 80-day Taft–Hartley cooling-off period.
2. The president would be given power to create a board that could require partial operation of a struck transportation industry.
3. A procedure for *final offer selection* would be initiated. This mechanism would establish a procedure by which the parties to a dispute would submit one or two final offers to the secretary of labor. The parties would then negotiate for five days on the basis of the final offers. If they failed to reach a settlement, the president would name a three-member panel of neutrals, which would select one of the final offers in its entirety, and order it into effect.[31]

According to the bill, the president was to be limited to only one option in a particular dispute, and Congress was to be given the power to reject the president's choice of options.

Although these proposals initially were criticized by both management and labor, the Association of American Railroads and the Air Transport Association showed signs of support for such legislation. Congressional reaction to the legislation was mixed. However, there was considerable speculation that the United Transportation Union selective strikes of July–August 1971 would force congressional action on the bill. But the strikes were settled one week before a congressional recess, and that development probably precluded such action. Similarly, the maritime strikes of 1971 and 1972 rekindled interest in antistrike measures. Once again, the parties to the dispute argeed one day prior to likely congressional intervention.

In view of the lack of favorable congressional reaction to this bill (when not confronted with an impending crisis), and undoubtedly influenced by the upcoming national election, the administration formally withdrew its support of the bill in mid-1972.[32]

Federal Role in Job Guarantees

The role of the federal government in transportation labor has not been limited to establishment of procedures for strike resolution. Congress has also played an active role in promoting job protection in the railroad industry. Congressional concern for worker security in cases of railroad mergers and consolidations was reflected in the Transportation Act of 1940. In part the act specified that

> as a condition of its approval [of a merger or consolidation] . . . the Commission shall require a fair and equitable arrangement to protect the interests of the railroad employees affected. In its order of approval the Commission shall include terms and conditions providing that during the period of four years from the effective date of such order such transaction will not result in employees of the carrier or carriers by railroad affected by such order being in a worse position with respect to their employment, except that the protection afforded to any employee pursuant to this sentence shall not be required to continue for a longer period, following the effective date of such order, than the period during which such employee was in the employ of such carrier or carriers prior to the effective date of such order.[33]

In cases that have come before the ICC, these provisions have been considered to constitute minimum coverage of employees, and broader protections have been given to employees in a number of instances.[34] Generally attrition programs are relied upon to eliminate jobs. The agreements also typically stipulate that workers can be transferred throughout the resulting system. If workers are unwilling to move, cash settlements are made. As might be expected, such extensive employee protection has been costly to the carriers involved. For instance, the total cost of the job protection provisions incorporated into the Penn Central consolidation was $78 million.[35]

In 1970, Congress applied the same basic pattern of employee protection to railroad workers affected by the creation of Amtrak, and extended the period of coverage to six years.[36] Congressional concern for employee protection also surfaced during hearings on the Northeast Railroad Reorganization. The line reductions discussed in these hearings implied major cutbacks in railroad employment in the region. Although Congress wished to extend employee protections as it had in the past, it was clear that the seven bankrupt railroads being reorganized were not financially strong enough to make such guarantees. Consequently, Congress established a $250 million federally financed protection plan, which contained the standard range of guarantees. The railroad unions were then expected to renegotiate all outstanding contracts with Conrail.

Unfortunately, the generosity of Congress backfired. Two solvent railroads, the Chessie System and the Southern Railway, were to acquire some of the bankrupt carriers' trackage in the region, and they were to provide competition for Conrail at many points. However, the Reorganization Act stipulated that such carriers had to reach mutually satisfactory arrangements with the unions that represented affected employees who would be transferred from the bankrupt lines. In their negotiations with the unions, the two solvent carriers sought to have the unions agree to the same work rules that applied to their existing employees. The unions refused because they had better *guarantees* under the federal program—their existing work rules would be honored as Conrail employees. Both solvent lines refused to accept these work practices "which contributed to the bankruptcy" of the predecessor lines.[37] Subsequently, the Chessie and the Southern withdrew from the reorganization plan. This significantly reduced the likelihood of rail competition for Conrail at many points in the region.

Congressional concern for the welfare of railroad employees is laudable. There is limited job potential for many long-term railroad employees who do not have readily transferable skills. However, experience with the guarantees accorded under the 1973 agreement illustrates that such guarantees can also be counterproductive. In return for its guarantees, Congress should have required substantial work rule and operating practice changes from the railroad unions. The reorganization provided an unprecedented opportunity to improve worker productivity in the region (which had been the lowest in the industry prior to the reorganization). This would have been a decisive movement toward the establishment of a viable railroad system in the region. Modification of long-standing work rules and practices in Conrail could have served as a pattern for future negotiations on a national basis. Unfortunately, the opportunity was mishandled by Congress, and the costs will be significant. It is hoped that the memory of these mistakes will remain with Congress in future consideration of railroad labor legislation.

SUMMARY

The significance of the labor component in transportation cannot be overstated. Employee compensation comprises a major portion of the cost structure of the industry and, consequently, has a decided impact on carrier prices. The work rules and job descriptions contained in labor contracts are major determinants of worker efficiency. Furthermore, work stoppages can have a quite negative impact on the flow of commerce in the United States.

The employment picture in transportation is mixed. A variety of factors, including technological changes, mergers, and abandonment of services in several modes, has combined to exert downward pressures on carrier employment. However, these pressures have been partially offset by the growth of aggregate demand for transportation services, which has accompanied U.S. economic expansion. Transportation workers are well paid in comparison with workers in other occupational categories. Wages have risen steadily and thus have contributed to higher rates and fares. In the post-World War II period, the productivity of transportation workers has tended to outpace that of workers in the aggregate private sector. However, the significance of these productivity figures is the subject of considerable debate; they must therefore be viewed with caution.

The transportation workforce is highly unionized, and bargaining has trended toward national negotiations between carrier organizations and major unions. Due to public dependency upon continued transportation service and the negative impact of strikes, the federal government has established guidelines under the Railway Labor Act and the Taft–Hartley Act for postponing or preventing major transportation strikes. However, experience under these acts in recent years has led to serious questions concerning their adequacy.

NOTES

1. Transit labor is examined in Chapters 19 and 20.
2. "Something to Be-Labor," *Handling and Shipping,* XI, No. 6 (September 1970), p. 14.
3. Robert C. Lieb, *Labor in the Transportation Industries* (New York: Praeger Publishers, Inc., 1974), p. 3.
4. American Waterway Operators, Inc., *Big Load Afloat* (Washington, D.C.: American Waterway Operators, Inc., 1966), 1973.
5. Carolyn S. Fehd, "Productivity in the Petroleum Pipeline Industry," *Monthly Labor Review,* XCIV, No. 4 (April, 1971), p. 48.
6. U.S. Department of Transportation, Office of the Secretary, *1974 National Transportation Report* (Washington, D.C.: U.S. Government Printing Office, 1975), p. 296.
7. Association of American Railroads, *Yearbook of Railroad Facts* (Washington, D.C.: the Association, 1976), p. 58; Air Transport Association, *Air Transport, 1976* (Washington, D.C.: the Association, 1976), p. 28; and Transportation Association of America, *Transportation Facts and Trends* (Washington, D.C.: the Association, 1976), p. 24.
8. The most widely cited BLS measurement of productivity is output per man-hour. However, man-hour data have not historically been made available to the BLS by several modes of carriage. Therefore, several of the transportation productivity series are only calculated in terms of output per employee.
9. Solomon Fabricant, *A Primer on Productivity* (New York: Random House, Inc., 1969), p. 5.

10. Lieb, op. cit., p. 93.
11. Joseph E. Dragonette and Chester Myslicki, "Air Transport: Trends in Output per Employee," *Monthly Labor Review,* XCI, No. 2 (February 1968), p. 13.
12. U.S. Interstate Commerce Commission, *Proceedings: Productivity Measurement Conference* (Washington, D.C.: the Commission, 1975).
13. "Unions Slip from Past Gains," *Business Week* (October 2, 1971), p. 77.
14. Conversation with John Wells, Personnel Director, St. Johnsbury Trucking Company, Cambridge, Mass., December 27, 1971.
15. Congressional intervention in a nationwide railroad strike is far more likely than intervention into a motor carrier strike of the same duration. This is so because much of trucking traffic can be diverted to either rail or private trucking in the short run, whereas heavy loading rail traffic is not as easily divertible. Thus a rail strike potentially has a more severe economic impact.
16. Todd E. Fandell, "Pan Am Quits Strike-Aid Pact with Industry," *Wall Street Journal,* New York, December 17, 1974, p. 6.
17. Ibid.
18. Much of the following discussion is based on Lieb, op. cit., pp. 36–43.
19. Dudley F. Pegrum, *Transportation: Economics and Public Policy,* rev. ed. (Homewood, Ill.: Richard D. Irwin, Inc., 1968), p. 505.
20. Ibid.
21. Hugh S. Norton, *Modern Transportation Economics,* 2nd ed. (Columbus, Ohio: Charles E. Merrill Publishing Company, 1971), p. 210.
22. Pegrum, op. cit., p. 507.
23. Ibid., p. 515.
24. Ibid.
25. Dwight L. Gentry and Charles A. Taff, *Elements of Business Enterprise,* 2nd ed. (New York: Ronald Press Company, 1966), p. 294.
26. Similar experience has been had with respect to the recommendations of airline emergency boards.
27. John Hoerr and Stephen H. Wildstrom, "Ripe for Oblivion: The Railway Labor Act," *Business Week* (December 15, 1975), p. 27.
28. Lieb, op. cit., p. 29.
29. Hoerr and Wildstrom, op. cit., p. 27.
30. Lieb, op. cit., p. 49.
31. U.S. Congress, Senate, *Emergency Public Interest Protection Act of 1971,* S. 560, 92nd Cong., 1st Sess., 1971.
32. "Anti-Strike Bills Blossom Out," *UTU News,* V, No. 9 (March 10, 1973), p. 3.
33. *Transportation Act of 1940,* 49 U.S.C. Sec. 5 (2)(f) (1940).

34. It should be noted that railroad workers have not historically been protected from job loss due to technological changes or reorganizations within a single railroad.
35. U.S. Interstate Commerce Commission, *Finance Docket No. 21989, Pennsylvania Railroad Company—Merger—New York Central Railroad Company,* April 6, 1966, p. 543.
36. U.S. Department of Labor, Office of Information, "Rail Worker Protection Plan Certified by Hodgson," April 16, 1971. (News release)
37. See "Chessie, Southern Drop from Plan to Revamp Rails," *Wall Street Journal,* New York, February 13, 1976, p. 2; also "The Rail Booby Trap," *Wall Street Journal,* New York, February 17, 1976, p. 22.

SELECTED REFERENCES

Brand, Horts. "Problems of Measuring Railroad Productivity." *Monthly Labor Review,* XCVII, No. 3 (March, 1974), pp. 9–14.

Carnes, Richard B. "Productivity Trends in Intercity Trucking." *Monthly Labor Review,* XCVII, No. 1 (January, 1974), pp. 53–57.

Cottrell, Fred. *Technological Change and Labor in the Railroad Industry.* Boston: D. C. Heath & Company, 1970.

Davis, Grant M., Martin T. Farris, and Jack J. Holder. *Management of Transportation Carriers.* New York: Praeger Publishers, Inc., 1975.

Dragonette, Joseph E., and Chester Myslicki. "Air Transport: Trends in Output per employee." *Monthly Labor Review,* XCI, No. 2 (February, 1968), pp. 13–16.

Fehd, Carolyn S. "Productivity in the Petroleum Pipeline Industry." *Monthly Labor Review,* XCIV, No. 4 (March, 1971), pp. 46–48.

Fehd, Carolyn. U.S. Department of Labor, Bureau of Labor Statistics, Office of Productivity and Technology. *Productivity Measures for the Transportation Industries.* Washington, D.C.: the Bureau, 1970.

Lieb, Robert C. *Labor in the Transit Industry.* Washington, D.C.: U.S. Government Printing Office, 1976.

Lieb, Robert C. *Labor in the Transportation Industries.* New York: Praeger Publishers, Inc., 1974.

Sampson, Roy J., and Martin T. Farris. *Domestic Transportation: Practice, Theory, and Policy.* Boston: Houghton Mifflin Company, 1975.
Chapter 26. "Society's Interest in Labor–Management Relations," pp. 424–36.

Task Force on Railroad Productivity. *Improving Railroad Productivity.* Final Report to the National Commission on Productivity and the Council of

Economic Advisers. Washington, D.C.: Task Force on Railroad Productivity, 1973.
Chapter 7. "Labor Relations," pp. 210–30.

U.S. Department of Labor, Bureau of Labor Statistics. *Airline Experience Under the Railway Labor Act.* Bulletin 1683. Washington, D.C.: U.S. Government Printing Office, 1971.

U.S. Interstate Commerce Commission. *Proceedings: Productivity Conference.* Washington, D.C.: the Commission, 1975.

DISCUSSION QUESTIONS

1. Discuss the nature and significance of selective strikes and mutual aid agreements in the transportation industries.
2. Why have carriers formed collective bargaining units such as the National Railway Labor Conference and Trucking Employers, Inc.?
3. Do you believe that binding arbitration of transportation labor disputes should be mandated? Explain the rationale of your answer.
4. Discuss the factors that can influence the productivity figures registered by workers in the transportation industries.

CHAPTER
16

Consolidations, Intermodal Ownership, and Conglomerate Combinations

The structure of an industry, including such characteristics as its competitive intensity and the size and diversity of market participants, is a major determinant of how business is conducted in the industry. In turn, that influences the economic performance of the industry. As a result, legislators and regulators have long been concerned with factors that might affect the structure of the transportation industries. One manifestation of this concern has been the establishment of federal policies governing carrier consolidations, intermodal ownership, and the conglomerate movement in transportation.

As used in this chapter, *consolidation* refers to any combination of two or more carriers of the same mode that results in their being managed as a unit.[1] In contrast, *intermodal ownership* involves combinations of carriers engaged in different forms of transportation, such as a railroad acquiring a motor carrier. A *conglomerate combination* in transportation involves the combination of a carrier with one or more firms engaged in nontransportation activities.

Each of these diverse forms of carrier combination has attracted increasing attention as existing transportation policies have come under closer scrutiny. Because of the significance of federal policies related to these structural issues, this chapter examines the motives that have led carriers to consider such combinations. It also explores the factors that have influenced federal policy formulation concerning carriers consolidations, intermodal ownership, and conglomerate combinations. Attention is also given to the impact that carrier combinations have had on the transportation industries.

CONSOLIDATION

The following discussion examines not only the major factors that have led carriers to consider consolidation opportunities, but also the extent of consolidation activity by mode.

Consolidation Motives

Many factors have influenced the degree of carrier interest in consolidations. The most important have been cost-reduction possibilities, financial considerations, and competitive implications.

Cost-Reduction Possibilities

Consolidation may make it possible for carriers to substantially reduce the overhead burden that was previously borne by individual companies. Intramodal combinations may provide a means of reducing the number of employees involved in clerical, statistical, and accounting operations. Similar cost reductions might also be realized through elimination of duplicate facilities, such as field sales offices, terminals, switching yards, and pickup and delivery operations. Operating cost savings may also be possible. If terminals and shops can be consolidated, some reduction in the number of operating personnel might be envisioned. However, as discussed in Chapter 15, employee cutbacks of this nature are generally subject to regulatory agency review.

Abandonment of duplicate routes can also generate cost savings. When the consolidation involves carriers with parallel route structures, it is often both feasible and desirable to eliminate certain routes and runs. Traffic may be rerouted over more economical and less circuitous routes. This has been an important consideration in a number of rail consolidation applications. By eliminating duplicate runs, it may be possible to generate greater traffic density while utilizing less equipment. This might permit more efficient use of equipment while allowing elimination of excess capacity. Proposals of this nature, however, are carefully scrutinized by the regulatory agencies, which seek to protect shipper interests against service deterioration. End-to-end consolidations may eliminate costly and time-consuming interchanges of traffic on multiple-line hauls. The reduction of traffic interchange might also lead to lower damage claims due to less handling.

Consolidations, Intermodal Ownership, and Conglomerate Combinations

Consolidations might also promote realization of economies of scale. Increasing size may have a positive effect on average costs. Economies may be realized either through management or machine specialization as firm size increases. Specialists may be hired in such areas as law, finance, and research, and this may have a positive effect on productivity. Similarly, as the scale of an enterprise is expanded, specialization in machinery becomes a distinct possibility, with possible resultant productivity benefits. Scale economies may also be realized in purchasing through quantity discounts on machinery and supplies and in financial operations. The nature of scale economies and their incidence in the various modes were discussed in Chapter 8.

Financial Considerations

Elimination of duplicate terminals, yards, and other transport-related facilities, which may be possible because of carrier consolidations, might provide capital gains through the sale of property. Such sales could produce considerable capital for carriers, particularly railroads, which have substantial property holdings in many major cities. Property taxes would also be reduced if such sales took place.[2] Consolidation may also offer a means of survival to carriers experiencing financial difficulties. In many instances, troubled carriers have sought financially stable consolidation partners to offset their financial woes. Properly conceived and implemented consolidations may assist the troubled carrier in establishing a sounder financial base, which is essential in attracting needed investment capital.

Competitive Considerations

Carriers may also seek consolidations to improve their competitive positions. To that end, consolidations may reduce the pressures of intramodal competition. However, these competitive reductions are among the major factors to be considered by the ICC and CAB in evaluating consolidation proposals.

End-to-end consolidations may broaden the territories served by the carrier, and may also allow the provision of through services to improve the carrier's competitive position. These considerations have played a major role in promoting a number of consolidations in both rail and motor carriage. Motor carriers have often utilized consolidations as a means of broadening territories served and to increase the range of commodities that they might carry.[3]

Railroad Consolidations

The discussions of Chapters 12 and 13 noted that federal regulatory policy concerning railroad consolidations has changed significantly over time. Consequently, the intensity of railroad consolidation activity has also varied considerably throughout the years.

Early Railroad Consolidations

Most early rail lines were local and served quite limited areas. However, as population grew and dispersed and industrialization decentralized, it became apparent that many rail lines were interdependent. As interline traffic expanded, railroad owners sought to consolidate local lines to improve efficiency in handling such traffic. This early consolidation movement was hindered somewhat by restrictive state charters and laws, but congressional pressures and the potential economic benefits of carrier consolidation combined to effectively eliminate most of these barriers by the mid-1860s.[4]

Railroad Consolidations and Antitrust

Although the Sherman Antitrust Act was passed in 1890, there was·a prevailing attitude that its provisions did not apply to railroad consolidations.[5] However, several court cases, the most important of which was the Northern Securities Company case of 1904, brought these consolidations within the domain of the antitrust laws.[6] In the 1904 case, the Supreme Court ruled that the Northern Securities Company, a holding company that had been formed to control the Great Northern and Northern Pacific Railroads, was in violation of the Sherman Antitrust Act due to its adverse impact on competition. The Court required dissolution of the holding company, and the railroads were forced to dispose of their security holdings in several other railroads. These court rulings, coupled with the passage of the Clayton Act in 1914, which strengthened the antitrust statutes, effectively prohibited further railroad consolidations until after World War I.

Consolidations and the Transportation Act of 1920

United States involvement in World War I placed considerable strain on the national railroad system; when the system failed to meet government performance expectations, the railroads were placed under direct federal control and operation in 1917. As discussed in Chapter 12, the rigors of the war effort left many railroads in precarious financial and physical condition. In an effort to prevent the financial collapse of the railroads, Congress passed the Transportation Act of 1920. The most important provision of that statute, in terms of the present discussion, was a directive to the ICC to formulate a plan to consolidate the U.S. railroads into a limited number of systems. These were to combine weak and strong roads in various regions to create railroads that were balanced in terms of earning power. All future consolidations were required to conform to the plan that the ICC was to formulate. The act also empowered the ICC to withdraw any railroad consolidation from the operation of the antitrust statutes. Thus the ICC could approve consolidations that might result in a lessening of competition between rail carriers. Federal policy concerning railroad consolidations therefore shifted from enforced intramodal competition and a prohibition of consolidations to active promotion of consolidations that might reduce such competition.

The ICC struggled with the master plan concept for nearly a decade, and several times during that period the commission petitioned Congress to relieve it of the burden. However, Congress did not respond to these requests. In 1929 the ICC adopted a *final* consolidation plan, which consisted of 21 systems. However, lack of agreement between carriers and Congress concerning the propriety of the plan, the fact that the carriers were not compelled to consolidate, and the Depression all combined to render the plan inoperable. It was not until 1940 that Congress abandoned the master plan concept and declared that the initiative in future railroad consolidation proposals should come from the carriers. The ICC was relieved of its responsibility of preparing a consolidation plan, and its role in future consolidation proposals was defined as determining if the proposals met the standards of the Interstate Commerce Act. In such cases the ICC was given the statutory charge to consider the impact of the proposed consolidation upon the following:

1. The public need for adequate transportation service.
2. Other carriers.
3. The fixed charges of the railroads involved.
4. Employees.[7]

Railroad Consolidations Since 1940

Between 1940 and 1958 relatively few consolidations were proposed by the railroads. However, between 1958 and 1968 the ICC was deluged with consolidation applications involving many major U.S. railroads. Rapidly escalating operating costs and the increasing intensity of intermodal competition provided the major impetus for this wave of applications, which generally sought to eliminate duplicate operations.

Many of these applications, which were reviewed according to the ICC's case-by-case approach, met the standards prescribed by the ICC and were approved. Major railroad consolidations approved during that period created the Penn Central, the Burlington Northern, and the Baltimore and Ohio–Chesapeake and Ohio systems, among others. Many of these consolidation cases were quite time consuming. For example, the proposal that sought to link the Pennsylvania and New York Central railroads into the Penn Central was originally submitted to the ICC in 1962, but was not finally decided by the commission until 1966.[8] Such delays resulted in widespread criticism of ICC procedures in handling consolidation cases.

The railroad consolidation movement slowed somewhat following the June 1970 bankruptcy of the Penn Central. Some congressmen blamed the collapse of the Penn Central on the consolidation, but it soon became apparent that the railroad's problems were the result of many factors. Among these were the changing economic conditions of the region, forced continuance of unprofitable services, and managerial infighting. As a result, the unofficial moratorium on railroad consolidations was rather short lived. In fact, as discussed in early chapters, Congress became actively involved in the massive consolidation of seven bankrupt railroads in the Northeast and Midwest in 1973. Further railroad consolidations were also actively supported by the DOT beginning in 1975. The department called for a new wave of consolidations, particularly of an end-to-end nature, to promote a more efficient U.S. railroad system.[9] Also, the Railroad Revitalization and Regulatory Modernization Act of 1976 contained provisions to accelerate ICC consideration of railroad consolidation applications. Under the provisions of the act, the ICC was given a 31-month time limit for processing such applications and rendering a final decision.[10] The prospect of more rapid processing of such proposals led to a new round of consolidation discussions among railroads, which made further consolidation activity likely.

Effects of Railroad Consolidations

The many railroad consolidations approved by the ICC have had a decided impact on the structure of the railroad industry. Although these consolidations have not conformed with the earlier master plan of the ICC, they have led to the emergence of a limited number of major systems and have promoted a much needed reduction of duplication within the industry. To date, there is a lack of sufficient data to quantitatively evaluate the effects of the most recent wave of railroad consolidations.

Motor Carrier Consolidations

The Motor Carrier Act of 1935 established ICC jurisdiction over consolidations involving regulated motor carriers. However, the statute stipulated that any consolidation involving fewer than 20 vehicles did not require ICC approval. In 1965 the provision was modified to exempt from ICC control any consolidation involving motor carriers whose combined annual gross revenues were less than $300,000. On several occasions the ICC has recommended to Congress that this exemption be extended to $500,000, but Congress has not responded to these requests.

The nature of the certificates granted to individual motor carriers by the ICC provides a major incentive for motor carrier consolidations. Often the certificates are quite limited in terms of commodities to be carried and territories to be served. To expand the base of their operations, carriers may either request new operating authority from the ICC or seek to consolidate with a company that has complementary operating authority. Given existing regulations, which limit entry into motor carriage, it may be easier to obtain ICC approval of a consolidation proposal than it is to obtain new operating authority.[11]

In a typical year the ICC approves an average of approximately 300 motor carrier consolidations. The majority of these consolidations are of an end-to-end nature. The intensity of motor carrier consolidation activity accelerated greatly in the late 1950s; as a result, a number of large motor carrier systems emerged. One of the most active carriers during that period was Consolidated Freightways, which used consolidations to become the largest U.S. trucking company with more than 64,000 route miles in the United States and Canada. Between 1955 and 1960 the company acquired 52 other companies, which were involved in local, specialized, or general-purpose trucking operations.[12] Through these acquisitions Consolidated became the first transcontinental motor carrier in the country. Several other carriers, including Navajo and Transcon, have since joined Consolidated in the ranks of transcontinental operators.

In commenting on the continuing interest in motor carrier consolidations, the ICC has stated that it believes that such activities are not only a function of the nature of the original certificates granted, but also a reaction to the growing competition of private trucking, which seems to make it "imperative . . . to improve, or extend, existing franchises as a matter of business survival."[13]

Effects of Motor Carrier Consolidations

Motor carrier consolidations have contributed to a growing concentration of intercity trucking activities. Several large motor carriers have emerged that rank among the largest U.S. transportation companies in terms of both assets and operating revenues. This trend toward increasing concentration in the industry has led to some criticism of ICC policies. Critics have contended that trucking is basically a competitive industry, and that the ICC should not be permitted to exempt motor carrier consolidations from the antitrust laws.[14]

Undoubtedly, motor carrier consolidations have led to a considerable lessening of intramodal competition in trucking. However, this competitive loss must be weighed against the service improvements that have resulted from single-line carriage, and the operating economies that have been realized through more balanced traffic flows and better equipment utilization. Any future ICC determination that service quality has deteriorated due to competitive reductions should lead to more liberal ICC entry standards in the markets involved.

Water Carrier Consolidations

There has been relatively little consolidaton activity involving those water carriers that are subject to ICC jurisdiction. Most consolidations that have occurred have been of an end-to-end nature. Combinations that have involved parallel lines have generally concerned dormant or little-used operating rights.

Pipeline and Freight Forwarding Consolidations

The ICC has no jurisdiction over pipeline consolidations. Although a limited number of pipeline consolidations have occurred in recent years, the structure of the industry was primarily defined by a series of consolidations that occurred in the latter part of the nineteenth century. The major consolidations during that period involved the Standard Oil Trust, which bought out the interests of the major eastern pipeline companies, and the combination of a number of western refiners, which resulted in the formation of the U.S. Pipe Line Company.

Consolidations involving surface freight forwarders are also beyond the ICC's control. Many consolidations have occurred and have led to a concentration of forwarding activities. United States Freight, a holding company, controls seven of the thirty largest surface forwarding companies in the United States.

Consolidations involving air freight forwarders are within the jurisdiction of the Civil Aeronautics Board. However, the majority of business combination activity related to air forwarding has involved the entrance of surface carriers into air forwarding. This trend toward expansion of intermodal ownership is discussed later in this chapter.

Air Carrier Consolidations

The Civil Aeronautics Act of 1938 brought airline consolidations within the jurisdiction of the CAB. In administering the consolidation provisions of the act, the board has attempted to protect competition whenever possible. Consequently, the board has denied several major consolidation proposals because it believed that the potential negative impact on competition outweighed the prospective carrier benefits.

Since 1938, 7 of the 19 domestic trunk lines that were granted grandfather rights have been consolidated into other systems.[15] The board has also generally permitted consolidations of local service lines when evidence has indicated that the transaction would lead to development of a stronger local carrier.[16] However, the CAB has sought to maintain a separation between local service and trunk-line carriers, and therefore has not looked favorably upon trunk-line proposals to acquire local service carriers.

Board decisions on major consolidation applications seem to have often been highly influenced by the financial condition of the applicant airlines. In 1961 the board approved the consolidation of Capital Airlines and United Airlines, even though the transaction seemed likely to cause considerable diversion of traffic from competing carriers.[17] However, at that time Capital was faced with the immediate prospect of bankruptcy, and the CAB believed that the proposed combination could lead to rehabilitation of Capital operations. Similar reasoning also seemed apparent in the 1971 board decision to allow American Airlines to acquire Trans Caribbean Airways. In that case American was financially sound while Trans Caribbean was experiencing considerable financial difficulty. More recently, the CAB has approved two other major consolidations that exhibited similar *strong–weak* characteristics. These cases involved the linkage of the strongest local service line, Allegheny Airlines, with the troubled Mohawk system, and the consolidation of the financially strong Delta Airlines with Northeast Airlines, which was on the brink of financial disaster. During 1974 and 1975, Pan American World Airways and Trans World Airlines conducted preliminary consolidation discussions, which were prompted by ridership and cost difficulties experienced by both lines.[18] However, these discussions ultimately led to a CAB-approved transfer of several routes between the two carriers rather than a consolidation.

Effects of Airline Consolidations

The airline consolidations approved in recent years have not only provided a means of salvaging financially troubled operations, but have also promoted improvements in through service and more efficient utilization of equipment and personnel. Although the consolidations have reduced competition over some routes, the competitive reductions have often been offset by CAB route awards to other carriers. In response to these developments, in 1975 Secretary of Transportation William Coleman called for a new wave of airline consolidations to further rationalize the domestic airline system.[19] Several years earlier, CAB chairman Secor Browne called for similar action.[20] Such measures appear rather unlikely, at least in the short run. The movement toward regulatory reform during the mid-1970s led to criticism of earlier CAB consolidation policies because of their negative impact on competition. At the same time the board, under considerable political pressures, also expressed interest in promotion of a more competitive airline environment.[21] Thus a more conservative CAB approach to airline consolidations might be expected.

INTERMODAL OWNERSHIP

Intermodal ownership provides carriers engaged in a given mode of carriage with the ability, either through direct ownership or security control, to operate or substantially influence the operations of a carrier engaged in another form of transportation. National transportation policy has generally restricted the extent of intermodal ownership in the United States. Nevertheless, many carriers have continued to express interest in multimodal operations, and they have lobbied for possible revisions in existing intermodal ownership policies.

Proponents

It has been suggested that, because carriers engaged in different forms of transportation fear each other and fail to cooperate, intermodal ownership is the only means available to improve coordination of multimodal movements such as piggybacking.[22] Advocates have asserted that such integration would reduce the economic waste that typifies the U.S. transportation system. It is proposed that this would be accomplished through abandonment of facilities whose functions might be more efficiently performed by another mode or combination of modes.[23]

It has also been suggested that multimodal companies would generate shipper benefits by handling the distribution needs of shippers in a more systematic manner, rather than treating the transportation task as a series of disjointed elements. The arguments continue that intermodal ownership could provide one-stop transportation service, and would make it possible to tailor rates and services to meet the varying needs of customers.[24]

Those favoring integration of the modes also believe that it would promote substantial carrier benefits. It is argued that these companies could

335

generate savings through common sales and promotional efforts. Proponents believe that intermodal companies, by combining the varying capabilities of the modes, might achieve a level of cost and service that is impossible under existing regulations.[25] Such savings might be passed on to shippers in the form of lower rates. It is further asserted that integrated companies would be financially stable, because the risk of failures caused by the decline of one type of service (mode) would be lessened.[26] Proponents also believe that integration might provide a means of channeling capital from the established modes into developmental efforts in refining new transportation technology.[27] This assertion is based on the premise that the airline and motor carrier industries would have matured sooner, to the public benefit, if intermodal ownership guidelines had not limited cross-modal capital flows.

Opponents

Those opposed to intermodal ownership believe that it would lead to disastrous changes in the transportation system. It has been proposed that integration of the modes would curtail modal development and would stifle the incentive to innovate.[28] It has also been suggested that, because of their superior size and financial strength, the railroads would dominate any environment in which more extensive intermodal ownership was permitted. The argument continues that railroad management would consequently dominate multimodal companies and, due to the heavy fixed investment in rail plant and equipment, would channel traffic away from other modes.[29]

Opponents believe that traffic would be channeled to rail operations by allowing the services of controlled modes to deteriorate, thereby making the rail alternative more attractive and leading to a phasing out of the other modes. It is predicted that destructive competition between multimodal companies and independent operators would prevail, and that the independents would be eliminated.[30] Those opposed to intermodal ownership propose that monopolistic conditions would result in the long run, and that this would not be consistent with the public interest.[31]

Federal Policy

Generally, the nature of federal policies governing intermodal ownership seems to reflect a belief in the arguments posed by opponents of the concept. However, no single statute or policy reflects the federal position concerning this matter.[32] Rather, this important regulatory issue is governed by the provisions of several statutes, including the Panama Canal Act of 1912, the Motor Carrier Act of 1935, the Civil Aeronautics Act of 1938, and the Freight Forwarder Act of 1942. The provisions of these statutes were subsequently incorporated into either the Interstate Commerce Act or the Federal Aviation Act.

Each of the four previously mentioned statutes was formulated during a period of extreme financial difficulty for the mode involved. The overriding intent of Congress seems to have been the protection of the newer, developing modes from the domination of carriers engaged in the more established forms of transportation. Typically, the governing provisions do not constitute a definite prohibition of intermodal ownership.[33] However, in many instances the legislative barriers do constitute a significant obstacle to integration efforts. The governing provisions are often inconsistent with respect to the various modes and modal combinations, and several contain special provisions that must be met by only the railroads.[34] The vagueness of the provisions has also caused continuing interpretative difficulties for the regulatory agencies.

Extent of Intermodal Ownership

Despite the legislative restrictions that govern intermodal ownership, there are a number of instances in which such integration has occurred. Typically, a company that controls several modes of transportation operates the separate modes as distinct operating subsidiaries.

Intermodal combinations have come about through a variety of circumstances. First, the statutes relating to the ownership of certain forms of transportation, such as pipelines, contain no provisions that limit intermodal ownership. Second, several legislative provisions that govern certain forms of transportation integration were accompanied by grandfather clauses which permitted operations that predated the legislation to be continued. This explains, for instance, the extensive participation of rail carriers in motor carriage. Third, integration has been accomplished through the process of applying to the proper regulatory agency and subsequently meeting the provisions of the relevant statute. As previously mentioned, in most instances the governing statute does not constitute a definite prohibition of such ownership, and the applicant may be successful in substantiating the public benefit of the proposed transaction. In such cases, shipper support has generally been quite important.

Water Carriage

The Panama Canal Act of 1912 sought to prevent railroad domination of water carriers that operated through the newly opened canal. However, the ICC interpreted the rather vague provisions of the act quite strictly, and the commission's decisions in the 1915 Lake Lines cases prac-

337

tically eliminated the participation of the railroads in domestic water carriage.[35] Although later ICC decisions in cases involving the Panama Canal Act exhibited a more moderate interpretation of the provisions of the act, the railroads have made few major attempts to re-enter domestic water carriage on a significant scale. One such effort was rebuffed by the ICC in the Hay case of 1962. The case involved a joint application by the Southern Pacific Company and the Illinois Central Railroad to acquire control, through joint stock ownership, of the John I. Hay Company. Hay was a major barge operator whose routes roughly paralleled those of the applicant railroads. In a sharply divided opinion the ICC denied the application, stating that intermodal competition would be lessened, and barge traffic would be channeled to the parent railroads if the proposal was approved.[36] However, the ICC has since demonstrated that it will approve such rail–barge relationships if there is not potential competition between the two controlled modes. The ICC has therefore approved supplemental services by rail-controlled barge operations in cases involving both the Southern Railway and Katy Industries, which is the parent company of the Missouri–Kansas–Texas Railroad.[37]

Although railroad interest in water carriage has been limited, other modes have shown a growing interest in the water mode. However, this interest has generally been in international shipping. By far the most extensive movement into domestic water carriage by a company engaged in another form of transportation was completed in 1968 when Texas Gas Transmission merged with American Commercial Barge Lines. As a result of the merger, the largest inland barge complex in the country is an operating division of a pipeline company that is engaged in the interstate transportation of natural gas. The pipeline company is not regulated by the ICC, but it has a motor carrier division which is subject to commission regulation. The water carrier operations of Texas Gas Transmission are conducted through its Inland Waterways Service Division. American Commercial Barge Lines is a major component of that division, which has over 8,000 miles of operating authority.

Pipeline Operations

Ten of the 104 common carrier oil pipeline companies regulated by the ICC in 1976 were either owned or controlled by railroads,[38] among them the Southern Pacific, the Sante Fe, and the Union Pacific. This form of intermodal ownership has been possible because such combinations are not regulated under the Interstate Commerce Act. In a number of instances rail–pipeline integration has provided a means of handling petroleum products more efficiently and economically.

Motor Carriage

The ownership or control of motor carrier operations by carriers primarily engaged in other modes is rather extensive. An interest in trucking activities has been established by a number of rail, water, and air carriers, as well as by surface forwarders. This is not surprising, because the truck is the most important vehicle involved in the promotion and coordination of intermodal service offerings. Most forms of coordinated transportation rely upon motor carriage at least for pickup and delivery activities, if not for performance of part of the line-haul movement itself.

Railroad Participation. Of the other modes of transportation, the railroads, by far, have the most extensive interest in trucking operations. Many class I railroads have controlling interest in some motor carrier operation. In fact, about 2 percent of the total operating revenues of ICC-regulated motor carriers are earned by railroad-controlled motor carriers.[39]

The participation of rail carriers in motor carriage may be divided into unrestricted and restricted operations. Unrestricted trucking operations conducted by railroads or their subsidiaries are not subject to the special provisions that are generally imposed upon railroad-controlled motor carriers. Restricted trucking operations conducted by railroads or their subsidiaries are activities subject to special provisions that have been developed by Congress and the ICC to apply to rail-controlled trucking operations.

Commission interpretation of the intermodal ownership provisions of the Motor Carrier Act has led to the development of five basic conditions that are generally imposed upon restricted trucking operation of railroads. These are as follows:

(1) The service to be performed shall be limited to service which is auxiliary to, or supplemental of, rails service [meaning that all traffic moving by the motor carrier must move on rail rates and rail billing and not on truck rates and truck billing]; (2) No motor service shall be rendered to or from any point not a station on the rail line of the railroad; (3) Shipments to be transported shall be limited to those on a through bill of lading, including a prior or subsequent movement by rail [usually, this is replaced by a key point restriction that prevents the movement of a shipment between any of two named points or through or to or from more than one of the designated points]; (4) All contractural arrangements between the applicant motor carrier and the parent railroad shall be reported to the Commission and shall be subject to revision; (5) The motor carrier service shall be subject to further conditions as the Commission in the future may find it necessary to impose, in order to insure that it will remain auxiliary and supplemental to rail service.[40]

These provisions apply only to rail carrier subsidiaries. Other forms of transportation may establish motor carrier operations without meeting such stipulations.

Railroads have gained access to unrestricted trucking authority in three ways. One source has been railroad involvement in purely intrastate motor carriage. Individual states have authority over these operations, but they have not generally followed the rather restrictive policies of the ICC. As a result, many rail-controlled motor carriers conduct unrestricted general freight service on an intrastate basis. As noted in one study:

> Railroad subsidiary motor carriers in . . . California, Texas, Nevada, and Oregon regularly participate in intrastate transportation over such distances as would compare with medium and long-distance interstate trucking on the Eastern Seaboard.[41]

Some railroads also acquired unrestricted motor carrier authority through the grandfather clause contained in the Motor Carrier Act of 1935. These railroads had established trucking subsidiaries prior to the passage of the statute; under its provisions, they were permitted to continue the operations.

The third way in which railroads have been able to enter trucking on an unrestricted basis is by means of an ICC finding that "special circumstances," such as poor service by existing motor carriers, justifies the granting of unrestricted authority to rail affiliates. Subsidiaries of several railroads have been granted unrestricted authority on this basis. In one case the ICC granted a significant expansion of the unrestricted trucking authority held by Pacific Motor Trucking, which is a subsidiary of the Southern Pacific Railroad. In the ICC's opinion, several large trucking companies were offering substandard service in the areas involved.[42]

In addition to these unrestricted trucking authorizations, many railroads have also been granted limited trucking authority that is auxiliary and supplemental to their rail operations. In certain instances railroads have also been permitted to substitute trucking operations for rail service and lightly traveled routes.

Other Modes. Companies engaged in other forms of intercity carriage have also expressed interest in motor carriage. In addition to its substantial interest in domestic water carriage, Texas Gas Transmission also has a rather extensive Trucking Services Division, which operates in 10 states.[43] One component of that division is Commercial Carriers, Inc., which is one of the nation's largest transporters of new autos and trucks.

Another integrated holding company, United States Freight, has also established a substantial interest in motor carriage. Besides owning a con-

340

tainership line and controlling seven domestic and two international freight forwarding operations, the company also controls nine trucking enterprises. These motor carriers conduct pickup and delivery operations for the parent company in metropolitan areas throughout the United States. Freight forwarders are forbidden to control intercity trucking operations, but may participate in trucking operations in terminal areas.

Air Carriage

The provisions of the Federal Aviation Act that govern surface carrier participation in air carriage have been strictly interpreted by the CAB. In fact, since the passage of the Civil Aeronautics Act in 1958, all surface carrier attempts to enter direct air carriage have been rebuffed by the board.

This separation of surface carriers from air transportation has not always been the case. There were several instances of railroad involvement in domestic air carriage during the early days of commercial aviation. For example, the Boston and Maine and Maine Central railroads financially participated in the development of Northeast Airlines. The airline was originally incorporated in 1931 as the Boston–Maine Airways. This rail–air relationship predated the Civil Aeronautics Act of 1938 and was thus protected under grandfather rights. However, the CAB ruled that the railroads would not be permitted to increase their control of the airline, and the original interest was eventually liquidated.[44]

During that same time period, the Pennsylvania Railroad also became involved in air transportation. In 1938 the railroad purchased a 20 percent equity interest in Transcontinental Air Transport, which later became part of Trans World Airlines. Through this interest in air carriage the railroad sought to develop coordinated passenger service, which would rely upon rail service during the night and air service during the day. However, after a series of administrative difficulties with the CAB following regulation, the railroad relinquished its interest in the airline.[45]

Freight Forwarding

As discussed in Chapter 13, the Freight Forwarder Act of 1942 was enacted in response to discriminatory pricing and the related abuses that had become common in freight forwarding activities. At the time that the legislation was passed, many large railroads, including the Pennsylvania, New York Central, and the Erie, were engaged in forwarding operations. However, the railroads developed their own through service, and forwarding activities declined in importance until motor and air carriage increased in volume.

Although railroad interest in forwarding activities has declined, carriers primarily engaged in other forms of direct carriage have expressed a growing interest in forwarding. This is illustrated by the fact that nearly one fourth of the surface freight forwarders regulated by the ICC are controlled by direct surface carriers.[46]

In recent years, the CAB has reversed a long-standing policy against surface carrier involvement in air freight forwarding, and has granted forwarding authorizations to many surface carriers. By 1976, approximately one third of the outstanding air forwarding authorizations were either owned or controlled by surface carriers.[47]

The majority of motor carriers involved in air forwarding are local service truckers with limited operating authority. Frequently, in such combined operations the air forwarder solicits traffic, which is ultimately to be shipped by air freight, and the trucking authority is used to perform the pickup and delivery operations. The 1969 approval by the CAB of applications by Consolidated Freightways, Navajo Truck Lines, and Pacific Intermountain Express to enter air forwarding substantially broadened the scope of motor carrier participation in air forwarding activities.[48] These truckers have extensive interstate certificates from the ICC, and their involvement in air forwarding has significantly expanded the number of cities that are offered the benefits of air freight service. This factor, expansion of the geographical area served by air freight, was of primary importance to the board in judging the surface carrier applications. By approving these applications, CAB provided a means of further coordinating motor and air service, and also provided an incentive to motor carriers to promote air service. Since that time the Southern Pacific, Sante Fe, and Burlington Northern railroads and a number of household goods moving companies have also been granted air freight forwarding authority by the CAB.

Experience with Intermodal Ownership

The arguments typically posed against intermodal ownership have not been validated by past experience with the concept, either in the United States or in Canada, where intermodal ownership is generally permitted. Multimodal operations have not stifled the development of the various modes of carriage. To the contrary, in a number of instances cross-modal capital flows have been instrumental in the development of newer forms of transportation. For example, it was not uncommon for up to 50 percent of the capital of the early regional bus companies to be subscribed by railroads.[49] That situation proved to be quite beneficial to the development of the intercity bus industry. Recent CAB approval of surface carrier entry into air forwarding has been based on the recognition of the value of such capital backing.[50]

Where intermodal ownership has been permitted, it has promoted a more rational assignment of transportation functions to the modes that are economically best suited to provide such services. Examples may be found in the railroads' channeling of various traffic types to pipeline and motor carrier subsidiaries, and in the willingness of motor carriers to direct many small, long-distance shipments to air freight forwarding subsidiaries. Railroad expansion of rail–motor piggybacking services has also promoted more efficient traffic allocation.

Intermodal ownership has not resulted in any significant disruption of competition, and has shown no tendency to create a monopolistic situation in the transportation marketplace.[51] Limited financial entry barriers in several modes of carriage and the ability of the regulatory agencies to grant new operating authority tend to negate any monopolistic tendencies that might exist.

The previously cited Doyle Report of 1960 recommended a revised federal policy toward intermodal ownership that would have eliminated the inconsistency and discrimination that typified existing intermodal policy.[52] Congress, however, did not act on the recommendation of the study group. Since that time the regulatory agencies have indicated that they are not philosophically opposed to intermodal ownership, but in some instances they are bound by the restrictive nature of existing policies.[53] At the same time, the Department of Transportation and many shipping and carrier groups have expressed a desire for a more liberal intermodal ownership policy.[54] As pressures mount for further rationalization of the U.S. transportation system and more efficient use of scarce transportation resources, such policy changes seem increasingly appealing.

CONGLOMERATES IN TRANSPORTATION

In recent years many carriers have sought to diversify their operations by expanding into nontransportation activities. The carriers who have participated in the *conglomerate* movement in U.S. industry have done so for several reasons.

First, the rate of return offered by many industries is substantially higher than that which has been generated in certain forms of transportation. For example, since 1945 the aggregate railroad industry has not earned an annual rate of return on investment in excess of 4 percent.[55] Over the same time period, the rate of return on stockholder investment in U.S. industry in general has averaged 9 to 12 percent after taxes.[56] An adequate rate of return that compares favorably with the rest of U.S. industry is necessary to obtain the investment capital required for modernization and expansion of transportation activities. Second, by diversifying into nontransportation activities, carriers may find it possible to combine different profit cycles, which might improve their cash flow positions. Third, diversification might improve the carriers' likelihood of survival in case of a business decline in a particular segment of its traffic. Fourth, the tax credits that many carriers have accumulated may be used to offset profits in other operations.

Federal Policy

The federal government has historically tended to limit carrier involvement in nontransportation activities. During the late nineteenth and early twentieth centuries, a number of railroads diversified into such businesses as lumber production and coal mining. In some cases the railroads would transport their own commodities, which were directly competitive with similar items produced by shippers who also used the railroads for transportation. By charging competitive shippers high rates, or by charging themselves artificially low rates to ship the same products, railroads were able to create an insurmountable competitive advantage for their own products.[57] The *commodities clause* of the Hepburn Act of 1906 sought to eliminate such discrimination. The clause prevented railroads engaged in interstate operations from transporting articles that they had produced, or had an interest in, over interstate routes. Timber products were exempted from the provisions of the act, which were essentially directed at abuses related to the production and shipment of anthracite coal.[58]

The act forced many railroads to divest themselves of nontransportation interests.[59] The commodities clause applied only to railroads, and was not subsequently extended to the other modes.

Federal control over carrier diversification was further tightened by the Transportation Act of 1920, which established ICC control over the issuance of railroad securities. This was significant, because in the pre-1906 period the railroads had often used security issues to acquire other companies.

Holding Companies

One means of circumventing much of the regulatory control over carrier diversification is the formation of holding companies. A *holding company* is a corporation that owns controlling interest in the voting stock of one or more companies. Companies controlled in this manner may be referred to as subsidiaries. The Emergency Transportation Act of 1933 gave the ICC power over holding companies that sought to gain control of two or more carriers, but one-carrier holding companies are exempt from the provisions of Section 5(2) of the Interstate Commerce Act, which governs carrier acquisitions. Therefore, a holding company that is formed to control a single carrier is free of ICC supervision of its activities, while its carrier subsidiary remains under ICC control.[60] The courts have not found the provisions of the commodities clause applicable to situations in which companies engaged in nontransportation activities are controlled by a holding company that also controls a railroad.[61]

Extent of Conglomerate Involvement

Although this loophole in regulatory policy governing carrier diversification existed for many years, it was not until 1962 that a significant number of carriers formed parent holding companies to be used as diversification vehicles. The first of the modern transportation holding companies was formed that year when the Bangor and Aroostook Company was established to control the Bangor and Aroostook Railroad. The parent company later merged with the Punta Allegre Sugar Company to form the Bangor Punta Company.

Since that time nearly two thirds of the class I railroads, many motor carriers, and several airlines have sought to participate in the conglomerate movement through formation of holding companies. Carriers have diversified into a wide range of businesses, including real estate development, equipment manufacturing, food processing, and financial services. The railroads have been the most active carrier group in conglomerate diversification. The extent of their movement into nontransportation interests has undoubtedly been influenced by the anemic rate of return that has been generated by many railroads since World War II. It has been suggested that there has been less motor carrier diversification because motor carriage still offers considerable growth potential and, therefore, is still an attractive investment.[62]

Recent Developments

The increasing movement of carriers into nontransportation endeavors has stimulated fears that carriers, attracted by the greater profit potential of other businesses, will channel vital funds from transportation operations into nontransportation activities. The sentiment of the ICC concerning regulated carrier participation in conglomerate combinations has been summarized as follows:

> Subject to some reservations, we are reasonably convinced that this conglomerate approach can be attributed to a desire to improve earnings through diversification. And, it may be argued that this policy could possibly result in a revitalization of the railroads, and, consequently, improved railroad transportation to the public. We are equally convinced, however, that the conglomerate restructuring of the railroad industry could pose a

threat to the public's interest in an adequate rail transportation system and complicate the Commission's regulatory and enforcement problems.[63]

Because of these concerns the ICC has undertaken several studies of the impact of conglomerate involvement on transportation companies. Based on these studies, a 1975 ICC report estimated that during the previous several decades the cash loss of transportation companies to conglomerate parents was approximately $3 billion.[64] Consequently, the ICC asked Congress to give it sufficient "regulatory tools to prevent such a financial drain."[65] Those supporting carrier diversification have contended that the capital flows have gone in the opposite direction, from nontransportation activities to the carriers.

The impact of carrier diversification on the structure and performance of the transportation industries is still unclear. The studies conducted to date have been quite limited in scope. However, the propriety of regulatory policies that have failed to provide many carriers, particularly the railroads, with an adequate rate of return to sustain viable operations and the restrictive intermodal ownership policies that have limited cross-modal movements might well be questioned. Modification of federal policies related to those matters might significantly lessen carrier interest in conglomerate combinations.

SUMMARY

Federal policies governing carrier consolidations have varied considerably both over time and with respect to the various modes. In evaluating consolidation proposals the regulatory agencies must weigh the potential cost, revenue, and service improvements against any adverse effects on shippers, competitors, or employees. The carrier consolidations approved by the ICC and CAB in recent years, many motivated by financial problems, have led to growing carrier concentration in many markets.

Congress has generally followed a restrictive policy toward intermodal ownership. Federal policies concerning the integration of the modes are rather vague and inconsistent with respect to different modal combinations. Despite the restrictive nature of prevailing policies, there are still a number of instances of intermodal ownership. Past experience with such integration and increasing emphasis on the potential of intermodal coordination have stimulated considerable interest in this concept. Several attempts have been made to modify existing intermodal ownership policies, but these legislative efforts have not met with congressional approval.

Conglomerate combinations have also aroused the interest of both carriers and those involved in the regulatory process. Existing statutes seek to limit the movement of carriers into nontransportation activities, but the holding company mechanism allows carriers to circumvent much of the regulatory agencies' authority over diversification. Consequently, many carriers have been attracted by the higher potential returns offered by other industries and have formed parent holding companies to diversify.

NOTES

1. The terms "consolidation" and "merger" are often used interchangeably. However, there is a significant difference in the financial implications of the two terms. In a consolidation, two or more firms combine to form a new corporation. A merger occurs when one company is absorbed into another, and the absorbed company ceases to exist.
2. Charles F. Phillips, "Railroad Mergers, Competition, Monopoly and Antitrust," *Washington and Lee Law Review,* XIX, No. 1 (Spring, 1962), pp. 14–15. (Reprint)
3. Nadreen A. Burnie, ed., *Transportation Mergers and Acquisitions* (Evanston, Ill.: Transportation Center, Northwestern University, 1962), p. 27.
4. U.S. Congress, Senate, Committee on Interstate and Foreign Commerce, Special Study Group on Transportation Policies in the United States, *National Transportation Policy* (Doyle Report), 87th Cong., 1st Sess., 1960 (Washington, D.C.: U.S. Government Printing Office, 1961), p. 230.
5. Burnie, op. cit., p. 34.
6. *Northern Securities Company* v. *United States,* 193 U.S. 197 (1904).
7. Interstate Commerce Act, Sec. 5(6)(c) (1969).
8. *Pennsylvania Railroad Company—Merger—New York Central Railroad Company,* 327 ICC 475 (1966).
9. "Fewer but Stronger Airlines, Railroads Is Goal of New Transportation Secretary," *Wall Street Journal,* New York, April 9, 1975, p. 2.
10. The lengthiest and probably the most complex railroad consolidation case ever considered by the ICC was the *Rock Island Merger Case,* 347 ICC 556 (1974). The case was before the ICC for nearly 10 years. Ironically, soon after the ICC gave its approval to the consolidation the Rock Island declared bankruptcy and the consolidation was never consummated.
11. Charles A. Taff, *Commercial Motor Transportation,* 3rd ed. (Homewood, Ill.: Richard D. Irwin, Inc., 1961), p. 567.

12. Consolidated Freightways, Inc., *Financial Review, 1959–1968* (San Francisco: Consolidated Freightways, Inc., 1969), p. 1.

13. Interstate Commerce Commission, *Report on Basic Policy Matters Under Consideration by the Interstate Commerce Commission* (Washington, D.C.: the Commission, 1970), p. 38.

14. Charles F. Phillips, *The Economics of Regulation,* rev. ed. (Homewood, Ill.: Richard D. Irwin, Inc., 1969), pp. 521–522.

15. Carl F. Fulda, *Competition in the Regulated Industries: Transportation* (Boston: Little, Brown and Company, 1961), p. 193.

16. *West Coast Case,* 8 CAB 636, 639 (1947).

17. *United–Capital Merger Case,* CAB Dkt. No. 11699, E-16605, April 3, 1961.

18. See "Subsidies for Pan Am and TWA Rejected, but CAB Will Study Pan Am Situation," *Wall Street Journal,* New York, September 19, 1974, p. 4.

19. "Fewer but Stronger Airlines, Railroads Is Goal of New Transportation Secretary," p. 2.

20. "Only Mergers Can Bail Out the Airlines," *Business Week* (January 9, 1971), p. 37.

21. "Less Regulation of Airline Sector Is Urged by Ford," *Wall Street Journal,* New York, October 9, 1975, p. 3.

22. Lee J. Melton, "An Integrated Approach to the Transportation Problem," *Southern Economic Journal,* XXIII (April, 1957), p. 406.

23. Ibid.

24. Alfred E. Perlman, Vice Chairman, Penn Central Company, "Toward a Space Age Transportation Policy," an address delivered to the Federal Bar Association, Washington, D.C., January 28, 1969, p. 3. (Mimeographed)

25. Letter from John Stenason, Vice President, Transport and Ships, Canadian Pacific Railway Company, January 16, 1970.

26. Paul W. Cherington and David Schwartz, "The Common Ownership Issue from Political Ideology to a Practical Consideration of the Practices and Goals for Public Service," *Transportation Law Journal,* I (January, 1970), pp. 1–10.

27. Ibid.

28. Peter T. Beardsley, "Intermodal Ownership of Transportation Facilities— A Motor Carrier View," an address delivered to the Federal Bar Association, Washington, D.C., March 20, 1969, p. 9. (Mimeographed)

29. D. Philip Locklin, *Economics of Transportation,* 6th ed. (Homewood, Ill.: Richard D. Irwin, Inc., 1963), p. 845.

30. "Panel Discussion: The Effects of Diversification into Other Modes of Transportation," *ICC Practitioners' Journal,* XXXVI, No. 6 (September–October, 1969), p. 2000.

31. Dudley F. Pegrum, *Transportation: Economics and Public Policy* (Homewood, Ill.: Richard D. Irwin, Inc., 1963), p. 429.

32. Robert C. Lieb, "Intermodal Ownership: Experience and Evaluation," *ICC Practitioners' Journal,* XXXVIII, No. 5 (July–August, 1971), p. 746.

33. Byron Nupp, "Regulatory Standards in Common Ownership in Transportation," *ICC Practitioners' Journal,* XXXIV, No. 1 (November–December, 1966), p. 21.

34. Ibid., p. 35.

35. *Lake Lines Applications Under the Panama Canal Act,* 33 ICC 699 (1915).

36. Finance Dkt. No. 20940, *Illinois Central Railroad Control—John I. Hay Co.,* 317 ICC 39 (1962).

37. "ICC Examiner Rules to Let Southern Road Operate a Barge Line," *Wall Street Journal,* New York, September 4, 1971, p. 6.

38. Annual reports to the ICC filed by railroads.

39. George L. Buland and Frederick E. Fuhrman, "Integrated Ownership: The Case for Removing Existing Restrictions on Ownership of Several Modes of Transportation," *George Washington Law Review,* XXXI (October, 1962), p. 73.

40. Ibid., p. 72.

41. Alan C. Furth and John MacDonald Smith, "Intermodal Segregation: Success or Failure?" *1968 Annual Report of the American Bar Association,* Section on Public Utility Law (Washington, D.C.: American Bar Association, 1969), p. 26.

42. "ICC Examiner Would Grant Motor Carrier Authority to SP Railroad Subsidiary," *Traffic World,* CXLI (January 17, 1970), p. 66.

43. *TTC–Purchase–Terminal Transport Co., Inc.,* 97 MCC 380 (1965).

44. *Boston and Maine and Maine Central Railroads Control Northeast Airlines, Inc.,* 4 CAB 379 (1943).

45. Robert C. Lieb, *Freight Transportation: A Study of Federal Intermodal Ownership Policy* (New York: Praeger Publishers, Inc., 1972), p. 121.

46. Annual reports to the ICC filed by freight forwarders.

47. Annual reports to CAB filed by air freight forwarders.

48. CAB Dkt. No. 16857, XIV (April, 1969).

49. Taff, op. cit., p. 641.

50. CAB Dkt. No. 16857, XIV (April, 1969).

51. Lieb, "Intermodal Ownership: Experience and Evaluation," p. 759.

52. U.S. Congress, Senate, *National Transportation Policy,* p. 221.

53. Interstate Commerce Commission, op. cit., p. 100.

54. Lieb, *Freight Transportation,* p. 193.

55. Association of American Railroads, *Yearbook of Railroad Facts* (Washington, D.C.: the Association, 1975), p. 20.

56. Jerome B. Cohen and Sidney M. Robbins, *Financial Manager* (New York: Harper & Row, Inc., 1966), p. 230.

57. Roy J. Sampson and Martin T. Farris, *Domestic Transportation: Practice, Theory, and Policy,* 3rd ed. (Boston: Houghton Mifflin Company, 1975), p. 327.

58. Ibid.

59. Locklin, op. cit., p. 462.

60. Robert W. Burdick, "A Study of Diversification in the Motor Carrier Industry," *Transportation Journal,* IX, No. 4 (Summer, 1970), p. 20.

61. 298 U.S. 492 (1936).

62. Burdick, op. cit., p. 23.

63. Interstate Commerce Commission, op. cit., p. 62.

64. "Congress Told $3 Billion in Railroad Assets Were Drained by Conglomerates," *Traffic World,* CLXV, No. 11 (March 15, 1976), pp. 42–43.

65. Ibid., p. 43.

SELECTED REFERENCES

Beardsley, Peter T. "Intermodal Ownership of Transportation Facilities—A Motor Carrier View." An address delivered to the Federal Bar Association, Washington, D.C., March 20, 1969. (Mimeographed)

Burdick, Robert W. "A Study of Diversification in the Motor Carrier Industry." *Transportation Journal,* IX, No. 4 (Summer, 1970), pp. 16–32.

Burnie, Nadreen A., ed. *Transportation Mergers and Acquisitions.* Evanston, Ill.: Transportation Center, Northwestern University, 1962.

Corsi, Thomas C. "The Policy of the ICC in Trucking Merger, Control, and Acquisition of Certificate Cases, 1965–1972." *ICC Practitioners' Journal,* XLIII, No. 1 (November–December, 1975), pp. 24–38.

Dewitt, William J. "The Railroad Conglomerate: Its Relationship to the Interstate Commerce Commission and National Transportation Policy." *Transportation Journal,* XII, No. 2 (Winter, 1972), pp. 5–14.

Eads, George C. "Railroad Diversification: Where Lies the Public Interest?" *Bell Journal of Economics,* V, No. 2 (Autumn, 1974), pp. 595–614.

Fulda, Carl H. *Competition in the Regulated Industries: Transportation.* Boston: Little, Brown & Company, 1961.

Healy, Kent T. "The Merger Movement in Transportation." *American Economic Review,* LII, No. 2 (May, 1962), pp. 436–44.

Heaver, Treavor D. "Multi-Modal Ownership—The Canadian Experience." *Transportation Journal*, XI, No. 1 (Fall, 1971), pp. 14–28.

Johnson, James C., and Terry C. Whiteside. "Professor Ripley Revisited: A Current Analysis of Railroad Mergers." *ICC Practitioners' Journal*, XLII, No. 4 (May–June, 1975), pp. 419–52.

Lackman, Conway L. "Implications of Conglomerates for Transportation in the 1970's." *Transportation Journal*, XIV, No. 1 (Fall, 1974), pp. 30–45.

Lieb, Robert C. "A Revised Intermodal Ownership Policy." *Transportation Journal*, X, No. 4 (Summer, 1971), pp. 48–53.

Lieb, Robert C. *Freight Transportation: A Study of Federal Intermodal Ownership Policy.* New York: Praeger Publishers, Inc., 1972.

Lieb, Robert C. "Intermodal Ownership: A Limited Reality." *Quarterly Review of Economics and Business*, XI, No. 2 (Summer, 1971), pp. 71–81.

Lieb, Robert C. "Intermodal Ownership: Experience and Evaluation." *ICC Practitioners' Journal*, XXXVII, No. 5 (July–August, 1971), pp. 746–59.

Nupp, Byron. "Regulatory Standards in Common Ownership in Transportation." *ICC Practitioners' Journal*, XXXIV, No. 1 (November–December, 1966), pp. 21–38.

Pegrum, Dudley F. *Transportation: Economics and Public Policy*, 3rd ed. Homewood, Ill.: Richard D. Irwin, Inc., 1973.
Chapter 18. "Consolidation and Integration," pp. 420–40.

Sampson, Roy J., and Martin T. Farris. *Domestic Transportation: Practice, Theory, and Policy*, 3rd ed. Boston: Houghton Mifflin Company, 1975.
Chapter 25. "Unification, Integration, and Diversification," pp. 405–24.

Smith, Jay A. "Concentration in Common and Contract Motor Carrier Industry—A Regulatory Dilemma." *Transportation Journal*, XII, No. 4 (Summer, 1973), pp. 30–48.

"The Great Railroad Robbery." *Modern Railroads*, XXIX, No. 9 (September, 1974), pp. 67–72.

U.S. Department of Transportation, Office of the Secretary. *Executive Branch Criteria for Domestic Airline Merger Proposals.* Washington, D.C.: the Department, 1971.

DISCUSSION QUESTIONS

1. Given your understanding of the conglomerate movement in transportation, do you believe that Congress should modify existing laws so that carriers are not permitted to form holding companies?

2. Trace briefly federal policy governing intermodal ownership in transportation.

3. What have been the basic motivating factors in most recent railroad consolidations?

4. Transportation workers are generally accorded comprehensive job guarantees in carrier consolidations. Do you believe that such guarantees are appropriate? Explain your reasoning.

Transportation Safety
and the Environment

The United States has developed the most extensive and modern transportation system in the world. It provides our population with unparalleled mobility and a variety of modal options for most trips. Thus the transportation system yields tremendous societal benefits.

However, the creation and operation of the U.S. transportation network has also been quite expensive in terms of both economic and social costs. In a typical year more than 45,000 Americans die, and millions more are injured, in transportation-related accidents.[1] Similarly, the pollution problems caused by transportation are all too obvious to us when we drive into a city or when we happen to be in the vicinity of a major airport. Furthermore, transportation also accounts for approximately one fourth of U.S. consumption of scarce energy resources.[2]

This chapter focuses on the impact of transportation on national safety and the environment, and also reviews government efforts to minimize the negative side effects of modern transportation.

SAFETY

The promotion of transportation safety has long been a public concern. As discussed in earlier chapters, safety considerations played a major role in the early development of transportation regulation in this country. It is fitting that the promotion of transportation safety is accorded a high national priority. Approximately one half of all accidental deaths in this country are transportation related.[3] Furthermore, the economic cost of transportation accidents is enormous. In the highway modes alone, traffic deaths, injuries, and property damage have been estimated at approximately $36 billion annually, more than $250 per capita.[4] To put these figures in proper perspective, it must be realized that they do not, and cannot, adequately reflect the cost of human suffering related to such accidents.

Many significant steps have been taken in recent years to foster transportation safety. Improvements in infrastructure, and efforts to prevent accidents and increase the likelihood of survival in accidents have been made in several modes. However, it must be realized that such measures generate sizable costs that are borne either directly or indirectly by the general public. Inclusion of safty features in new automobiles gives added protection, but also adds hundreds of dollars to the sticker prices of these vehicles. For example, the price of a 1975 Pinto included $325 in safety equipment that had been mandated by the federal government.[5] Other government directives, such as requiring improved braking systems on intercity trucks, generate additional carrier costs, which will ultimately be reflected in freight rates.

Thus the government and the general public are faced with a massive transportation safety cost–benefit analysis. The results of such calculations are unclear not only because of the number of variables included in the analysis, but also due to the difficulty involved in quantifying certain cost and benefit elements. What is the true cost of a human life—$40,000 or $1 million? There are no simple answers to such questions, and therefore debate is inevitable each time new safety measures are proposed. Inclusion of the initial safety devices such as seat belts offered sizable safety returns at limited costs, but it is clear that as more safety equipment is added the marginal protection benefits diminish. At what point should modifications be suspended? In terms of cost–benefit analysis, one might assert that modifications should continue until potential costs offset potential benefits. However, as noted, there are serious questions concerning the quality of such estimates. Resolution of this problem is clearly beyond the scope of this book, but this dilemma will continue to be a significant decision-making issue in future transportation safety programs.

Safety Promotion and Regulation

Many parties, including government agencies, equipment manufacturers, carriers, unions, and the general public are involved in the promotion and regulation of transportation safety.

Role of Government

In attempting to protect the public interest, government plays a major role in the promotion and regulation of transportation safety. Early regulation and promotion emerged at the state level, but the federal government now dominates such activities.

Previous chapters outlined the development of safety regulation by mode, and noted that federal regulation and promotion of transportation safety was centralized within the Department of Transportation on April 1, 1967. State involvement in transportation safety has remained vested in a variety of state agencies and commissions. However, federal and state transportation safety programs are often interdependent. In many instances, DOT must rely upon state agencies to enforce federal safety standards if the standards are to be effective. At the same time, a substantial portion of the funds utilized by states in such efforts as upgrading highway facilities and rehabilitating convicted drunken drivers is supplied under DOT grant programs.

Federal involvement in transportation safety is multidimensional. Through its numerous funding programs, the DOT finances expansion and upgrading of transportation facilities, such as highways, airports, and air navigation facilities, which promote transportation safety. The department also plays a major regulatory role in developing and enforcing operating procedures, qualification standards for operators, and equipment standards. Additionally, the agency finances extensive research into safety-related issues and technology, and then disseminates information to equipment manufacturers, other government agencies, carriers, and the general public. Specific federal safety activities are outlined later in this chapter.

Role of Equipment Manufacturers

Equipment failure can lead to serious transportation accidents. Naturally, no manufacturing firm strives to develop faulty transportation equipment. However, manufacturers are sensitive to the impact that improved safety systems will have on equipment prices. Consequently, unless all manufacturers adopt similar safety features, there will tend to be a lag in the introduction of new safety features because they reduce a company's price competitiveness. As a result, the DOT often finances research into new safety features for transportation equipment, and establishes equipment standards that must be met by all manufacturers.

A slightly different situation exists in the market for private automobiles. A number of manufacturers have sought to *sell* safety features to the consumer as a differentiating factor. For example, many of the advertising appeals used by foreign automobile producers and tire manufacturers have stressed the safety features of their products (which are often more expensive than competitive models). Nevertheless, the DOT has mandated inclusion of numerous safety devices as standard equipment in new automobiles.

Role of Carriers and Unions

Carrier management and the unions that represent transportation personnel also influence transportation safety. A company's efforts in the selection and training of operating personnel will have an impact on the safety performance of the carrier. Similarly, management views, both official and unofficial, concerning such matters as compliance with federal and state safety standards will also be reflected by operating personnel. Carriers can also seek to influence equipment manufacturers in terms of future vehicle designs and modifications of existing systems that pose safety hazards. Organized labor has also played an important role in promoting transportation safety. For instance, in their contract negotiations, the Teamsters have long influenced industry policies on equipment adoption and operating practices, and the objections of the Airline Pilots Association to the carriage of hazardous materials on commercial flights ultimately led to more stringent handling requirements and the diversion of a large volume of hazardous traffic to all-cargo flights.[6] Similarly, a 1976 strike of the Canadian airline system was prompted by pilot concern about the adequacy of air traffic control systems at major airports.[7] Such active union involvement is quite desirable because of the familiarity of operating personnel with potential hazards, which might not be readily apparent to management.

Role of the General Public

As is the case in many aspects of transportation policy, the general public plays a limited role in the promotion of transportation safety except through individual efforts as operators of transportation vehicles. That role, however, should not be underestimated because driver and pilot errors are major causes of accidents involving automobiles and general aviation, respectively. For that reason operator training programs are quite important.

Beyond that operating contribution to safety, the individual's role is limited. To date little effort has been made to systematically research the views of the public on such matters as automobile safety programs, even though these programs affect not only the individual's safety but also his expenditures.[8] Instead, to a great extent, the DOT has substituted its judgment for that of the public. However, there are signs that this orientation is changing. In A Statement of National Transportation Policy issued by the DOT in 1975, the agency stated that

> as long as there is adequate public understanding and candor, the consumer should have some choice about how much he is willing to pay for additional safety, especially in private transportation systems.[9]

If such public participation is to be realized, the DOT must endeavor to improve the level of public knowledge about safety matters, and then systematically determine public attitudes that might be reflected in the governmental decision-making process.

Modal Developments

Governmental desire to further facilitate transportation safety has led to a steady expansion of public sector involvement in that realm. Given the breadth and depth of federal, state, and local government involvement in the promotion and regulation of transportation safety, it is beyond the scope of this book to recount all relevant developments. However, the following discussion highlights those recent developments that have had the most significant impact on the safety performance of the major modes of intercity carriage.

Highway Safety

As the national highway system has expanded in scope, and vehicle registrations and average speeds have risen, potential safety hazards have increased. Reflecting the dominance of the automobile in passenger transportation, nearly 90 percent of the fatal accidents in transportation involve automobiles.[10] The severity of the highway safety problem is illustrated by the fact that by 1976 nearly 2 million Americans had lost their lives on our country's highways.[11] That number of deaths exceeds the total combat fatalities experienced by the United States in all wars.[12] Furthermore, as noted earlier in this chapter, the economic and social costs of highway accidents are staggering.

In response to this national problem, a number of steps have been taken at both the federal and state level to further promote highway safety. Several of the more important developments are reviewed in the following discussion.

Centralization of Federal Controls. The establishment of the Department of Transportation in 1967 led to a centralization of federal highway safety activities within the department. Several organizational components of the

DOT are actively involved in highway safety matters. Safety of vehicles, drivers, passengers, and pedestrians is the responsibility of the National Highway Safety Traffic Administration, which is organizationally housed in the office of the secretary. Also, two bureaus of the department's Federal Highway Administration (FHA) manage certain highway safety activities. The Bureau of Public Roads oversees construction and highway design safety; the Bureau of Motor Vehicle Safety is charged with responsibility for commercial motor carrier safety. Additionally, the independent National Transportation Safety Board, which is administratively housed in the DOT, is responsible for investigating, ascertaining, and reporting on the probable cause of accidents in any mode of carriage. However, to date the board has placed its major emphasis on aviation.[13]

The centralization of these highway safety activities within the DOT has provided a consistency and continuity that did not exist prior to the agency's creation. Several federal agencies, including the ICC and the Department of Commerce, had formerly played fragmented roles in highway safety. The leadership of the DOT in this field is illustrated by the fact that now all states have comprehensive highway safety programs based on national highway safety standards established by the department.[14]

The effectiveness of the DOT efforts is partially a function of two 1966 statutes which gave the DOT substantial highway safety powers beyond those which had previously been administered by other federal agencies. The National Traffic and Motor Vehicle Safety Act authorized the secretary of transportation to issue federal performance standards for new and used motor vehicles and their equipment. That act has led to the development of numerous DOT standards pertaining to such matters as motor vehicle tire strength and braking systems. The Highway Safety Act authorized the secretary to issue federal safety performance standards for various state highway programs to which the states must conform, provided federal grants-in-aid are given to assist in implementation of the standards. Since that time numerous federal standards have been issued covering such state programs as periodic vehicle inspection, driver education, highway design construction and maintenance, and traffic control devices.[15]

DOT Activities. In addition to its efforts in developing highway safety standards, the DOT has also sought to substantially upgrade the highway system. As discussed in Chapter 4, the DOT dispenses federal highway funds to the states under various aid programs. These outlays have dramatically improved the U.S. highway system, and DOT studies have indicated that accident and fatality rates tend to decline significantly following upgrading of a particular highway link.[16]

The DOT has also focused considerable attention on highway accident prevention. One major target of the DOT has been the drunken driver. Extensive use of alcohol is the single largest contributing factor to serious crashes on U.S. highways. It has been estimated that nearly one half of all highway fatalities are caused by intoxicated drivers.[17] In responding to this problem, the DOT has initiated a number of programs, including the Alcohol Safety Action Project (ASAP). Under the provisions of ASAP, grants are made to state and local government agencies for special patrol units to detect drunken drivers before they cause accidents. Funds are also made available for special education programs for convicted drunken drivers. In an effort to further reduce the incidence of drunken driving, the DOT has also conducted research into a variety of ignition interlock systems that would make it difficult for an intoxicated person to operate an automobile.

In attempting to prevent highway accidents, the DOT has also focused attention on pedestrian safety and driver education. Pedestrian fatalities account for nearly 20 percent of all highway deaths.[18] The DOT has therefore mounted a broad public information effort, particularly aimed at children, concerning such matters as proper usage of street crossings and bicycle operation. Federal outlays for driver education efforts recognize that many accidents are the result of driver error. Therefore, these programs stress such factors as vehicle braking distances and proper signaling.

With the volume of traffic handled by the contemporary highway system, some accidents are inevitable. Consequently, the DOT has also devoted attention to accident survival. Extensive testing of vehicles and safety features is conducted by the agency. Major changes in construction standards for doors, roofs, and bumpers have been mandated by DOT in recent years, and it has mounted a concerted effort to improve seat-belt utilization. The emphasis on seat belts has been partially stimulated by the 23 percent decline in automobile fatalities in Australia during that country's first year of mandatory seat-belt utilization.[19] Similar mandatory-use programs have been considered in this country, but the proposals have not been able to overcome the opposition of those parties who believe that such laws constitute infringements on personal liberty. The debate poses a question that cannot be answered in this book. The question is how far a government can or should go in attempting to protect an individual from his own negligence. The death of an individual caused by his failure to take normal precautionary safety steps generates enormous social and economic costs, which are not limited to that individual.

Because many automobile occupants fail to use active safety restraint systems (those which the individual activates, such as seat belts), the DOT has conducted extensive research into passive restraint systems, such as concealed *airbags* that automatically inflate upon impact to protect passengers. Although Congress mandated inclusion of a passive restraint system in all new automobiles by 1977, disputes concerning system reliability between the DOT and equipment manufacturers have led to postponement of such action.[20] It is ironic that, although some government officials and manufacturers believe that the most effective occupant protection system consists of a seat belt and shoulder harness, the majority of the driving public refuses to utilize it.

DOT and state efforts, coupled with equipment recalls and the 55 mile per hour speed limit mandated by Congress during the energy crisis, have combined to produce a significant improvement in highway safety (see Tables 17–1 and 17–2). Table 17–1 examines the highway fatality rate per 100 million vehicle miles traveled, and therefore reflects all highway fatalities incurred in automobile, truck, and bus accidents.

Table 17–1

Highway Fatalities per 100 Million Vehicle Miles Traveled

Year	Fatality Rate
1971	4.68
1972	4.53
1973	4.27
1974	3.60
1975	3.30[a]

[a] Estimate.

SOURCE: U.S. Department of Transportation, Office of the Secretary, *A Statement of National Transportation Policy* (Washington, D.C.: U.S. Government Printing Office, 1975), p. 35.

In contrast, Table 17–2 compares the fatality rates experienced only by passenger modes in terms of deaths per 100 million passenger miles traveled. These figures exclude truck-only and pedestrian deaths.

Aviation Safety

The tremendous growth that has occurred in both commercial and general aviation since World War II has naturally led to growing national emphasis on aviation safety. Such concern for aviation safety is not new. It may be recalled that deteriorating airline safety conditions during the

Table 17–2

Comparative Modal Safety Records, 1970–1975[a]

Passenger Fatalities per 100 Million Passenger Miles	1975	1974	1973	1972	1971	1970
Scheduled Airlines						
Fatalities	113	159	128	160	174	0
Rate	0.09	0.13	0.10	0.13	0.16	0.0
Buses						
Fatalities	3	12	29	29	14	2
Rate	0.02	0.06	0.17	0.17	0.08	0.02
Railroads						
Fatalities	8	8	6	47	17	10
Rate	0.08	0.08	0.07	0.56	0.23	0.09
Automobiles						
Fatalities	26,500[b]	26,800	33,700	35,200	34,200	34,800
Rate	1.2	1.3	1.7	1.9	1.9	2.1

[a] These figures exclude deaths of pedestrians killed by transportation vehicles and fatalities of crew members killed in commercial operations.
[b] Estimate.

SOURCE: Air Transport Association, *Air Transport 1976* (Washington, D.C.: the Association, 1976), p. 28.

mid-1930s was one major reason for passage of the Civil Aeronautics Act of 1938.

Prior to 1966 the independent Federal Aviation Administration and the Civil Aeronautics Board were charged with promotion and regulation of air safety. When the DOT was established, the FAA became an operating administration of the department and was given control over all aspects of aviation safety except accident investigation, which was transferred to the National Transportation Safety Board. As a result, the FAA has become the dominant force in both promoting air safety and enforcing safety regulations. The FAA's safety orientation is reflected by the fact that 100 percent of its annual expenditures are either directly or indirectly related to aviation safety.[21]

FAA Activities. The FAA's involvement in air safety takes many forms. Its most significant task involves the funding and operation of the national airway system. According to the FAA:

the Nation's airway system is managed by the close integration of the terminal air traffic control, enroute air traffic control, and flight service systems. The terminal and enroute systems provide for separation of aircraft, flow control (temporary limitation of traffic into congested airspace), navigation and approach guidance, and information service to airway users. The flight service system provides weather and other preflight information service and inflight information assistance, and accepts flight-related inputs from airmen.[22]

The FAA also funds airport expansion and safety improvements. Under the provision of the Airport and Airway Development Act of 1970, the FAA has extended grants of more than $1.2 billion to airports for construction of runways and taxiways, lighting, approach aids, emergency vehicles, and many other safety-related improvements.[23]

Responsibilities of the agency also include the testing and certification of airmen. As might be expected, quite rigid medical and skill standards are applied to such personnel. Airports that serve certified air carriers must themselves be certified by the FAA or they must discontinue such operations. This requirement is intended to assure that those airports are adequately equipped to provide safe air transportation. Approximately 500 airports have been so certified; they account for nearly 99 percent of annual revenue passenger enplanements in the United States.[24]

The FAA is also responsible for certification of new equipment before it is introduced into use, and the agency issues minimum performance standards for aircraft equipment. In recent years the FAA has issued new or updated standards on such equipment as altimeters, flight data recorders, distance-measuring equipment, and fire detectors. Safety rules and regulations are also administered by the FAA. Some matters receiving FAA attention have been the development of standards requiring the use of nontoxic and nonflammable materials in aircraft passenger compartments and the establishment of improved operator training and procedures for aircraft emergency evacuations.

Safety Performance and Problem Areas. The FAA activities outlined in the preceding discussion and the combined efforts of the commercial airlines and equipment manufacturers have led to a marked improvement in commercial aviation safety. In fact, the three fatal accidents registered by U.S. air carriers in 1975 marked the industry's best performance since such records were first recorded in 1949.[25] Over that period of time the domestic air carrier fatality rate declined by approximately 90 percent.[26]

This industry performance is admirable, and comprises one of the best records compiled by any mode of intercity carriage. However, there are still several significant problem areas in aviation safety. Predominant among these are airport congestion and the relatively high fatality rate of general aviation.

Many major airports are quite congested, and community resistance makes it rather difficult to increase the physical capacity of these facilities. Stacking of aircraft above these airports poses a threat to safety, and numerous near misses are recorded each day. The FAA believes that the increasing automation of air traffic control systems will improve this situation through elimination of possible human errors.[27]

Although the fatality rate of general aviation has improved substantially in recent years, it still greatly exceeds that experienced by the other intercity modes. Whereas the fatality rate per 100 million passenger miles registered by the scheduled airlines during the 1971–1973 period was 0.13, general aviation's rate was 19.0 for the same time span.[28] The efforts of the FAA to improve this situation include development of educational materials for private pilots and more stringent crashworthiness standards for small planes.

FAA–Industry Interaction. The FAA's relationship with the commercial airlines has been a subject of controversy. Critics have charged that the agency has been reluctant to require equipment modifications that involve substantial carrier costs. The intensity of these allegations increased following several commercial crashes in the mid-1970s that involved equipment malfunctions. Prior to two of those crashes, the FAA had recommended, but not required, modification of equipment units that were directly implicated in the crashes. In neither case had the airlines made the suggested modifications. These developments led to major personnel changes within the FAA and fostered an extensive DOT review of FAA policies and practices.

Railroad Safety

Prior to the creation of the DOT, several federal bodies, including the ICC, the Department of Commerce, and the Department of the Interior, were involved in railroad safety enforcement. When the DOT was established, its organization structure included the Federal Railroad Administration (FRA), which assumed federal control over railroad safety. The authority of the FRA was subsequently expanded with the passage of the Rail Safety Act of 1970, which gave the agency broader powers in such matters as establishment of track and equipment safety standards.

FRA safety programs are administered by its Bureau of Railroad Safety. The primary programs enforced by the bureau are locomotive inspection, equipment inspection, and investigation of accidents. Other safety-related activities of the FRA include development of track and equipment standards, development of operating procedures, and investigation of complaints. The agency also conducts extensive research into railroad safety matters.

The passenger safety record of the railroad industry has been outstanding (see Table 17–2). However, the industry has experienced continuing difficulties with derailment of freight trains and grade-crossing accidents.

Throughout the years, railroad maintenance outlays have tended to vary with carrier profitability. Consequently, derailments have generally been a more serious problem during periods of low carrier profitability. The establishment and monitoring of track safety standards by the FRA has partially offset this railroad tendency toward cyclical maintenance. But it might be expected that financially troubled carriers would minimally comply with such standards. However, the infusion of federal monies into Conrail and the establishment of loan and loan guarantee programs under the Railroad Revitalization and Regulatory Reform Act of 1976 should contribute to improved track conditions, and this might be expected to lower derailment rates.

There are still more than 180,000 unguarded railroad grade crossings in the United States.[29] Each year accidents at these crossings result in approximately 1,500 deaths and 3,700 injuries.[30] The FRA is committed to substantially reducing that safety hazard; it has embarked upon a grant program aimed at either eliminating such crossings or improving signaling systems at existing crossings.

Oil Pipeline and Waterway Safety

Promotion of safety in both commercial and recreational boating is the responsibility of the U.S. Coast Guard, which is a component of the Department of Transportation. The safety-related activities of the Coast Guard are quite varied.

Under the provisions of the Boat Safety Act of 1971, the agency was empowered to regulate the design, manufacture, and use of boats. Subsequently, the agency has played a major role in this area. This has been particularly true with respect to development of construction standards aimed at preventing the swamping or capsizing of small boats. That statute also provided the Coast Guard with authority to extend grants to public and private interests to promote boating safety.

Coast Guard involvement in boating safety also increased with passage of the 1972 Port and Waterway Safety Act. The provisions of the act have led to Coast Guard establishment of vessel traffic systems for areas of heavy marine traffic concentration, and have also promoted improvements of navigational aids for the waterway system.

364

Other Coast Guard safety activities include search and rescue efforts, certification of marine vessels, vessel inspection through its marine inspection units, and training of state and local law enforcement officers. Responsibility for investigation of serious marine accidents has been transferred to the National Transportation Safety Board.

The Department of Transportation's Office of Pipeline Safety maintains regulatory responsibilities over liquid pipeline systems operated by carriers engaged in interstate commerce. Although this mode handles no passengers and poses little direct threat to human life, the hazardous nature of many of the commodities handled poses an indirect threat. Nevertheless, the oil pipeline industry has compiled an outstanding safety record.

Congress has granted the DOT broad powers in regulating pipeline safety. The Office of Pipeline Safety has been given authority to develop standards for design, construction, operation, and maintenance of pipeline systems. Additional activities of the office have included pipeline inspection, the issue of periodic information bulletins, and the offering of safety seminars for state and local regulatory officials.

TRANSPORTATION AND THE ENVIRONMENT

Public awareness of environmental issues has grown steadily in recent years. Environmental concerns are now widespread; they include not only efforts to preserve scarce resources, but also attempts to minimize the negative impact of man's activities on the physical environment. The interrelationship between man and the environment is clearly illustrated in the transportation sector. Our expanding transportation system has caused numerous environmental problems.

Transportation accounts for nearly one fourth of U.S. daily energy consumption and more than one half of U.S. petroleum usage.[31] Also, the energy conversion process utilized in the various modes (primarily the internal combustion engine) has historically been responsible for approximately one half of the total pollutants emitted into the atmosphere.[32] The significance of this is illustrated by the fact that the costs of air pollution have been estimated at up to $16 billion annually, and transportation has been implicated in approximately two thirds of these costs.[33] The operation of transportation vehicles has tended to be rather noisy, and this has contributed to noise-level problems. Furthermore, transportation facilities, such as highways, airports, and terminals, have consumed tremendous parcels of land, and have in the process led to social problems related to population dislocations.

These extensive transportation–environment interactions have led to increasing governmental efforts to minimize the harmful side effects of transportation progress. Such efforts have occurred at the federal, state, and local levels, and have often involved the active cooperation of several governmental units. At the federal level, environmental protection efforts related to transportation have been primarily conducted by the DOT and the Environmental Protection Agency (EPA).

Within the DOT, environmental responsibilities are held by the assistant secretary for environment, safety, and consumer affairs. The assistant secretary provides policy advice to the secretary on environmental matters, and also monitors and coordinates DOT environmental programs. Development and enforcement of specific DOT environmental standards have generally been delegated to the modal administrations, such as the FAA, of the department. Because of the important role that the DOT plays in financing transportation infrastructure, it must necessarily be sensitive to the potential environmental impact of such outlays. Therefore, the DOT requires quite detailed environmental impact statements on all major projects before work can be commenced.

When the EPA was established by Congress in 1970, it was given broad responsibilities and powers to foster environmental protection. Two basic charges were improvement of air quality and reduction of noise levels in our cities. EPA efforts in these areas naturally have had a heavy transportation orientation. As a result, the EPA and the DOT have actively cooperated on numerous projects.

Modal Developments

Due to unique operating characteristics, each mode has had a different impact on the environment and thus has attracted a varying degree of government attention. The major environmental developments of recent years related to the intercity modes are traced in the following discussion.

Highway Modes

The combined efforts of the DOT and the EPA have significantly reduced the negative environmental impact of the highway modes. Vehicle emission control standards established by the EPA have greatly reduced emission levels. During the first five years of its existence, the EPA developed standards that fostered a 25 percent reduction in sulfur dioxide emissions, and 1976 model automobiles gave off 83 percent less hydrocarbons and carbon monoxide than 1970 models.[34]

Highway noise pollution has also been a target of the DOT and the EPA. Noise level standards have been issued for use in planning and designing federally assisted highways, and quantitative models have been developed to estimate air and noise pollution levels associated with specific highway project proposals. Additionally, the two federal agencies have jointly developed noise level standards that have been applied to motor carriers.

Because of the highway modes' tremendous consumption of petroleum products, extensive research has been conducted by the DOT and the EPA into methods of promoting greater fuel efficiency. Attention has been given not only to alternative engine types, such as the rotary and the Wankel, but also to alternative energy sources, such as electricity, steam, and hydrogen. The automotive industry has also significantly improved automobile fuel efficiency in the years following the Arab oil embargo. Similarly, the ICC has contributed to improved fuel efficiency by permitting intercity motor carriers to eliminate some of the circuity contained in their certificates.[35]

Aviation

To date the major federal concern with the environmental impact of aviation has involved noise pollution. Recognition of the significance of that problem led Congress, in 1968, to charge the Federal Aviation Administration with responsibility for controlling aircraft noise. The FAA's subsequent efforts have included development of programs to reduce aircraft engine noise and the establishment of takeoff and landing procedures to minimize airport-vicinity noise levels. Additionally, the agency has actively cooperated with state and local authorities on such matters as soundproofing programs for homes, schools, and hospitals in airport zones and the establishment of property buffer zones around airports.

Aviation air pollution has also received the attention of both the FAA and the EPA. Their combined efforts have led to major reductions in engine emissions, which have been primarily accomplished through retrofit programs. Also, in-flight fuel dumping, which was a standard aviation practice, has been discontinued due to its adverse impact on air quality.

The FAA has also become actively involved in the promotion of improved aviation fuel efficiency. FAA efforts have included

revision of gatehold and air traffic flow procedures, increased use of optimum cruising speeds and altitudes, use of flight simulators for training and check flights, accelerated installations of instrument landing capability on approach runways and improving runway and taxiway technology.[36]

The energy implications of the DOT's proposals for changes in the economic regulation of air carriage are unclear. Although cutbacks in service to low-density markets would improve carrier fuel utilization rates, greater competitive intensity over trunk routes could lead to increased consumption of aviation fuel.

367

Supersonic Transport. As discussed in Chapter 6, the U.S. SST project was terminated in 1971 in direct response to questions concerning the environmental impact of such aircraft. The British–French and Russian efforts continued, and by early 1976 commercial SST services were being offered on a limited scale.

Following extensive deliberations, Secretary of Transportation Coleman permitted the British–French Concorde to land at several U.S. airports on an experimental basis. These flights began in May 1976. The secretary's decision prompted widespread public criticism because of the potential environmental hazards. Various environmental and citizens' groups initiated legal actions to block SST landings, but the courts ruled that the flights were legal.

Political pressures undoubtedly played a major role in Coleman's decision. The British and French governments had invested heavily in the Concorde project, and had depended upon U.S. landing rights to provide a major share of SST operating revenues. Threats of a British–French boycott of U.S. goods and possible retaliation against U.S. airlines serving Britain and France preceded Coleman's decision. Similarly, the State Department strongly advocated extension of landing rights to the Concorde.

The secretary's ruling in this matter was rather inconsistent with the DOT's strong stand against other environmentally questionable projects. It again illustrated the complexity of the transportation policy decision-making process. It also reaffirmed the DOT's continuing interest in supersonic aircraft, and seemed to indicate that efforts to rekindle U.S. involvement in future SST development would be forthcoming.

Rail Carriage

Railroad diesel engines contribute relatively little to air pollution compared with the internal combustion engines on U.S. highways, and they are not as noisy as many types of jet aircraft. Therefore, it is not surprising that the railroads have not received as much environmental attention as the highway and air modes. However, the Federal Railroad Administration has issued operating and equipment standards that have reduced railroad noise and emission levels.

There has been much controversy concerning the relative fuel efficiency of the various modes of intercity carriage. Numerous conflicting reports have been released. However, it is important to note that the DOT believes that railroads are more fuel efficient than trucks in moving bulk commodities over long distances. As a result, the DOT has sought to promote railroad movement of such commodities.[37] The pricing flexibility granted the railroads under the DOT's Railroad Revitalization and Regulatory Reform Act of 1976 reflected this DOT commitment.

It may be expected that the fuel efficiency of the railroads might be further improved in the near future because of the consolidation and branch-line abandonments promoted by the Northeast railroad reorganization. These developments should lead to higher-density movements and hence improved fuel efficiency.

Water Carriage

In the marine environment the Coast Guard is the primary agency responsible for enforcement of federal antipollution laws and treaties. Thus far, the major threat to the marine environment has been oil spills.

In the past the Coast Guard has tended to emphasize development of adequate cleanup capability for removing oil and hazardous materials from the water. To facilitate such efforts the Coast Guard maintains a National Response Center, which coordinates cleanup activities. More recently the emphasis of the Coast Guard has shifted to prevention of spills through regulation of not only vessel construction and operation, but also oil transfer facilities. The Coast Guard has also worked toward development of separated sea lanes to offer improved protection against spills caused by collisions and groundings.

In addition to these activities, the Coast Guard also conducts extensive research into the potential causes of water pollution and prevention techniques. The agency also is responsible for environmental impact studies related to specific waterway projects, and provides technical assistance on pollution control techniques to various domestic and international organizations.

Oil Pipelines

Potential oil pipeline malfunctions also pose environmental threats. However, the industry and the DOT's Office of Pipeline Safety have worked closely to develop elaborate shut-off and safety systems to minimize potential environmental hazards. Rigid standards have also been developed for materials and construction procedures to be used in pipeline systems.

The Alaskan Pipeline project posed a series of environmental threats. In addition to the threat of system malfunctions resulting in oil spills, there were also potential threats to Alaska's delicate permafrost, because the oil was to be heated as it moved through the pipeline. Furthermore, aboveground segments of the pipeline threatened to impede the migratory patterns of arctic animals. The resolution of these environmental concerns delayed the construction of the Alaskan Pipeline for nearly five years. Although the delay was quite costly, it did result in a tremendous reduction of the potential environmental threat posed by the project.

SUMMARY

Development, operation, and maintenance of a modern transportation system produces a number of undesirable side effects. These include threats to the safety of the general public and environmental degradation. Steps can be taken to minimize these problems, but safety and environmental controls are generally quite expensive. Therefore, government and the general public must carefully weigh the costs and potential benefits of such policy alternatives. Such calculations are rather complex, not only because of the number of variables included in the analysis, but also because it is difficult to quantify many safety and environmental considerations.

Significant strides have been taken in recent years to improve transportation safety and to minimize transportation's pollution and energy consumption problems. However, there is much room for improvement, which can only be accomplished through the active cooperation of government, equipment manufacturers, carriers, and the general public.

NOTES

1. U.S. Department of Transportation, Office of the Secretary, *A Statement of National Transportation Policy* (Washington, D.C.: U.S. Government Printing Office, 1975), p. 35.

2. U.S. Department of Transportation, Office of the Secretary, *Energy Statistics: A Supplement to the Summary of National Transportation Statistics* (Springfield, Va.: National Technical Information Service, 1973), p. 73.

3. U.S. Department of Transportation, Office of the Secretary, *1972 National Transportation Report* (Washington, D.C.: U.S. Government Printing Office, 1972), p. 62.

4. U.S. Department of Transportation, *Seventh Annual Report* (Washington, D.C.: U.S. Government Printing Office, 1974), p. 25.

5. Brooks Jackson and Evans Witt, "Controls Can Be Life Savers," *Boston Globe,* March 18, 1976, p. 26.

6. For a discussion of the steps taken by the FAA to lessen this hazard, see U.S. Department of Transportation, *8th Annual Report* (Washington, D.C.: U.S. Government Printing Office, 1975), p. 21.

7. "Air Canada Widened Its Loss in First Half Due to Work Stoppage," *Wall Street Journal,* New York, August 11, 1976, p. 18.

8. For an analysis of consumer views concerning government safety programs, see Robert C. Lieb and Frederick Wiseman, "Consumer Attitudes Toward Automobile Safety Programs," Technical Paper 73-ICT-36, pre-

sented at the 1973 Intersociety Conference on Transportation, Denver, Colo. (New York: American Society of Mechanical Engineers, 1974).

9. Department of Transportation, *A Statement of National Transportation Policy,* p. 35.

10. Ibid.

11. U.S. Congress, House, *Message from the President of the United States Transmitting a Proposal for a Cabinet-Level Department of Transportation Consolidating Various Existing Transportation Agencies,* House Doc. 399, 89th Cong., 2nd Sess., 1966, p. 54. (Updated.)

12. Ibid.

13. Grant M. Davis and Martin T. Farris, "Federal Transportation Safety Programs—Misdirected Emphasis and Wasted Resources," *Transportation Journal,* XI, No. 4 (Summer, 1972), p. 9.

14. Department of Transportation, *Seventh Annual Report,* p. 24.

15. Charles A. Taff, *Commercial Motor Transportation,* 4th ed. (Homewood, Ill.: Richard D. Irwin, Inc., 1969), p. 400.

16. Department of Transportation, *Seventh Annual Report,* p. 24.

17. Ad Hoc Committee, *Cumulative Regulatory Effects on Cost of Automobile Transportation,* a report prepared for the President's Office of Science and Technology (Washington, D.C.: U.S. Government Printing Office, 1972), Appendix II-E, p. II-E2.

18. Department of Transportation, *1972 National Transportation Report,* p. 62.

19. Department of Transportation, *Seventh Annual Report,* p. 18.

20. U.S. Department of Transportation, National Highway Traffic Safety Administration, *The Case for Seat Belts* (Washington, D.C.: U.S. Government Printing Office, 1973), p. 1.

21. Davis and Farris, op. cit., p. 9.

22. Department of Transportation, *1974 National Transportation Report,* p. 316.

23. Air Transport Association, *Air Transport, 1976* (Washington, D.C.: the Association, 1976), p. 7.

24. Department of Transportation, *Seventh Annual Report,* p. 13.

25. Air Transport Association, op. cit., p. 5.

26. Department of Transportation, *A Statement of National Transportation Policy,* p. 35.

27. Ibid., p. 36.

28. Ibid., p. 35.

29. Harvey Ardman, "The Terrible Condition of America's Freight Railroads," *American Legion Magazine* (December, 1971), p. 8.

30. Ibid.

31. Department of Transportation, *Energy Statistics,* p. 73.

32. U.S. Department of Transportation, Office of the Secretary, *A Statement of National Transportation Policy* (Washington, D.C.: the Department, 1971), p. 14.

33. Ibid.

34. Jackson and Witt, op. cit., p. 26.

35. U.S. Interstate Commerce Commission, *The Regulatory Issues of Today* (Washington, D.C.: the Commission, 1975), pp. 16–26.

36. Department of Transportation, *A Statement of National Transportation Policy* (1975), p. 34.

37. Ibid.

SELECTED REFERENCES

Ad Hoc Committee. *Cumulative Regulatory Effects on Cost of Automobile Transportation.* A report prepared for the president's Office of Science and Technology. Washington, D.C.: U.S. Government Printing Office, 1972.

Harper, Donald V. "The Dilemma of Aircraft Noise at Major Airports." *Transportation Journal,* X, No. 3 (Spring, 1971), pp. 5–28.

Lieb, Robert C., and Frederick Wiseman. "Consumer Attitudes Toward Automobile Safety Programs." Technical Paper 73-ICT-36 presented at the 1973 Intersociety Conference on Transportation, Denver, Colorado. New York: American Society of Mechanical Engineers, 1974.

Lieb, Robert C., and Frederick Wiseman. "Drunken Driving: The Public Viewpoint." *Court Review,* XIII, No. 6 (January, 1975), pp. 27–31.

Sampson, Roy J., and Martin T. Farris. *Domestic Transportation: Practice, Theory, and Policy,* 3rd ed. Boston: Houghton Mifflin Company, 1975. Chapter 3. "Environmental and Sociological Aspects of Transportation," pp. 40–48.

Smerk, George M. "The Environment and Transportation." *Transportation Journal,* XII, No. 1 (Fall, 1972), pp. 40–49.

U.S. Department of Transportation, Office of the Secretary. *Energy Statistics: A Supplement to the Summary of National Transportation Statistics.* Springfield, Va.: National Technical Information Service, 1973.

DISCUSSION QUESTIONS

1. You have just been appointed the president's special adviser on the transportation–energy interface. Realizing that private and for-hire transportation are the greatest users of petroleum in the United States, the president has

asked you to develop a five-year plan to reduce energy consumption by transportation activities. What would your program consist of? Why did you select the various components, and what would their impact be?

2. In your opinion, should the inclusion of further safety equipment in private automobiles be required or optional? Explain your reasoning.

3. Given your understanding of the airline industry and environmental concerns, should the United States build a supersonic aircraft to be used in commercial markets?

CHAPTER
18

Policy Trends and Considerations in Intercity Transportation

In the aggregate, federal transportation policy consists of a myriad of policies governing transportation regulation and promotion. The recent financial and service problems experienced within the national transportation system make it likely that the coming years will witness extensive reevaluation of existing transportation policies. The development of a systematic transportation policy review process is quite desirable, because industrial and economic conditions change over time and policies should be appropriately modified. Although Congress will continue to play the dominant role in transportation policy formulation, the DOT, the regulatory agencies, shipper groups, carrier associations, and other interested parties should actively participate in the policy review and critique process.

Previous chapters have outlined numerous trends in federal transportation policy related to such diverse matters as environmental concerns, labor relations, and carrier consolidations. This chapter seeks to identify several basic aspects of transportation policy that are likely to receive closest attention in the near future. It also examines the issue of railroad nationalization as a policy alternative, and reflects upon the process by which policy changes are likely to occur.

REGULATORY POLICY

As discussed in Chapter 17, federal involvement in the regulation of transportation safety has increased steadily, and there are no signs that this

374

trend will soon be reversed. However, there are mounting pressures to reduce the degree of economic regulation in transportation. The Department of Transportation, the president's Council of Economic Advisers, and many economists have long advocated major reductions in economic regulation; however, Congress has been quite reluctant to act. But, as the severity of our national transportation problems has increased, it has become apparent that many of these problems are at least partially related to existing economic regulations. As a result, Congress has shown growing receptivity to proposals that deal with changes in the economic regulation of transportation. Three major regulatory issues that seem certain to receive considerable attention in the coming years are government controls over carrier pricing, entry, and abandonment of service.

Pricing Controls

The movement toward greater carrier pricing freedom initiated in the Railroad Revitalization and Regulatory Reform Act of 1976 appears likely to continue. The pattern of gradual expansion of carrier pricing freedom contained in that bill was subsequently incorporated into DOT proposals related to the airline and motor carrier industries.[1]

Such relaxation of pricing controls on a gradual basis permits a limited test of carrier desire to be price competitive, and reduces regulatory agency involvement in carrier pricing decisions. Consumer interests are still protected against monopolistic pricing practices through provisions that allow regulatory agency intervention in cases involving limited competition.

The Canadian transportation network has operated under such a *zone of reasonableness* pricing system since the late 1960s, and no major market distortions have yet been observed.[2] That experience and congressional acceptance of a related pricing model in the 1976 railroad bill have increased the likelihood of similar action in motor and air carriage.

Entry Controls

The propriety of existing entry controls in air and motor carriage has long been debated. Critics of entry controls have argued that more liberal entry policies would not only increase the number of market participants, but would also promote improved services and lower prices.[3] Those supporting existing entry standards (usually the carriers and the regulatory agencies) have claimed that elimination of entry controls would lead to industry chaos, and that carrier earnings would suffer. Furthermore, they contend that industrial stability and service quality would deteriorate.[4]

Although some modification may be made in entry regulations, it seems clear that entry standards will not be totally abolished. At the minimum, the requirement of some demonstration that the applicant is "fit, willing, and able" will be maintained. The shipping public has been most vehement in expressing its desires to retain such qualification standards.[5] Shippers would therefore not support total deregulation of entry, and such a significant regulatory change stands little chance of enactment without shipper support.

In terms of political reality, it does not appear likely that entry into air and motor carriage will be opened to all interested parties that could meet the "fit, willing, and able" standards. Existing carriers have strong vested interests, and have invested enormous sums of money in developing their markets. Thus they are threatened by the prospect of new entrants. These carriers and their lobby associations are very vocal and well organized in their efforts to convey these sentiments to Congress. Consequently, it appears far more likely that, if substantial new market entry is to be permitted, it will involve expansion of the operating rights of existing carriers rather than market entry of new transportation companies. Although existing companies may face new market competition, this would be partially offset by their ability to also move into other markets that offer substantial traffic potential.

Such an approach was incorporated into the DOT's Aviation Act of 1975. Under the provisions of the act, each year existing carriers were to be permitted to expand their operations by a percentage (5 to 10 percent) of their previous year's available seat miles. Such limited movements into new markets were to be beyond CAB control.[6] This proposal was criticized by some parties because it simply permitted existing carriers to get larger; it would not stimulate the entrance of new companies into the industry.

The 1975 airline and motor carrier bills of the DOT did not receive favorable reaction from Congress, but it is likely that similar efforts to liberalize entry controls in these two modes will be submitted to Congress in the near future. The DOT has incorporated such liberalization of entry into its regulatory philosophy, and may be expected to continue to reflect this in its future legislative initiatives.

Discontinuance of Service

It may also be expected that increasing attention will be devoted to federal policies that have required continuance of noncompensatory services. By forcing carriers to continue to provide such services, the ICC and CAB have often used the carriers as instruments of public policy. Although these services have produced certain economic, social, and political benefits, they have also drained much-needed resources from many carriers.

The resolution of this problem seems quite simple: allow the carriers to discontinue the noncompensatory services. However, this issue is far too complex to be resolved so simply. Those consuming groups, industries, and geographic regions that have historically benefited from such indirect subsidization have come to expect it. Location patterns, business relationships, and pricing structures have developed that are based on the existence of those services and their related prices. Consequently, discontinuance of these services may have quite adverse effects on certain interest groups.

Once again, gradual action appears to be warranted. The transitional costs of dramatic service reductions over a short time span are too high. One gradual approach to service discontinuance was contained in the Railroad Revitalization and Regulatory Reform Act of 1976. The act provided $360 million in federal money to finance a five-year program of federal assistance to local railroad service. Under the provisions of the act, the federal government agreed to pay 100 percent of a branch line's deficit in the first year, 90 percent in the second, 80 percent in the third, and 70 percent in each of the next two years.[7] Federal financial participation ceases after five years; at that point the communities involved must decide how any future deficits are to be financed. For example, financing may be accomplished through price increases in which shippers bear the additional costs or by some combination of state and local government subsidies. In any event, the intent of the program is clear. That is, the true costs of such services should be ultimately borne by those who directly benefit from them. The five-year time frame provides adequate time for assessment of the real worth of these services to the communities involved. Under the provisions of the 1976 statute, if the communities do not agree to underwrite the deficits following termination of the federal funding involvement, the rail services may be abandoned.

The Aviation Act of 1975 also dealt with the abandonment issue. It stipulated that an air carrier could abandon a route if either:

1. The carrier has operated the route below fully allocated cost (including a reasonable return) for at least one year.

or

2. The carrier has operated the route below the direct costs for a period of at least three months.[8]

Although the bill was not enacted by Congress, the DOT has expressed its intention to resubmit similar legislation in the future.

PROMOTIONAL POLICY

The promotional role of the Department of Transportation is extremely broad and includes such diverse elements as the funding of the transportation infrastructure, financing technological research, and coordination of shipper, carrier, and governmental activities. Because of this diversity, it is impossible to comment on the direction of all federal promotional programs. However, two specific aspects of the DOT's future promotional role should be mentioned. These are the DOT's expressed intentions to minimize government subsidization in transportation and to improve the quality of interaction among various governmental units.

Minimization of Public Aid

The DOT has consistently called for more evenhanded federal treatment of the several modes of intercity carriage. From a funding standpoint, such treatment entails elimination of both direct and indirect subsidization whenever possible and the establishment of user-charge systems to finance modal developments.

Toward that end, the DOT has called for a reduction of federal funding of Amtrak and local service airline operations. It has further advocated extension of the user-charge concept to the domestic waterway system.[9]

Realization of a more equitable funding treatment of the intercity modes will not be easily accomplished. Any cutbacks of federal promotional programs that have historically benefited certain interest groups will surely be vigorously opposed by those groups. As a result, DOT faces a formidable challenge in attempting to convince Congress of the merits of its views. However, the accomplishment of this end would promote a system of modal self-sufficiency, which would serve to eliminate the many market distortions that have evolved throughout the years.

Although the DOT is firmly committed to minimizing federal subsidization, it does believe that subsidies may be necessary under extreme circumstances

> when a clearly defined national interest requires the development, modernization or maintenance of essential transportation service.[10]

Improved Governmental Interaction

Since its establishment, the DOT has played a quite important role in funding state and local transportation projects. By establishing funding criteria, the DOT has had a major influence on the specific nature of many

378

of these projects. This has led to debate concerning the proper role to be played by the DOT versus state and local governments in project planning efforts. The debate has revolved around state and local desire for local self-determination and the DOT's orientation toward approving or disapproving specific projects.

There has been a decided trend toward an expanded local decision-making role in federal funding programs outside transportation, and there is growing evidence that similar developments are occurring in transportation. The DOT now conducts a systematic National Transportation Needs Study every two years in which it attempts to gauge the needs of specific areas based on data supplied by state and local government units. Also, several highway and transit funding programs now involve federal grants that may be used for a variety of transportation projects.[11] The exact application of these funds is ultimately decided by state and local officials. In view of these developments, it might be reasonably expected that state and local officials will play an expanded planning role in future federal funding projects involving transportation.

RAILROAD NATIONALIZATION AS A POLICY ALTERNATIVE

Thus far this chapter has focused on the direction of federal transportation policy in the context of private ownership and operation of transportation facilities. However, the railroad bankruptcies of the Northeast and Amtrak's continuing financial difficulties have led to considerable discussion of railroad nationalization as a policy alternative.[12] Because of the importance and implications of any movement toward government provision of transportation services, it is appropriate that some attention should be devoted to that topic.

Arguments for Nationalization

The consideration of railroad nationalization as a policy alternative necessitates a review of arguments favoring such a course of action. It might be argued that nationalization would provide a ready source of investment capital to finance railroad modernization and expansion. The substitution of federal government credit for that of individual railroads would lower industry capital costs, due to the lower interest rates typically associated with federal securities.[13]

Nationalization might also provide a means of coordinating railroad services and eliminating duplication. Such coordination might simplify interlining and reduce circuity, thereby cutting operating costs and improving service.[14] The savings envisioned through such coordination might lead to lower rates, which would make rail carriage a more viable competitor in the transportation marketplace. Nationalization might also eliminate the need for the costly regulatory process, and would therefore reduce taxpayer burdens.

Foreign Experience with Nationalization

Railroad nationalization is not an untried concept. In fact, most railroads and airlines in other countries are government owned and operated. The degree of government involvement is a function of a number of considerations, including the desire to support military objectives, attempts to promote national unity, and the lack of private investment capital in emerging nations.

The earnings performance of most nationalized railroads has been dismal (see Table 18–1). In contrast, the U.S. railroad system in the aggregate has averaged annual profits of more than $400 million in recent years.[15]

Table 18–1

Financial Statistics of Selected Nationalized Railroad Systems, 1973

System	Profit (Loss) in Millions
South African Railways	$ (118)
Canadian National Railways	(174)
British Railways	(336)
French National Railways	(1,624)
Italian State Railways	(1,743)
Japanese National Railways	(1,945)
German Federal Railways	(2,686)

SOURCE: Union Pacific Railroad Company, *A Brief Survey of Railroads of Selected Industrial Countries* (New York: the Company, 1975), p. ix.

Although the foreign deficit figures are startling, it must be remembered that the railroads of other nations are not realistically comparable with the U.S. railroad system. In some countries the railroad system is composed of a seemingly disjointed collection of lines that appear to have little relationship to each other. Similarly, differences in system size, national traffic flow patterns, the traffic mix, and competitive conditions preclude meaningful comparisons. Also, it must be remembered that nationalized systems are often used to realize a variety of governmental goals, and their deficits are generated in the provision of socially desirable services.

United States Experience with Nationalization

There has also been limited experience with the concept of railroad nationalization in the United States. As discussed in Chapter 12, in December 1917 the railroads of the United States were placed under federal control to facilitate the war effort. During the next three years the railroad system incurred a deficit of nearly $1.5 billion (nearly $2 million per day), and the physical plant deteriorated steadily.

However, neither of these developments was necessarily due to poor management. The federal government, in attempting to both halt an inflationary spiral and promote the movement of needed commodities, held railroad rates down during the conflict.[16] Despite these measures, prices continued to climb, and although the government spent more for maintenance than the railroads had during a similar prewar period, inflation actually led to a decline in maintenance work.[17]

It has often been noted that without direct federal control during World War II the railroads moved twice as much freight, and paid the government nearly $3 million per day in taxes. Once again, however, it must be remembered that, although the profitability of the government-controlled operations during World War I was poor, the government was primarily concerned with goals other than profitability. Traffic volume records were set, and the rail system remained viable during the conflict.

Appraisal of the Nationalization Alternative

Any movement toward nationalization of the railroads of the United States would pose numerous problems. One major consideration would be the cost of acquisition. Railroad nationalization would necessitate a tremendous federal outlay to compensate existing owners. The Association of American Railroads has estimated that the fair market value of railroad properties is approximately $60 billion.[18] Furthermore, in attempting to promote system improvements, the federal government would encounter the same opposition from labor and other interest groups that has troubled the privately owned railroads. In fact, it is likely that expenditures for railroad capacity would become even more responsive to political pressures than they are now, and that performance would vary even further from economic norms.

Nationalization would not eliminate the need for regulation. A federal agency would still be needed to handle such matters as shipper complaints and rate proposals. Furthermore, the other modes would still be regulated.

Nationalization could also lead to considerable tax losses for federal, state, and local government units. In 1975 alone, railroads paid more than

$1.59 billion in taxes.[19] In many small communities railroads are the largest component of the tax base; nationalization would seriously impair this situation.

The scope of a national railroad system would make coordination quite complicated, and could lead to diseconomies of scale. Other organizational difficulties would include the problems of political patronage in staffing the upper levels of the organization and the lack of a profit motivation for employees of the nationalized system.

A final danger posed by railroad nationalization is that it might promote further restrictions on the operations of other modes. In a major study of transportation policy alternatives, Owen and Dearing addressed that issue and suggested that

> it would be difficult to conceive that complete government ownership of this segment [railroads] of the national transportation system would not lead to extensive controls over other forms of transportation as a means of preserving railroad investments.[20]

Such governmental action has followed nationalization of railroad operations in a number of countries.[21]

The potential problems associated with railroad nationalization should clearly make it an extremely low priority policy alternative. It runs counter to basic U.S. economic philosophy, which generally relies upon the private sector to own and operate major industrial enterprises. The majority of the benefits offered by nationalization might also be realized through other policy measures that are far less drastic than transfer of the railroads into the public sector.

Although the issue of railroad nationalization has been given some national attention, the concept has few supporters. However, Congress and the ICC are faced with the task of creating an environment in which the railroads can earn an adequate return so that nationalization can be avoided. The regulatory and promotional modifications discussed earlier in this chapter would make significant contributions toward that end.

REGULATORY CHANGE PROCESS

If changes in transportation regulation do occur, they will come about gradually. Past attempts to promote regulatory change in transportation have been hindered by mismanagement of legislative proposals.[22] Too little attention has been devoted to the process by which regulatory changes are sold to legislative bodies.

To promote significant regulatory changes in transportation, the supporting agency (usually the DOT) must involve shippers, carriers, consumer groups, lobby associations, and other government agencies in the policy analysis process as early as possible. Empirical data concerning the views of these groups may well identify and refine areas that should be addressed by forthcoming legislative initiatives. Also, agencies should avoid the "massive legislative package" approach to fostering regulatory change due to the inherent aversion of legislative bodies to such far-reaching bills. A common belief appears to be that submission of a massive regulatory change bill assures the supporting agency of getting some part of the package enacted. However, experience indicates that this has not been the case. To the contrary, when an agency is discredited on any segment of the package, this tends to jaundice the legislature's views concerning the balance of the legislation. Consequently, nothing is enacted.

It is a simple fact that massive regulatory changes brought about simultaneously might cause massive problems. Uncertainty is unavoidable, and most individuals and groups (including legislative bodies) like to take uncertainty in small doses. Consequently, advocates of regulatory change in transportation should consider formulation of their proposals in such a manner as to introduce change gradually. This minimizes the magnitude of any negative effect that might occur initially. Attention should be given to the possibility of incorporation of an escape clause, which would allow termination of a particular experiment after a review period. This legislative management approach by an agency advocating regulatory change in transportation might substantially improve the likelihood of such changes occurring.

CONGRESSIONAL APPROACH TO POLICY FORMULATION

As Congress focuses on the development of future transportation policy, it must deal with many difficult issues. Too often in the past it has tended to throw money at problems, through such devices as carrier loan guarantee programs, in hopes that the problems would disappear. However, unless action is taken to eliminate the fundamental causes of the problems that are plaguing the carriers, these problems are likely to resurface. We have witnessed that pattern time and again.

The pattern must be changed. Congress, with the assistance of the DOT, must play an anticipatory role in transportation policy development. More attention must be devoted to forecasting and preventing problems. In the past, Congress has not generally responded to transportation problems until well after they had taken on disastrous proportions. Reflection on the conditions that preceded almost any significant piece of transportation legislation reveals this to be the case. In recent memory the creation of Amtrak, the Northeast Railroad Reorganization, and the Railroad Revitalization and Regulatory Reform Act of 1976 were all enacted after conditions had gotten so bad that steps had to be taken. The costs of this congressional lag are enormous.

There is no question that it is difficult for Congress to play a more aggressive policy formulation role in transportation, given the other demands placed on the time of individual congressmen. Because of this, it is critical that the DOT and the congressional committees involved in transportation strive toward establishment of a true working relationship. All too frequently in the past, these parties have automatically adopted adversary positions on transportation matters. This relationship can only be improved through mutual efforts on behalf of both congressmen and DOT officials. This does not entail congressional surrender of policy formulation authority to the DOT, but rather acceptance of the department's legitimate role in supplying expert opinion.

SUMMARY

The coming years are likely to witness growing pressures to modify certain aspects of federal regulatory and promotional policies in transportation. In terms of economic regulation, the aspects of policy that are most likely to be modified are controls over entry, pricing, and discontinuance of service. It is very unlikely that these controls will be abolished, because the concept of total deregulation has not attracted the support of either carrier or shipper groups. Therefore, the changes that do occur will probably be marginal in nature.

In the realm of promotional policy, the DOT has expressed its intention to promote a more evenhanded federal treatment of the several modes of intercity carriage. From a funding standpoint, such treatment entails elimination of both direct and indirect subsidies whenever possible and reliance upon user charges to finance system improvements and operations. To promote such equity, the department will have to overcome the strong opposition of those interest groups that have historically benefited from these subsidies. If the DOT is successful in this effort, it could significantly contribute to the elimination of many of the market distortions that have surfaced throughout the years.

To be successful in fostering regulatory and promotional changes, the DOT will have to adopt a more gradual and limited approach to the formulation of legislative proposals. Congress has not accepted and will not accept massive change proposals that seek to make numerous simultaneous changes in federal programs or regulations.

In a related matter, Congress and the DOT must strive to develop an effective working relationship, which avoids the adversary posture that they automatically adopted all too frequently in the past. Hopefully, by working together these parties can reduce the congressional lag that has threatened the viability of the U.S. transportation system.

NOTES

1. For a discussion of these legislative proposals, see U.S. Department of Transportation, *Statement of John W. Snow, Administrator, National Highway Traffic Safety Administration Before the House Committee on Public Works and Transportation, Subcommittee on Surface Transportation, on Motor Carrier Regulatory Reform,* presented September 14, 1976 (Washington, D.C.: the Department); also U.S. Department of Transportation, *Aviation Act of 1975—Section-by-Section Analysis* (Washington, D.C.: the Department, 1975).

2. For a discussion of the Canadian experience, see H. M. Romoff, "Deregulation: The Canadian Experience," *Transportation and Distribution Management,* XIII, No. 4 (April, 1973), p. 18.

3. U.S. Department of Transportation, Office of the Secretary, *Executive Briefing: Transportation Regulatory Modernization and Assistance Legislation* (Washington, D.C.: the Department, 1972), pp. 45–47.

4. For a concise summary of these pro-entry control arguments, see James C. Nelson, "The Effects of Entry Control in Surface Transport," in *Transportation Economics* (New York: National Bureau of Economic Research, 1965), p. 383.

5. For a discussion of shipper reaction to such proposals, see Robert C. Lieb, "Relaxing Motor Carrier Regulation: The Massachusetts Attempt," *Logistics and Transportation Review,* XI, No. 2 (Fall, 1975), pp. 193–201.

6. Department of Transportation, *Aviation Act of 1975—Section-by-Section Analysis,* pp. 11–14.

7. Association of American Railroads, *Basic Provisions of Railroad Revitalization and Regulatory Reform Act of 1976* (Washington, D.C.: the Association, 1976), p. 2.

8. Department of Transportation, *Aviation Act of 1975—Section-by-Section Analysis,* pp. 9–10.

9. During 1976 the Senate Public Works Committee approved a bill that called for the imposition of a user-charge system for the domestic waterway system. However, the user-charge provision was stricken from the waterway bill by the Senate.

10. U.S. Department of Transportation, Office of the Secretary, *A Statement of National Transportation Policy* (Washington, D.C.: the Department, 1975), p. 19.
11. This federal–local government interaction is discussed further in Chapter 20.
12. The issue of railroad nationalization had been considered several times by Congress. The Windom Report of 1874 recommended nationalization to eliminate the railroad abuses that were uncovered during the Granger movement. Similarly, following World War I, Congress considered nationalization as a means of improving the industry's financial condition.
13. D. Philip Locklin, *The Economics of Transportation*, 6th ed. (Homewood, Ill.: Richard D. Irwin, Inc., 1966), pp. 589–90.
14. Ibid., p. 591.
15. Association of American Railroads, *Yearbook of Railroad Facts* (Washington, D.C.: the Association, 1976), p. 19.
16. Walter S. Splawn, *Government Ownership and Operation of the Railroads* (New York: Macmillan Publishing Co. Inc., 1928), pp. 375–82.
17. Ibid., p. 381.
18. Association of American Railroads, *Nationalization—A Costly Idea* (Washington, D.C.: the Association, 1970), p. 2.
19. Association of American Railroads, *Yearbook of Railroad Facts*, p. 17.
20. Charles L. Dearing and Wilfred Owen, *National Transportation Policy* (Washington, D.C.: Brookings Institution, 1949), p. 130.
21. Ibid.
22. For a discussion of this issue, see Robert C. Lieb, "Promoting Change in Transportation Regulation," *Business Horizons*, XVIII, No. 3 (June, 1975), pp. 91–94.

SELECTED REFERENCES

Davis, Grant M., ed. *Transportation Regulation: A Pragmatic Assessment.* Danville, Ill.: Interstate Printers and Publishers, Inc., 1976.

Davis, Grant M., and Linda J. Combs. "Some Observations Regarding Value-of-Service Pricing in Transportation." *Transportation Journal*, XIV, No. 3 (Spring, 1975), pp. 49–58.

Douglas, George W., and James C. Miller. *Economic Regulation of Domestic Air Transportation: Theory and Policy.* Washington, D.C.: Brookings Institution, 1974.

Eads, George C. *The Local Service Airline Experiment.* Washington, D.C.: Brookings Institution, 1972.

Eastman, Samuel E. "The Administration's Regulatory Dilemma." *Transportation Journal*, XV, No. 3 (Summer, 1976), pp. 5–13.

Fair, Marvin L., and Ernest W. Williams. *Economics of Transportation and Logistics*. Dallas, Tex.: Business Publications, Inc., 1975.
Chapter 26. "National Transportation Policy," pp. 518–36.

Friedlaender, Ann F. *The Dilemma of Freight Transport Regulation*. Washington, D.C.: Brookings Institution, 1969.
Chapter 6. "Alternatives to Present Policies," pp. 127–62.

Heads, John. "Some Lessons from Transportation Deregulation in Canada." *ICC Practitioners' Journal*, XLII, No. 3 (March–April, 1975), pp. 270–80.

Johnson, James C., and Donald V. Harper. "The Potential Consequences of Deregulation of Transportation." *Land Economics*, LI, No. 1 (February, 1975), pp. 58–71.

Munro, John M. "A Comparative Evaluation of Canadian and U.S. Transport Policy." *Transportation Journal*, XII, No. 4 (Summer, 1973), pp. 5–26.

Nelson, James C. "The Effects of Entry Control in Surface Transport," in *Transportation Economics*. New York: National Bureau of Economic Research, 1965, pp. 381–422.

Sampson, Roy J., and Martin T. Farris. *Domestic Transportation: Practice, Theory, and Policy*, 3rd ed. Boston: Houghton Mifflin Company, 1975.
Chapter 29. "Conflicts in National Transportation Policy," pp. 474–90.

Spychalski, John C. "Criticisms of Regulated Freight Transport: Do Economists' Perceptions Conform with Institutional Realities?" *Transportation Journal*, XIV, No. 3 (Spring, 1975), pp. 5–17.

U.S. Congress, Senate, Committee on the Judiciary, Subcommittee on the Judiciary. *Civil Aeronautics Board Practices and Procedures*. 94th Cong., 1st Sess. Washington, D.C.: U.S. Government Printing Office, 1975.

U.S. Department of Transportation, Office of the Secretary. *A Statement of National Transportation Policy*. Washington, D.C.: U.S. Government Printing Office, 1975.

DISCUSSION QUESTIONS

1. Would you favor total deregulation of the economic aspects of transportation?

2. You are the assistant secretary for policy development of the federal Department of Transportation. Assume that during the current legislative session you have the ability to bring about *one* major change in transportation policy. Given that ability, what aspect of policy would you change, and how would the change affect the industry? For the purposes of this discussion,

assume that total deregulation is not one change, but rather a series of changes.

3. At a Department of Transportation meeting a staff member states, "I believe that any carrier engaged in any form of transportation should be permitted to curtail any or all of its services following a 30-day notice to the appropriate regulatory agency. I believe that we should include such a recommendation in our next legislative proposal to Congress." Do you agree with him? Explain your answer.

4. For many years people have discussed the desirability of creating a single federal transportation trust fund. Creation of such a fund would involve the dissolution of other modal funds, such as the Highway Trust Fund. Do you believe that such a step would be desirable?

PART
6

Metropolitan Transportation

CHAPTER 19

Problems of Metropolitan Transportation

Some of the most pressing national transportation problems exist in our cities and their surrounding metropolitan areas. Among these problems are the pollution and congestion caused by growing automobile usage and the financial decline of the transit industry.[1] These and related problems have posed serious threats to the quality of urban life.

This chapter outlines and examines the major transportation problems that exist in the metropolitan sector of the U.S. transportation system. In doing so it stresses the interrelationship between transportation and other matters of metropolitan concern such as population shifts and land use patterns. The chapter also addresses the importance of freight movements in metropolitan traffic flows, and identifies the interface that exists between metropolitan and intercity transportation. Chapter 20 then explores the efforts that have been made to remedy metropolitan transportation problems.

METROPOLITAN INTERRELATIONSHIPS
INVOLVING TRANSPORTATION

The transportation system of a metropolitan area is closely interrelated with the area's development pattern and its economic dynamics. An understanding of these interrelationships is extremely important to those engaged in metropolitan area planning. Several of the more important of these inter-relationships are examined in the following discussion.

Population Trends

The U.S. population has become increasingly urban as a steady population shift has taken place from rural to urban locations. In 1900 the Census Bureau considered only 40 percent of the population to be urbanized.[2] However, by 1970 it was reported that 73.5 percent of the population resided in urban areas, and it has been estimated that by 1980 the degree of urbanization will approach 80 percent.[3]

In recent years a related population shift has occurred. It has involved the dispersion of urban population over wider metropolitan areas. This development, often referred to as suburbanization, has fostered lower population densities in many of our central cities. Suburbanization has been both a function of transportation availability and a cause of serious metropolitan transportation problems.

Before the development of large-scale public transportation in urban areas, it was generally necessary for workers to reside close to their places of employment. That situation, coupled with the early clustering of industrial activities in our central cities, led to high urban population density. However, as public transportation became available, it was possible for workers to live apart from their job locations, and commutation emerged. The related population dispersal was reinforced by the development of the automobile; today, widespread automobile ownership and the advanced highway system make it possible for people to live many miles from their jobs. Transportation improvements have therefore increased population mobility, which in turn has promoted suburbanization.

Unfortunately, the suburbanization process has also created several serious transportation problems. As population disperses more widely from the central city it becomes increasingly less likely that it can be adequately served by transit systems. Density diminishes, and the potential number of origin–destination pairs becomes too great. Consequently, more people rely upon the automobile for commutation, and transit patronage and revenues decline. This pattern has been observed in many of our major metropolitan areas. Besides contributing to the decline of transit, increased automobile commutation has also led to serious pollution, congestion, and energy consumption problems. It has also promoted higher automobile accident and insurance rates in our cities.

Land Use Patterns

Transportation development and land use patterns in metropolitan areas are also closely intertwined. The mobility created by transportation improvements has significantly increased land values in suburban areas as "bedroom communities" have emerged. However, there are several related problems. Transportation facilities have become major consumers of metropolitan land. In most cities, approximately one third of all land is devoted to streets, railroad yards, terminals, airports, and parking facilities.[4] Consequently, the amount of unused land and open space has seriously diminished in many cities. Properties that are adjacent to transportation facilities have often become blighted; this has lowered property values and has had a negative impact on the quality of urban life.

Tax Base Considerations

Transportation development has also influenced the tax base of our cities. New transportation facilities have often displaced residents and businesses, thereby eroding the tax base. This has aggravated an existing problem, because many cities already had high concentrations of tax-exempt properties such as churches and schools.[5]

Furthermore, the commuting mobility of the middle and upper income classes has left our cities with major concentrations of the elderly and the poor. These people depend quite heavily upon social services, but they cannot afford to underwrite them through taxes. These same core dwellers tend to be quite dependent upon transit to meet their transportation needs. Unfortunately, rising transit deficits have often led to service cutbacks, which have further impaired the ability of these people to reach work locations. This problem has intensified with the relocation of many industrial activities to the suburbs. These developments have combined to economically trap the poor in our cities and have contributed to increasing welfare needs.

Environmental Considerations

Transportation has also contributed to air and noise pollution and congestion problems in our metropolitan areas. The street systems of many of our large cities were not designed to handle the volume of contemporary traffic flows. Nor do they effectively separate vehicle and pedestrian flows. The resulting congestion increases travel time and vehicle fuel consumption rates. As congestion worsens, exhaust fumes increase and pollution problems intensify. The impact of traffic congestion is illustrated by the fact that average automobile speeds in U.S. cities range from 16 miles per hour in Boston and St. Louis to 22 miles per hour in San Francisco and Milwaukee.[6] Public buses, which must share the street system with other vehicle classes, run much slower.[7]

The severity of urban pollution problems led Congress in 1970 to direct the Environmental Protection Agency to develop plans to reduce air and noise pollution levels in our cities. As discussed in Chapter 17, the agency has brought about major reductions in urban pollution.

The obvious linkage between increased urban automobile usage and a variety of socioeconomic and environmental problems that exists in metropolitan areas has prompted federal, state, and local officials to reassess transit's role in metropolitan transportation. However, the transit industry has also experienced serious problems.

STATUS OF THE TRANSIT INDUSTRY

While public interest in transit operations has increased dramatically in recent years, the industry has experienced financial difficulties that have threatened the viability of transit service in many cities. Among the problems faced by the industry have been decreased ridership and earnings, rapidly escalating costs, and the heavy concentration of demand during peak hours. The industry has also suffered due to stringent local regulation and the historical highway orientation of government transportation spending programs.

Ridership and Earnings

Mass transit ridership declined by nearly 60 percent between 1950 and 1975 (see Table 19–1). Several factors contributed to the long-term decline in transit patronage. Among these were the trend toward low-density development, growing affluence, increasing highway spending programs, and heavy utilization of the automobile.[8] In all but a few cities the automobile has emerged as the dominant mode of urban passenger movement. It should be noted, however, that transit ridership trended upward between 1973 and 1975, thus reversing the long-term downtrend in ridership. The reasons for that development and its importance are discussed in Chapter 20.

The transit industry has incurred steadily growing deficits (see Table 19–2). The aggregate loss for the industry exceeded $1.7 billion in 1975. Numerous transit properties have declared bankruptcy, and many medium-sized communities have lost transit service completely.[9] One major cause of the industry deficit has been a rapidly rising cost spiral.

Industry Costs

Transit industry costs have escalated steadily in recent years. Equipment and supply cost increases have been significant, but rising labor costs have been far more important. Labor compensation is the major operating cost

Table 19–1

Transit Ridership, 1950–1975

Year	Total Revenue Passengers (millions)
1950	13,845.0
1955	9,189.0
1960	7,521.0
1965	6,698.0
1970	5,931.7
1971	5,497.0
1972	5,253.3
1973	5,293.9
1974	5,605.9
1975	5,625.8

SOURCE: American Public Transit Association, *Transit Fact Book* (Washington, D.C.: the Association, 1976), p. 33.

Table 19–2

Transit Operating Income (Deficit), 1950–1975

Year	Income or Deficit (000)
1950	$ 66,370
1955	55,710
1960	30,690
1965	(10,610)
1970	(288,212)
1971	(411,400)
1972	(513,126)
1973	(738,499)
1974	(1,299,673)
1975[a]	(1,703,526)

[a] Projected.

SOURCE: American Public Transit Association, *Transit Fact Book* (Washington, D.C.: the Association, 1976), p. 28.

element in most transit activities, comprising nearly 65 percent of industry operating expenses in 1975.[10] The importance of the magnitude of labor compensation is illustrated by the fact that in several of the largest U.S. transit systems employee compensation exceeds the operating revenues of the properties involved.[11]

Despite the industry's financial downturn, transit labor succeeded in increasing average hourly wage rates by 73.3 percent between 1967 and 1974.[12] Average annual wages of transit workers reached $13,993 during 1975.[13] However, despite the fact that transit wages have risen rapidly in recent years, much of the increase has been absorbed by inflation. As a result, the increases in real wages experienced by many transit workers have been quite modest.[14]

Labor Productivity

Although the impact of wage increases can often be reduced through increased productivity, several studies have indicated that the transit industry has experienced constant or declining worker productivity since 1950.[15] Further research has found little relationship between system size and worker productivity.[16] Similarly, there does not appear to be any significant difference in productivity between public and private transit systems.[17]

Constant or declining labor productivity, coupled with steadily rising labor costs, poses a most perplexing problem for transit management. Labor inputs have become increasingly more expensive, but not more productive. This problem has led to consideration of many technological changes in the industry, but few have been implemented. For example, no major innovations in bus operations have occurred in more than 20 years.[18] Utilization of express bus lanes in several cities has improved driver productivity, but these projects have been quite limited in scope. These efforts are discussed further in Chapter 20.

Management desire to reduce labor costs while increasing labor productivity in transit has been one of the major motivating factors in rekindling interest in fixed-rail rapid transit systems. Operations such as the Bay Area Rapid Transit (BART) system in the San Francisco Bay area and the Lindenwold Line, which serves Philadelphia, have been partially sold to the public on this basis. While BART has been plagued with a variety of technical and political problems, the Lindenwold Line's performance has been reassuring to rapid transit advocates. One study has indicated that the capital-intensive system has achieved a considerably lower labor to operating cost ratio than typical bus operations.[19] Similarly, labor productivity increased impressively during the early years of the system's operation.[20] Such performance is encouraging, but the high capital costs of such systems and the need for major population concentrations along corridors served limit the opportunity for feasible applications of this technology. Even though several new rapid transit systems are being built, they will not carry a sufficient volume of passengers to significantly improve aggregate industry productivity.

Peak Hour Problems

The transit industry is troubled by peak hour problems. Although transit ridership has fallen dramatically in many cities, service still tends to be quite heavily used during the peak commutation periods of 7 to 9 A.M. and 4 to 6 P.M. In most major cities, transit facilities are used to capacity during those periods, but ridership falls off precipitously during off-peak hours. For example, on the rapid transit lines of Chicago, Cleveland, and Philadelphia, 58 percent of normal weekday volume is handled during the four peak hours.[21] Similarly, nearly 70 percent of the weekday volume of rail commuter operations in Chicago, Washington, and Philadelphia is concentrated in the peak hours.[22] Consequently, transit systems must still meet the manpower and equipment levels dictated by peak demands, but are then faced with the prospect of underutilized personnel and equipment during off-peak periods.

To combat this problem, many transit companies now use buses for charter services during the slack periods, and in some cities transit unions have agreed to work split shifts so that a single group of workers can handle both the morning and evening rushes. Several cities have experimented with lower off-peak fares as a means of both limiting peak demand and stimulating off-peak utilization. One such program, Boston's MBTA Dime Time experiment, lowered the fare from 25 cents to 10 cents between the morning and evening rush periods. However, although ridership increased during the slack period, demand was not sufficiently elastic to increase revenues, and the program was discontinued.[23] The results of other experimental off-peak fare programs have been mixed.

Transit Regulation

The transit industry has also been troubled by rather stringent local regulations. When the transit industry emerged during the late nineteenth century, it was primarily financed and operated by private companies. In most instances these companies were granted charters by the local government. Under the provisions of these charters, the rates charged and services offered were generally controlled by public authorities. In subsequent years these charter stipulations were to cause serious difficulties for many private transit companies. Rates were often held at rather low levels despite increasing costs, and the companies were often forced to continue noncompensatory services. These regulatory controls contributed heavily to the many bankruptcies that occurred in the transit industry, and they accelerated the movement toward public ownership of transit properties.

Regulation of transit fares and services has generally continued following the private-to-public ownership transition. If anything, the public systems are under even greater political pressures than their private predecessors to maintain fare levels. This has contributed to the revenue deficiencies experienced by many publicly owned transit systems. As discussed in Chapter 20, continuing deficits of public (and private) systems have led to increasing reliance upon governmental subsidies to keep these systems operational.

Highway Spending and Transit

Government spending programs in transportation have historically been skewed toward the highway modes. This has been particularly true of expenditures at the federal level. Substantial federal aid has been available for urban highway programs for many years, but federal outlays for transit were miniscule prior to 1970. Transit tended to be viewed as a local matter. Due to these funding inequities, state and local transportation planners gravitated toward highway solutions to metropolitan transportation problems. As improved urban highway systems attracted more riders from transit operations, the automobile often became a superior alternative to transit systems that were underfunded and deteriorating in service quality. The highway orientation of metropolitan transportation programs, particularly after World War II, contributed heavily to the problems of the transit industry.

Future Role of Transit

It has become increasingly obvious that metropolitan commutation needs can no longer be satisfied through increased reliance upon the automobile. The societal costs of the continued pursuit of the "highway solution" are too great. As a result, the federal government has embarked on a major program to revitalize transit. The nature of the federal commitment and its interaction with state and local programs are explored extensively in Chapter 20.

METROPOLITAN FREIGHT MOVEMENTS

No examination of the transportation problems of U.S. metropolitan areas would be complete without reference to the movement of freight. To the present time, little systematic attention has been devoted to freight movements within metropolitan areas. This is unfortunate, because freight movements have a decided impact on traffic flows and environmental issues.

Historically, cities have served as freight transportation hubs in which outbound traffic was consolidated for movement to other cities and inbound freight was sorted for local delivery. Therefore, the terminal facilities of both intercity modes and local cartage companies tended to cluster near the center city to facilitate traffic interchange. This led to considerable mixing of passenger and freight vehicles in the metropolitan traffic flow.

The decentralization of industry and urban highway expansion has fostered a shift of many freight terminals to suburban locations. This development has reduced freight traffic volume within cities, but it cannot possibly eliminate them. Retail establishments still require the replenishment of inventory and customer deliveries. Supplies of food must still be delivered to stores that service urban residents.

There is a heavy concentration of trucks in urban areas to serve such needs. Nearly two thirds of all trucks registered in the United States are operated locally in urban areas.[24] Although more than one half of all urban truck trips involve freight pickup and delivery, trucks are also engaged in such diverse urban activities as construction, mail delivery, and the provision of maintenance services.[25]

Most city streets were not designed to cope with truck movements. They are often narrow, and off-street loading and unloading facilities are frequently inadequate. Consequently, many local pickup and delivery vehicles obstruct traffic flows each time they stop. This greatly contributes to the congestion problems experienced in central cities. Aggravating the situation still further is the fact that many of these trucks carry partial loads.

Public officials in some cities have considered modification of freight pickup and delivery patterns to combat congestion problems. Suggestions have been made to establish union terminals where the pickup and delivery functions of the line-haul and local carriers could be coordinated. However, the coordination of these carriers is a massive undertaking, and little progress has been made in implementing this concept. Proposals to restrict local truck services to periods before and after the normal business day have also been considered in several cities. Such restrictions would reduce congestion and pollution problems during the day. However, such restrictions have been strongly opposed by both merchants and local truckers. Merchants contend that their operating hours and employment needs would be adversely affected by such arrangements; truckers oppose the change in their work patterns that the restrictions would necessitate. Consequently, such plans have not been implemented.

METROPOLITAN–INTERCITY TRANSPORTATION INTERFACE

Metropolitan transportation problems cannot be addressed in isolation because of the complex interrelationship that exists with intercity freight and passenger movements. The bulk of pickup and delivery activities of intercity truckers occurs within metropolitan areas. Local traffic congestion increases carrier running time and costs, and reduces worker productivity. Furthermore, the ability of intercity carriers to meet freight delivery schedules is quite dependent upon ease of local movement. Therefore, congestion problems that appear to be local transportation issues can lead to cost and service difficulties for intercity carriers.

Similarly, those intercity travelers who use for-hire modes must generally enter the metropolitan traffic stream. Unfortunately, intercity passenger services, particularly airline operations, also experience heavy peak hour demands, which coincide with the peaking of local commutation traffic. This often creates serious traffic congestion problems near intercity passenger terminals, which inconveniences both intercity and local travelers who must share common highway facilities. Furthermore, many intercity passengers reaching destination terminals are quite dependent upon local transit and taxi services to complete their trips.

The freight and passenger terminals of intercity carriers also consume major parcels of metropolitan land, thereby contributing to the land use and blight problems discussed earlier in this chapter. Metropolitan operations of intercity carriers are also a significant cause of noise and air pollution problems.

In view of the degree and importance of the interaction of metropolitan and intercity transportation systems, increasing attention has been devoted to comprehensive transportation planning at the federal, state, and local levels. These planning efforts are discussed in detail in the next chapter.

SUMMARY

A strong interrelationship exists between the passenger and freight transportation systems of a metropolitan area and such matters as population trends and land use patterns. Additionally, the space demands of the transportation network can lead to erosion of the area's tax base, while vehicle operations contribute to pollution, congestion, and energy consumption problems. Consequently, it is not surprising that metropolitan transportation has attracted growing national attention in recent years.

In most metropolitan areas the automobile has emerged as the dominant form of passenger carriage. Besides intensifying environmental difficulties, this development has also led to major declines in transit ridership and revenues. The combination of automobile competition, rising costs, and stringent regulation has threatened the viability of the transit industry.

Although given little planning emphasis in the past, freight movements within metropolitan areas are quite important. They are necessary to supply businesses and consumers, but they also cause difficulties, because our central cities were not designed to accommodate major flows of truck traffic.

An important interface exists between metropolitan and intercity transportation. An intercity carrier's service and cost performance are significantly influenced by the nature of local transportation facilities and the degree of congestion encountered when making local pickup and delivery stops. At the same time, the presence of intercity vehicles in the metropolitan traffic stream contributes to congestion and pollution.

These metropolitan transportation problems and interrelationships have created a need for integrated transportation planning involving local, state, and federal officials. These planning efforts and the funding programs established to promote metropolitan transportation development are the major topics of discussion in Chapter 20.

NOTES

1. As used in this book, the term "transit" includes local bus, subway, commuter rail, and other forms of fixed-rail metropolitan service.

2. George M. Smerk, *Urban Mass Transportation: A Dozen Years of Federal Policy* (Bloomington, Ind.: Indiana University Press, 1974), p. 5.

3. Ibid.

4. Wilfred Owen, *The Metropolitan Transportation Problem,* rev. ed. (Washington, D.C.: Brookings Institution, 1966), p. 190.

5. Ibid., pp. 151–53.

6. The Editors of *Fortune, The Exploding Metropolis* (Garden City, N.Y.: Doubleday & Company, Inc., 1958), pp. 79–80.

7. Ibid.

8. Robert C. Lieb, *Labor in the Transit Industry* (Washington, D.C.: U.S. Government Printing Office, 1976), p. 1.

9. Owen, op. cit., p. 93.

10. American Public Transit Association, *Transit Fact Book* (Washington, D.C.: the Association, 1976), p. 38.

11. For example, during 1975 Boston's MBTA system generated $52.7 million in transportation revenues while incurring wage and fringe benefit costs of $134.5 million.

12. Bureau of National Affairs, "Wage Rates for Local-Transit Operating Employees," *Daily Labor Report,* Economic Section, No. 88 (May 6, 1975), p. B-1.

13. American Public Transit Association, op. cit., p. 38.

14. Mary Kay Rieg, "Price Hikes Dampen Wage Gains for Transit Employees," *Monthly Labor Review,* XCVII, No. 7 (July, 1974), p. 56.

15. See Lieb, op. cit., pp. 46–57; also Darold T. Barnum, *Collective Bargaining and Manpower in Urban Mass Transit Systems* (Springfield, Va.: National Technical Information Service, 1972), p. 53.

16. Barnum, op. cit., p. 388.

17. Barnum, op. cit., p. 50.

18. Ibid.

19. John T. Berg, Stanley Miller, and Edward Fleishman, "Labor Costs and Productivity for the Lindenwold Rapid Rail Line and the Shirley Highway Rapid Bus Demonstration Project: Some Preliminary Findings," *Transportation Journal,* XIV, No. 1 (Fall, 1974), p. 48.

20. Ibid.

21. John R. Meyer, John F. Kain, and Martin Wohl, *The Urban Transportation Problem* (Cambridge, Mass.: Harvard University Press, 1965), p. 95.

22. Ibid.

23. "MBTA Report: Dime Time Fails, Zone Fares Likely," *Boston Globe,* July 12, 1975, p. 3.

24. Wilbur Smith and Associates, *Motor Trucks in the Metropolis* (New Haven, Conn.: Wilbur Smith and Associates, 1969), p. v.

25. Ibid., pp. 46–47.

SELECTED REFERENCES

Buel, Ronald A. *Dead End: The Automobile in Mass Transportation.* Englewood Cliffs, N.J.: Prentice-Hall, Inc., 1972.

Catonese, Anthony (ed.). *New Perspectives in Urban Transportation Research.* Lexington, Mass.: D. C. Heath & Company, 1972.

Fair, Marvin L., and Ernest W. Williams. *Economics of Transportation and Logistics.* Dallas, Tex.: Business Publications, Inc., 1975.
Chapter 8. "Urban Logistics: Human and Goods," pp. 123–42.

Foster, Jerry R., and Martin F. Schmidt. "Rail Terminals and the Urban Environment." *Transportation Journal,* XV, No. 1 (Fall, 1975), pp. 21–28.

Lieb, Robert C. *Labor in the Transit Industry.* Washington, D.C.: U.S. Government Printing Office, 1976.

McDermott, Dennis R. "An Alternative Framework for Urban Goods Distribution: Consolidation." *Transportation Journal,* XV, No. 1 (Fall, 1975), pp. 29–39.

Meyer, John R., John F. Kain, and Martin Wohl. *The Urban Transportation Problem.* Cambridge, Mass.: Harvard University Press, 1965.

Miller, David R. *Urban Transportation Policy: New Perspectives.* Lexington, Mass.: D. C. Heath & Company, 1972.

Norton, Hugh S. *Modern Transportation Economics,* 2nd ed. Columbus, Ohio: Charles E. Merrill Publishing Company, 1971.
Chapter 4. "The Urban Transport Dilemma," pp. 83–98.

Owen, Wilfred. *The Accessible City.* Washington, D.C.: Brookings Institution, 1972.

Owen, Wilfred. *The Metropolitan Transportation Problem,* rev. ed. Washington, D.C.: Brookings Institution, 1966.

Pegrum, Dudley F. *Transportation: Economics and Public Policy,* 3rd. ed. Homewood, Ill.: Richard D. Irwin, Inc., 1973.
Chapter 23. "The Urban Transportation Problem," pp. 534–68.

Schreiber, Arthur F., Paul K. Gatons, and Richard B. Clemmer. *Economics of Urban Problems: An Introduction.* Boston: Houghton Mifflin Co., 1971.
Chapter 5. "Transportation," pp. 81–100.

Smerk, George M. *Urban Mass Transportation: A Dozen Years of Federal Policy.* Bloomington, Ind.: Indiana University Pres, 1974.

Smerk, George M. *Urban Transportation: The Federal Role.* Bloomington, Ind.: Indiana University Press, 1965.

Smith, Wilbur, and Associates. *Motor Trucks in the Metropolis.* New Haven, Conn.: Wilbur Smith and Associates, 1969.

Weiner, Paul, and Edward J. Deak. *Environmental Factors in Transportation Planning.* Lexington, Mass.: D. C. Heath & Company, 1972.

DISCUSSION QUESTIONS

1. Discuss the factors that have influenced transit patronage in the post-World War II period.
2. What is the peak-hour problem in the transit industry?
3. How has transportation affected land use patterns in metropolitan areas?

CHAPTER
20

Solving Metropolitan Transportation Problems

Chapter 19 stressed the significance and the problems of metropolitan transportation, and in this chapter we trace the responses of local, state, and federal government units to these problems. Attention is devoted both to those programs that have sought to revitalize transit and to those that have promoted integration of the highway modes into metropolitan planning. Additionally, the impact of these programs is reviewed, and the movement toward coordinated transportation planning in metropolitan areas is explored.

LOCAL AND STATE ROLE IN TRANSIT

During the formative years of the transit industry, the involvement of local government in transit was primarily limited to chartering private companies to provide the services and the regulation of their activities. However, the financial problems experienced by many private transit companies and the local desire to promote continuity of service necessitated a growing local government involvement in transit financing.

Bankruptcies of private transit systems led to public acquisition of transit facilities in many of our large cities, including New York, Chicago, Detroit, Boston, Pittsburgh, and San Francisco. Only 35 percent of all U.S. transit systems are publicly owned, but public systems carry 90 percent of the industry's revenue passengers and employ 86 percent of the transit workforce (see Table 20–1).

Table 20–1

Statistics of Publicly Owned Transit Systems

	Calendar Year 1975	Industry Total (%)
Number of Systems	333	35
Operating Revenue (millions)	$1,729	86
Vehicle Miles Operated (millions)	1,706	86
Revenue Passengers (millions)	5,090	90
Employees	138,212	86
Passenger Vehicles Operated	51,964	83

SOURCE: American Public Transit Association, *Transit Fact Book* (Washington, D.C.: the Association, 1976), p. 25.

In addition to its ownership and operation role in transit, local government has become extensively involved in the subsidization of public and private transit system deficits. It has become increasingly difficult for transit systems to be self-sufficient at the fare box. As costs have risen and ridership has declined, transit systems have often resorted to fare increases. As a result, the average transit fare in the United States rose from 10.02 cents in 1950 to 33.07 cents in 1975.[1] Although such fares have yielded increased revenues per rider, each successive price increase tends to further erode the transit ridership base.[2] Additionally, transit fare hikes tend to be rather regressive and place a disproportionate burden on lower-income groups, which rely quite heavily upon transit services. In view of the negative ramifications of fare increases, in recent years public officials in many cities have opted to establish or increase public subsidies to transit systems rather than to continue to raise fares.

These subsidy programs have been financed by various means. Among the financial arrangements used have been tax assessments to the communities served, local sales tax levies earmarked for transit subsidies, and transit taxes on automobiles registered in metropolitan areas. Such arrangements have provided a means of preserving transit system operations, but they have not supplied adequate funding for significant improvements in transit service. The competition for local tax dollars has been intense, and transit upgrading necessarily has been weighed against expenditures for such programs as public education, housing, and health care. At the same time, local taxpayers have protested loudly against increased taxes. As a result

405

of these pressures, local public officials have increasingly turned to state and federal government units for transit assistance.

State government has progressively been drawn into the mass transit issue. Thirty-two states have enacted legislation that is directly concerned with the protection of public transportation systems in metropolitan areas.[3] Twenty-one states provide direct financial subsidies to those systems. The form of subsidization varies widely, and the subsidies draw upon a wide range of tax programs.[4] For example, California utilizes a combination of real estate taxes and a sales tax to finance transit projects; Oregon uses payroll taxes for the same purpose.[5] Such state assistance has been useful, but it has not provided the capital infusion necessary to revitalize transit. That burden has increasingly fallen upon the federal government.

FEDERAL ROLE IN TRANSIT

Prior to 1960 there was little federal involvement in transit affairs. While billions of dollars were spent on highway, airport–airway, and waterway projects, federal transit funding was nonexistent. The prevailing attitude in Washington appeared to be that transit was a local matter. This situation has changed significantly since 1960. The federal government now plays a major role not only by providing capital grant assistance to transit companies, but also by extending planning grants to cities and contributing funds to offset a portion of transit operating deficits. The evolution of the federal role in transit is examined in the following discussion.

Housing Act of 1961

The late 1950s and early 1960s were marked by a growing public awareness of the problems of our cities. The deterioration of the quality of urban life was apparent. This led to a substantial expansion of the federal role in urban affairs. Numerous programs were established to channel federal funds into urban areas. With increasing attention being devoted to the urban setting, the role of transit in achieving urban objectives began to attract congressional attention. A coalition of urban interest groups, transit officials, and local politicians intensified their lobbying efforts for federal transit funding. These efforts were reinforced by two major federal reports on transportation issues, which were released in 1960.[6] Both studies called for increased federal involvement in solving the commutation problems of our cities.

In response to these developments, Congress took several steps to create transit support in the Housing Act of 1961. The transit-related provisions of that statute were as follows:

1. Twenty-five million dollars was authorized for mass transit demonstration grants. The federal share of such demonstration projects was to be two thirds of the project cost, with the balance to be funded by local and state government.
2. Cities were directed to include mass transportation planning as an integral part of comprehensive urban planning under the act's planning grants program.
3. Fifty million dollars in low-interest loans were made available to the transit industry. The loan program was to be administered by the Housing and Home Finance Agency (which was incorporated into the Department of Housing and Urban Development in 1966).[7]

The amount of money committed to transit under the act was modest, but it marked a major victory for transit supporters in that an initial federal funding commitment had been made to transit. A number of small-scale demonstration grants were awarded. Among the projects funded under the program were improvements in the bus system of Detroit, the operation of low-fare commuter rail services in the Philadelphia area, and minibus operations in the central business district of Washington, D.C. However, both the absolute amount of federal money available and the nature of the projects funded indicated that the 1961 act was primarily concerned with limited experimentation, rather than large-scale improvements in transit systems.

Urban Mass Transportation Act of 1964

Encouraged by their success in 1961, transit advocates continued to press for expanded federal funding. They found a strong ally in President John F. Kennedy. In his 1962 transportation message to Congress, the president recommended

> that the Congress authorize the first installment of a long-range program of Federal aid to our urban regions for the revitalization and needed expansion of public mass transportation . . . [through] a capital grant authorization of $500 million to be made available over a 3-year period, with $100 million to be made available in fiscal 1963 . . . .[8]

Initial efforts to obtain congressional support for these measures were unsuccessful. Furthermore, the assassination of the president in November 1963 and the period of political transition that it caused lowered the priority accorded to transit matters by the White House.[9] However, by mid-1964 transit legislation was again being actively promoted by the White House. This time Congress responded favorably to the legislative proposal, and on July 9th the Urban Mass Transportation Act of 1964 was signed into law by President Johnson.[10] The act sought not only to provide improvement and development aid to mass transit systems, but also to encourage integrated transportation planning. The statute was to become the basic foundation of future federal transit involvement.

The demonstration and loan programs established in 1961 were continued. More importantly, the 1964 act established a capital grant program that provided federal transit funds on a two-thirds federal, one-third state and local funding basis. The funds could be used for practically any transit-related project. All capital grants were to be made to public agencies, but private interests were encouraged to work with the agencies in jointly securing funds. The act further stipulated that no state was to receive more than 12.5 percent of the total funds disbursed during a given year.

The act provided $375 million in capital grant funds over a three-year period, and established relocation allowances for businesses and residents that might be displaced by transit projects. Also of major importance was Section 13(c) of the statute, which provided job protection guarantees to transit workers who might be adversely affected by federal grants. These worker protection guidelines have been the subject of controversy in recent years; they are examined later in this chapter.

The importance of the Urban Mass Transportation Act's capital grant provisions should not be underestimated. The transit industry had suffered from capital shortages for many years, and funds had not been available to upgrade and expand transit facilities. The new federal capital grants program made such efforts possible, providing that local and state interests could raise their one-third share of project costs. The 1964 capital grants program and later additions have been of major importance in attempts to promote a revitalization of transit facilities.

Federal Developments, 1964–1969

The next several years witnessed a number of significant legislative developments that were to influence the future role of the federal government in transit development. Although the concept of federal participation in transit financing had been firmly established in 1964, the absolute amount of funding provided under the Urban Mass Transportation Act was still quite modest in comparison with transit needs. In 1966, Congress addressed this issue by making several modifications in the 1964 act. Capital grants provided under the act were extended at the rate of $150 million per year in fiscal 1967, 1968, and 1969. Increases in demonstration project funding were also approved, and federal funds were made available for planning, engineering, and designing mass transit projects. The latter appropriations marked a congressional response to the cities which contended that they could not finance the extensive planning process which was a prerequisite for funding applications.

The next significant development occurred the following year when the DOT commenced operations. One year later, in 1968, the transit funding program was transferred from HUD to the DOT. The Urban Mass Transportation Administration (UMTA) was then established within the DOT to administer federal transit programs. The scope of UMTA's operations has expanded substantially since that time, and it has become increasingly involved in the formulation of DOT policies related to all forms of metropolitan transportation development.

Also of importance during that period was the congressional enactment of the National Environmental Policy Act in 1969. The act, mirroring growing national concern with environmental issues, established strict prerequisites on urban transportation construction for the protection and enhancement of the environment. It also required the preparation of environmental impact statements for all major federally funded projects.[11] Although this stipulation has generally resulted in longer and more expensive planning efforts in metropolitan transportation projects, it has also led to greater sensitivity to the possible adverse effects of such projects.

Urban Mass Transportation Assistance Act of 1970

Transit advocates were pleased that federal outlays for transit were increasing, but they believed that the federal commitments were too short term. Representatives of urban areas contended that establishment of a long-term federal commitment to transit would make it much easier to raise local transit funds. Some suggested the creation of a transit trust fund similar to the existing Highway Trust Fund; others proposed yearly appropriations from the Highway Trust Fund for transit projects. Both proposals met with strong opposition. The Bureau of the Budget (now the Office of Management and Budget) adamantly objected to the creation of a transit fund because of the rigidity of such spending programs, and highway interests fought to protect existing highway expenditure programs.[12]

Although President Nixon opposed the creation of a special transit fund, he did favor a substantial increase in transit funding.[13] Consequently, in 1969 he announced his intention to support a $10 billion, 12-year program of transit assistance. The proposal quickly attracted the support of transit and urban interest groups, including the U.S. Conference of Mayors and the National League of Cities. Furthermore, highway interests were convinced to support the proposal in return for the support of the urban interest group coalition when the Highway Trust Fund came up for renewal in 1972.[14] Given that solid block of support, the Urban Mass Transportation

Assistance Act of 1970 proceeded through Congress and was signed into law by President Nixon on October 15, 1970.[15]

In the bill, which modified many provisions of the 1964 statute, Congress responded to requests for long-term transit funding by expressing an intention to provide $10 billion to transit over the next 12 years. The initial $3.1 billion of that amount was appropriated by the act to be awarded during fiscal 1971.

In addition to providing a major increase in federal transit funding, the act also reflected growing congressional concern with the side effects of transportation projects. Applicants for capital grants were directed to hold public hearings on the economic, social, and environmental impacts of proposed transit projects. These considerations were to be weighed in final project deliberations. Furthermore, the secretary of transportation was directed to consult with the heads of other federal agencies with regard to projects affecting the environment to assure that federal transit commitments were prudent.

Highway Act of 1973

The mass transit lobby had succeeded in obtaining a sizable long-term commitment from Congress in 1970, but it still had two other major goals. The first was establishment of a program of operating subsidies to transit, and the second was diversion of Highway Trust Fund monies to major transit projects.[16]

The administration strongly opposed transit operating subsidies, because it was feared that such payments would reinforce inefficiency in transit operations. However, it did favor the diversion of some highway money into transit projects. These issues were debated extensively in Congress, and on August 13, 1973, were finally legislatively settled with the passage of the Federal Highway Act of 1973.

The act contained several important transit provisions. In dealing with the existing transit funding program, Congress appropriated $3 billion more of the $10 billion program initiated in 1970. Also, the federal share of transit project funding was increased from two thirds to 80 percent.[17] To facilitate improved transit planning, the act gave the secretary of transportation the power to fund transit planning up to 100 percent of planning costs.

In terms of new programs, the act permitted certain highway authorizations (Highway Trust Fund allocations to the Federal-Aid Urban System) to be used for either highway or public mass transit projects. If used for transit purposes, the funds could be used to finance either transit-related facilities or the purchase of buses or rail transit rolling stock. The total amount of discretionary funding available was set at $780 million in fiscal 1974, and $800 million for each of the next two fiscal years. Another provision of the 1973 act permitted substitution of transit projects for proposed Interstate Highway segments, if the segments were withdrawn from the interstate system.

Congress did not approve transit operating subsidies in 1973. However, the issue was to arise again during the following year.

National Mass Transportation Assistance Act of 1974

The energy crisis, prompted by the Arab oil embargo, and steadily increasing transit deficits prompted further congressional transit action. It took the form of the National Mass Transportation Assistance Act of 1974.[18]

The act significantly increased federal transit funding by authorizing $11.8 billion over a six-year period. Of that total, $7.3 billion was to be made available for capital assistance to transit systems, and $500 million was earmarked for rural mass transportation projects. The remaining $4 billion was to be allocated to urban areas according to a formula based on population and population density. These funds could be used for either capital or operating assistance. Thus federal transit operating assistance became a reality.

As a result of the 1974 legislation, federal transit assistance had become quite comprehensive. It included not only a multibillion dollar capital assistance program, but also planning grants and operating assistance. Funds were available not only through direct congressional appropriations, but also through limited diversion from the Highway Trust Fund. The metamorphosis that the federal transit role had undergone following the passage of the Housing Act of 1961 had been dramatic, and it profoundly influenced the industry.

IMPACT OF FEDERAL TRANSIT PROGRAMS

The expansion of the federal role in transit since 1961 has influenced the transit industry in several ways. It has provided funds not only to modernize and expand transit services in our cities, but also to promote experimentation with new forms of transit service. Federal aid has also sponsored management development in the industry. Additionally, the federal transit statutes have influenced intergovernmental relationships and accorded extensive job protection to transit workers who might be adversely affected by federal grants.

411

Modernization and Expansion Funds

Since 1961, federal transit funding programs have provided billions of dollars to an industry that had suffered from chronic capital shortages. These funds have allowed many cities to modernize existing transit facilities and others to expand transit capability. As a result of this growing support, the industry's vehicle fleet and service offerings have expanded, thereby reversing long-term industry downtrends. The related service improvements have also likely contributed to the industry's recent reversal of the declining ridership pattern which it experienced in the post-World War II period.

Nevertheless, transit advocates believe that the work has just begun. They contend that federal transit funding has increased too slowly and that more than $40 billion is required to truly revitalize the industry.[19] As a result, the recent lobbying efforts of the industry have not only focused on increasing the absolute size of the federal transit commitment, but also upon obtaining that commitment as soon as possible. This is important because of the significant lag time between the commitment of federal funds and the implementation of improved transit services.

Transit Experimentation

Since its creation, UMTA has financed experimentation with new forms of transit technology such as moving sidewalks, people moving systems, and high-speed rail technology. Such experimentation has attracted considerable public attention, but it has often been criticized as being impractical.[20] More recently, UMTA has tended to gravitate toward less capital intensive experimentation with transit services, and has concentrated upon more marginal modifications of basic transit services. As a result, such programs as development of exclusive busways and implementation of paratransit services are being given higher priorities.[21]

Exclusive busways, which separate commuter bus operations from the normal traffic flow, have been federally supported in a number of metropolitan areas, including Boston, San Francisco, Milwaukee, Seattle, and Washington, D.C.[22] Generally, these projects have stimulated increases in bus ridership by improving the effective speed of buses which operate over exclusive rights-of-way on limited routes.

UMTA has also become heavily involved in promotion of paratransit services, which involve organized ride-sharing activities, ranging from private automobiles to conventional transit modes.[23] Paratransit services operate directly in response to demand without fixed schedules or routes, except where they are prearranged as in subscription and charter bus operations. The most significant forms of paratransit are daily and short-term car rental, taxicabs, dial-a-ride systems, jitneys, carpools, and sub-scription and charter bus systems.[24] In promoting paratransit services UMTA has not envisioned these services as a substitute for mass transit. Rather, paratransit has been seen as meeting demands that are not easily accommodated by mass transit. Numerous paratransit experiments have been funded by UMTA, and it is likely that such services will play an in-creasingly important role in our metropolitan areas.

Management Development

Federal funding has also been used in an attempt to upgrade the level of management skills in the transit industry. If transit is to be effectively revitalized and expanded, the industry will necessarily have to attract and hold talented managers. However, most transit systems have historically devoted little attention to these matters. Management recruiting and train-ing expenditures have often been viewed as unnecessary outlays.[25] The in-dustry has relied quite heavily upon promotion from within to managerial ranks; consequently, many transit managers have lacked adequate educa-tional backgrounds and functional skills to perform effectively. Highlight-ing this problem, a 1973 survey noted that 93 percent of U.S. transit managers were not college graduates.[26]

In responding to this problem, UMTA has established an Office of Tran-sit Management, which sponsors and funds continuing education programs for transit industry managers. Another important step in this direction was taken in 1975 when the trade association of the industry, the American Public Transit Association, established a Task Force on Education and Manpower Development to work closely with UMTA in developing the industry's human resources.[27]

Federal–Local Government Interaction

The extension of federal transit funds to our cities has necessitated ex-tensive interaction between UMTA and local government officials. In some instances this interaction has led to disputes concerning the relative roles to be played by each in transit planning. The basic conflict involves resolution of UMTA's desire to play a strong leadership role in transit development and the desire of local government for self-determination.

This conflict manifested itself during UMTA's early years in the agency's views concerning fixed rail transit proposals. Officials of several major cities believed that their transit needs could be best served by fixed-rail rapid transit systems, but UMTA was strongly opposed to funding such systems due to the magnitude of their cost and their inflexibility. As a result, the agency generally refused to grant funds to new rail projects, and concen-

413

trated its funding on projects involving bus service. The UMTA posture infuriated officials of cities that were denied transit funding.

UMTA's antirail policy softened considerably during the mid-1970s in response to energy considerations; in fact, during fiscal 1974 rail projects received 53 percent of the agency's capital grants.[28] The largest commitment of these funds involved construction of new rapid transit facilities in Atlanta and Baltimore.

The technology selection conflict was but one manifestation of the basic dispute concerning the relative role of UMTA versus local government in transit development. The intensity of this dispute appears to be lessening. Many federal funding programs are now moving toward greater local self-determination. Revenue-sharing plans that involve funding grants based on population and density exemplify this philosophy, and this pattern is spreading to transportation. The Department of Transportation's position on this issue was summarized in its 1975 Statement of National Transportation Policy:

> A Federal–local partnership . . . should be premised on the principle that each urban area is unique—with different needs and different development objectives—and each should be free to choose for itself the transportation solutions that best serve its objectives. Federal support for mass transportation must therefore be flexible, relying on local ability to assess requirements, identify and evaluate opportunities for improvement and initiate needed action.[29]

Therefore, although UMTA will continue to play a major role in transit planning through its funding decisions, it may well be expected that local government will play an expanded future role in that process.

Labor Protection

Federal involvement in transit has also affected industry labor relations. Prior to the passage of the 1964 transit statute, Congress was concerned that federal capital grants to transit might lead to a substitution of capital for labor in the industry, thereby exerting further downward pressure on transit employment.[30] In responding to that potential problem, Congress included Section 13(c) in the Urban Mass Transportation Act. Under its provisions, transit workers were guaranteed continuation of their bargaining rights, compensation levels, and working conditions. They were also given priority for employment or reemployment. Training or retraining would be provided if necessary. These benefits were patterned after those previously included under Section 5 of the Interstate Commerce Act, which governed railroad consolidations.

414

Whereas the benefits that Section 13(c) accords to labor are obvious, transit management has been quite critical of the guidelines. Before a transit system can obtain a capital grant (or operating assistance) from UMTA, it must sign a 13(c) agreement with the transit unions. Management has contended that this stipulation has effectively given labor the power to veto UMTA grants, and has forced transit systems to agree to steadily escalating 13(c) benefits.[31] However, the transit systems have failed to document the specific costs of the 13(c) guidelines, and very few transit grants have been denied because of the failure of management and labor to reach a 13(c) accord.[32] Congress has demonstrated little interest in changing the labor protection guidelines, and is unlikely to do so unless transit system officials can clearly document the cost inefficiencies caused by Section 13(c).

COPING WITH THE AUTOMOBILE

Despite steady transit improvements, the automobile will continue to dominate metropolitan passenger movements in the forseeable future unless public policy restricts automobile usage. Transit cannot match the flexibility of the automobile, and does not possess the physical capacity to handle any large-scale increases in patronage, particularly during peak hours. Therefore, the relevant public policy issues related to future metropolitan automobile usage involve better integration of the automobile into metropolitan transportation planning.

Highway Expansion

It appears likely that urban planners will rely less heavily upon new highway projects in meeting future metropolitan transportation needs. Growing emphasis on environmental issues and increased availability of federal transit funding should combine to slow new highway construction in these areas. These developments have reinforced the "freeway revolt" of the early 1970s.[33] The revolt consisted of intense lobbying activities by urban interest groups that opposed highway expansion due to its adverse social and environmental impact. As a result of the intensity of this community resistance, many highway projects were canceled, and several cities instituted highway building moratoriums.

Such community activism was a relatively new phenomenon in the early 1970s, but it is now an established force to be reckoned with in the future. The growing participation of citizen interest groups in future metropolitan transportation planning efforts will also likely lead to increased use of discretionary federal transportation funds for transit rather than highway projects. Consequently, a major concern in the coming years will be better utilization of existing highway facilities.

Utilizing Metropolitan Highway Capacity

Efforts to increase the effective capacity of existing metropolitan highways and streets have taken several forms. In many cities, on-street parking has been banned on major commuting arteries during rush hours. Demand-responsive traffic signaling systems have also been utilized on a limited basis. Similarly, serious attention is being given to the possible reduction of urban truck movements during normal business hours.

Although such efforts are important, probably the most promising area of potential utilization improvement is car pooling. The automobile is the dominant vehicle in the metropolitan traffic flow, and its capacity has generally been underutilized. Surveys conducted by the Federal Highway Administration have indicated that the average automobile occupancy rate for the home-to-work trip in our major metropolitan areas is 1.4 occupants.[34] Furthermore, nearly 75 percent of home-to-work automobile trips contain only one person.[35]

Improved automobile occupancy rates would not only tend to lessen congestion problems, but would also contribute to improved environmental conditions. As a result, the DOT and the Environmental Protection Agency have worked with many communities in promoting car pool programs. Computer matching services are now available in many cities. The DOT contends that the potential for carpooling is the greatest

> where trip origins and destinations are concentrated in small areas separated by a relatively long trip, and where there is some disincentive to private automobile travel such as long, time consuming trips, severe highway congestion, high parking charges or restrictions, or limited access to a private automobile.[36]

To increase the attractiveness of car pooling, some cities have extended special parking privileges to high-occupancy vehicles, and on some urban expressways car pools have been given access to express lanes. Increasing attention is also being given to the concept of differential tolls for car pools versus single-occupant automobiles on urban expressways.

Parking Facilities

The availability of parking spaces within a city naturally influences the commuters' modal choice decision. Consequently, city officials must develop a strategy related to parking, and it must be treated as a major component of local transportation planning. This entails decision making related not only to the management of the supply of parking facilities, but also to the level of parking fees.

Any increase in the supply of parking facilities gives the commuter an added incentive to drive. As a result, public officials in many cities have considered placing a moratorium on new parking facility construction. The EPA has also advocated such a strategy for several cities in attempting to improve urban air quality. Although a moratorium on new parking facilities tends to increase the relative attractiveness of transit, it must be realized that such proposals generally encounter stiff opposition. Several groups that have generally opposed plans to restrict parking expansion are businesses located within the city, urban residents, and construction interests. Collectively, these groups can and have mounted substantial political pressure against such action.

Therefore, to date public officials have found it quite difficult to place a ceiling on urban parking facilities. However, they have increasingly turned to tighter controls over illegal parking. In most cities illegal parking spaces comprise a sizable portion of the available parking space. For example, several studies conducted in Boston have indicated that nearly one fourth of parking spaces in use during business hours are illegal.[37] In response to this situation, officials in several cities have significantly increased parking fines and promoted more aggressive vehicle-towing campaigns. Over an extended period, as drivers become more selective in parking their vehicles, these actions can effectively reduce the stock of available parking spaces.

Given the existing supply of parking spaces in a city, public officials can make driving less attractive by raising parking fees in public parking facilities. Major increases can significantly influence the total cost of driving. In the past, proposed parking fee increases have generally been strongly opposed by retailers, who fear a related contraction of business, and other organizations with many employees who drive to work. As a result, parking fee increases have typically been quite gradual.

Although strategies related to tightening parking restrictions in our cities have been widely discussed in recent years, a DOT study indicated that planners in our major cities forecasted an 87.6 percent increase in metropolitan parking facilities by 1990.[38] However, emphasis seems to be shifting to fringe parking facilities, which provide a link with a line-haul transit operation. Whereas planners forecasted a 46.9 percent increase in central business district spaces by 1990, they projected a 422 percent increase in fringe parking facilities serving transit.[39]

In any event, public decisions concerning parking facilities will continue to exert an influence on urban modal selection. The direction of future parking policies will likely be a function of the intensity of environmental and energy problems and related federal programs.

Automobile Disincentives

As discussed earlier in this chapter, there has been a short-term increase in national transit demand in recent years. However, the magnitude of this increase has been small, and it has had little impact on urban traffic flows. This development has raised questions concerning the commuting public's long-term willingness to switch to improved transit services.

If the public is reluctant to voluntarily forsake the automobile for commutation, and if environmental and energy considerations require more limited automobile usage, it may be necessary to rely upon disincentives. Such disincentives, which would be aimed at decreasing the relative attractiveness of the automobile, might take many forms. Steps could be taken to increase the cost of automobile usage through increased tolls on urban expressways, bridges, and tunnels (particularly during rush hours), higher parking fees, or increased excise taxes on gasoline. Other actions might be aimed at decreasing the automobile's access to the city. Cutbacks in parking facilities, creation of auto-free zones, and outright bans on automobile usage would increase the relative attractiveness of transit. Such policy decisions would be politically unpopular, but they may be necessary if national goals necessitate a major shift in commutation patterns from the automobile to transit.

NEED FOR INTEGRATED PLANNING

Attempts to solve metropolitan transportation problems have historically been troubled by organizational difficulties. Typically, several local and state agencies have controlled the various components of the metropolitan transportation system. This has increased the difficulty of developing a multimodal planning posture that attempts to efficiently meet metropolitan transportation needs. Further complicating the situation has been the multiplicity of political jurisdictions within a given metropolitan area. The intensity of this problem is illustrated by the fact that more than 18,000 political and administrative jurisdictions are represented in the 212 metropolitan areas recognized by the Department of Commerce.[40] It has been extremely difficult to coordinate these governmental units in a transportation planning framework. This problem is even more complicated in the 32 metropolitan areas that extend across one or more state lines.[41] Similarly, the growing involvement of the federal government in metropolitan transportation funding has necessitated even greater intergovernmental coordination. At the same time, it must be recognized that transportation planning must be integrated with other metropolitan community planning efforts.

418

Federal Promotion of Integrated Planning

The federal government has used its funding leverage to promote metropolitan transportation planning that is not only multimodal in nature, but also geographically comprehensive and related to other community planning efforts. Toward that goal, the Urban Mass Transportation Act specifies that no federal assistance will be provided unless it is

> needed for carrying out a program . . . for a unified or officially coordinated urban transportation system as a part of the comprehensively planned development of the urban area, and [is] necessary for the sound, economic, and desirable development of such area.[42]

Furthermore, the DOT has stressed that it will give transit funding preference to communities that

> demonstrate how transportation planning responds to long-term metropolitan planning objectives in meeting urban problems, assuring effective processes for resolving conflicts among jurisdictions and interest groups and harmonizing with land use and community development objectives.[43]

As a result of these statutory and institutional policies, public officials in metropolitan areas have been given additional incentives to promote coordinated solutions to transportation problem solving.

Metropolitan Response

In recognition of the potential benefits of coordinated transportation planning, many major metropolitan areas have established metropolitan transportation planning agencies. One such agency is the Metropolitan Transportation Commission (MTC), which operates in the San Francisco Bay Area. It was created by the California legislature in 1970 to facilitate local government cooperation in planning transportation development in the Bay Area.[44] The MTC is charged with preparation of an overall transportation plan for the area, and is empowered to review and approve allocation of transportation funds to various projects.

Although the MTC has no authority to regulate or prescribe prices or to enact new sources of transportation revenue, it is required to maintain a financial plan for Bay Area transportation that covers revenues from all sources. Consequently, the MTC continually interacts with other transportation agencies in pricing decisions.

Similar metropolitan transportation planning bodies have surfaced in other communities. Their responsibilities and powers differ, but they have come to play an important role in overall community planning.

SUMMARY

For many years the transportation problems of our metropolitan areas were treated as strictly local matters. This placed considerable pressure on local officials, who lacked sufficient funds to bolster failing transit systems. At the same time, they found it difficult to cope with the urban highway system's voracious appetite for property and its related pollution and congestion problems.

However, beginning in the early 1960s, congressional efforts to improve the quality of urban life led to a substantial increase in federal assistance to our cities. In recognition of the important role that transit can play in supporting local objectives, Congress began limited funding of transit projects in 1961. Since that time, growing national concerns with both improvement of environmental conditions and energy conservation have prompted a tremendous expansion of federal transit funding. At the same time, the Department of Transportation has used the federal funding of transit and urban highway projects for leverage in promoting integrated metropolitan transportation planning.

The cooperative efforts of federal, state, and local government units have at least partially alleviated several of the major metropolitan transportation problems. Air pollution levels have been substantially reduced in many of our cities, and federal funds have promoted major improvements in transit services. Furthermore, the long-term downtrend in transit ridership has been reversed. However, much remains to be done, and it can only be accomplished through continued cooperative efforts and long-term federal funding commitments.

NOTES

1. American Public Transit Association, *Transit Fact Book* (Washington, D.C.: the Association, 1976), p. 42.

2. For a discussion of this issue, see George M. Smerk, "Mass Transit Management," *Business Horizons*, XIV, No. 6 (December, 1971), p. 10.

3. W. G. Roeseler and Peter S. Levi, "State Subsidies for Public Transit: An Overview of Current Legislation," *Urban Lawyer*, Vol. 4, No. 1 (Winter, 1972), p. 62.

4. Ibid.

5. Ibid.

6. See James M. Landis, Report on Regulatory Agencies to the President-

Elect, submitted by the Chairman of the Subcommittee on Administrative
Practice and Procedure to the Committee on the Judiciary of the U.S.
Senate, 86th Cong., 2nd Sess., 1960 (Washington, D.C.: U.S. Government
Printing Office); also U.S. Senate, Committee on Interstate and Foreign
Commerce, Special Study Group on Transportation Policies in the United
States, *National Transportation Policy* (Doyle Report), 87th Cong., 1st
Sess., 1960 (Washington, D.C.: U.S. Government Printing Office, 1961),
pp. 552–635.

7. George M. Smerk, *Urban Mass Transportation: A Dozen Years of Federal
Policy* (Bloomington, Ind.: Indiana University Press, 1974), pp. 48–49.

8. *The Transportation System of Our Nation,* message from the president of
the United States, April 5, 1962, House of Representatives, Doc. No. 384,
87th Cong., 2nd Sess. (Washington, D.C.: U.S. Government Printing
Office, 1962), p. 10.

9. Smerk, *Urban Mass Transportation,* pp. 54–55.

10. Public Law 88-365 (1964).

11. U.S. Department of Transportation, *1974 National Transportation Report*
(Washington, D.C.: U.S. Government Printing Office, 1975), p. 155.

12. Smerk, *Urban Mass Transportation,* p. 76.

13. Ibid.

14. Ibid.

15. Public Law 91-453 (1970).

16. Department of Transportation, *1974 National Transportation Report,* p.
155.

17. The Federal-Aid Highway Acts of 1968 and 1970 permitted the states to
divert some of the funds they received from the Highway Trust Fund to
transit-related projects, such as exclusive or preferential bus lanes, parking
facilities, or bus stops. However, the funds could not be used for major
capital projects.

18. Public Law 93-503 (1974).

19. "Attacking the Mass Transit Mess," *Business Week* (June 3, 1972), p. 62.

20. Department of Transportation, *1974 National Transportation Report,* pp.
145–55.

21. U.S. Department of Transportation, Office of the Secretary, *Implementing
Transportation Policy* (Washington, D.C.: the Department, 1973), pp.
14–15.

22. GMC Truck and Coach Division of General Motors, *Progress Report:
Exclusive Busways,* 1971.

23. Department of Transportation, *1974 National Transportation Report,* p.
140.

24. Ibid., p. 145.

25. Robert C. Lieb, *Labor in Mass Transit* (Washington, D.C.: U.S. Government Printing Office, 1976), p. 6.

26. Ray A. Mundy and John C. Spychalski, *Managerial Resources and Personnel Practices in Urban Mass Transportation* (University Park, Pa.: Pennsylvania State University, Pennsylvania Transportation and Traffic Safety Center, 1973), p. 216.

27. Lieb, op. cit., p. 8.

28. U.S. Department of Transportation, *Eighth Annual Report* (Washington, D.C.: U.S. Government Printing Office, 1975), p. 41.

29. U.S. Department of Transportation, Office of the Secretary, *A Statement of National Transportation Policy* (Washington, D.C.: U.S. Government Printing Office, 1975), pp. 27–28.

30. Lieb, op. cit., p. 29.

31. See "Over 400 Learn Ins and Outs of Transit Act During ATA Transit Seminar," *Passenger Transport* (December 18, 1970), p. 4, as cited by Darold T. Barnum, *Collective Bargaining and Manpower in Urban Mass Transit Systems* (Springfield, Va.: National Technical Information Service, 1972), p. 320.

32. Ibid.

33. Department of Transportation, *1974 National Transportation Report*, p. 159.

34. Ibid.

35. Ibid., p. 137.

36. Ibid., p. 148.

37. Wilbur Smith and Associates, *Summary Report: An Access Oriented Parking Strategy for the Boston Metropolitan Area* (Boston: Wilbur Smith and Associates, 1974), p. 16.

38. Department of Transportation, *1974 National Transportation Report*, p. 179.

39. Ibid.

40. Information supplied by the U.S. Department of Commerce.

41. Wilfred Owen, *The Metropolitan Transportation Problem*, rev. ed. (Washington, D.C.: Brookings Institution, 1966), p. 179.

42. Urban Mass Transportation Act of 1964, Section 4(a).

43. Department of Transportation, *A Statement of National Transportation Policy*, p. 28.

44. For an extensive discussion of this matter, see Richard H. Carll, "Some Observations on Urban Transport Pricing and Its Relationship to Comprehensive Transportation Planning," *Transportation Journal*, XIV, No. 3 (Spring, 1975), pp. 18–29.

SELECTED REFERENCES

American Public Transit Association. *Transit Fact Book*. Washington, D.C.: the Association. 1976.

Banks, R. L., and Associates. *Study and Evaluation of Local Transit Regulation and Regulatory Bodies*. Springfield, Va.: National Technical Information Service, 1972.

Barnum, Darold T. *Collective Bargaining and Manpower in Urban Transit Systems*. Springfield, Va.: National Technical Information Service, 1972.

Carll, Richard R. "Some Observations on Urban Transport Pricing and Its Relationship to Comprehensive Transportation Planning." *Transportation Journal*, XIV, No. 3 (Spring, 1975), pp. 18–29.

Charles River Associates. *An Evaluation of Free Transit Service*. Cambridge, Mass.: the Associates, 1968.

Hilton, George W. *Federal Transit Subsidies: The Urban Mass Transportation Assistance Program*. Washington, D.C.: American Enterprise Institute for Public Policy Research, 1974.

Kirby, Ronald F., Kiran U. Bhatt, Michael A. Kemp, Robert C. McGillivray, and Martin Wohl. *Para-Transit: Neglected Options for Urban Mobility*. Washington, D.C.: Urban Institute, 1975.

Lieb, Robert C. *Labor in Mass Transit*. Washington, D.C.: U.S. Government Printing Office, 1976.

Mundy, Ray A., and John C. Spychalski. *Managerial Resources and Personnel Practices in Urban Mass Transportation*. University Park, Pa.: Pennsylvania State University, Pennsylvania Transportation and Traffic Safety Center, 1973.

Schneider, Lewis M. *Marketing Urban Mass Transit*. Boston: Harvard University, Graduate School of Business Administration, Division of Research, 1965.

Smerk, George M. "An Evaluation of Ten Years of Federal Policy in Urban Mass Transportation." *Transportation Journal*, XI, No. 2 (Winter, 1971), pp. 45–57.

Smerk, George M. "Mass Transit Management." *Business Horizons*, XIV, No. 6 (December, 1971), pp. 5–16.

Smerk, George M. *Urban Mass Transportation: A Dozen Years of Federal Policy*. Bloomington, Ind.: Indiana University Press, 1974.

U.S. Department of Transportation. *1974 National Transportation Report*. Washington, D.C.: U.S. Government Printing Office, 1975.
Chapter 4. "Trends in Urban Transportation," pp. 129–60.
Chapter 5. "Urban Transportation Plans, Programs, and Alternatives," pp. 161–276.

423

U.S. Department of Transportation, Urban Mass Transportation Administration. *An Urban Transportation Bibliography*. Springfield, Va.: National Technical Information Service, 1971.

Vickrey, William. "The Pricing of Urban Transportation: Economic Desiderata, Technological Possibilities, and Political Constraints." A paper presented at the Intersociety Conference on Transportation, Denver, Colo., September, 1973.

DISCUSSION QUESTIONS

1. Do you believe that people can be attracted back to transit through system improvements? If you are not presently a regular transit patron, what would it take to make such services attractive to you?

2. Given that most major transit properties presently incur deficits, why aren't fares raised to make the services self-supporting?

3. As mayor of a large northeastern city, you have been approached by the members of the city council with a suggestion to ban automobile traffic in the central business district. You are scheduled to meet with the council tomorrow to inform them of your reaction. In deciding whether or not to support the proposal, discuss the benefits that such a program might foster, and the problems that it might cause. Be complete in your discussion and include all relevant factors. Furthermore, crafty politician that you are, you begin to weigh the matter in terms of votes. Who would provide support for such an automobile ban? Who would oppose you if you decided to support the proposal?

4. As chairman of the Transportation Advisory Committee of a midwestern metropolitan area of approximately 1 million residents (core plus suburbs), you must make a report to the rest of the committee and the mayor concerning the selection of the future transit system of your city. Your presentation essentially involves the choice of the most appropriate technology —fixed rail versus bus operations. What factors will you consider in formulating your recommendations?

Index of Subjects

Index

Index

Index

Index of Names

Index